ALTERNATIVE
ASSESSMENT
TECHNIQUES
FOR READING
& WRITING

Wilma H. Miller

JOSSEY-BASS
A Wiley Imprint
www.josseybass.com

Published by Jossey-Bass
A Wiley Imprint
989 Market Street, San Francisco, CA 94103-1741   www.josseybass.com

Jossey-Bass books and products are available through most bookstores. To contact Jossey-Bass directly call our Customer Care Department within the U.S. at 800-956-7739, outside the U.S. at 317-572-3986 or fax 317-572-4002.

Jossey-Bass also publishes its books in a variety of electronic formats. Some content that appears in print may not be available in electronic books.

Library of Congress Cataloging-in-Publication Data

Alternative assessment techniques for reading & writing / by Wilma H. Miller.

    p. cm.

    ISBN 0-87628-141-2

    1. Language arts (Elementary)—United States—Abilty testing—
Handbooks, manuals, etc. 2. Reading (Elementary)—United States—
Ability testing—Handbooks, manuals, etc. 3. English language—
United States—Composition and exercises—Ability testing—
Handbooks, manuals, etc. I. Center for Applied Research in Education.

LB1576.A6154 1995   95-826

372.6'044—dc20

FIRST EDITION

PB Printing 10   9   8   7   6   5

To the memory of my beloved parents, William and Ruth Miller,
and
Win Huppuch, Vice-President of C.A.R.E. and my dear
friend and professional advisor for twenty-five years

Acknowledgments

I would like to gratefully acknowledge a number of people who have made it possible for me to write *Alternative Assessment Techniques for Reading & Writing*. I first would like to acknowledge the memory of my beloved late mother Ruth K. Miller who worked with me on all my writing projects until the age of eighty. She remains an inspiration to me in all of my writing activities. I also would like to thank all of my present and former undergraduate and graduate students at Illinois State University for being a constant source of information and motivation for me. I also very much thank Dr. Paula Smith, Dean Sally Pancrazio, and Former Provost David Strand for granting me a sabbatical leave from Illinois State University during the fall of 1994 to complete the writing of this handbook. Finally, I would like to express my deepest gratitude to the following people at The Center for Applied Research in Education for their help and inspiration: Win Huppuch, Susan Kolwicz, Diane Turso, Louise Rothman, and Eileen Gerne Ciavarella. (A special thank you to Maggie and John Paul Ciavarella for their art and writing samples.) Without your help, this manuscript would not have been possible.

About the Author

A former classroom teacher, Wilma H. Miller, Ed.D., has been teaching at the college level for more than 30 years. She completed her doctorate in reading at the University of Arizona under the direction of the late Dr. Ruth Strang, a nationally known reading authority.

Dr. Miller has contributed numerous articles to professional journals and is the author of more than sixteen other works in the field of reading education. Among the latter are *Identifying and Correcting Reading Difficulties in Children* (1972), *Diagnosis and Correction of Reading Difficulties in Secondary School Students* (1973), *Reading Diagnosis Kit* (1975, 1978, 1986), and "Corrective Reading Skills Activities File" (1977), *Reading Teacher's Complete Diagnosis & Correction Manual* (1988), and *Reading Comprehension Activities Kit* (1990), and *Complete Reading Disabilities Handbook* (1993), all published by The Center for Applied Research in Education.

She is also the author of an inservice aid for teachers entitled *Reading Activities Handbook* (1980), several textbooks for developmental reading, *The First R: Elementary Reading Today* (1977), and *Teaching Elementary Reading Today* (1983), published by Holt, Rinehart & Winston, Inc., and of a guide to secondary reading instruction, *Teaching Reading in the Secondary School*, published by Charles C. Thomas.

The Practical Help This Book Offers

While standardized tests of all types provide the literacy teacher with some insights into a student's literacy strengths and weaknesses, the *sole* use of standardized devices to evaluate the performance of students has many inherent dangers. Over the years much harm has been done to students from using only standardized test scores to evaluate their performance. Perhaps two true incidents will clearly illustrate the great potential harm of using *only* standardized tests to evaluate students.

When I was a beginning doctoral student at the University of Arizona many years ago, I was required to take the Graduate Record Examination to be admitted into the program. I received a 99 percentile on the qualitative (language) portion of the test; however, I received only a 6 percentile on the quantitative (mathematics) portion of the test. The latter score was *well below* the minimum level for acceptance into the doctoral program. I was admitted to the program only because of the personal intervention of the Head of the Graduate Program in Education whom I had as an instructor at that time. In spite of my low quantitative score on the test, I received an **A** in both statistics courses that were required for the doctorate.

One of my undergraduate students recently told the class she had been ill when she took an aptitude test that was given early in her high school career. Since her test score was fairly low, she was allowed to only pursue classes in the non-academic track, even though both she and her parents requested that she be allowed to take an alternate form of the test again. This *one test score* made it extremely difficult for her to later enter any college. In her high school, the results from only one test were the sole criterion for what "track" a student was allowed to pursue.

These two true incidents clearly indicate why it is crucial that literacy teachers attempt to assess a student's reading, writing, and spelling strengths and weaknesses by using many *informal means*. It is my experience that informal assessment of literacy skills is generally much more accurate and helpful than are standardized test scores. Informal assessment also reflects literacy learning in whole language (literature-based) programs much more effectively than do standardized tests. Although I understand why standardized test scores are required by administrators and the public, informal assessment must be pursued just as often as possible to ensure the optimum literacy instruction for all students.

This handbook will greatly help literacy teachers make an accurate, useful assessment of a student's specific literacy strengths and weaknesses and attitudes toward it. If such informal assessment then were followed up by prescriptive, motivating literacy instruction, great progress could be made in improving the literacy skills of all students.

Just examine the following statistics that clearly indicate how essential it is to improve literacy instruction in our nation today:

- approximately 60,000,000 Americans are thought to be reading below the eighth-grade level
- about 85% of the juveniles in the court system are functionally illiterate
- approximately 50% of the inmates in American prisons are believed to be functionally illiterate

These figures clearly indicate why it is essential for teachers to be provided with the best assessment tools possible so that they can accurately determine each student's literacy competencies and weaknesses to ensure that an excellent program is then provided for them.

Alternative Assessment Techniques in Reading & Writing has been written for classroom literacy teachers, Chapter I reading teachers, teachers of learning-handicapped students, reading specialists and supervisors, and administrators. Everyone involved in the teaching of literacy (reading, writing, and spelling) should find it a very valuable source of informal assessment devices of all types.

Written in a *practical and easy-to-understand manner*, it contains a multitude of classroom-tested *informal assessment devices* of all kinds. The descriptions and reproducible examples of a wide variety of informal assessment devices should save the literacy teacher countless time and energy in making a useful assessment of all aspects of any student's literacy ability.

The handbook opens with an introductory chapter about using informal devices in assessing literacy skills. It provides a definition of literacy that is mainly based on the contemporary whole language philosophy. The chapter then briefly describes how informal assessment and evaluation can be used in any literacy program, and explains the great importance of continually integrating assessment with instruction. Instruction should always be based on a student's assessed literacy strengths and weaknesses to ensure that he or she receives the best possible literacy instruction. The chapter also describes why it is essential to use informal assessment in any whole language program, as standardized tests do not evaluate most contemporary literacy programs very effectively. The chapter briefly describes the limitations of using informal assessment and then explains the hope that literacy teachers will rely more heavily on informal assessment in literacy skills in the future than they have in the past.

Part One of this handbook is devoted to the informal assessment of competencies and weaknesses in *reading*. Chapter 2 opens with a detailed discussion about why it is crucial for all teachers to be expert "kid-watchers" or observers of children's behavior. Such ethnographic observation is very important to the success of the whole language program. The chapter then contains numerous classroom-tested checklists of various types for assessing a student's abilities in letter-name knowledge and other aspects of emergent literacy as well as the various techniques of word identification such as sight-word recognition and identification, graphophonic (phonic) analysis, structural analysis, semantic (contextual) analysis, and also of oral reading. In addition, the chapter contains a checklist designed to assess a student's self-monitoring abilities while using the word-identification techniques.

Chapter 3 contains many classroom-tested reproducible checklists of various types for assessing competencies and weaknesses in vocabulary, the various elements of comprehension, the basic study skills, and silent reading. The various checklists are designed for use in the primary grades, the intermediate grades, and the middle–upper levels. The chapter also includes a detailed description of how to use retelling as an informal measure of comprehension ability; a self-monitoring checklist of reading comprehension ability; a checklist for evaluating reading competencies in an intermediate-grade whole language program; and a checklist for pleasure reading.

Variations of miscue analysis are described and illustrated in detail in Chapter 4. Miscue analysis is a contemporary means of assessment that fits in exceedingly well with the whole language philosophy. The chapter first describes miscue analysis in an easy-to-understand manner and then discusses its advantages and limitations. The following variations of miscue analysis are described and concretely illustrated in this chapter: miscue analysis as used in the two forms of the Individual Reading Inventory included in this handbook and miscue analysis as described by Susan B. Argyle. The chapter contains several reproducible examples of how miscue analysis can be carried out. The chapter closes by explaining how to use miscue analysis most effectively in any literacy program.

Chapter 5 is devoted to the variations of the traditional, but still very useful, Individual Reading Inventory (IRI). The chapter opens with a description of a typical IRI, discusses the advantages and limitations of an IRI, and describes how to construct, administer, and evaluate an IRI. The chapter then contains two forms entitled Form L and Form M of a completely new Individual Reading Inventory with graded word lists and graded oral-silent reading passages that can be used from the primer level through the twelfth-grade reading level. (Readers of my earlier publications in this field will notice a number of differences between my previous IRIs and the IRI included in this handbook.) The IRI assesses a student's prior knowledge and interest before reading, contains an innovative evaluation scheme, and evaluates a student's self-monitoring of comprehension ability after reading. Thus, the inventory has been designed to more accurately reflect whole language instruction. The chapter also contains a comprehensive list of other commercial Individual Reading Inventories; and describes and contains reproducibles of interest inventories and content reading inventories.

Chapter 6 describes how to use inventories and other informal devices to assess competencies and weaknesses in the word-identification techniques of letter-name knowledge, sight-word identification, graphophonic (phonic) analysis, structural analysis, and semantic (contextual) analysis. The chapter contains numerous ready-to-duplicate examples of inventories and other informal devices in these important reading skills at various grade levels from the emergent literacy level through the intermediate-grade reading level. In addition to the inventories constructed for this chapter, it includes a copy of Fry's Instant Words, and reproducible copies of the San Diego Quick Assessment Test, the Quick Survey Word List, the El Paso Phonics Survey, and the Name Test.

Chapter 7 presents many alternative and innovative ways of assessing literacy ability in vocabulary, the various aspects of comprehension, the basic study skills, and silent reading. The chapter describes various types of teacher-pupil reading conferences and interviews; explains the importance of assessing and activating prior knowledge before reading; and includes a description of the Pre-Reading Procedure (Plan), which is sometimes called PReP. The chapter describes how to use questionnaires and inventories in assessing prior-knowledge abilities and includes a sample reproducible questionnaire-inventory for assessing prior knowledge. It next includes a reproducible schema assessment device, and briefly describes reading comprehension and explains questioning strategies or "QARs" in detail. It then provides descriptions and reproducible examples of a Self-Monitoring (Metacognitive) or Self-Correction Assessment Device; a Simple Metacognitive Checklist; "Think-Alouds"; creative book sharing; story frames; a QAD Chart; reading autobiographies; a self-appraisal of reading abilities; and a book selection device.

Part Two of this handbook is devoted to assessing competencies and weaknesses in *writing and spelling*. Chapter 8 describes and includes reproducibles for emergent writing behaviors; creative and content writing; creative expression, narration, exposition, persuasion, and description; checklists in writing at the primary-grade, intermediate-grade, and middle–upper levels; and checklists for assessing ability in computer word processing and editing behaviors.

Chapter 9 is devoted to describing and illustrating the holistic scoring of writing used in this handbook. The chapter explains the following criteria used in holistic scoring: clarity, support, organization, mechanics, and overall rating. The chapter includes actual children's compositions at the first-grade, second-grade, third-grade, fourth-grade, fifth-grade, and sixth-grade levels that have been holistically scored by several different raters (teachers) using the criteria recommended in this handbook. The chapter then provides examples of actual children's compositions at these grade levels that the literacy teacher can score using the criteria contained in the chapter; he or she later can compare the scores assigned to each of these compositions with the scores given by several trained raters (teachers). The chapter also briefly describes and offers a reproducible for an Individual Writing Inventory.

Chapter 10 includes a number of innovative ways of assessing writing and spelling abilities. It describes the usefulness of having a child at the emergent writing level write all of the words he or she can on a sheet of paper to assess his or her writing and spelling abilities; explains how to analyze writing by using *T-units* as an evaluative measure; explains coaching/conferencing as a writing assessment technique and includes a reproducible sheet for recording information about a student's writing; describes a writing survey and includes a reproducible writing survey; discusses and illustrates dialogue journals; describes and includes a Developmental Spelling Test; and concludes with a discussion of and a reproducible example of sentence combining.

Part Three of this handbook provides a very comprehensive discussion and illustration of how to use a portfolio assessment in any literacy program. Although portfolio assessment is exceedingly useful in a whole language program, it also should be useful if a literacy teacher uses a more traditional approach such as basal readers. Chapter 11 describes some of the basic characteristics of portfolio assessment and then describes some of the elements that can comprise a good **working portfolio**. Some of these are as follows: the portfolio holder, table of contents, reading/writing log, drafts of all types of writing, reading response journals, a dialogue journal, writing done outside of class, tape-recorded oral reading protocols, audiotapes, student-teacher conference notes, self-assessment devices of various types, teacher anecdotes and observations, and graphs (records) of progress. The chapter also discusses whether or not to include standardized test scores of various types in a working portfolio; presents the advantages and limitations of using portfolio assessment in any literacy program and the special importance of using portfolio assessment in a whole language program; presents some guidelines for helping a literacy teacher to begin implementing portfolio assessment in his or her program; discusses the importance of student self-assessment of the materials included in his or her portfolio; and concludes with the following reproducible devices that should save the literacy teacher much time and effort in implementing portfolio assessment: a letter to parents before beginning portfolio assessment, My Portfolio Table of Contents, How I Can Organize My Portfolio, This Is My Portfolio, My Reading/Writing Log, Student-Teacher Literacy Portfolio Conference Notes, Self-Assessment Device, What I Think About My Reading and Writing, Classmate Review Sheet, a Parent Portfolio Review Form, and an Evaluation of a Portfolio.

Part Four, (Chapter 12) is called "Closing Thoughts." The chapter presents a very brief review of the contents of this handbook, and again makes the plea for using **informal assessment devices** as much as possible in any literacy program. The chapter discusses grading in a whole language program and provides a model of a contemporary report card that evaluates some important literacy behaviors.

Literacy teachers will find the following to be unique about *Alternative Assessment Techniques for Reading & Writing*:

- It is published in a spiral-bound format that makes reproducing the material very simple.

- It emphasizes the importance of being a "kid-watcher" in literacy assessment.

- It contains numerous classroom-tested assessment devices in reading, writing, and spelling.

- It emphasizes the whole language (literature-based) philosophy which is so popularly used at this time. **Whole language proponents have stated that there is a great need for informal assessment devices** since standardized tests do not accurately reflect this philosophy.

- It contains numerous ready-to-duplicate devices for the informal assessment of literacy skills, which should save the literacy teacher monumental time and effort in assessing a student's strengths and weaknesses.

- It is the *only resource* of which I am aware that contains numerous ready-to-duplicate examples of such a variety of informal assessment devices in all of the important elements of literacy.

- It contains descriptions and reproducible examples of countless innovative assessment strategies in literacy of which a number of teachers are not aware due to the fairly recent introduction of the whole language philosophy.

- It contains the only Individual Reading Inventory that includes numerous other ready-to-duplicate assessment devices. The typical IRI contains only graded word lists and graded passages and possible phonic tests.

- It includes two forms of an Individual Reading Inventory that uses evaluation procedures that are very contemporary and reflect the latest research in assessing prior knowledge and self-monitoring of reading behaviors.

- It is designed to be used from the emergent literacy level through the middle–upper level. Thus, it should be of help to many literacy teachers.

Standardized tests simply have been unfair to far too many students in the past. This is not to say that they have no value. However, literacy teachers need to have access to many *informal means* of assessing literacy ability. If such informal assessment were conducted on a regular basis, and the results were then acted upon effectively by literacy teachers, many cases of reading, writing, and spelling disabilities could effectively be prevented and children also would enjoy literacy instruction much more. If this handbook can help literacy teachers achieve these goals, it will have served its purpose very well.

Wilma H. Miller

CONTENTS

Chapter 10   Other Alternative Means of Assessing Writing and Spelling Ability   424

PART THREE   PORTFOLIO ASSESSMENT   441

Chapter 11   Using Portfolio Assessment in Any Literacy Program   443

CHAPTER ONE

Using Informal Devices in Assessing Reading and Writing Ability

In a true incident indicating why standardized test scores never should be used as a sole assessment technique, I remember very well one of my teacher-trainees who came to my office in tears because she had failed for the fourth time the reading portion of a pre-professional test for teachers that she was required to pass before she could student teach. After counseling her and helping her to obtain assistance in preparing to take this test for the fifth time, I still did not feel confident that she would pass it. Although her reading skills were adequate for her to easily pass the test, by this time she had developed many negative feelings about the entire experience. Fortunately, I received a letter from her about six weeks after she took the test in early May. Yes, she had passed the test on her fifth try—scoring 173 points—*only one point over the minimum score of 172 to pass the test*. Yet, I believe that she will be a fine primary-grade teacher. This incident clearly indicates why **informal assessment of literacy always should be used along with standardized evaluation**. In many instances, it is much more valid and useful.

Definition of Literacy as Used in This Handbook

As most literacy teachers are aware, the whole language (literature-based) philosophy is becoming more and more popular. It is now used as a major approach in many primary-grade and intermediate-grade classrooms throughout North America. It has been popular in the British Isles, Australia, and New Zealand for many years.

Literacy can be defined as attaining competencies in the language arts of *listening, speaking, reading, writing,* and *spelling.* Literacy is best taught and practiced in real settings and by integrating the learning of all of its elements. Literacy skills also are best presented and reinforced when students clearly see purposes for what they are learning, as by using appropriate thematic units in the content areas of social studies and science.

Skills presented and taught in whole language approaches emphasize literacy as a global, language-based process in which all of the skills are presented and used when needed. Often in these approaches literacy skills rarely are taught in isolation except possibly to learning-handicapped and other "at-risk" children. In whole language approaches, children become aware of the need to learn important literacy skills.

Literacy also is said to begin at birth and progress forward from that point. The concept of *emergent literacy* states that all children begin literacy learning in infancy, and that children in kindergarten and first grade have reading, writing, and spelling skills that can be used as a starting point from which to proceed. Emergent literacy also states that all of the literacy skills should be presented and practiced together. There should rarely be a time, for example, when reading and writing are taught as separate, discrete skills.

Since all of the literacy sills are considered of equal importance, the improvement of competencies in *reading, writing,* and *spelling* will be addressed in this handbook. The handbook also emphasizes the fact that these elements of literacy are strongly rooted in listening and speaking competency. Often instruction and practice in one of the elements of literacy will result in improvement in the remainder of them.

However, although all of the elements of literacy should be presented and practiced together whenever possible, I have found it desirable to teach and reinforce them in isolation once in a while. This may be particularly helpful with disabled readers, learning-handicapped children, and other "at-risk" children. Although these students too often greatly profit from whole language approaches, they sometimes need to have the various reading, writing, and spelling skills presented to them in isolation and also sometimes need isolated practice.

Definition of Assessment and Evaluation as Used in This Handbook

It may be useful to define the terms *assessment* and *evaluation* as they are used in this handbook. *Assessment* can be defined as gathering information to meet the particular reading needs of a child. It involves looking at which children can and cannot achieve. Although it is obvious that assessment is often informal, it still can be very useful.

Evaluation is judging or evaluating the information that is gathered by assessment. It is evaluating the responses that the child gave, and often may be more formal than assessment. For example, *standardized tests* are an example of evaluating a student for the purpose of making a diagnosis of his or her competencies and weaknesses. Having a child retell a tradebook is an example of *assessment*, while evaluating the child's retelling to assign a quantitative or qualitative score is an example of *evaluation*.

The major purpose of assessment is to provide literacy teachers and students with information that is useful in promoting a student's growth in literacy. On the other hand, evaluation is tests that are used to measure growth. *Summative evaluation, which occurs at the end of a predetermined period,* evaluates the impact of instruction. The final exam that students take at the end of a course is an example of summative evaluation. When teachers evaluate children's learning summatively, the evaluation often is expressed in the form of a grade. *Formative evaluation is ongoing and is used to improve instruction.* Teacher-made tests are an example of formative evaluation when the results of those tests are used to plan instruction.

Donald Graves has described an evaluator as being either an *adversary* or an *advocate*. The *adversary* sits opposite the student on a higher chair, takes the student's paper without waiting for it to be given, and makes little eye contact. The adversary always has all the right answers and is clearly the center of the evaluation. The adversary role often places the student in an ego-threatening, defensive position. On the other hand, an *advocate* is likely to sit next to the child at the same height, wait to be offered the student's paper, and makes considerable eye contact. The advocate's responses are generally nonjudgmental. In many instances, teachers of the majority of children, especially those with literacy problems, should attempt to be an advocate as much as possible.[1]

In summary, although both assessment and evaluation are useful in literacy classrooms and clinics, often assessment is more helpful because it more directly points the way toward appropriate instruction. The literacy teacher always should know why he or she is either assessing or evaluating students and neither should be done without concern for improved instruction. Although this handbook mainly emphasizes reproducible models of informal assessment devices, some of the devices included also can be used for informal evaluation of students' progress. However, the handbook describes no standardized tests. If you want a description and listing of some standardized tests of various kinds, consult the following source:

> Wilma H. Miller, *Complete Reading Disabilities Handbook*. West Nyack, NY: The Center for Applied Research in Education, 1993, pp. 105-120.

Definition of Informal Assessment and Evaluation

Informal assessment always must be considered an essential part of instruction and therefore should occur continuously. Informal assessment often is more useful in determining a child's literacy strengths and weaknesses than are standardized tests such as norm-reinforced and criterion-referenced tests of various types, especially if the informal assessment is done by an experienced teacher. Informal assessment usually is recommended by contemporary literacy specialists and proponents of the whole language approach. Certainly whole language approaches are not evaluated effectively by most standardized tests. Indeed, whole language proponents have often expressed the need for process-oriented measures of literacy that will better address the needs of students

---

[1]Donald Graves, *Writing: Teachers and Children at Work*. Portsmouth, NH: Heinemann, 1983.

and teachers who use these approaches. This handbook contains a multitude of these types of informal assessment devices which should help whole language teachers.

In many instances, process-oriented assessment of literacy competencies and weaknesses is much more likely to be accurate and useful than is standardized testing. The use of informal assessment devices is likely to be more commonly used in the future *if administrators, school board members, state boards of education, and parents will accept it.* Certainly I recommend that informal assessment devices be much more commonly used than standardized tests. Far too many people place too much faith in standardized test scores, which correspondingly discourages the use of informal teacher assessment.

Standardized tests can be influenced by far too many extraneous factors to ever be used as a sole criterion for grouping children, promoting children, grading children, or evaluating teachers and schools. Such test scores can be greatly influenced by factors such as examiner–examinee rapport, the student's health on the day of the test, the test format, the physical conditions in the classroom, and even the time of year.

Informal assessment should be conducted on an individual or group basis and should be the basis for subsequent prescriptive instruction of literacy for an individual child or a group of children. Assessment never should be conducted without being followed up by appropriate instruction. Without follow-up the assessment is a waste of time and effort.

Informal assessment can take many different forms. It can be in the form of surveys, checklists, miscue analysis, various types of informal inventories, conferences and interviews of various types, retellings, dialogue and response journals, creative book reports, autobiographies of various kinds, holistic scoring of writing, and portfolio assessment. Reproducible examples of many variations of all of these informal assessment devices are included in this handbook. Some of these devices are solely used for informal assessment, while others also can be used for informal evaluation of student's progress in the various aspects of literacy.

Importance of Integrating Assessment with Instruction

This chapter already has briefly described why it is essential to integrate or link literacy assessment with literacy instruction. All informal and standardized assessment should direct subsequent instruction. Without such direction, assessment has no place in the school curriculum. Far too many standardized test results simply are included in a school district's annual report or a child's cumulative folder. If they are only going to be used in this way, they should not be given.

Appropriate assessment followed by appropriate instruction can save a teacher and student much time and effort. Why should time be spent on literacy skills that already have been mastered or that are relatively unimportant?

Integrating assessment with instruction makes it likely that information gained from assessment will be used. If literacy teachers continually assessed children's literacy progress and acted upon the results of this assessment, many cases of reading, writing, and spelling disability could be effectively presented.

Advantages of Using Informal Assessment Devices

There are a number of advantages of using informal assessment devices which often make them more useful than standardized tests. However, they usually should be used along with some standardized tests since the latter are required by administrators, school boards, state boards of education, and parents.

Here are the *major advantages* of using informal assessment devices in any literacy program:

- They are more authentic in evaluating many literacy programs.
- They are often more relevant to the information that is being taught in the classroom or special reading program.
- They better reflect the modern approaches such as the *whole language approach*. whole language approaches are not well assessed or evaluated by traditional tests that view reading as a group of discrete subskills and also do not evaluate students' attitudes toward literacy activities.
- They emphasize the *process aspects* of literacy rather than the product aspects as traditionally is done by standardized tests of various types.
- They are able to assess the affective (emotional or attitudinal) aspects of reading fairly effectively.
- They usually more accurately reflect the accomplishments and attitudes of "at-risk" children than do standardized tests. "At-risk" children such as minority-group children, learning-handicapped children, and slow-learning children often are discriminated against by standardized tests.
- They usually reflect different styles of teaching and learning more effectively than do standardized tests.
- They do not have the prescribed directions and time limits that typically are found on standardized tests. Such tests, for example, often penalize the slow, but accurate, reader.

Limitations of Using Informal Assessment Devices

Here are the *major limitations* of using informal assessment devices in any literacy program:

- They usually are neither statistically reliable nor valid. However, this does not indicate that they are not useful; they usually simply do not meet the statistical requirements for reliability and validity. A possible exception may be some commercial Individual Reading Inventories (see Chapter 5).
- They can be time-consuming to construct and/or evaluate.
- Their results often do not meet the requirements of administrators, school boards, state boards of education, or parents.

- They may make it difficult to evaluate children by predetermined criteria such as traditional report cards and grades. That is why holistic report cards such as that described and illustrated in Chapter 12 often should be used along with informal assessment.

- They may require considerable time and effort if a literacy teacher is to become adept at administering and evaluating them.

- They are not always easy to locate. However, the informal assessment devices included in this handbook should greatly help literacy teachers to locate and reproduce many appropriate informal assessment devices.

However, in spite of these limitations, literacy instruction would improve significantly if literacy teachers relied more heavily on informal assessment devices in the future. I hope they will be allowed to do so by administrators, school boards, state boards of education, and parents.

The Future of Informal Assessment Devices

It is very difficult to predict what the future holds about how common informal assessment devices will be in elementary literacy programs. As stated earlier, whole language advocates consistently express the need for less use of standardized tests and more use of informal assessment devices such as those included in this handbook.

However, in spite of all the inherent limitations of standardized tests, they still seem to be more commonly used instead of less widely used for a number of reasons. For example, in Illinois, the state in which I teach, elementary-school students routinely must take standardized achievement tests, the Illinois Goal Assessment Program (IGAP—a process-oriented measure of reading comprehension), and basal reader tests among others. The state issues various kinds of reports about school achievement on a regular basis. Many times the test scores of various school districts are published in local newspapers as an indication of how those schools are doing.

As stated earlier, administrators, school boards, state boards of education, and parents place far too much emphasis on standardized test scores. This over-reliance on test scores as an indicator of student performance seems to be even more common now than it was in the past due to the *accountability movement* in education. Both teachers and students often are under inordinate pressure to achieve well on these tests. This is extremely disturbing when one remembers how much test scores can vary depending upon so many extraneous circumstances.

Therefore, I hope that informal assessment devices such as those contained in this handbook will be used more commonly in the future. I understand that informal assessment devices never can completely replace standardized tests because there must be some accountability in education. However, standardized tests should not be allowed to drive instruction nor receive undue emphasis.

Brief Case Summaries

The following brief case summaries will help to illustrate how the informal assessment devices included in this handbook can be effectively implemented.

CHRIS

Chris was a second-grade student whom two of my teacher-trainees tutored in literacy skills. One teacher-trainee tutored him during the fall semester, while the other worked with him during the spring semester. Chris was a nice-appearing boy from a single-parent family that probably would be considered upper-lower class. Since his mother worked full time, Chris attended a day-care center after school and on vacation days while she was working. He lived in a low-rent apartment and was somewhat hyperactive and extremely difficult to motivate. Although he did not want to read or write anything at all, he was not a true behavior problem but just a reluctant student. He attended an elementary school that qualified for Chapter I funding.

Through informal observation the following were determined to be Chris's literacy strengths and weaknesses.

Literacy Strengths

- adequate stock of sight words
- fairly good literal (explicit) comprehension if he could identify the words
- fair oral-reading fluency if he could identify the words
- fairly cooperative—not a true behavior problem

Literacy Weaknesses

- no real method of word attack
- weak graphophonic (phonic) analysis skills
- weak beginning structural analysis skills
- weak interpretive (implicit) comprehension skills
- weak in self-monitoring his reading
- weak in self-correction while reading orally and silently
- reluctant reader who wouldn't read any type of material unless he was forced to do so
- weak spelling skills
- didn't want to do writing of any kind

Here are some of the *informal assessment devices,* which are included in this handbook, that may be indicated for assessing Chris's specific literacy strengths and weaknesses. Not all of these would ever be used with a child, as such extensive diagnosis would be overwhelming and frustrating for a child who already had negative attitudes toward reading. They are included just for the purpose of illustrating what kind of devices might be selected.

- "Interest Inventory" in Chapter 5 (This should be given in as creative a manner as possible such as in the form of the questions being placed on puzzle pieces, placed on paper fish with paper clips to be pulled out with a magnet, or placed in a game.)

- portion of the "Second-Grade Checklist in Word-Identification Techniques" in Chapter 2 that assesses competencies and weaknesses in graphophonic (phonic) analysis and structural analysis (An alternative to the "Second-Grade Checklist in Word-Identification Techniques" can be the "Second-Grade Graphophonic Inventory" and the "Second-Grade Structural Analysis Inventory" in Chapter 6. I would not give both the checklist and the inventories as they are duplicative.)
- "Checklist for Self-Monitoring While Using the Word-Identification Techniques" in Chapter 2
- portion of the "Primary-Grade Checklist for Assessing Comprehension and the Basic Study Skills" in Chapter 3 that analyzes ability in interpretive (implicit) comprehension
- miscue analysis as described by Susan B. Argyle in Chapter 4 (This type of miscue analysis is especially useful in assessing competencies in graphophonic (phonic) analysis (whether the area of difficulty is in word beginnings, word middles, or word endings) and in assessing ability in self-correction. **NOTE:** An alternative to miscue analysis can be Form L or M of the "Individual Reading Inventory" in Chapter 5. I would *not* use both an IRI and miscue analysis with Chris. If the IRI is to be used, he should begin at primer level and continue through about the third-reader level in both the graded word lists and oral reading passages. This IRI also evaluates Chris's use of prior knowledge and his self-monitoring while reading.)
- "Primary-Grade Writing and Spelling Checklist" in Chapter 8
- Chris can be motivated (if possible with a hands-on activity) to write his own story, and the literacy teacher can holistically score the story using the examples and criteria contained in Chapter 9.
- If the literacy teacher wanted, the "Developmental Spelling Test" in Chapter 10 could be given.

IMPORTANT: As stated earlier, under no circumstances should all of the above-mentioned informal assessment devices be used with a child, and assessment and correction (remediation) should always be continuous. It is very detrimental to a child to over-diagnose him or her at any point during instruction. It is also important to begin instruction as soon as possible in any kind of literacy program.

Suggestions for Chris's Corrective (Remedial) Literacy Program

Here are some of the strategies and materials my teacher-trainees used with Chris during the year-long tutoring program. They were fairly successful especially during the spring semester, and Chris did improve his reading, writing, and spelling skills and his attitude toward literacy although he still was a somewhat reluctant reader/writer when the tutoring sessions were finished.

- Much oral and silent reading of easy, highly motivating *tradebooks* on his low instructional and independent reading levels. The tutor always gave him a choice of one of three tradebooks to read in order to empower him and give him some control of the tutoring. These tradebooks often had hidden figures, were pop-up books, or were beautifully illustrated to be especially motivating for Chris.

- Prediction and activation of prior knowledge always was used before and during reading a tradebook.

- Retelling of the tradebook and a few *interpretive (implicit) questions* were used after reading.

- *Important* unknown phonic elements and generalizations were presented and practiced. Normally they were presented in a *whole language context*, although they also were presented and reinforced in isolation occasionally. The following phonic elements were presented to Chris:

  > short vowel sounds
  > word middles (received the major emphasis)
  > consonant blends
  > common vowel digraphs
  > word families (phonograms)

- Teacher-made *games* were very useful in helping Chris master these phonic elements. He especially liked the motivation and competition of playing these games with his tutor.

- A few highly motivating activity sheets were made more interesting by having the tutor cut them out of the book and place cut-out seasonal illustrations on them, such as Christmas trees and Santa Clauses around Christmas time.

- Chris read along orally with tutor-made tapes from motivating, appropriate tradebooks.

- Alternate reading in which Chris read one page orally, and his tutor read the next page orally, was done. This was more motivating for him than having to read an entire tradebook himself.

- Simple structural analysis skills such as common suffixes and a few very useful prefixes were presented and practiced.

- Semantic (contextual) analysis was emphasized in silent and oral reading especially in combination with graphophonic (phonic) analysis.

- Cloze procedure, which combined phonic analysis and contextual analysis

- Fix-up strategies such as rereading, visual imagery, use of context, and asking for assistance

- Portfolio assessment as illustrated in Chapter 11 was used with Chris. His portfolio contained the following:

  > tutor-completed checklists
  > taped oral-reading protocols
  > writing samples
  > tutor anecdotes

notes from miscue analysis
graphs of progress

In summary, in tutoring Chris my teacher-trainees attempted to provide him with as many hands-on activities as possible and to empower him by giving him choices of tradebooks to read and activities in which to participate.

MATT

Matt was a fourth-grade student whom my teacher-trainees tutored for two consecutive semesters. He was a nice-appearing boy from a stable, intact middle-class family. He lived in a middle-class neighborhood in a modern, comfortable home. Although both of his parents worked, they seemed to provide a good home environment for Matt and his siblings. Matt attended a neighborhood school that did not qualify for Chapter I funding. Most of the children in the school came from stable, middle-class families.

Although Matt was a well-behaved boy, he seemed very passive and disinterested in all school activities. He didn't enjoy doing any type of school work. Usually he rushed through his work marking anything that came to mind. We found this to be especially true with the activity sheets that his tutor had him complete during the fall semester. The second semester of tutoring my teacher-trainee involved Matt in as many activities as possible.

From informal observation the following were determined to be Matt's literacy strengths and weaknesses.

Literacy Strengths

- good stock of sight words
- adequate word-identification skills in the areas of graphophonic (phonic) analysis and structural analysis
- adequate oral reading fluency
- adequate literal comprehension skills
- adequate spelling skills
- a fairly cooperative attitude (not belligerent or hostile)

Literacy Weaknesses

- very poor interpretive (implicit) comprehension skills especially while reading social studies and science textbooks
- only fair use of semantic (contextual) cues especially while reading social studies and science textbooks
- very weak in self-monitoring of reading comprehension
- very reluctant reader/writer
- passive student

- careless work habits
- dislike of all reading/writing activities

Here are some of the *informal assessment devices,* which are included in this handbook, that may be indicated for assessing Matt's specific literacy strengths and weaknesses. Certainly not all of them would be used with any student as such extensive assessment would be detrimental for a student who already had negative feelings toward literacy activities. They are included just for the purpose of illustrating what kind of devices might be selected.

- "Interest Inventory" found in Chapter 5 (It should be given in as creative a manner as possible, such as in the form of a game or the role playing of a newspaper reporter while asking the student the questions and recording his or her responses.)
- interpretive (implicit) elements of the "Intermediate-Grade Checklist for Assessing Vocabulary, Comprehension, and the Basic Study Skills" in Chapter 3
- "Checklist for Metacognition (Self-Monitoring) of Reading Comprehension" in Chapter 3
- "Individual Reading Inventory" in Chapter 5 if the literacy teacher wants to determine the student's approximate independent, instructional, and frustration reading levels (With Matt I recommend giving the *graded passages* (not the word lists) of both Forms L and M and having him read one set of passages silently and the other set orally to make a comparison between his silent and oral reading. The assessment of prior knowledge and self-monitoring included in these IRIs is useful.)
- "Fourth-Grade Semantic (Contextual) Analysis Inventory" in Chapter 6
- "Pre-Reading Plans" (PReP) in Chapter 7 to assess his prior knowledge since this is very useful to good comprehension skills
- extensive use of the "Think and Search" and "On My Own" QARs (questioning) strategies in Chapter 7
- "Self-Monitoring or Self-Correction Assessment Device" in Chapter 7
- "Intermediate-Grade Writing and Spelling Checklist" in Chapter 8
- Matt should write stories with mainly self-selected topics, and these stories can be scored holistically as described and illustrated in Chapter 9
- coaching/conferencing through editing in Chapter 10
- portfolio assessment as described and illustrated in Chapter 11 to help Matt and his tutors evaluate his literacy achievements

IMPORTANT: As stated earlier, all of the above-mentioned informal assessment devices never should be used with a student, and assessment and correction (remediation) always should be continual. It is very damaging to a student to assess him or her too much before or during instruction. It is crucial to begin instruction just as soon as possible in any kind of literacy program.

Suggestions for Matt's Corrective (Remedial) Literacy Program

Here is a sampling of the strategies and materials my teacher-trainees used with Matt during his year-long tutoring program. The tutor especially during the spring semester was very successful, and Matt greatly improved his interpretive (implicit) comprehension skills and work habits. Although he still remained a somewhat reluctant reader/writer, he made some improvement in these areas also.

- Matt read tradebooks and social studies and science textbooks on his independent and low instructional reading levels. It was very important to empower Matt and give him a feeling of control over his reading improvement program by allowing him a choice in his reading materials and the strategies used with him.

- Alternate reading was used so Matt did not have to read every page of a tradebook or textbook himself.

- **Request Procedure (Reciprocal Questioning)**—Matt very much enjoyed *reciprocal questioning* in which he and his tutor both read various portions of narrative or content material and then asked each other interpretive (implicit) comprehension questions about alternate passages or paragraphs in the material. Matt especially enjoyed tricking his teacher by reading so carefully that she could not always answer all of his questions, although she really tried to do so! *Request Procedure (Reciprocal Questioning) was the single most effective strategy we used with Matt.* When doing activity sheets the previous semester, he rushed through them marking anything without even reading the material.

- Prediction activities before and during reading

- Anticipation Guide

- PReP Plan (Pre-Reading Plan)

- Helping Matt to always activate his prior knowledge

- Directed Reading-Thinking Activity (DR-TA)

- Appropriate QARs—"Think and Search" and "On My Own"

- Semantic mapping of selected portions of social studies and science textbooks

- Guided Reading Procedure

- Dialogue journals

- Response journals

- Process writing with mainly self-selected topics and published books that his classmates and parents could read

- GIST Procedure (Generating Interactions Between Schemata and Text) for practice in effective summary writing

- Concrete reinforcement such as graphs of progress (It was also helpful to give Matt praise to build his self-esteem about literacy and to motivate him to read/write for information and pleasure.)

- Matt's portfolio contained such items as the following:

tutor anecdotes
tutor-completed checklists
Individual Reading Inventory results
graphs of progress
writing samples
samples of various kinds of book reports

In summary, Matt's tutors mainly tried to keep him active and involved in his instruction by using reciprocal questioning, self-selection of high-motivating materials of various types, and providing praise for his improvement.

NOTE: The following resources provide detailed examples and ready-to-duplicate samples of all the strategies and materials mentioned in the preceding two brief case summaries:

Wilma H. Miller, *Complete Reading Disabilities Handbook.* West Nyack, NY: The Center for Applied Research in Education, 1993.

Wilma H. Miller, *Reading Comprehension Activities Kit.* West Nyack, NY: The Center for Applied Research in Education, 1990.

Wilma H. Miller, *Reading Teacher's Complete Diagnosis & Correction Manual.* West Nyack, NY: The Center for Applied Research in Education, 1988.

PART ONE

Assessing Competencies and Weaknesses in Reading

Using Checklists and Other Informal Devices to Assess Competencies and Weaknesses in Visual Perception Ability, Emergent Literacy Skills, Word Identification Skills, and Oral Reading

Pete was a second-grade child whom my teacher-trainees recently tutored for two consecutive semesters. At the beginning of the tutoring it was very obvious that he had significant reading problems as well as a very negative attitude toward all literacy activities. Pete was hyperactive, very distractible, fairly uncooperative, and unable to read on grade level.

Since Pete had a significant reading disability, I felt that an Individual Reading Inventory would be much too difficult for him and that his first tutor instead should assess his specific word-identification strengths and weaknesses by using an informal checklist. His tutor did so and was able to determine fairly accurately with which literacy skills he needed help. He needed to attain competency in the sight words found on the Dolch Basic Sight Word List and in the graphophonic (phonic) elements of consonant blends, short vowel sounds, consonant digraphs, and word families (phonograms). His tutor also determined through observation that she must help him change his negative attitude about all literacy activities and help him learn to stay on task more effectively.

During the two semesters of tutoring, amazingly, Pete made excellent progress. He learned the basic sight words through about the third-reader level, learned all of the graphophonic elements that he needed to know, and perhaps, most important, greatly improved his interest in reading and ability to stay on task. No, he did not always concentrate and pay attention nor always value literacy activities; however, he certainly made significant progress. At the end of two semesters of tutoring, Pete told me that he really hoped that he could have another tutor in third grade, but I told him that I doubted that he needed one! Indeed, I found out the next year that he did not.

The Importance of Being an Expert "Kid Watcher" or Observer of Children's Behavior

Perhaps the most significant contribution of whole language approaches and the Reading Recovery™ Program is that they have clearly demonstrated the great importance of a literacy teacher's being a consistent and expert observer of children's literacy behaviors. No longer can literacy teachers rely solely on prescribed teacher behaviors such as those found in basal reader or phonic program teacher's manuals. Instead, they must carefully observe children's literacy behaviors on a daily basis and act on the results of this observation to modify instruction. It is my sincere belief that if literacy teachers observed a child's literacy behaviors regularly and acted upon those observations, countless cases of literacy disabilities could effectively be prevented. In addition, children would enjoy all reading/writing activities much more.

The term *"kid watching"* was introduced by Yetta Goodman of The University of Arizona, a proponent of the whole language philosophy. She has stated that "kid watching" is direct or informal observation of a child in various classroom settings. It is based on the premise that literacy development is a natural process. "Kid watching" allows teachers to explore these two questions:

1. What evidence exists that literacy development is occurring?
2. What does a child's unexpected production of literacy behaviors say about the child's knowledge of literacy?[2]

"Kid watching" or informal teacher assessment consists of these three aspects:

- *Observation*—carefully watching activities of a single child's, group of children's, or the entire class's literacy use and social behaviors
- *Interaction*—this takes place when the teacher raises questions, responds to journal writing, and conferences with children in order to stimulate further literacy and cognitive growth
- *Analysis*—the teacher obtains information by listening to a child read or discuss and by considering a child's written work. The teacher then applies knowledge of learning principles to analyze the child's literacy abilities

Expert "kid watchers" demonstrate the following behaviors:

- They understand the reading and writing processes in great detail. They also have excellent knowledge of children's and adolescents' literature. This extensive knowledge of the literacy processes is one of the reasons why Reading Recovery™, the early intervention program for "at risk" first-grade children, has been so successful.

---

[2]Yetta Goodman, "Kid Watching: An Alternative to Testing." *National Elementary Principal,* 57 (June 1978), pp. 41-45.

- They recognize important patterns of behavior differences in competencies exhibited by different children.

- They listen attentively and perceptively to children.

- They continuously evaluate while teaching.

- They accept responsibility for curriculum development—they do not place undue emphasis on standardized test scores.

- They keep detailed records of a child's literacy competencies, weaknesses, and progress. This also is an important reason for the success of Reading Recovery™. Running records at those used in Reading Recovery™ and miscue analysis are explained in detail in Chapter 4. Some teachers keep records by jotting dated notes on self-stick tags while meeting with children and later placing them in the child's files. Teachers also can use class sheets with a square for each name as in the form of a calendar. As a teacher writes these notes, he or she sticks them on the child's name. Other teachers carry clipboards on which they have class lists with space for important comments. These comments later are placed in the child's file but must first be transcribed or cut apart and glued on each child's record sheet. Here is a sample of this kind of recordkeeping.

OBSERVATIONAL CHECKLIST FOR CLASS

Activity_____ Date_____

Name	**Comment**
Apful, Stacy	_____
Barry, Colleen	_____
Decker, Sam	_____
Flanagan, Mary	_____
Goldberg, David	_____

Anecdotal records and teacher-completed checklists can also be part of the recordkeeping that is required for effective "kid watching." On the other hand, standardized test scores provide little help in "kid watching" or moment-to-moment decision making in literacy teaching. Based on effective "kid watching" (informal observation and hunches), literacy teachers can modify teaching strategies, clarify explanations, give extra help, and provide appropriate reinforcement (teacher-made and commercial games, creative teacher-made and commercial activity sheets, and computer software, among others.)

Effective "kid watching" is crucial to successful whole language programs for these main reasons:

- They are unstructured in comparison to traditional basal reader or phonic approaches.

- The teacher himself or herself, not the prescribed program, must determine in which precise literacy skills a child needs instruction and reinforcement and also how to effectively teach or reinforce those particular literacy skills.
- There is no real guide that tells a literacy teacher what skills to teach or how to teach them.

Reading Recovery™ is similar to whole language approaches in that it also requires the teacher to be an expert observer of a child's literacy behaviors. It has no true sequence of tradebooks that the child is required to read; the skills presented are not sequenced; and the Reading Recovery™ teacher is not told which specific strategies to present or reinforce. The Reading Recovery™ teacher must determine all of these elements himself or herself.

"Kid watching" or informal assessment of literacy behaviors is a difficult, demanding task. However, it can be made easier by the reproducible informal assessment devices included in this handbook.

Importance of Language Development to Success in Literacy

Literacy (reading, writing, and spelling) ability greatly depends upon competency in oral language. Without good oral language skills, a child usually has considerable difficulty with both beginning reading, writing, and spelling skills. To be a good reader/writer/speller, a child should have a large, precise vocabulary, should use complex sentence structure, and should use correction grammatical structures.

The mentally handicapped child often may have underdeveloped oral language skills. A mentally handicapped child, for example, of five sometimes has oral language skills that are more like that of a child who is several years younger. I am very well acquainted with a young woman of seventeen who has Down's syndrome, for example, who has somewhat limited oral language skills. Her literacy skills also are not nearly as well developed as are those of a student her age who has average or above-average intelligence.

Children who speak non-standard English, who have a dialect which is very different from that used by the typical middle-class child, or who speak English as a second language may well have more difficulty with literacy skills than do children who speak standard English. This especially may be the case if a literacy teacher does not accept the child's language differences and does not make adequate provisions for it. However, if this occurs, usually a child will not have undue difficulties. Normally if a child does not speak English, that child is first taught to read and write in his or her native language. Only after the child has adequate oral English skills should he or she be taught literacy skills in English.

Speech defects such as improper articulation, lisping, or stuttering occasionally may be related to reading problems. If a child cannot articulate the sounds in exactly the way in which his or her teacher does, that child *may* have some difficulty with graphophonic (phonic) analysis. If a child has a speech defect of any type, such as improper articulation or stuttering or stammering, he or she probably will dislike reading orally. Such children also may develop a low self-esteem which may make it even more difficult for them to learn to read effectively.

My teacher-trainees tutored a second-grade student named Jeff for two semesters who had a significant speech defect especially in articulating such initial consonant sounds as /r/ and /s/. I believe that Jeff's literacy problems were mainly caused by his self-consciousness about this speech defect while reading orally. Although Jeff made good improvement during his year-long tutoring sessions, his speech defect did not improve even with regular speech correction.

REPRODUCIBLE "LANGUAGE DEVELOPMENT CHECKLIST"

This is a reproducible "Language Development Checklist" designed for the emergent literacy level (kindergarten and first-grade levels). You can duplicate it and use it in its present form or modify it in any way you wish, depending upon the needs of your own pupils. (See page 22.)

Description of Visual Perception Ability

Perception is the interpretation of incoming sensations by the brain, which selects, groups, organizes, and sequences them. When the eyes are stimulated, *visual perception* occurs. Meaningful interpretations of incoming visual sensations should lead to appropriate responses or actions. The perceptual aspects of reading are complex because the mind must act on a succession of stimuli in which both spatial and temporal patterns must be perceived.

The following terms often are used in the literature of perception and reading:

- *Figure-ground relationships*—one unit or group of units is perceived against a background only vaguely. For example, in reading, the print is perceived clearly while the background of the printed page is seen only vaguely.

- *Discrimination*—the ability to discriminate among visual stimuli. This ability usually improves with maturation; for example, a child is able to make the difficult discrimination between the letters *b* and *d* more easily with maturation.

- *Closure*—the mind has a strong desire to complete the missing part or to perceive wholes.

- *Sequence*—understanding the sequence of visual stimuli to be able to read. A child must learn the arbitrary conventions of left-to-right progression and reading from top to bottom.

- *Mind set*—a student's mind set helps him or her to anticipate what is going to occur next in reading. This mind set enables a child to make effective *predictions* while reading.

A number of learning-handicapped children have considerable difficulty with visual perception. Although these children may have adequate visual acuity (vision), they do not have good visual perception ability due to a weak visual modality (channel). Such children may have considerable difficulty with beginning literacy activities especially if they must learn to read by a predominantly visual method (the sight word method). If such children have an adequate auditory modality (channel), graphophonic

Name _____ Grade _____ Teacher _____ Date _____

LANGUAGE DEVELOPMENT CHECKLIST
(Emergent Literacy Level)

	Always	Sometimes	Never
Is able to pronounce the consonant sounds correctly	❑	❑	❑
Is able to pronounce consonant blends and consonant digraphs correctly	❑	❑	❑
Is able to pronounce the short and long vowel sounds correctly	❑	❑	❑
Is able to speak in one-word sentences	❑	❑	❑
Is able to speak in two-word sentences	❑	❑	❑
Is able to speak in sentences of three or more words	❑	❑	❑
Is able to identify familiar sounds	❑	❑	❑
Is able to identify similar sounds	❑	❑	❑
Is able to understand the language of adults when spoken to	❑	❑	❑
Is able to understand the language of peers when spoken to	❑	❑	❑
Is able to follow oral directions	❑	❑	❑
Does not have significant speech defects such as with articulation or stuttering	❑	❑	❑
Has appropriate vocabulary for his/her level of maturity	❑	❑	❑
Speaks in complete sentences	❑	❑	❑
Uses varied syntactic (grammatical) structures	❑	❑	❑
Is able to be understood by adults	❑	❑	❑
Is able to be understood by peers	❑	❑	❑

Teacher Comments:

_____

_____

(phonic) analysis probably should receive considerable emphasis in their beginning literacy program.

Here are the results of some studies on visual perception that you may want to consider in teaching this skill to all children, but especially, to learning-handicapped children:

1. Lower-case letters can be recognized more quickly than can upper-case letters.
2. Initial letters can be perceived the best visually, final letters the next best, while middle letters usually cause the most difficulty.
3. Overall form or contour is not a very effective strategy in word perception. That is why the technique of *configuration* may not be useful, although it now is presented in some whole language programs.
4. Special features such as lines and curves in different positions are fairly important in word perception.[3]

STRATEGIES FOR IMPROVING VISUAL PERCEPTION ABILITY

There are a number of useful strategies for improving visual perception ability. Very briefly, here are a few:

- Have the child draw, copy, and then reproduce various geometric figures from memory.
- Use *templates* to help a child learn to draw the various geometric figures. A template can be made from cardboard, oaktag, linoleum, or plywood.
- Have the child assemble simple and then more difficult jigsaw puzzles.
- Have the child complete an incomplete picture.
- Have the child work with a pegboard.
- Have the child string beads.
- Have the child do all kinds of tracing, cutting, and pasting activities.
- Have the child locate and trace a figure in the ground.

- Have the child work with a balance beam walking both forward and backward on the beam in a toe-to-heel position.
- Have the child scribble and draw on a chalkboard.

---

[3]Eleanor J. Gibson and Harry Levin, *The Psychology of Reading.* Cambridge, MA: MIT Press, 1975, p. 16 and pp. 195-197.

- Have the child catch and throw different sizes of balls and beanbags.

- Suspend and swing a ball at eye level. The child has to follow the swinging ball with his or her eyes.

- Have the child make his or her own body into the shape of a letter.

- Have the child make geometric figures into pictures.

- Have the child do various kinds of chalkboard exercises such as dot-to-dot, incomplete pictures, drawing various geometric figures, and printing letters and words.

- Have the child discriminate between non look-alike letters; for example:

    f   g   r   f

- Have the child discriminate between look-alike letters; for example:

    b   d   b   g

- Have the child discriminate between non look-alike words; for example:

    man   tan   van   man

- Have the child discriminate between look-alike words; for example:

    was   was   saw   saw

- Use a commercially available visual-perception program such as:

    Frostig Program for the Development of Visual Perception
    Consulting Psychologists Press, Inc.
    577 College Avenue
    Palo Alto, CA 94306

    Techniques and Diagnostic Criteria for the Optometric Care of Children's Vision
    Optometric Extension Program Foundation
    Duncan OK 73533

INFORMAL VISUAL PERCEPTION TEST

This informal visual perception test (see page 25) is designed for average children about 4-6 years old and for learning-handicapped children about 4-7 years old. It consists of five figures to be copied and then reproduced from memory by the child. The five figures are a *circle* (typically mastered by a three-year-old child), a *cross* (typically mastered by a four-year-old child), a *square* (typically mastered by a five-year-old child), a *diamond* (typically mastered by a six-year-old child), and *three letters* (typically mastered by a seven-year-old child).

Directions for Administering

1. Place a copy of the test in front of the child in the usual writing position—do not allow the child to rotate the paper.

2. Have the child count the number of figures on the page: 1–2–3–4–5.

3. Have the child look at the circle and have him or her copy it as well as look at the rest of the figures and copy them also. (You can have a preschool child imitate each figure after you have drawn it as a model.)

Name _____ Grade _____ Chronological Age _____
yr.   mo.

Date of Test _____ Examiner _____ Visual Perception Test Age _____

Observations: _____ Figure Recall _____

_____ Adequate 4+ _____

VISUAL PERCEPTION TEST[4]

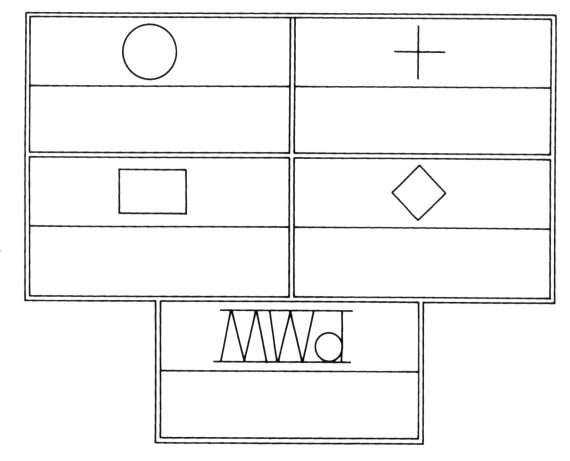

---

[4]This test was adapted from the "Developmental Visual Perception Test" in the following source: Margaret H. LaPray, Ph.D., *On-the-Spot Reading Diagnosis File*. West Nyack, NY: The Center for Applied Research in Education, ©1978, pp. 10-15. Adapted with permission of The Center for Applied Research in Education.

4. When the test sheet is complete, take it away.

5. Place a clean sheet of paper in front of the child and have him or her draw as many of the five figures as he or she can.

Directions for Scoring

While the child is taking the test, watch for signs of difficulty such as the following:

- poor line control—shaky or wobbly

- inability to draw distinct angles

- lack of closure or completion

- figure rotation of 45 degrees or more

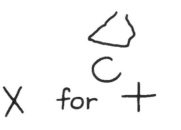

To score the test, see the "Visual Perception Scoring Sheet" on page 27. Most students are able to pass all of the tests until the first failure and then will fail all the figures beyond this point. For such students, the *Age Norm* is the highest figure passed.

However, when a student fails at one level and passes a level beyond, add one year for each level passed.

EXAMPLE

Mark, aged six, passed the first two figures but failed the third figure. However, he passed the fifth figure which is supposed to be the most difficult.

1. Highest level consecutively passed	4-year-old level
2. Plus 1 year for each level passed beyond this point regardless of the failures in between	+1 year for passing figure 5

VPT Age	**5-year-old level**
Chronological Age	**6 years old**

This score shows a deficit of *one year in visual perception ability.*

When tested on immediate recall, Mark remembered only **two** of the five figures; therefore, his performance in immediate recall of the figures is marked as follows:

VISUAL PERCEPTION SCORING SHEET

1. Three-year-old children usually start at the bottom of the circle this way:

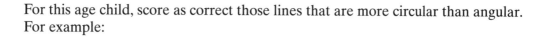

For this age child, score as correct those lines that are more circular than angular. For example:

   + if mainly circular   − if mainly angular

2. Four-year-old children have very little difficulty with the vertical line, but they have two main problems with this figure: one with the horizontal line and the other with intersecting the vertical line.

3. Five-year-old children usually can draw parallel lines and are able to reproduce slightly more of a square than a rectangle.

4. Six-year-old children usually elongate the diamond and sometimes make concave lines when doing this.

5. Seven-year-old children typically copy these three letters **accurately** within the space provided without reversals.

+ M W d   − W M b

self-confident	_____	insecure	_____ ✕ _____
cooperative	_____ ✕ _____	reluctant	_____

4 figures or more—adequate
3 figures or less—inadequate

Quality: as expected _____   above _____   below ___✕____

In interpreting Mark's score informally, it is probable that he was given practice in copying letters before he learned closure and angles as required in copying the square and the diamond.

Description of Alphabet Knowledge

The "Alphabet Knowledge Checklist" contained in this chapter can be used to assess abilities in letter matching, letter recognition, and letter identification. Although *letter matching* is the easiest of the three for children to master, it also is not particularly relevant to reading success. Although *letter recognition* also is quite easy for most children to master, it too is not truly significant to reading achievement. The following is an example of *letter recognition:*

Put an X on the capital **R**.

On the other hand, this is an example of *letter identification:*

What is the name of this letter?

R

It is obvious that *letter identification,* not letter recognition, is required in actual reading. Therefore, although letter-matching and letter-recognition activities may be valuable at the beginning stages of reading instruction, letter identification should receive the primary amount of stress.

Although research has discovered that ability in letter identification is highly related to success in beginning reading, it is not a true prerequisite to early reading success. A number of emergent literacy activities such as reading to the child, the language-experience approach, various other kinds of writing experiences, and the learning of environmental print can precede direct instruction in the letter names.

However, it is fairly important for children to learn the letter names early in the reading program for a number of reasons. A child needs to know the letter names in order to call them by a name in beginning reading. He or she cannot, for example, call a lower-case *b* a "circle and a tall stick." I also am sure that a child who can identify the letter names probably has come from a home environment in which all the literacy skills have received a great deal of emphasis.

IMPROVING ALPHABET KNOWLEDGE ABILITY

Here are a few ways in which letter matching, letter recognition, and letter identification can be practiced. For more detail on how to implement these strategies and also to locate many ready-to-duplicate activity sheets in this area, you can consult the following resources:

Wilma H. Miller, *Complete Reading Disabilities Handbook.* West Nyack, NY: The Center for Applied Research in Education, 1993, pp. 214-238.

Strategies and Materials

- Matching capital and lower-case letter name puzzles
- Tactile strategies such as a sand tray, a salt tray, instant pudding, shaving cream, hair gel, fingerpaints, clay play dough, magnetic letters, and edible alphabet pretzels
- Stringing macaroni letters
- Games of various types such as *Alphabet Bingo, Bang, Old Maid Letter Name Game, Letter Chairs,* and *Jump-Up*
- Predictable books
- Dictated and child-written language-experience stories
- Tradebooks that reinforce specific letter names
- Songs and fingerplays
- Teacher-made and commercial activity sheets
- Computer software (these can be very useful in reinforcing both letter recognition and letter identification)

REPRODUCIBLE "ALPHABET KNOWLEDGE CHECKLIST"

Here is a reproducible "Alphabet Knowledge Checklist" on page 30. You can reproduce and use it in its present form or modify it in any way you wish. It assesses ability in letter matching, letter recognition, and letter identification at the emergent literacy level.

Description of Concepts About Books

It is important that children at the emergent literacy level understand various *concepts about books.* Although many children enter kindergarten with very good understanding of these concepts, others do not because of a lack of this type of exposure. Such children need specific instruction and practice in these important concepts at the emergent literacy level.

Concepts about books include such understandings as:

- the purpose of a book
- where to begin reading a book

Name _____ Grade _____ Teacher _____ Date _____

ALPHABET KNOWLEDGE CHECKLIST
(Emergent Literacy Level)

	Always	**Sometimes**	**Never**

Letter Matching

	Always	Sometimes	Never
Is able to match corresponding capital (upper-case) and lower-case letter pairs such as <u>Aa, Bb, Cc, Dd, Ee, Ff, Gg, Hh, Ii, Jj, Kk, Ll, Mm, Nn, Oo, Pp, Qq, Rr, Ss, Tt, Uu, Vv, Ww, Xx, Yy, and Zz</u>	❑	❑	❑

Letter Recognition

	Always	Sometimes	Never
Is able to <u>recognize</u> the capital (upper-case) letter names in isolation	❑	❑	❑
Is able to <u>recognize</u> the capital (upper-case) letter names in context	❑	❑	❑
Is able to <u>recognize</u> the lower-case letter names in isolation	❑	❑	❑
Is able to <u>recognize</u> the lower-case letter names in context	❑	❑	❑

Capital (Upper-Case) Letter Identification

	Always	Sometimes	Never
Is able to identify the capital (upper-case) letter **A** both in isolation and context	❑	❑	❑
Is able to identify the capital (upper-case) letter **B** both in isolation and context	❑	❑	❑
Is able to identify the capital (upper-case) letter **C** both in isolation and context	❑	❑	❑
Is able to identify the capital (upper-case) letter **D** both in isolation and context	❑	❑	❑
Is able to identify the capital (upper-case) letter **E** both in isolation and context	❑	❑	❑
Is able to identify the capital (upper-case) letter **F** both in isolation and context	❑	❑	❑
Is able to identify the capital (upper-case) letter **G** both in isolation and context	❑	❑	❑

ALPHABET KNOWLEDGE CHECKLIST
(Emergent Literacy Level) (Cont.)

	Always	Sometimes	Never
Is able to identify the capital (upper-case) letter **H** both in isolation and context	❏	❏	❏
Is able to identify the capital (upper-case) letter **I** both in isolation and context	❏	❏	❏
Is able to identify the capital (upper-case) letter **J** both in isolation and context	❏	❏	❏
Is able to identify the capital (upper-case) letter **K** both in isolation and context	❏	❏	❏
Is able to identify the capital (upper-case) letter **L** both in isolation and context	❏	❏	❏
Is able to identify the capital (upper-case) letter **M** both in isolation and context	❏	❏	❏
Is able to identify the capital (upper-case) letter **N** both in isolation and context	❏	❏	❏
Is able to identify the capital (upper-case) letter **O** both in isolation and context	❏	❏	❏
Is able to identify the capital (upper-case) letter **P** both in isolation and context	❏	❏	❏
Is able to identify the capital (upper-case) letter **Q** both in isolation and context	❏	❏	❏
Is able to identify the capital (upper-case) letter **R** both in isolation and context	❏	❏	❏
Is able to identify the capital (upper-case) letter **S** both in isolation and context	❏	❏	❏
Is able to identify the capital (upper-case) letter **T** both in isolation and context	❏	❏	❏
Is able to identify the capital (upper-case) letter **U** both in isolation and context	❏	❏	❏
Is able to identify the capital (upper-case) letter **V** both in isolation and context	❏	❏	❏

ALPHABET KNOWLEDGE CHECKLIST
(Emergent Literacy Level) (Cont.)

	Always	Sometimes	Never
Is able to identify the capital (upper-case) letter **W** both in isolation and context	❏	❏	❏
Is able to identify the capital (upper-case) letter **X** both in isolation and context	❏	❏	❏
Is able to identify the capital (upper-case) letter **Y** both in isolation and context	❏	❏	❏
Is able to identify the capital (upper-case) letter **Z** both in isolation and context	❏	❏	❏

Lower-Case Letter Identification

	Always	Sometimes	Never
Is able to identify the lower-case letter **a** both in isolation and context	❏	❏	❏
Is able to identify the lower-case letter **b** both in isolation and context	❏	❏	❏
Is able to identify the lower-case letter **c** both in isolation and context	❏	❏	❏
Is able to identify the lower-case letter **d** both in isolation and context	❏	❏	❏
Is able to identify the lower-case letter **e** both in isolation and context	❏	❏	❏
Is able to identify the lower-case letter **f** both in isolation and context	❏	❏	❏
Is able to identify the lower-case letter **g** both in isolation and context	❏	❏	❏
Is able to identify the lower-case letter **h** both in isolation and context	❏	❏	❏
Is able to identify the lower-case letter **i** both in isolation and context	❏	❏	❏
Is able to identify the lower-case letter **j** both in isolation and context	❏	❏	❏
Is able to identify the lower-case letter **k** both in isolation and context	❏	❏	❏

ALPHABET KNOWLEDGE CHECKLIST
(Emergent Literacy Level) (Cont.)

	Always	Sometimes	Never
Is able to identify the lower-case letter **l** both in isolation and context	❏	❏	❏
Is able to identify the lower-case letter **m** both in isolation and context	❏	❏	❏
Is able to identify the lower-case letter **n** both in isolation and context	❏	❏	❏
Is able to identify the lower-case letter **o** both in isolation and context	❏	❏	❏
Is able to identify the lower-case letter **p** both in isolation and context	❏	❏	❏
Is able to identify the lower-case letter **q** both in isolation and context	❏	❏	❏
Is able to identify the lower-case letter **r** both in isolation and context	❏	❏	❏
Is able to identify the lower-case letter **s** both in isolation and context	❏	❏	❏
Is able to identify the lower-case letter **t** both in isolation and context	❏	❏	❏
Is able to identify the lower-case letter **u** both in isolation and context	❏	❏	❏
Is able to identify the lower-case letter **v** both in isolation and context	❏	❏	❏
Is able to identify the lower-case letter **w** both in isolation and context	❏	❏	❏
Is able to identify the lower-case letter **x** both in isolation and context	❏	❏	❏
Is able to identify the lower-case letter **y** both in isolation and context	❏	❏	❏
Is able to identify the lower-case letter **z** both in isolation and context	❏	❏	❏

- differences between print and pictures
- the function of the title, author, and illustrator of a book

IMPROVING ABILITY IN CONCEPTS ABOUT BOOKS

The concepts about books that you can informally evaluate by using the following checklist can perhaps best be taught by informal individual or small-group instruction with actual tradebooks at the emergent literacy level.

The child or small group of children can be taught the various elements that comprise tradebooks by informal instruction and practice using actual appropriate tradebooks. Although the instruction is easy to do, it must be fairly direct for some children, while others can pick it up informally.

REPRODUCIBLE "CONCEPTS ABOUT BOOKS CHECKLIST"

Here is a reproducible "Concepts About Books Checklist" on page 35. You can use it in its present form or modify it in any way you wish.

Description of Concepts About Print

"Concepts About Print" is a checklist that informally assesses the *basic* emergent and early primary-grade reading skills. It is a general checklist that can be used to assess competencies and weaknesses in knowledge of environmental print, knowledge of the function of letters and words, letter-name knowledge, rudimentary graphophonic (phonic) analysis, and rudimentary structural analysis.

Many of these literacy skills are assessed in much more depth in the checklists found later in this chapter. However, the "Concepts About Print Checklist" assesses ability in them in a more general way. The checklist, however, can be useful as an initial screening device near the beginning stages of reading.

IMPROVING ABILITY IN THE SKILLS ASSESSED BY THE "CONCEPTS ABOUT PRINT CHECKLIST"

A number of the elements that are evaluated first in this checklist can be taught and practiced informally by the use of dictated and child-written language-experience stories. Sight word recognition and identification, graphophonic (phonic) analysis, structural analysis, and semantic (contextual) analysis are briefly described in this chapter before the checklists in various word identification techniques. Strategies and materials for improving competency in all of these skills are described later in this chapter also.

However, detailed descriptions of all the word identification techniques and countless strategies, ready-to-duplicate activity sheets, and materials for improving ability in each of them can be found in the following resources among many others:

Wilma H. Miller, *Complete Reading Disabilities Handbook.* West Nyack, NY: The Center for Applied Research in Education, 1993, pp. 238-338.

Name _____ Grade _____ Teacher _____ Date _____

CONCEPTS ABOUT BOOKS CHECKLIST
(Emergent Literacy Level)

	Always	Sometimes	Never
Understands that a book is for reading	❏	❏	❏
Is able to identify the front and back of a book	❏	❏	❏
Is able to identify the top and bottom of a page in a book	❏	❏	❏
Knows where to begin reading on a page	❏	❏	❏
Knows that a person reads print, not pictures	❏	❏	❏
Is able to turn the pages of a book properly	❏	❏	❏
Knows what the title of a book is	❏	❏	❏
Knows what the author of a book is	❏	❏	❏
Knows what the illustrator of a book is	❏	❏	❏

Wilma H. Miller, *Reading Teacher's Complete Diagnosis & Correction Manual.* West Nyack, NY: The Center for Applied Research in Education, 1988, pp. 168-238.

REPRODUCIBLE "CONCEPTS ABOUT PRINT CHECKLIST"

Offered here beginning on page 37 is a ready-to-use checklist for assessing competencies in overall concepts about print. You can duplicate and use it in its present form or modify it in any way you want.

Brief Description of Sight Word Recognition and Sight Word Identification*

Sight words can be described in several different ways. They can be designated as those words that a reader recognizes immediately upon seeing them. In addition, sight words can be described as those words that do not have a regular sound-symbol relationship. Therefore, these kinds of words cannot be analyzed effectively but are best recognized as a *total unit.* Some examples of sight words are *love, of, mother, father, does,* and *once.*

A sight word is not usually recognized by its individual letters or word parts. Sight-word recognition or identification consists of such subskills as recognizing a word by its total shape, its first few letters, its special characteristics such as *ascenders (b, d, l), descenders (g, y, p)* or its length. *Configuration* or drawing a frame around the word is another subskill of sight-word recognition or identification. Although configuration had not commonly been presented as a technique for teaching sight words for a number of years, it recently has been fairly common in whole language programs.

Two different subskills comprise sight words: sight word recognition and sight word identification. *Sight word recognition* requires the child to select a sight word that the teacher pronounces from several other similar-appearing words. Although it may have some use to emergent literacy, it is not really related to reading since sight word recognition does not occur during actual reading. Here is an example of sight word recognition:

Put an X on the word **have.**

gave   have   love   had

---

*Descriptions and ways to improve ability in the word identification techniques of sight word recognition and identification, graphophonic (phonic) analysis, structural analysis, and semantic (contextual) analysis are presented in this chapter. They are not discussed again in Chapter 6.

Name _____ Grade _____ Teacher _____ Date _____

CONCEPTS ABOUT PRINT CHECKLIST
(Primary-Grade Level)

	Always	Sometimes	Never
Is able to read environmental print such as <u>STOP, Alpha-Bits, Crest, Cheerios</u>, etc.	❏	❏	❏
Knows what a letter is and can point to a letter on a page	❏	❏	❏
Knows what a word is and can point to a word on a page	❏	❏	❏
Knows that print goes from left to right (left-to-right progression)	❏	❏	❏
Know that there are spaces between words (word boundaries)	❏	❏	❏
Knows the purpose of a period	❏	❏	❏
Knows the purpose of a comma	❏	❏	❏
Knows that oral language can be written down and then read by someone	❏	❏	❏
Can recognize such common sight words as <u>mother, dog</u>, and <u>cat</u>.	❏	❏	❏
Can give a rhyming word to a word that is supplied (<u>rat—sat—mat—bat</u>)	❏	❏	❏
Can identify the upper-case letter names	❏	❏	❏
Can identify the lower-case letter names	❏	❏	❏
Associates consonants with their initial and final sounds	❏	❏	❏
Associates consonant blends with their sounds (<u>cl, fl, br, st, dr, pr, sl</u>, etc.)	❏	❏	❏

CONCEPTS ABOUT PRINT CHECKLIST
(Primary-Grade Level) (Cont.)

	Always	Sometimes	Never
Associates vowels with their matching long and short sounds (a-apron, apple; e—each, egg; i—ice, igloo; o—ocean, octopus; u—use, up)	❏	❏	❏
Knows the consonant digraph sounds (ch, sh, voiced and voiceless th, ph and wh)	❏	❏	❏
Can blend phonemes into words	❏	❏	❏
Can segment phonemes found in words	❏	❏	❏
Uses context and syntax to identify unknown words	❏	❏	❏
Can count the number of words in a syllable (up to three syllables in a word)	❏	❏	❏
Uses picture clues as a word identification technique	❏	❏	❏
Can predict unknown words by using context in combination with letter-sound relationships	❏	❏	❏
Can identify common prefixes such as un-, in-, and re-	❏	❏	❏
Can identify common prefixes such as -s, -ed, ing, -ly, and -es	❏	❏	❏

Although *sight word identification* is a more difficult skill for most children, it is the skill required in actual reading. Therefore, it should receive the greatest amount of stress in reading instruction. Here is an example of sight word identification:

What is this word? (have)

have

To be an effective reader a child must have a large stock of sight words that can be recognized instantly. Often these are the words that comprise a sight word list. In addition, a number of words that are first decoded by using another word-identification technique such as graphophonic (phonic) analysis or structural analysis should eventually become part of a child's stock of sight words. Many reading teachers believe a child may need *20–140 meaningful exposures of a word before it becomes part of his or her sight word bank.* Some disabled readers and learning-handicapped students may need even more exposures than that before a sight word is recognized instantly.

The most common sight words are found in a number of different sight word lists. There is considerable overlap among all of the lists although the words contained on each list varies somewhat depending upon the sources from which it was taken (children's reading or writing or a combination of both of them).

The most common sight word list is the *Dolch Basic sight word List* which was formulated by the late Edward Dolch of the University of Illinois. This list of 220 service words is said to make up about *70%* of the words found in most first readers and about *65%* of the words contained in second and third readers. Most of the words in any sight word list are *structure or function words,* which means that they have no referent. Structure or function words usually are more difficult for most children to remember than are *content words* which have a concrete referent. This probably is especially true for learning-handicapped students and the majority of disabled readers.

Here is a way to determine a child's *approximate instructional reading level* as established by his or her performance on the Dolch Basic sight word List:

Words Recognized	*Reading Level*
0–75	Preprimer
76–120	Primer
121–170	First Reader
171–210	Second Reader
Above 210	Third Reader or above[5]

The Dolch Basic Sight Word List

Here is the Dolch Basic Sight Word List in alphabetical order. It should be completely mastered to the level of automaticity by the end of the third-reader level.

---

[5]Maude McBroom, Julia Sparrow, and Catherine Eckstein, *Scale for Determining a Child's Reader Level.* Iowa City, IA: Bureau of Publications, Extension Service, University of Iowa, 1944, p.11. Used by permission of the University of Iowa.

a	done	I	out	these
about	don't	if	over	they
after	down	in	own	think
again	draw	into	pick	this
all	drink	is	play	those
always	eat	it	please	three
am	eight	its	pretty	to
an	every	jump	pull	today
and	fall	just	put	together
any	far	keep	ran	too
are	fast	kind	read	try
around	find	know	red	two
as	first	laugh	ride	under
ask	five	let	right	up
at	fly	light	round	upon
ate	for	like	run	us
away	found	little	said	use
be	four	live	saw	very
because	from	long	say	walk
been	full	look	see	want
before	funny	made	seven	warm
best	gave	make	shall	was
better	get	many	she	wash
big	give	may	show	we
black	go	me	sing	well
blue	goes	much	sit	went
both	going	must	six	were
bring	good	my	sleep	what
brown	got	myself	small	when
but	green	never	so	where
buy	grow	new	some	which
by	had	no	soon	white
call	has	not	start	who
came	have	now	stop	why
can	he	of	take	will
carry	help	off	tell	wish
clean	her	old	ten	with
cold	here	on	thank	work
come	him	once	that	would
could	his	one	the	write
cut	hold	only	their	yellow
did	hot	open	them	yes
do	how	or	then	you
does	hurt	our	there	your[6]

[6]Edward W. Dolch, "Basic Sight Vocabulary." *Elementary School Journal.* 36, March 1936, pp. 456-460. Published by The University of Chicago Press, Copyright 1936 by The University of Chicago. All rights reserved.

The Instant Words

Edward B. Fry, Professor Emeritus of Rutgers University, has compiled an updated version of the *Instant Words* which he first compiled in 1957. This sight word list was revised in 1980 based on a modification of the Carroll (American Heritage) data. The first 100 words make up half of all written material and should be mastered by the end of the first-reader level, while the 300 words together comprise *65%* of all written materials. The first 200 words should be mastered by the end of the second-reader level, while all 300 of the words should be mastered by the end of the third-reader level.

Fry has graciously given all textbook authors permission to reprint the revised Instant Words in the hope that this sight word list will help in the improvement of reading instruction. You will find a complete copy of Fry's Instant Words in Chapter 6 of this handbook.

IMPROVING ABILITY IN SIGHT WORD RECOGNITION AND SIGHT WORD IDENTIFICATION

There are many strategies, materials, and games my teacher-trainees and inservice teachers have used to teach and/or reinforce sight word recognition and identification. Since this handbook deals mainly with assessment, it will mention only a few of the most useful ones. (This also is the case in graphophonic analysis, structural analysis, and semantic analysis.) However, you will find many additional strategies, reproducible activity sheets, and directions for games in the two following sources among many others:

Wilma H. Miller, *Complete Reading Disabilities Handbook.* West Nyack, NY: The Center for Applied Research in Education, 1993, pp. 244-275.

Wilma H. Miller, *Reading Teacher's Complete Diagnosis & Correction Manual.* West Nyack, NY: The Center for Applied Research in Education, 1988, pp. 171-188.

NOTE: sight word identification is best presented and practiced in word and sentence context. Presenting and reinforcing sight word identification in context is in keeping with the whole language philosophy that is widely used in elementary classrooms today. It is very effective with above-average, average, and many disabled readers. However, some disabled readers and learning-handicapped students also need to have sight words emphasized in isolation with tracing strategies, activity sheets, and appropriate games.

Wide Reading

Wide reading is the single most effective way of improving sight word identification at both the primary-grade and intermediate-grade reading levels. The more widely that a child reads from a variety of materials, the larger the stock of sight words that he or she is likely to have. Such wide reading can take place in predictable books, Big Books, child-dictated and child-written experience stories, tradebooks, content textbooks, and children's magazines and newspapers. It is obvious that reading is a skill that best improves with motivated practice.

Additional information about all of the strategies, reproducible examples of all of the activity sheets, and directions for constructing and playing all of these games are found in Wilma Miller's *Complete Reading Disabilities Handbook* (West Nyack, NY: The Center for Applied Research in Education, 1993, pp. 244-275).

Strategies

- Tracing of kinesthetic strategies for hard-to-remember sight words. These can include a colored chalk sand tray, a colored chalk salt tray instant pudding, fingerpaints, shaving cream, oobleck, macaroni, rice, dried beans, pipe cleaners, clay, play dough, magic modeling clay, edible alphabet pretzels, and commercially available magnetic letters.
- Flashcards
- Computer software
- Word bank (often comprised of the important sight words from child-dictated or child-written language-experience stories)
- Sight word puzzles

Activity Sheets

Use creative teacher-made and commercial activity sheets such as the following:
- Locating and Writing Difficult Sight Words
- Locating Hidden Sight Words
- Sight word Search

Games

- Sight Words on Dice
- Word Sort
- Grab Bag Game
- Vocabulary Sewing Cards
- Word Wheels
- Sight Word Crossword Puzzles
- Sight It
- Cover It All
- Sight Word Tic-Tac-Toe
- Newspaper Relay
- Feed the Monkey with Sight Words
- Magician's Hat
- Pick a Chip
- Sight Word Checkers
- Treasure Chest

Brief Description of Graphophonic (Phonic) Analysis

Graphophonic (phonic) analysis can be defined as using the phonic elements in a word to determine its pronunciation and meaning. It is important for a child to learn the *most important graphophonic elements* such as *consonants, consonant blends, long and short vowel sounds,* and *word families (phonograms)* if he or she has the requisite auditory discrimination to do so. However, students in the intermediate grades and junior high school as well as adult readers rarely use graphophonic analysis in decoding an unknown word except *in rare instances* when it may be used along with context cues.

Most of the common graphophonic rules are taught to the typical child by the end of the third-reader level. If a child has not mastered them by that time, it is best to present only the most important graphophonic elements such as those mentioned earlier.

This chapter contains a very brief description of graphophonic elements you may find helpful. *Phonemes* can be defined as the *sounds* that occur in a language. There are about *44* or *45* phonemes in English. When you see a written symbol such as an /f/, you know that this is an example of a phoneme because of the slash marks placed around it. *Graphemes* can be defined as the written symbol for phonemes or sounds. A grapheme can be composed of one letter or more than a letter, depending upon the phoneme of which it is composed. As an example, it takes the two letters *s* and *h* to represent the phoneme /sh/. There are about 251 graphemes or different ways to spell the phonemes of which oral English is composed. Thus, it is obvious that English does not have a completely regular phoneme-grapheme relationship.

If you want definitions and examples of these graphophonic elements, you may consult the *Complete Reading Disabilities Handbook* for information:

- consonants
- consonant blends (consonant clusters)
- consonant digraphs
- vowels
- schwa sound
- diphthongs
- vowel digraphs
- word families (phonograms)
- homophones (homonyms)
- homographs

IMPROVING ABILITY IN GRAPHOPHONIC (PHONIC) ANALYSIS

There are a multitude of strategies, materials, and games that can be used to present and reinforce graphophonic analysis. Graphophonic analysis can be presented both in word context and in isolation.

NOTE: For many children graphophonic analysis probably is best presented and practiced in word context, which is in keeping with the whole language philosophy When it is presented and practiced in the context of reading, the skills usually are much more meaningful for children. However, disabled readers and learning-handicapped students may benefit from isolation instruction and practice in graphophonic analysis.

In such whole language context, graphophonic analysis can be presented and practiced by using predictable books, child-dictated and child-written experience stories, tradebooks, content textbooks, and children's magazines and newspapers. Reading Recovery™, for example, uses predictable books as the main basis for teaching graphophonic analysis. For a description of how this is done, you can consult the *Complete Reading Disabilities Handbook,* pp. 268-274.

Additional information about all of the strategies, reproducible examples of all of the activity sheets, and directions for constructing all of these games are found on pp. 281-298 of that same book.

Strategies

- Mnemonic devices (teaching a child a key word for each different consonant phoneme and vowel phoneme)
- Have several children make and use a code in which numbers are substituted for vowels.
- Word wheels
- Have the child search for and circle a designated phonic element or elements in a school newspaper, local newspaper, or magazine.
- Computer software
- Monkey tachistoscope
- Place large letters on the floor and have the child "skate" from one to another while saying the letter sounds aloud, or have the child stretch a rubber band between words.
- Have the child sort small objects by placing each object into a correct box according to the initial sound of that object.
- Place cards with one phonogram on each spot on the target and paste a consonant blend or consonant digraph on each dart. Have the child hit the phonogram with the dart and pronounce the word formed by the consonant blend or consonant digraph and phonogram.

Activity Sheets

Use creative teacher-made and commercial activity sheets such as the following:

- Double Consonant Substitution
- Diphthong Puzzle
- Omitted Vowels

Games

- The Magic E
- Circle Vowel Game
- Rhyming Worm
- Sound Block
- Supermarket
- Ring-a-Blend
- Beach Ball Bounce

Brief Description of Structural Analysis

Structural analysis can be defined as using word structure or word parts to determine the pronunciation and meaning of unknown words that are met during reading. This word identification technique can be very helpful in improving a child's meaning vocabulary, especially if it is used along with semantic cues and graphophonic analysis. Although it is helpful at the primary-grade reading level, it may be especially helpful in the intermediate grades and above when students can learn many vocabulary terms from word structure.

Structural analysis consists of the following subskills:

- base or root words
- prefixes
- suffixes
- inflections
- syllabication
- accent
- compound words
- word origins

As stated earlier, the study of the most useful prefixes, suffixes, word roots, and word origins may be a very useful aspect of structural analysis since this type of study can add many words to a child's meaning vocabulary, thus subsequently enhancing his or her comprehension ability. The *Complete Reading Disabilities Handbook* (pp. 299-301) contains a comprehensive list of the more common prefixes, suffixes, and word roots and their meanings which you should find useful.

However, the following includes an even more comprehensive list of prefixes, suffixes, word roots, and their meanings:

Edward R. Fry, Jacqueline K. Kress, and Dona Lee Fountoukidis, *The Reading Teacher's Book of Lists,* second edition. Englewood Cliffs, NJ: Prentice-Hall, 1993.

The *Complete Reading Disabilities Handbook* also contains a list of the most useful structural and accent generalizations that should be presented to children. These sixteen generalizations are found on page 302 of that book.

IMPROVING ABILITY IN STRUCTURAL ANALYSIS

This portion of the chapter presents a very brief sampling of the strategies, materials, and games that can be used to present and reinforce the various elements of structural analysis.

> **NOTE:** With the contemporary emphasis of reading as a global, language-based process that stresses comprehension of what is read from the beginning, in many instances structural analysis should be presented and practiced as much as possible within the context of meaningful reading.

Often structural analysis may be more useful than graphophonic analysis since it deals with larger, more meaningful word elements. *However, structural analysis skills probably should be presented in isolation on occasion, especially to disabled readers and learning-handicapped students.*

To reflect the whole language philosophy, structural analysis skills can be taught and reviewed by using such materials as predictable books, child-dictated and child-written experience stories, and content textbooks. Therefore, the single most effective way to improve ability in the use of structural analysis is for the child to read widely from a variety of interesting materials on his or her instructional or independent level. The child, for example, may learn many new vocabulary words by reading material containing prefixes and suffixes that give clues to word meaning.

Additional information about all of the strategies, reproducible examples of all of the activity sheets, and directions for constructing all of these games are found in Wilma Miller's *Complete Reading Disabilities Handbook* (West Nyack, NY: The Center for Applied Research in Education, 1993, pp. 303-318).

Strategies

- Have the child use clay or play dough to construct objects that indicate comparison—*big, bigger, biggest.*
- Construct compound-word puzzles in which the two halves of a compound word are printed on a word card and then cut apart.
- Write parts of a compound word on the chalkboard. Give the child a sheet of paper and have him or her write down as many compound words as possible using different combinations.
- Computer software
- Have the child select real compound words from a list of words that contains true compound words and make-believe compound words; for example:

blackberry   treebark

- Have the child illustrate appropriate compound words in a humorous way; for example:

  catfish   dragonfly   ponytail

- Have the child read material containing homographs correctly and incorrectly depending upon the placement of the accent.
- Contraction crossword puzzle
- Affix card file (this file should contain affixes, their meanings, their origins, and sentences using the affixes)
- Make three columns on a sheet of paper and label them *prefixes, suffixes,* and *root words.* Have children cut words out of the newspaper and paste them into the correct columns.
- Word wheels for prefixes and suffixes
- Select ten one-syllable words and write the words in a column down the left side of a sheet of notebook paper. Have the child think of two-, three-, and four-syllable words that have the same meaning or nearly the same meaning as the one-syllable root. Have a child work with a partner on this activity.

  join   unite   congregate   affiliate

- Print sentences or a paragraph on the chalkboard or the word processor that are variations of the cloze procedure but have deleted morphemes Have the child complete these variations of the cloze procedure.
- Etymology (the study of word origins) may interest some students in the intermediate grades and junior high school.

Activity Sheets

Here is a sampling of the activity sheets that can be used to improve ability in structural analysis:

- Constructing Compound Words
- Deducing Compound Words from Two Clues
- Determining the Meaning of Derivatives
- Using Words Containing a Greek or Latin Word Root

Games

Here are some games that can be constructed to improve ability in structural analysis:

- Construction Clothespins
- Plastic Egg Puzzle
- Stacks
- Prefix and Suffix Baseball
- Making Plurals

- Word Flight
- Affix Relay
- Contraction Tic-Tac-Toe
- Ice Cream Syllabication Rule Scoop
- Butterflies and Root Words

Brief Description of Semantic (Contextual) Analysis

Semantic analysis is a word identification technique in which the reader determines the meaning, and less often, the pronunciation of unknown words by examining the context in which they are found. That context can be the sentence, the adjacent sentences, the paragraph, or occasionally the entire passage.

> **IMPORTANT:** With the current emphasis on whole language and the emphasis upon reading as a global, language-based process that stresses comprehension of what is read from the emergent literacy level, it is obvious that semantic analysis is the single most useful and important word identification technique. Structural analysis may be especially useful when it is used in combination with structural and phonic analysis and when there are not too many unknown words in the reading material. Usually there should not be more than about *1 in 50* unknown words in the material if semantic cues are to be used successfully.

It is very important that all children in the elementary school be taught that semantic analysis is not merely guessing at the meaning of unknown words. It instead is a calculated estimate of the meaning of unknown words which demands interpretive thinking on the reader's part. Since semantic analysis best represents reading as a language-based process that emphasizes comprehension, it undoubtedly should receive the greatest amount of stress as a word identification technique with all children in the elementary school. However, if possible, all children also need to develop some competency in the *important elements* of structural analysis and graphophonic analysis. This may be especially true with learning-handicapped children.

IMPROVING ABILITY IN SEMANTIC (CONTEXTUAL) ANALYSIS

The chapter now very briefly lists some of the strategies and materials that can be used to improve ability in semantic analysis. Additional information about all of the strategies and reproducible examples of the activity sheets are found in Wilma Miller's *Complete Reading Disabilities Handbook,* pp. 320-334.

Strategies

- ***Wide reading of various kinds of materials is the single most important way of improving ability in semantic analysis.*** This reading can take place in predictable books, child-dictated and child-written experience books, tradebooks of all types, content textbooks, various types of newspapers, children's magazines, and reference books. The reading material usually should be on the child's independent or instructional reading level. Have the child listen to tape-recorded material and indicate when a disruption occurs and also indicate why that miscue is inappropriate.

- Teach the child that words *after* the unknown word provide more help in determining the unknown word than words that precede it.

- Print a number of sentences on the chalkboard or a transparency. Each sentence should have an omitted word that could reasonably be replaced by a number of different alternatives. Have a child read a sentence aloud, completing it with one option. Other children in the group can suggest alternative options.

- Crossword puzzles (these can now be constructed by a computer software program)

- Print a number of sentences on the chalkboard or a transparency. Each sentence should contain an irrelevant word. Have the child cross out the irrelevant word and then read the sentence with this word omitted.

- Set a goal of 500 words in context for each lesson. Avoid having a mini-lesson in word analysis during the context reading. Chart the number of words that a student reads in context during a lesson.

- Encourage children to always monitor their silent and oral reading. This monitoring (metacognition) is a *mind-set* in which a child consistently thinks about what he or she is reading. When the child thinks that he or she is not comprehending effectively, he or she should apply appropriate fix-up strategies.

- All of the variations of the cloze procedure (explained in detail in Chapter 7)

- Place a sentence on the chalkboard or a transparency containing a nonsense word. Have the child suggest a word that could be used in that sentence. This activity helps the child use both semantic cues and syntactic cues; for example:

  <u>vrtom</u>　　I saw a <u>vrtom</u> on the way to school yesterday.

- Riddles; for example:

  I am a large black animal that lives in the woods.

  People are often afraid of me.

  I am a b_____. (bear)

Activity Sheets

- Deducing a Mystery Word from Story Context
- Locating and Correcting Incorrect Words in a Story

Description of Oral Reading

Before 1910 the only type of reading instruction in American schools was oral. Even today oral reading receives considerable emphasis especially in the primary grades. At the emergent literacy level it may help a child to read aloud since word pronunciation is then emphasized. It also helps the emergent literacy teacher to assess the child's reading progress.

However, as the child progresses through the primary grades into the intermediate grades, oral reading should receive less emphasis. It is obvious that an adult does very little oral reading but a great deal of silent reading. Therefore, silent reading should receive much more emphasis than oral reading at every level except the emergent literacy level.

Oral reading has a number of unique benefits. Here are some of them:

- to diagnose the characteristics of a child's reading (These include such characteristics as major and minor oral reading miscues, self-corrections, omissions, substitutions, mispronunciations, hesitations, repetitions, reversals, disregard of punctuation, word-by-word reading, and reading without adequate expression. All of these characteristics of oral reading are explained and illustrated in detail in Chapters 4 and 5, which deal with miscue analysis and the Individual Reading Inventory.)
- to read aloud to answer a specific question
- to read aloud in an audience situation
- choral reading
- part-reading as in a play

However, *reading around the circle or "round-robin reading"* is not a justified practice in most cases. It has persisted in elementary reading instruction because it is easy to implement with children. When it is used, most children only pay attention to the part they have to read aloud, and reading often becomes only word identification instead of comprehension. However, reading around the circle may be occasionally acceptable with below-average readers who seem to derive a kinesthetic reinforcement from it. It just must not be used too often.

IMPROVING ABILITY IN ORAL READING

Here are some of the strategies my teacher-trainees have used in tutoring to improve children's oral reading. However, oral reading usually should not receive much emphasis above the primary-grade reading level.

- Have the child tape record his or her oral reading and listen to the tape, monitoring it as he or she follows along with the print.
- Use read-along tapes. We have found teacher-recorded tapes of very motivational tradebooks to be the best since many of the commercially available read-along tapes are paced too rapidly for most children.
- Practice reading in groups of two, three, or four words instead of in a word-by-word manner. Word-by-word reading often interferes with comprehension.
- Encourage the child to observe punctuation marks such as commas and periods.

- Use a marker under each line of material if the child loses his or her place while reading aloud.

- Read aloud often to the child (children) to model excellent oral reading.

- Encourage the child to use appropriate expression while reading orally. However, do not overemphasize oral reading expression.

REPRODUCIBLE CHECKLISTS IN THE WORD-IDENTIFICATION TECHNIQUES AND ORAL READING

The following reproducible checklists beginning on page 52 are designed to help you assess competencies in sight word knowledge, graphophonic (phonic) analysis, structural analysis, and semantic (contextual) analysis. They are designed for use at the first-grade, second-grade, third-grade, and intermediate-grade level. You can duplicate and use any of them in their present form or modify them in any way you want, depending on the needs of your students.

Name _____ Grade _____ Teacher _____ Date _____

CHECKLIST IN THE WORD IDENTIFICATION TECHNIQUES AND ORAL READING
(First-Reader Level)

	Always	**Sometimes**	**Never**
I. Sight Word Recognition and Sight Word Identification			
A. Is able to <u>recognize</u> about <u>170</u> words on the Dolch Basic Sight Word List	❑	❑	❑
B. Is able to <u>identify</u> about <u>170</u> words on the Dolch Basic Sight Word List	❑	❑	❑
C. Is able to <u>recognize</u> the first <u>100</u> words on Fry's Instant Words	❑	❑	❑
D. Is able to <u>identify</u> the first <u>100</u> words on Fry's Instant Words	❑	❑	❑
E. Seems to remember a sight word the day after or several days after it was presented	❑	❑	❑
F. While reading orally or silently at approximately the first-reader level, seems able to recognize most of the words encountered on an automatic basis	❑	❑	❑
G. If used, is able to effectively learn hard-to-retain sight words by using some type of tracing strategy such as felt letters, sandpaper letters, a sand tray, a salt tray, instant pudding, or shaving cream	❑	❑	❑
II. Graphophonic (Phonic) Analysis			
A. Is able to provide the sounds of each of these consonants and is able to provide a word that begins with each of them: <u>b, hard c, soft c, d, f, hard g, soft g, h, j, k, l, m, n, p, r, s, t, v, w, y,</u> and <u>z</u>	❑	❑	❑
B. Is able to pronounce the consonant <u>x</u> correctly when it is found at the end of a word, such as <u>box</u>, and is able to supply a rhyming word to <u>box</u>	❑	❑	❑

CHECKLIST IN THE WORD IDENTIFICATION TECHNIQUES AND ORAL READING
(First-Reader Level) (Cont.)

	Always	Sometimes	Never
C. Is able to pronounce each of the following consonant blends (clusters) and is able to provide a word that begins with that blend: <u>br, fl, gl, pl, sl, sc, sp, sr</u>, and <u>tr</u>	❑	❑	❑
D. Is able to pronounce each of the following consonant digraphs and provide a word that begins with that digraph: <u>th</u> and <u>wh</u>	❑	❑	❑
E. Understands that the <u>k</u> is silent in <u>kn</u>	❑	❑	❑
F. Is able to give the long sound of each vowel (<u>a, e, i, o, u</u>) and provide a word containing each long sound	❑	❑	❑
G. Is able to give the short sound of each vowel (<u>a, e, i, o, u</u>) and provide a word containing each short sound	❑	❑	❑
H. Is able to provide a word that rhymes with each of these phonograms (word families): <u>-ack, -ake, -ame, -ed, -end, -ill, -ime, -in, -ing, -og, -ump</u> (Primer Level) ·	❑	❑	❑
<u>-ail, -air, -alk, -ear, -eek, -ine, -oat, -ope, -unch, -ung</u> (First-Reader Level)	❑	❑	❑

III. Structural Analysis

	Always	Sometimes	Never
A. Is able to identify (recognize by sight) these contractions: <u>aren't, can't, couldn't, didn't, don't, hadn't, haven't, isn't, weren't, won't, wouldn't</u>	❑	❑	❑
B. Is able to add the following suffixes to regular base words: <u>-s, -ed, -ing</u>	❑	❑	❑
C. Exhibits readiness for later syllabication (is able to clap properly for a one- or two-syllable word)	❑	❑	❑

CHECKLIST IN THE WORD IDENTIFICATION TECHNIQUES AND ORAL READING
(First-Reader Level) (Cont.)

	Always	Sometimes	Never
IV. Semantic Analysis			
A. Usually substitutes unknown words for known words that make sense in sentence context and that are grammatically correct	❑	❑	❑
B. Usually is able to pronounce words correctly in context that cannot be pronounced accurately in word lists	❑	❑	❑
C. Is able to correctly complete a modified cloze procedure with the deleted words at the bottom of the sheet in random order (First-Reader Level)	❑	❑	❑
V. Oral Reading			
A. Seems to enjoy reading orally	❑	❑	❑
B. Uses adequate expression while reading orally	❑	❑	❑
C. Is able to stay on the correct line while reading orally	❑	❑	❑
D. Does not reread a line or skip a line while reading orally	❑	❑	❑
E. Observes punctuation marks, such as periods and commas, while reading orally	❑	❑	❑
F. Does not usually lose his/her place while reading orally	❑	❑	❑
G. Comprehends fairly well what he/she has read orally	❑	❑	❑
H. Appears to have no significant speech disorder while reading orally	❑	❑	❑

CHECKLIST IN THE WORD IDENTIFICATION TECHNIQUES AND ORAL READING
(Second-Reader Level)

	Always	Sometimes	Never
I. Sight Word Recognition and Sight Word Identification			
A. Is able to <u>recognize</u> about <u>210</u> words on the Dolch Basic Sight Word List	❏	❏	❏
B. Is able to <u>identify</u> about <u>210</u> words on the Dolch Basic Sight Word List	❏	❏	❏
C. Is able to <u>recognize</u> the first <u>200</u> words on Fry's Instant Words	❏	❏	❏
D. Is able to <u>identify</u> the first <u>200</u> words on Fry's Instant Words	❏	❏	❏
E. Seems to remember a sight word the day after or several days after it was presented	❏	❏	❏
F. While reading orally or silently at approximately the second-reader level, seems able to recognize most of the words encountered on an automatic basis	❏	❏	❏
G. If used, is able to effectively learn hard-to-retain sight words by using some type of tracing strategy	❏	❏	❏
II. Graphophonic (Phonic) Analysis			
A. Is able to pronounce each of the following consonant blends (clusters) and is able to provide a word that begins with that blend: <u>bl, cl, cr, dr, fr, gl, pr, qu, sc, scr, sm, sn, spl, str, squ, thr,</u> and <u>tw</u>	❏	❏	❏
B. Is able to pronounce each of the following consonant digraphs and provide a word that begins with that digraph: <u>ch, ph,</u> and <u>sh</u>	❏	❏	❏
C. Is able to pronounce each of these ending consonant clusters and provide a word that ends with that cluster: <u>ck, ng, ld, mp, nd, nt, st, ft</u>	❏	❏	❏

© 1995 by John Wiley & Sons, Inc.

CHECKLIST IN THE WORD IDENTIFICATION TECHNIQUES AND ORAL READING
(Second-Reader Level) (Cont.)

	Always	Sometimes	Never
D. Understands that <u>w</u> is silent in <u>wr</u>, <u>g</u> is silent in <u>gn</u>, and <u>b</u> is silent in <u>mb</u>	❑	❑	❑
E. Is able to pronounce each of these vowel digraphs and provide a word containing that vowel digraph: <u>ai, ea (each), ee, oa, ay, ow (bowl), ea (head), ae, oo (book), oo (goose), ie</u>	❑	❑	❑
F. Is able to pronounce each of these r-controlled vowel combinations and provide a word containing that r-controlled vowel combination: <u>ar, er, ir, or, ur, air</u>	❑	❑	❑
G. Is able to pronounce each of these diphthongs and provide a word containing that diphthong: <u>voi, ou, oy, ow (owl), ew</u>	❑	❑	❑
H. Is able to pronounce each of these special vowel combinations and provide a word containing that special vowel combination: <u>au</u> and <u>aw</u>	❑	❑	❑
I. Is able to provide a word that rhymes with each of these phonograms: <u>-ace, -ade, -arm, -each, -edge, -eep, -eld, -elp, -ew, -idge, -ile, -ince, -ive, -oak, -old, -ore, -ork, -ought, -ouse, -out, -uck, -ust</u>	❑	❑	❑
J. Is able to apply these two rules for <u>y</u>: <u>y</u> at the end of a multisyllabic word records the long <u>e</u> sound (<u>baby</u>); <u>y</u> at the end of a single-syllable word records the long <u>i</u> sound (<u>fly</u>)	❑	❑	❑
K. Is able to apply the following graphophonic rules:			
1. a single vowel in a closed syllable is usually short	❑	❑	❑
2. a single vowel at the end of a word is usually long	❑	❑	❑

CHECKLIST IN THE WORD IDENTIFICATION TECHNIQUES AND ORAL READING
(Second-Reader Level) (Cont.)

	Always	Sometimes	Never
3. when there are two vowels side by side, the long sound of the first vowel <u>may</u> be heard, while the second vowel <u>may</u> be silent	❑	❑	❑
4. when the same two consonants are located side by side, only one consonant is heard	❑	❑	❑
5. when a word contains two vowels, one of which is final <u>e</u>, the first vowel is long and the final <u>e</u> is silent	❑	❑	❑

III. Structural Analysis

	Always	Sometimes	Never
A. Is able to identify (recognize by sight) these contractions: <u>wasn't, he'll, here's, I'll, I'm, it's, let's, she'll, that's, there'll, there's, they'll, we'll, what's, where's, what'll, you'll, doesn't, hasn't, he's, I've, she's, they're, they've, we're, we've, you're, you've</u>	❑	❑	❑
B. Understands the basic function of prefixes and can add the following prefixes to base words: <u>a-, re-, un-</u>	❑	❑	❑
C. Understands the basic function of suffixes and can add the following suffixes to base words: <u>-en, -er, -es, -est, -ful, -ly, -y</u>	❑	❑	❑
D. Understands and is able to apply these syllabic principles:			
1. when two like consonants stand between two vowels, the word is usually divided between the two consonants let/ter VC/CV	❑	❑	❑
2. when two unlike consonants stand between two vowels, the word is usually divided between the two consonants sand/wich VC/CV	❑	❑	❑

	Always	Sometimes	Never
E. Understands the use of the possessive, such as <u>father's</u>	❏	❏	❏
F. Has readiness for later syllabication	❏	❏	❏
G. Understands the principle of doubling the final consonant in a short word before adding the suffix	❏	❏	❏
H. Understands and is able to apply the principle of changing <u>y to i</u> before adding the suffix <u>es</u>	❏	❏	❏
I. Uses structural analysis skills before applying graphophonic analysis skills in decoding an unknown word when this is applicable	❏	❏	❏

IV. Semantic Analysis

	Always	Sometimes	Never
A. Usually substitutes words for unknown words that make sense in sentence context and that are grammatically correct while reading silently and orally	❏	❏	❏
B. Usually can pronounce words correctly in context that cannot be pronounced correctly in isolated word lists	❏	❏	❏
C. Is able to complete about <u>80%</u> or more of the deleted words correctly from a cloze procedure that combines graphophonic analysis and semantic analysis (see Chapter 7)	❏	❏	❏
D. Is able to complete a semantic analysis inventory correctly at the second-reader level, such as the following:	❏	❏	❏

Barry saw a mother d_____
with twin fawns crossing the road one
summer day.

      draw
      deer
      duck

CHECKLIST IN THE WORD-IDENTIFICATION TECHNIQUES AND ORAL READING
(Second-Reader Level) (Cont.)

	Always	Sometimes	Never
E. Seems to use semantic cues when meeting an unknown word while reading	❑	❑	❑
V. Oral Reading			
A. Seems to enjoy reading orally	❑	❑	❑
B. Uses good expression while reading orally	❑	❑	❑
C. Is able to stay on the correct line while reading orally	❑	❑	❑
D. Does not reread a line or skip a line while reading orally	❑	❑	❑
E. Has made a beginning in reading in phrases or groups of words instead of reading in a word-by-word manner	❑	❑	❑
F. Observes punctuation marks, such as periods and commas, while reading orally	❑	❑	❑
G. Comprehends adequately what he/she has read orally	❑	❑	❑
H. Appears to have no significant speech disorders while reading orally	❑	❑	❑

CHECKLIST IN THE WORD IDENTIFICATION TECHNIQUES AND ORAL READING
(Third-Reader Level)

	Always	**Sometimes**	**Never**
I. Sight Word Recognition and Sight Word Identification			
A. Is able to <u>recognize</u> all <u>220</u> words on the Dolch Basic Sight Word List	❑	❑	❑
B. Is able to <u>identify</u> all <u>220</u> words on the Dolch Basic Sight Word List	❑	❑	❑
C. Is able to <u>recognize</u> all <u>300</u> words on Fry's Instant Words	❑	❑	❑
D. Is able to <u>identify</u> all <u>300</u> words on Fry's Instant Words	❑	❑	❑
E. Seems to remember a sight word the day after it was presented	❑	❑	❑
F. While reading orally or silently at approximately the third-reader level, seems able to recognize most of the words encountered on an automatic basis	❑	❑	❑
G. If applicable, is able to effectively learn hard-to-retain sight words by using some type of tracing strategy	❑	❑	❑
II. Graphophonic (Phonic) Analysis			
A. Is able to pronounce each of the following consonant blends (clusters) and is able to provide a word that begins with that blend: <u>gr, sch, shr, sk,</u> and <u>sw</u>	❑	❑	❑
B. Understands that the <u>gh</u> is silent in <u>ght</u> (might)	❑	❑	❑
C. Is able to provide a word that rhymes with each of these phonograms: <u>-ab, -amp, -ape, -eap, -earn, -eer, -ept, -id, -inch, -int, -iss, -oast, -ob, -oil, -ool, -oss, -ube, -umb, -une, -usk</u>	❑	❑	❑

CHECKLIST IN THE WORD IDENTIFICATION TECHNIQUES AND ORAL READING
(Third-Reader Level) (Cont.)

	Always	Sometimes	Never
D. Understands and can use the _schwa_ sound	❏	❏	❏
E. Is able to apply the following grapho-phonic rules:			
1. y at the end of a single syllable word usually records the long i sound	❏	❏	❏
2. y at the end of a multisyllabic word usually records the long e sound (except in some dialects it records the short i sound)	❏	❏	❏

III. Structural Analysis

	Always	Sometimes	Never
A. Is able to identify (recognize by sight) these contractions: _anybody'd, he'd, I'd, she'd, they'd, we'd, who'd, you'd_	❏	❏	❏
B. Understands the basic function of prefixes and can add the following prefixes to base words: _be-, ex-, in-, dis-, pre-_	❏	❏	❏
C. Understands the basic function of suffixes and can add the following suffixes to base words: _-able, -less, -ment, -ness, -th, -tion_	❏	❏	❏
D. Is able to divide words of two or three syllables correctly	❏	❏	❏
E. Understands and is able to apply these syllabic principles:			
1. prefixes and suffixes are usually separate syllables	❏	❏	❏
2. when a word ends in a consonant and _le_, the consonant usually begins the last syllable	❏	❏	❏
3. divide a compound word between the two words that comprise it	❏	❏	❏

CHECKLIST IN THE WORD IDENTIFICATION TECHNIQUES AND ORAL READING
(Third-Reader Level) (Cont.)

	Always	Sometimes	Never
4. do not divide between the letters in a consonant blend or consonant digraph	❏	❏	❏
F. Understands and is able to apply these accent generalizations:			
1. in two-syllable words the first syllable is usually accented	❏	❏	❏
2. in inflected or derived forms of a word, the primary accent usually falls on the root word	❏	❏	❏
G. Use structural analysis skills before using graphophonic skills in decoding an unknown word when this is applicable	❏	❏	❏

IV. Semantic Analysis

	Always	Sometimes	Never
A. Usually substitutes words for unknown words that make sense in sentence context and that are grammatically correct while reading silently and orally	❏	❏	❏
B. Usually can pronounce words correctly in context that cannot be pronounced correctly in isolated word lists	❏	❏	❏
C. Is able to complete about <u>80%</u> or more of the deleted words correctly or with an acceptable synonym from a traditional cloze procedure at approximately the third-reader level	❏	❏	❏

CHECKLIST IN THE WORD IDENTIFICATION TECHNIQUES AND ORAL READING
(Third-Reader Level) (Cont.)

		Always	Sometimes	Never
D.	Is able to complete a semantic analysis inventory correctly at about the third-reader level, such as the following:	❏	❏	❏

Mario thinks that it is very hard
to do_____

arithmetic
airport
already

problems in his third-grade class.

		Always	Sometimes	Never
E.	Seems to use semantic cues when meeting an unknown word while reading	❏	❏	❏

V. Oral Reading

		Always	Sometimes	Never
A.	Seems to enjoy reading orally	❏	❏	❏
B.	Uses good expression while reading orally	❏	❏	❏
C.	Is able to stay on the correct line while reading orally	❏	❏	❏
D.	Does not reread a line or skip a line while reading orally	❏	❏	❏
E.	Is somewhat competent in reading in phrases or groups of words	❏	❏	❏
F.	Observes punctuation marks, such as periods and commas, while reading orally	❏	❏	❏
G.	Comprehends adequately what he/she has read orally	❏	❏	❏
H.	Appears to have no significant speech disorders while reading orally	❏	❏	❏
I.	Usually avoids fingerpointing while reading orally	❏	❏	❏

Name _____ Grade _____ Teacher _____ Date _____

CHECKLIST IN THE WORD IDENTIFICATION TECHNIQUES AND ORAL READING
(Intermediate-Grade Level)

	Always	**Sometimes**	**Never**
I. Sight Word Recognition and Sight Word Identification			
A. Is able to <u>recognize</u> all of the words on any basic sight word list	❏	❏	❏
B. Is able to <u>identify</u> all of the words on any basic sight word list	❏	❏	❏
C. Is able to <u>recognize</u> all of the words on the Harris-Jacobson Core List (a sight word list encompassing the sixth-reader level) or any other equally comprehensive list	❏	❏	❏
D. Is able to <u>identify</u> all of the words on the Harris-Jacobson Core List (a sight word list encompassing the sixth-reader level) or any other equally comprehensive list	❏	❏	❏
E. Seems to be able to remember a new word the day after or several days after it was presented	❏	❏	❏
F. While reading orally or silently, seems able to recognize most of the words encountered on an automatic basis	❏	❏	❏
G. Seems able to <u>recognize</u> and <u>identify</u> the majority of the words in content textbooks, such as social studies and science, at the appropriate reader level on an automatic basis	❏	❏	❏
II. Graphophonic (Phonic) Analysis			
A. Is able to effectively use all of the <u>consonant elements</u> that were presented and reinforced in the primary grades to decode unknown words	❏	❏	❏
B. Is able to effectively use all of the <u>vowel elements</u> that were presented and reinforced in the primary grades to decode unknown words	❏	❏	❏

		Always	Sometimes	Never
C.	Is able to blend a series of sounds into a recognizable word (skill in auditory blending)	❑	❑	❑
D.	Is able to determine on which occasions it is the most appropriate to use graphophonic analysis as the most effective word-identification technique	❑	❑	❑
E.	Understands and is able to <u>effectively apply</u> (but not necessarily state) the major graphophonic rules that were presented in the primary grades	❑	❑	❑
F.	Seems to be equally competent in using graphophonic analysis in decoding unknown words both in narrative and content material	❑	❑	❑

III. Structural Analysis

		Always	Sometimes	Never
A.	Understands the basic function of prefixes and can add the following prefixes to base words: <u>a-, ad-, anti-, com-, con-, de-, dis-, im-, inter-, mid-, mis-, non-, over-, pre-, post-, sub-, trans-</u>	❑	❑	❑
B.	Knows the meaning of the following prefixes: <u>dis-, de-, ex-, pre-, en-, sub-</u>	❑	❑	❑
C.	Understands the basic function of suffixes and can add the following suffixes to base words: <u>-al, -an, -ance, -ant, -ation, -ence, -hood, -ible -ic, -ion, -ish, -ist, -ity, -ive, -or, -ous, -ship, -some, -ty, -ure, -ward</u>	❑	❑	❑
D.	Is able to correctly syllabicate multisyllabic words	❑	❑	❑
E.	Is able to use primary, secondary, and tertiary accents	❑	❑	❑

CHECKLIST IN THE WORD IDENTIFICATION TECHNIQUES AND ORAL READING
(Intermediate-Grade Level) (Cont.)

	Always	Sometimes	Never
F. Understands and is able to apply the following accent generalizations:			
1. if two vowels are together in the last syllable of a word, it is a clue to an accented final syllable	❏	❏	❏
2. if there are two unlike consonants within a word, the syllable before the double consonant is usually accented	❏	❏	❏
G. Is able to use the meaning of prefixes, suffixes, or word roots to determine the approximate meaning of unknown vocabulary terms found in content reading	❏	❏	❏
H. Uses structural analysis <u>before</u> using graphophonic analysis in decoding unknown words	❏	❏	❏

IV. Semantic Analysis

	Always	Sometimes	Never
A. Usually substitutes words for unknown words that are semantically and syntactically correct while reading silently and orally	❏	❏	❏
B. Usually is able to pronounce words correctly in context that cannot be pronounced correctly in isolation	❏	❏	❏
C. Is able to complete about <u>70-80%</u> of the omitted words correctly or with a synonym from a traditional cloze procedure on the fourth-, fifth-, or sixth-reader level	❏	❏	❏
D. Is able to complete a semantic analysis inventory at the fourth-, fifth-, or sixth-reader level, such as the following:	❏	❏	❏

It can be very exciting to go _____

rollerblading
ranch
research

if a person likes fresh air and exercise.

CHECKLIST IN THE WORD IDENTIFICATION TECHNIQUES AND ORAL READING
(Intermediate-Grade Level) (Cont.)

	Always	Sometimes	Never
E. Is able to use semantic cues equally effectively in narrative and content material	❑	❑	❑
F. Seems to use semantic cues when meeting an unknown word while reading silently and orally	❑	❑	❑

V. Oral Reading

	Always	Sometimes	Never
A. Seems to enjoy reading aloud before an audience	❑	❑	❑
B. Uses good expression while reading orally	❑	❑	❑
C. Does not appear to be tense while reading orally	❑	❑	❑
D. Reads aloud equally well from narrative and content material	❑	❑	❑
E. Observes punctuation marks while reading aloud	❑	❑	❑
F. Reads aloud in thought units or groups of words	❑	❑	❑
G. Is able to comprehend what has been read orally	❑	❑	❑
H. Usually avoids inhibiting factors, such as fingerpointing and head movements, while reading orally	❑	❑	❑

CHECKLIST IN THE WORD IDENTIFICATION TECHNIQUES AND ORAL READING
(Middle-Upper Level)

	Always	Sometimes	Never
I. Sight Word Identification			
A. Is able to <u>identify</u> the general vocabulary words found in narrative and content reading	❏	❏	❏
B. Is able to <u>identify</u> the specialized vocabulary terms encountered in reading various genres of literature	❏	❏	❏
C. Is able to <u>identify</u> the specialized vocabulary terms encountered in reading social studies materials	❏	❏	❏
D. Is able to <u>identify</u> the specialized vocabulary terms encountered in reading science materials	❏	❏	❏
E. Is able to <u>identify</u> the specialized vocabulary terms encountered in reading mathematics materials	❏	❏	❏
II. Graphophonic (Phonic) Analysis			
A. Is able to apply graphophonic analysis <u>when applicable</u> to deduce the pronunciation of general vocabulary terms	❏	❏	❏
B. Is able to apply graphophonic analysis <u>when applicable</u> to deduce the pronunciation of specialized vocabulary terms in the content areas of literature, social studies, science, and mathematics	❏	❏	❏
C. Is able to determine on what occasions it is the most effective to use graphophonic analysis as a word identification technique	❏	❏	❏
III. Structural Analysis			
A. Understands the basic function of prefixes and can add the following prefixes to base words: <u>ambi-, ante-, auto-, be-, bene-, bi-, centi-, circum-, contra-, counter-, di-, e-, em-, en-, extra-, hyper-, hypo-, intra-, micro-, mille-, mono-, over-, poly-, post-, tele-, trans-, with-</u>	❏	❏	❏

© 1995 by John Wiley & Sons, Inc.

CHECKLIST IN THE WORD IDENTIFICATION TECHNIQUES AND ORAL READING
(Middle-Upper Level) (Cont.)

		Always	Sometimes	Never
B.	Knows the <u>meaning</u> of such useful prefixes for vocabulary development as these: <u>ante-, anti-, bene-, bi-, circum-, extra-, micro-, mono-, post-, pro-, trans-</u>	❏	❏	❏
C.	Understands the basic function of suffixes and can add the following suffixes to base words: <u>-able, -arian, -eer, -ent, -ess, -fy, -ism, -ment, -ness, -phobia, -ship, -tude</u>	❏	❏	❏
D.	Knows the <u>meaning</u> of such useful suffixes for vocabulary development as these: <u>-able, (-ible, -ble), -ance, -ar, -ation, -en, -er, -hood, -ment, -ness, -phobia, -ty, -y</u>	❏	❏	❏
E.	Knows the meaning of common word roots such as these which can aid vocabulary development: <u>aero, aud, biblio, bio, cardi, dem, dict, foc, geo, gen, hydr, loc, miss, neo, ped, port, psych, spec, urb, vid</u>	❏	❏	❏
F.	Uses the meanings of prefixes, suffixes, and word roots to determine the approximate meaning of unknown vocabulary terms found in the content areas of literature, social studies, science, and mathematics	❏	❏	❏
G.	Is able to correctly syllabicate multisyllabic words (especially those found in the content areas of literature, social studies, science, and mathematics)	❏	❏	❏
H.	Is able to use primary, secondary, and tertiary accents and is able to apply accents to general and specialized vocabulary terms	❏	❏	❏
I.	Uses good judgment about when to apply structural analysis skills as a word identification technique	❏	❏	❏
J.	Uses structural analysis skills before graphophonic skills in decoding unknown words	❏	❏	❏

CHECKLIST IN THE WORD IDENTIFICATION TECHNIQUES AND ORAL READING
(Middle-Upper Level) (Cont.)

	Always	Sometimes	Never
IV. Semantic Analysis			
A. Usually substitutes words for unknown words that are semantically and syntactically correct while reading silently and orally	❏	❏	❏
B. Usually is able to pronounce words correctly in context that cannot be pronounced correctly in isolation	❏	❏	❏
C. Is able to pronounce about 70-80% of the omitted words correctly or with a synonym from a traditional cloze procedure	❏	❏	❏
D. Is able to use semantic cues effectively while reading narrative material such as literature	❏	❏	❏
E. Is able to use semantic cues effectively while reading content material such as social studies, science, and mathematics	❏	❏	❏
F. Seems to use semantic cues effectively while reading silently and orally	❏	❏	❏
V. Oral Reading			
A. Seems to enjoy reading aloud before an audience	❏	❏	❏
B. Has good expression while reading orally	❏	❏	❏
C. Does not appear to be tense while reading orally	❏	❏	❏
D. Reads aloud equally well from narrative and content material	❏	❏	❏
E. Observes punctuation marks while reading orally	❏	❏	❏
F. Reads aloud in thought units or groups of words	❏	❏	❏
G. Is able to comprehend what has been read orally	❏	❏	❏
H. Usually avoids inhibiting factors such as fingerpointing and head movement while reading orally	❏	❏	❏

Name _____ Grade _____ Teacher _____ Date _____

CHECKLIST FOR SELF-MONITORING (SELF-EVALUATION) WHILE USING THE WORD IDENTIFICATION TECHNIQUES
(Intermediate-Grade and Middle-Upper Level)

After you read each sentence, put a ✓ in the box under the word **Yes** or **No**.

	Yes	**No**
1. I can identify almost immediately most of the words in the tradebooks that I read.	❏	❏
2. I can identify almost immediately most of the words in the content textbooks that I read.	❏	❏
3. I can sound out words that I can't pronounce while I'm reading.	❏	❏
4. I usually know <u>when</u> I should sound out a word that I can't identify while I'm reading.	❏	❏
5. I know what a base or root word is.	❏	❏
6. I know what a prefix is and can attach a prefix to a base (root) word.	❏	❏
7. I know what a suffix is and can attach a suffix to a base (root) word.	❏	❏
8. I can divide an unknown word into syllables to help me identify it.	❏	❏
9. I know that I usually should divide a longer word into syllables before I try to sound it out.	❏	❏
10. I usually know which syllable of a word is accented.	❏	❏
11. I usually can figure out the meaning of a word that I don't know by using the other words in the sentence to help me.	❏	❏
12. If I meet a word whose meaning I don't know while I'm reading, I usually read to the end of the sentence to help me figure out the meaning of that word.	❏	❏
13. What I read usually makes sense to me.	❏	❏
14. Even if I don't know the exact meaning of an unknown word, I usually can make a good guess about its meaning.	❏	❏
15. When I meet an unknown word while I'm reading, I usually know what the best way is for me to try to figure out its pronunciation and meaning.	❏	❏

CHAPTER THREE

Using Checklists and Other Informal Devices to Assess Competencies and Weaknesses in Vocabulary, Comprehension Skills, the Basic Study Skills, and Silent Reading

Most students in the intermediate grades and middle school have a fairly good sight-word bank and adequate application of graphophonic elements (although they often cannot correctly name most of the graphophonic elements or state the rules). They usually also are fairly competent in structural analysis and literal (explicit) comprehension.

However, most disabled readers and learning-handicapped students whom my teacher-trainees have tutored are weak both in semantic (meaning) analysis and interpretive (implicit) comprehension. One such disabled reader whom one of my teacher-trainees recently tutored was a fifth-grade student named Dan.

Along with using an Individual Reading Inventory to determine Dan's independent, instructional, and frustration reading levels, the teacher-trainee also assessed his specific literacy strengths and weaknesses through observation by using a structured checklist. This mainly was done to verify and expand upon the results of the IRI. The use of a checklist gave the teacher-trainee additional valuable information that she could use in planning the tutoring sessions.

She found that Dan's main difficulty was with interpretive (implicit) comprehension. He was especially weak in using prior knowledge and effective prediction strategies. He also had considerable difficulty while reading social studies materials. He had less difficulty with interpretive comprehension when he read science and narrative materials. He also found the cause-effect relationships, which are important to effective comprehension in social studies, very challenging.

Dan could not find directly stated main ideas in paragraphs, much less locate the implied main ideas often found in content textbooks. He also was not competent in the use of semantic cues, especially when reading social studies, but was somewhat better in using them in narrative and science materials. Dan was a reluctant reader who did not like to read any type of materials for pleasure. However, he was a cooperative, well-mannered, pleasant boy who tried hard to improve.

Dan's teacher-trainee used a variety of strategies and materials to help him improve his interpretive comprehension ability. Many of them are listed later in this chapter. She also tried to empower him by always giving him a choice of tradebooks or magazine articles. He especially liked to read articles from the magazine *Ranger Rick*. Dan made considerable progress during the course of the tutoring both in his interpretive comprehension skills and in developing a more positive attitude toward reading for pleasure and information.

Brief Description of Vocabulary Knowledge*

Meaning vocabulary can be defined as the number of words to which an individual can attach one or more meanings. There also are several different kinds of meaning vocabularies in which a child should gain competence. They are: the *listening vocabulary*, the *speaking vocabulary*, the *reading vocabulary*, the *writing vocabulary*, and the *potential or marginal vocabulary* (all the words the child can determine the meaning of on a specific occasion by using context cues; the meaning of prefixes, suffixes, or word roots; or by understanding derivatives).

Reading comprehension is considered by most contemporary researchers to be a *global language-based process* that cannot be subdivided into discrete levels. Indeed, research has discovered that reading comprehension actually is composed of only two major areas: *vocabulary knowledge (word meaning)* and *understanding the printed material*.

Thus, it is obvious that an extensive meaning vocabulary is essential to effective reading comprehension. Although a well-developed meaning vocabulary is very helpful to comprehension at all reading levels, it is essential in comprehending material at the intermediate-grade reading level and beyond.

The traditional view of meaning vocabulary states that *words* are of primary importance in reading comprehension, and without adequate comprehension of individual words there can be no adequate comprehension. Although this seems logical, there is more to the comprehension of printed material than the meaning of individual words taken together. Today many reading specialists believe that because of the *redundancy* in language, cues within written material provide the information needed for comprehension, and that knowledge of individual word meanings really is not that important. While it is true that redundancy (word-order cues) in language does provide important clues to word meanings, the following example indicates that a reader also often must know the meanings of individual words to ensure comprehension of what is read.

---

*Descriptions of and ways to improve ability in vocabulary knowledge, the comprehension skills, and the basic study skills are presented in this chapter. They are *not* discussed again in Chapter 7.

- That smart child is fun to talk with since she knows so much.
- That erudite juvenile is joyous to converse with due to the fact that she is cognizant of a multitude of knowledges.

It is obvious that although the sentence structure and content of the second sentence is nearly the same as that of the first one, the vocabulary in the second sentence would be much more difficult for an elementary-school child to understand.

Content areas such as social studies, science, and arithmetic contains many specialized vocabulary terms that a student must be able to understand in order to effectively comprehend content textbooks and reference materials in the area. Since a number of content textbooks also are written at a level higher than the reading level of some students who are to read them, they indeed are very difficult for a number of students.

IMPROVING ABILITY IN VOCABULARY KNOWLEDGE

There are many strategies and materials that can be used to improve ability in meaning vocabulary from the emergent literacy level and beyond. Some are briefly mentioned here.

- Direct and first-hand experiences such as school trips to various places (including the zoo, fire station, post office, dairy, airport, hospital, museum, or planetarium, among many others) depending upon your location. Direct experiences probably are the single best way to improve meaning vocabulary.
- Vicarious or second-hand experiences such as videotapes, computer software, demonstrations, scientific experiments, pictures, guest speakers, actual objects, models, role playing, and creative dramatics. Vicarious experiences also are a very good way to improve meaning vocabulary although normally not quite as effective as direct experiences. However, a child cannot, for example, today experience a trip on the Oregon Trail but might learn a number of new vocabulary terms from using the computer simulation about it. The *whole language philosophy* is very well suited to helping students learn many new vocabulary terms from direct and vicarious experiences while participating in a classroom study of a subject such as the rain forest.
- Prediction strategies used both before and during narrative and content reading. Prediction of story, book, or chapter content is very effective in helping a child learn a number of new vocabulary terms.
- Pre-Reading Plan (PReP)
- Activation of prior knowledge before reading
- Semantic maps or webs constructed with the teacher, a partner, or independently before or after reading
- Semantic features analysis grid
- Semantic categories

- Emphasis on context cues
- Word-connection procedure
- Discussing and illustrating figurative language

Descriptions and ready-to-use examples of many of these strategies are found in the following resource:

Wilma H. Miller, *Reading Comprehension Activities Kit.* West Nyack, NY: The Center for Applied Research in Education, 1990, pp. 19-20 and 91-112.

Brief Description of Reading Comprehension

Reading comprehension is constructing and reconstructing meaning from the printed material. It is an *interactive process* that requires the use of the *prior knowledge* a reader has in combination with the reading material. It therefore is obviously necessary to consider both the characteristics of the reader and the printed material. In most cases prior knowledge is more important to the understanding of the reading material than is the material. The more extensive a reader's prior knowledge, the less he or she has to rely on the printed material. That is why an historian, for example, usually can read a history textbook more rapidly and effectively than can a person with less prior knowledge in history.

One aspect of contemporary research in comprehension is called *schema theory.* Schema theory attempts to explain how a person stores information or knowledge in his or her mind, how the knowledge currently possessed is used, and how new knowledge is acquired by a person.

Another aspect of comprehension is *metacognition or self-monitoring* of what is read. Self-monitoring is concerned with a child's awareness of his or her own thinking while trying to understand the printed material. It is very important to teach a child to monitor his or her comprehension while reading. Good readers usually are very adept at self-monitoring, while poor readers are not competent. They often are not concerned whether or not a sentence or paragraph makes sense.

Today most researchers consider comprehension to be a *global, language-based process* that cannot be subdivided into levels. They state that reading comprehension is composed of only two major areas: *vocabulary knowledge (word meaning)* and the *understanding of the printed material.*

Some researchers say that since comprehension cannot be divided into subskills in research studies, the various levels of comprehension, therefore, should not be taught to children, However, I think it is still important to teach the most useful elements of comprehension separately, at least at times, to ensure that both adequate and disabled readers achieve mastery in them. I agree, though, that much of the time these comprehension skills should be taught in the context of meaningful material at the appropriate reading level.

In any case, here are the main subskills of reading comprehension.

Explicit (Literal or Factual) Comprehension

- responding to explicit or literal questions; these questions are called *"Right There"* or *reading the lines*
- locating the directly stated main idea in a paragraph
- locating significant and irrelevant details in a paragraph
- placing a number of items in correct order or sequence
- reading and carrying out directions

Implicit (Interpretive or Inferential) Comprehension

- responding to implicit or interpretive comprehension questions; these questions are called *"Think and Search"* or *reading between the lines*
- interpreting, inferring, and drawing conclusions and generalizations
- predicting outcomes
- sensing an author's mood and purpose
- summarizing what is read
- understanding cause-effect and comparison-contrast relationships
- locating the implied main idea

Critical (Implicit or Evaluative) Reading

- Some reading specialists consider this an aspect of interpretive comprehension. However, there is *judging or evaluating* involved in critical reading. Critical reading is *"Think and Search"* and *reading between the lines.*
- discriminating between real and make-believe or between fact and fantasy
- evaluating the accuracy and truthfulness of the reading material
- comparing materials from several sources
- interpreting figurative language
- sensing an author's biases
- recognizing the various propaganda techniques such as testimonials, the bandwagon effect, glittering generalities, emotionally-toned words, and the halo effect

Creative (Schema Implicit or Applied) Comprehension

- Creative comprehension requires combining prior knowledge with the knowledge, attitudes, or insights gained from reading to develop a new product. It is *"On My Own"* and *reading between the lines.*
- application of reading to one's own life for problem-solving
- cooking and baking activities after reading simplified recipes
- creative writing of prose and poetry
- art activities as a follow-up to reading
- construction activities as a follow-up to reading

- rhythm activities as a follow-up to reading
- creative dramatics and sociodrama
- scientific experiments
- demonstrations
- puppetry
- creative book reports
- reading materials that appeal to the emotions or the affective domain

IMPROVING ABILITY IN READING COMPREHENSION

There are many strategies and materials that can be used to present and reinforce the various elements of comprehension. Comprehension skills can be presented and practiced both in story context and by using various types of especially-designed activity sheets.

> **NOTE:** For many children the various comprehension skills can best be taught and practiced in story context using predictable books, picture storybooks, other kinds of tradebooks, chapter books, and content textbooks, which is in keeping with the whole language philosophy. When these skills are presented and reinforced in the context of actual reading, they usually are much more meaningful for children. However, I believe the various elements of comprehension also can be presented and practiced at times by using strategies and activity sheets that are not always directly related to one particular tradebook or content textbook.

Complete descriptions of all these strategies and ready-to-duplicate activity sheets are found in the following two resources:

Wilma H. Miller, *Complete Reading Disabilities Handbook*. West Nyack, NY: The Center for Applied Research in Education, 1993, pp. 342-377.

Wilma H. Miller, *Reading Comprehension Activities Kit*. West Nyack, NY: The Center for Applied Research in Education, 1990.

Strategies

- Language-experience approach, predictable books, and Big Books (the emergent literacy level)
- Wide reading of relevant, interesting narrative and expository (content) materials at the independent and low-instructional reading level
- Prediction strategies used both before and during reading
- Pre-Reading Plan (PReP)
- Anticipation Guide
- Directed Reading Activity (DRA)
- Directed Reading-Thinking Activity (DR-TA)

- Story impressions
- Semantic maps (semantic webs or story maps)
- K-W-L and K-W-L Plus (both very good for expository (content) reading at the intermediate-grade and middle-school level)
- QARs (questioning strategies)
- Concept Question Chain
- ReQuest Procedure (reciprocal questioning)
- Self-monitoring of reading comprehension
- Visual imagery
- Herringbone Technique
- Knowledge and use of punctuation marks
- Variations of the cloze procedure
- Maze technique
- Fix-up strategies
- Guided Reading Procedure
- A study strategy such as Survey Q3R, Survey Q4R, and PQRST
- The retelling technique
- Text lookbacks
- All types of *writing activities*, such as summary writing, Generating Interactions Between Schemata and Text (GIST) Procedure, and response journals, can help improve comprehension skills since reading and writing skills are related.

Brief Description of the Study Skills

The different content areas require competence in a number of unique study skills. Although there is considerable overlap how these skills are used in different content areas, there also are some differences that should be considered when they are presented in literature, social studies, science, and arithmetic. It is important that students in the intermediate grades and middle school have instruction and practice in the important strategies required in comprehending and remembering content material effectively.

The study skills may be organized in categories such as these:

- knowing specialized vocabulary
- selecting information
- organizing information
- using graphic aids
- following directions
- improving reading rate and flexibility

For a complete description of the subskills that comprise all of the study skills elements in different content areas, you can consult the following resources:

> Wilma H. Miller, *Reading Teacher's Complete Diagnosis & Correction Manual.* West Nyack, NY: The Center for Applied Research in Education, 1988, pp. 276-280.

Improving Ability in the Study Skills

Many of the strategies included in the previous section on how to improve ability in the comprehension skills are equally applicable for improving ability in the study skills. Since reading is a tool, expository (content) materials such as literature, social studies, science, and arithmetic are very effective in giving students the opportunity to learn and practice reading strategies. Many of the ready-to-use activity sheets included in the following three resource books were constructed from the content areas of social studies and science:

> *Complete Reading Disabilities Handbook,* pp. 342-377
> *Reading Comprehension Activities Kit*
> *Reading Teacher's Complete Diagnosis & Correction Manual,* pp. 239-297

These *strategies* seem especially well suited for use in content materials:

- Pre-Reading Plan (PReP)
- Anticipation Guide
- Semantic webs (vocabulary overviews or graphic organizers)
- Directed Reading-Thinking Activity (DR-TA)
- K-W-L and K-W-L Plus
- ReQuest Procedure (reciprocal questioning)
- QARs (questioning strategies)
- Concept Question Chain
- Herringbone Technique
- Guided Reading Procedure
- Semantic Features Analysis
- Text Lookbacks
- Idea Mapping
- C/T/Q Strategy
- A study strategy such as Survey Q3R, Survey Q4R, PQRST, OK4R, POINT, C2R, and REAP
- Learning about different text structures such as simple listing, ordered listing, problem and solution, cause and effect, and comparison and contrast

- SEARCH (**s**et goals, **e**xplore sources and information, **a**nalyze and organize information, **r**efine and **r**ehearse, **c**ommunicate with others, and **h**elp yourself to improve)
- Inquiry Method
- Teaching a note-taking system such as NSL
- Teaching study habits
- Writing summaries

Reproducible Checklists

The following checklists (see pages 81–112) assess competencies and weaknesses in vocabulary, comprehension skills, the basic study skills, and silent reading. You may duplicate and use any of these checklists in their present form or modify them in any way you wish to suit your students' particular needs and interests.

Description of Assessment Using the Retelling Technique

The *retelling technique* also can be called the *tell-back strategy*. This strategy first was used around 1920 as the major way of assessing comprehension. Retelling was discontinued after a time due to the difficulty of accurately assessing a child's responses on the first standardized reading tests that were given around that time. Instead, such tests used multiple-choice items to assess comprehension skills because they were easier to evaluate. However, today retelling is used quite commonly especially in whole language programs because it assesses holistic comprehension in an informal way. It is an example of what is called *process comprehension*.

Allowing a listener or reader to retell a story or book offers active participation in a literacy experience that helps a child develop language structures, comprehension, and a sense of story structure. Retelling in either an oral or written form engages the child in holistic comprehension and organization of thought. It also encourages personalization of thinking as children merge their own life experiences into the retelling.

Retelling is different than asking a child to respond to comprehension questions since it emphasizes holistic comprehension instead of isolated pieces of information. With practice in retelling, children also begin to understand the concept of *story structure*. They learn to introduce a story with its beginning and its setting. They learn to recall its theme, plot episodes, and resolution. They also demonstrate understanding of story details and sequence.

Improving Ability in the Retelling Technique

To use this simple, but valuable, technique, it is important to tell a child before he or she reads a story or book that he or she is going to be asked to retell it. Even then it is not an easy task for many primary-grade children, but with practice they make rapid improvement. Further guidance depends upon the teacher's purpose in the retelling. If the intent is to teach or assess sequential ability, the child should be told to concentrate

Name _____ Grade _____ Teacher _____ Date _____

EMERGENT LITERACY CHECKLIST
EVALUATING VOCABULARY AND COMPREHENSION
(Emergent Literacy Level)

	Always	Sometimes	Never
I. Vocabulary Development			
A. Has appropriate vocabulary for his/her level of maturity	❑	❑	❑
B. Uses interesting, precise vocabulary	❑	❑	❑
C. Understands the meaning of the words used by his/her teacher	❑	❑	❑
D. Understands the meaning of the words used by his/her peers	❑	❑	❑
E. Learns new vocabulary terms easily from various settings such as field trips, demonstrations, computer software, videotapes, guest speakers	❑	❑	❑
F. Speaks in complete sentences	❑	❑	❑
G. Uses varied syntactical (grammatical) structures	❑	❑	❑
H. Uses "book language" while retelling a story	❑	❑	❑
I. Understands the vocabulary of predictable books, Big Books, picture storybooks, realistic literature, and information books that are read aloud to him/her	❑	❑	❑
II. Comprehension			
A. Pays attention while predictable books, Big Books, picture storybooks, realistic literature, and information books are read aloud to him/her either on a large-group or individual basis	❑	❑	❑
B. Enjoys hearing predictable books, Big Books, picture storybooks, realistic literature, and information books that are read aloud to him/her	❑	❑	❑

EMERGENT LITERACY CHECKLIST
EVALUATING VOCABULARY AND COMPREHENSION
(Emergent Literacy Level) (Cont.)

		Always	Sometimes	Never
C.	Is able to make plausible predictions from a story or book title that is read aloud to him/her	❑	❑	❑
D.	Participates in story reading by narrating as the teacher reads	❑	❑	❑
E.	Is able to retell a story in a general (overall) manner	❑	❑	❑
F.	Includes some general elements as these in story retellings: 1. setting 2. theme 3. plot episodes 4. resolution	❑	❑	❑
G.	Responds to text after listening with literal (explicit) comments or questions	❑	❑	❑
H.	Is able to answer literal (explicit) comprehension questions after hearing a predictable book, Big Book, picture storybook, realistic book, or information book read aloud to him/her	❑	❑	❑
I.	Responds to text after listening with interpretive (implicit) comments or questions	❑	❑	❑
J.	Is able to answer interpretive (implicit) comprehension questions after hearing a predictable book, Big Book, picture storybook, realistic book, or information book read aloud to him/her	❑	❑	❑
K.	Responds to text after listening with critical (evaluative) comments or questions	❑	❑	❑
L.	Is able to answer critical (evaluative) questions after hearing a predictable book, Big Book, picture storybook, realistic book, or information book read aloud to him/her	❑	❑	❑

Teacher Comments:

CHECKLIST FOR ASSESSING VOCABULARY, COMPREHENSION, THE BASIC STUDY SKILLS, AND SILENT READING
(Primary-Grade Reading Level)

	Always	Sometimes	Never
I. Vocabulary			
A. Uses vocabulary appropriate for his/her grade level	❑	❑	❑
B. Uses interesting, precise vocabulary terms	❑	❑	❑
C. Is able to understand the vocabulary used by his/her teacher	❑	❑	❑
D. Is able to understand the vocabulary while reading or listening to narrative materials	❑	❑	❑
E. Uses prediction strategies and activates prior knowledge before reading to improve his/her vocabulary	❑	❑	❑
F. Is able to understand the vocabulary contained in content materials such as social studies and science while reading or being read to	❑	❑	❑
G. Is able to understand figurative language (figures of speech and personification) at a very elementary level	❑	❑	❑
H. Is able to learn new vocabulary terms easily from direct and second-hand experiences such as field trips, videotapes, computer software, guest speakers, and demonstrations	❑	❑	❑
I. Uses newly learned vocabulary terms in his/her speaking and/or writing	❑	❑	❑
J. Uses "book language" when retelling a story or book	❑	❑	❑

II. Some Elements of *Overall* Comprehension Ability

A. Use of Prequestioning Skills

© 1995 by John Wiley & Sons, Inc.

CHECKLIST FOR ASSESSING VOCABULARY, COMPREHENSION, THE BASIC STUDY SKILLS, AND SILENT READING
(Primary-Grade Reading Level) (Cont.)

	Always	Sometimes	Never
1. Is able to form his/her own purposes for reading a narrative selection	❏	❏	❏
2. Is able to form his/her own purposes for reading an expository (content) selection	❏	❏	❏
3. Is able to formulate his/her own questions before reading narrative or expository (content) passage	❏	❏	❏

B. Use of Prediction Strategies

	Always	Sometimes	Never
1. Is able to predict the story content of a narrative story from its title	❏	❏	❏
2. At appropriate stopping points in a narrative story is able to predict what is going to happen next; i.e., "What do you think is going to happen now?"	❏	❏	❏
3. Upon finishing reading the material is able to evaluate if his/her predictions prior to reading were accurate	❏	❏	❏
4. Usually makes predictions prior to reading that were determined to be accurate following the reading	❏	❏	❏
5. Has some understanding of the Directed Reading-Thinking Activity (DR-TA) (second- and third-reader levels)	❏	❏	❏

C. Use of Self-Monitoring Skills

	Always	Sometimes	Never
1. Has a positive attitude toward reading and a good self-perception about his/her reading ability	❏	❏	❏
2. Is able to understand the purpose of reading	❏	❏	❏

CHECKLIST FOR ASSESSING VOCABULARY, COMPREHENSION, THE BASIC STUDY SKILLS, AND SILENT READING
(Primary-Grade Reading Level) (Cont.)

	Always	Sometimes	Never
3. Is able to modify his/her reading strategies for different purposes	❏	❏	❏
4. Is able to consider how new information relates to what is already known	❏	❏	❏
5. Is able to evaluate the reading material for clarity, completeness, and consistency	❏	❏	❏
6. Is able to determine the important information in a passage	❏	❏	❏
7. Is able to determine after reading how well the material was understood	❏	❏	❏

D. Several Other Important Elements of Comprehension

	Always	Sometimes	Never
1. Is able to complete a partially completed semantic map at the appropriate reading level	❏	❏	❏
2. Is able to make useful images while reading narrative material	❏	❏	❏
3. Observes punctuation marks, such as the period and comma, while reading	❏	❏	❏

III. Comprehension Skills

A. Explicit (Literal or Factual) Comprehension

	Always	Sometimes	Never
1. Is able to answer explicit (literal, recall, or factual) questions from narrative or expository material at the first-reader, second-reader, or third-reader level that the child has read for him-/herself	❏	❏	❏
2. Is able to retell a story or book on approximate grade level	❏	❏	❏

CHECKLIST FOR ASSESSING VOCABULARY, COMPREHENSION, THE BASIC STUDY SKILLS, AND SILENT READING
(Primary-Grade Reading Level) (Cont.)

	Always	Sometimes	Never
3. Includes these elements in a story retelling:			
a. setting	❑	❑	❑
b. theme	❑	❑	❑
c. plot episodes	❑	❑	❑
d. resolution	❑	❑	❑
4. Is able to orally state the main idea of a picture storybook (tradebook) that he/she has read	❑	❑	❑
5. Seems more competent with explicit than implicit comprehension	❑	❑	❑
6. Is able to carry out oral or written directions of about 3-5 steps in correct order	❑	❑	❑
7. Is able to place 3-8 steps in sequential order (depending on grade level)	❑	❑	❑
8. Is able to select the most important details in a picture storybook (tradebook)	❑	❑	❑
9. Is able to locate the directly stated main idea in a paragraph at the appropriate reading level if it is found in the topic sentence of that paragraph	❑	❑	❑

B. Implicit (Interpretive) Comprehension

	Always	Sometimes	Never
1. Is able to answer implicit (interpretive) comprehension questions at the first-reader, second-reader, or third-reader level. These questions call for predicting outcomes, interpreting, inferring, drawing conclusions and generalizations, and summarizing	❑	❑	❑

CHECKLIST FOR ASSESSING VOCABULARY, COMPREHENSION, THE BASIC STUDY SKILLS, AND SILENT READING
(Primary-Grade Reading Level) (Cont.)

	Always	Sometimes	Never
2. Understands that sometimes a question can have multiple acceptable responses that make sense	❑	❑	❑
3. Is able to orally or in writing summarize a picture storybook in one or two sentences	❑	❑	❑
4. Is able to orally or in writing summarize a content selection from a social studies or science textbook	❑	❑	❑
5. Is able to understand and apply simple cause-effect relationships	❑	❑	❑
6. Is able to orally state an author's purpose for writing a picture storybook (tradebook)	❑	❑	❑
7. Is equally competent in implicit and explicit comprehension	❑	❑	❑
C. Critical (Implicit) Comprehension			
1. Is able to answer questions that call for critical or evaluative responses from material at the first-reader, second-reader, or third-reader level	❑	❑	❑
2. Is able to discriminate between real and make-believe (fact and fantasy)	❑	❑	❑
3. Is able to recognize and understand the feelings, motives, and actions of story characters with some degree of competence	❑	❑	❑
4. Is able to evaluate the actions of individuals or groups with some degree of competence	❑	❑	❑

CHECKLIST FOR ASSESSING VOCABULARY, COMPREHENSION, THE BASIC STUDY SKILLS, AND SILENT READING
(Primary-Grade Reading Level) (Cont.)

	Always	Sometimes	Never
D. Creative (Script or Schema Implicit) Comprehension	❏	❏	❏
1. Is able to relate what he/she reads or hears read to improve his/her own life in some way	❏	❏	❏
2. Is able to follow up reading in a problem-solving way such as by cooking or baking activities, art activities, construction activities, dramatic play, creative dramatics, rhythm activities, or creative writing of prose or poetry	❏	❏	❏
3. Is able to relate reading and writing activities in a creative manner	❏	❏	❏

IV. Study Skills

	Always	Sometimes	Never
A. Is able to use a table of contents at the first-reader, second-reader, or third-reader level	❏	❏	❏
B. Is able to use the page numbers in a tradebook or content textbook to find the required page	❏	❏	❏
C. Is able to interpret pictures in narrative and content materials	❏	❏	❏
D. Is able to interpret simple maps	❏	❏	❏
E. Is able to use these elements of a simplified dictionary: guide words, entry words, and selecting the correct definition. At this level, these reading skills should be mastered only at a fairly rudimentary level	❏	❏	❏
F. Is able to use alphabetical sequence by the first letter in a very rudimentary way (first-reader level)	❏	❏	❏

CHECKLIST FOR ASSESSING VOCABULARY, COMPREHENSION, THE BASIC STUDY SKILLS, AND SILENT READING
(Primary-Grade Reading Level) (Cont.)

	Always	Sometimes	Never
G. Is able to use alphabetical sequence by the first letter in a longer series of words (second-reader level)	❏	❏	❏
H. Is able to use alphabetical sequence by the first 2-3 letters in a fairly short list of words (third-reader level)	❏	❏	❏
V. Silent Reading			
A. Seems to enjoy reading silently as evidenced from reactions	❏	❏	❏
B. Comprehends material read silently adequately	❏	❏	❏
C. Reads somewhat more rapidly silently than orally (later first-reader, second-reader, and third-reader levels)	❏	❏	❏
D. Uses word identification skills independently to decode unknown words	❏	❏	❏
E. Has proper posture and book position while reading silently	❏	❏	❏
F. Avoids vocalizing (lip movements) while reading silently (second-reader and third-reader levels)	❏	❏	❏
G. Avoids fingerpointing (second-reader and third-reader levels)	❏	❏	❏
H. Avoids head movement while reading silently (second-reader and third-reader levels)	❏	❏	❏

CHECKLIST FOR ASSESSING VOCABULARY, COMPREHENSION, THE BASIC STUDY SKILLS, AND SILENT READING
(Intermediate-Grade Reading Level)

	Always	Sometimes	Never
I. Vocabulary			
A. Uses vocabulary appropriate for his/her grade level	❑	❑	❑
B. Uses interesting, precise vocabulary terms	❑	❑	❑
C. Is able to understand the vocabulary while reading narrative materials	❑	❑	❑
D. Is able to understand the specialized vocabulary contained in content materials such as social studies, science, and mathematics on the appropriate reading level	❑	❑	❑
E. Uses prediction strategies and activates prior knowledge before reading to improve his/her vocabulary	❑	❑	❑
F. Is able to learn new vocabulary terms easily from various kinds of experiences and reading	❑	❑	❑
G. Uses newly learned vocabulary terms in his/her speaking and/or writing	❑	❑	❑
H. Understands figurative language such as the <u>metaphor</u> (She is a gazelle in her personality as well as in her appearance), the <u>simile</u> (She is as slow as a turtle), and <u>hyperbole</u> (You're so bright that you make the sun look dim)	❑	❑	❑
I. Is able to interpret such figurative language as the following:	❑	❑	❑

I. Is able to interpret such figurative language as the following:

My father is as sharp as a tack.
He's running around like a chicken with its
  head chopped off.
Dave is as crazy as a loon.

CHECKLIST FOR ASSESSING VOCABULARY, COMPREHENSION, THE BASIC STUDY SKILLS, AND SILENT READING
(Intermediate-Grade Reading Level) (Cont.)

	Always	Sometimes	Never

II. Some Elements of _Overall_ Comprehension Ability

A. Use of Prequestioning Skills

	Always	Sometimes	Never
1. Is able to formulate his/her own explicit (literal) comprehension questions prior to reading a narrative or expository (content) selection	❑	❑	❑
2. Is able to formulate his/her own implicit (interpretive) comprehension questions prior to reading a narrative or expository (content) selection	❑	❑	❑
3. Is able to formulate his/her own purposes for reading a narrative or expository (content) selection	❑	❑	❑

B. Use of Prediction Strategies

	Always	Sometimes	Never
1. Is able to predict the content of narrative or expository (content) material from its title	❑	❑	❑
2. At appropriate stopping points in a narrative story, is able to accurately predict what is going to happen next	❑	❑	❑
3. Is able to determine if his/her predictions prior to reading were accurate upon finishing the reading material	❑	❑	❑
4. Is able to use the Directed Reading-Thinking Activity (DR-TA) successfully with both narrative and content material	❑	❑	❑
5. Is able to formulate predictions prior to reading that were determined to be accurate following reading	❑	❑	❑

	Always	Sometimes	Never
C. Use of Self-Monitoring (Metacognitive) Skills			
1. Has a positive attitude toward reading and a good self-perception about his/her reading ability	❑	❑	❑
2. Is able to understand the purpose of reading	❑	❑	❑
3. Is able to formulate his/her own questions while reading	❑	❑	❑
4. Usually self-corrects his/her own word-identification errors while reading	❑	❑	❑
5. Is able to modify reading strategies for different purposes	❑	❑	❑
6. Knows which fix-up strategies to use when he/she does not understand the material well	❑	❑	❑
7. Is able to consider how new information relates to what is already known	❑	❑	❑
8. Is able to determine the important information in a passage	❑	❑	❑
D. Several Other Important Elements of Comprehension			
1. Understands the purpose of semantic maps or webs	❑	❑	❑
2. Is able to formulate a semantic map from narrative or expository (content) material at the appropriate reading level	❑	❑	❑
3. Is able to use visual imagery as a comprehension strategy while reading narrative or expository (content) material	❑	❑	❑

CHECKLIST FOR ASSESSING VOCABULARY, COMPREHENSION, THE BASIC STUDY SKILLS, AND SILENT READING
(Intermediate-Grade Reading Level) (Cont.)

	Always	Sometimes	Never
4. Observes punctuation marks, such as periods, commas, exclamation points, semicolon, and colon, while reading	❑	❑	❑
5. Is able to understand and apply such elements of <u>story grammar</u> as the setting, the characters, the theme or plot, a few episodes in the plot, and the resolution of the problem that motivated the characters to action	❑	❑	❑
6. Is competent in using such guide words as <u>because, if, so, as, for, when, until, meanwhile, before, after, during, following,</u> and <u>always</u>	❑	❑	❑
7. Understands anaphoric relationships such as: The woman and <u>her</u> younger brother both got a cold since both <u>she</u> and <u>he</u> went to a football game together in the rain. Who got a cold? Answer: the woman and her younger brother	❑	❑	❑

III. Comprehension Skills

A. Explicit (Literal or Factual) Comprehension

	Always	Sometimes	Never
1. Is able to answer explicit (literal) comprehension questions from narrative material at the appropriate reading level	❑	❑	❑
2. Is able to answer explicit (literal) comprehension questions from expository (content) material at the appropriate reading level	❑	❑	❑
3. Is able to understand the purpose of <u>who, what, when, where,</u> and <u>why</u> questions at the appropriate reading level	❑	❑	❑

CHECKLIST FOR ASSESSING VOCABULARY, COMPREHENSION, THE BASIC STUDY SKILLS, AND SILENT READING
(Intermediate-Grade Reading Level) (Cont.)

	Always	Sometimes	Never
4. Is able to competently use retelling of narrative or expository (content) material	❏	❏	❏
5. In narrative material includes these elements in a story retelling:			
a. setting	❏	❏	❏
b. theme	❏	❏	❏
c. plot episodes	❏	❏	❏
d. resolution	❏	❏	❏
6. Is able to locate the directly stated main idea and/or topic sentence in a paragraph	❏	❏	❏
7. Is able to write a statement of the main idea of a tradebook, basal reader story, or expository (content) selection	❏	❏	❏
8. Is able to read and carry out directions at the appropriate reading level correctly	❏	❏	❏
9. Is able to locate the significant details in a paragraph at the appropriate reading level	❏	❏	❏
10. Is able to locate the irrelevant details in a paragraph at the appropriate reading level	❏	❏	❏
11. Seems more competent with explicit than implicit comprehension	❏	❏	❏

B. Implicit (Interpretive) Comprehension

	Always	Sometimes	Never
1. Is able to answer implicit (interpretive) comprehension questions from narrative material at the appropriate reading level. These questions require predicting outcomes, interpreting, inferring, drawing conclusions and generalizations, and summarizing	❏	❏	❏

CHECKLIST FOR ASSESSING VOCABULARY, COMPREHENSION, THE BASIC STUDY SKILLS, AND SILENT READING
(Intermediate-Grade Reading Level) (Cont.)

	Always	Sometimes	Never
2. Is able to answer implicit (interpretive) comprehension questions from expository (content) material at the appropriate reading level. These questions require predicting outcomes, interpreting, inferring, drawing conclusions and generalizations, and summarizing	❏	❏	❏
3. Is able to summarize in writing narrative or expository (content) material in a paragraph or short passage	❏	❏	❏
4. Is able to apply fairly complex cause-effect relationships	❏	❏	❏
5. Is able to apply comparison-contrast relationships	❏	❏	❏
6. Is able to determine an author's purpose for writing a narrative or expository (content) selection	❏	❏	❏
7. Is able to verify in writing predictions about a selection that were made before reading it	❏	❏	❏
8. Is able to locate the implied main idea in a paragraph	❏	❏	❏
9. Understands that sometimes a question can have multiple acceptable responses that make sense	❏	❏	❏
10. Is equally competent in implicit and explicit comprehension	❏	❏	❏
C. Critical (Implicit) Comprehension			
1. Is able to answer questions that require critical (implicit or evaluative) responses from narrative material at the appropriate reading level	❏	❏	❏

CHECKLIST FOR ASSESSING VOCABULARY, COMPREHENSION, THE BASIC STUDY SKILLS, AND SILENT READING
(Intermediate-Grade Reading Level) (Cont.)

	Always	Sometimes	Never
2. Is able to answer questions that require critical (implicit or evaluative) responses from expository (content) material at the appropriate reading level	❑	❑	❑
3. Is able to distinguish between fact and opinion	❑	❑	❑
4. Is able to read parts of the newspaper critically such as editorials, letters to the editor, and advertisements	❑	❑	❑
5. Is able to recognize such common propaganda techniques as testimonials, the bandwagon effect, and emotionally-charged words	❑	❑	❑
6. Is able to compare materials from several sources such as a content textbook and a tradebook	❑	❑	❑
7. Is able to evaluate the actions of book characters	❑	❑	❑
8. Is able to determine an author's biases while reading any type of selection	❑	❑	❑
9. Is able to estimate the answer to a verbal problem in arithmetic	❑	❑	❑
10. Does equally well with this element of implicit comprehension as with explicit comprehension	❑	❑	❑

D. Creative (Script or Schema Implicit) Comprehension

	Always	Sometimes	Never
1. Is able to combine his/her own prior knowledge (experiences or scripts) with the printed material in the understanding and application of what is read	❑	❑	❑

CHECKLIST FOR ASSESSING VOCABULARY, COMPREHENSION, THE BASIC STUDY SKILLS, AND SILENT READING
(Intermediate-Grade Reading Level) (Cont.)

	Always	Sometimes	Never
2. Is able to relate what he/she has read in some way that contributes to his/her improvement	❏	❏	❏
3. Is able to relate reading and writing activities in a creative manner	❏	❏	❏
4. Is able to follow up reading in a problem-solving manner such as by cooking or baking activities, art activities, construction activities, dramatic play, creative dramatics, sociodrama, storytelling, and pantomiming	❏	❏	❏
5. Does equally well with this element of implicit comprehension as with explicit comprehension	❏	❏	❏

IV. Study Skills

	Always	Sometimes	Never
A. Is able to use such textbook aids as the table of contents, index, glossary, appendices, subheadings, and footnotes	❏	❏	❏
B. Is able to interpret various kinds of maps, charts, diagrams, pictures, tables, graphs, and schedules	❏	❏	❏
C. Is able to use all the elements of a dictionary at the appropriate reading level to locate the pronunciation or meaning of unknown words that are met in narrative or content reading. Such elements are alphabetical sequence, guide words, diacritical marks, and most important, selecting the correct definition for use in the actual situation	❏	❏	❏
D. Is able to use a thesaurus effectively	❏	❏	❏

CHECKLIST FOR ASSESSING VOCABULARY, COMPREHENSION, THE BASIC STUDY SKILLS, AND SILENT READING
(Intermediate-Grade Reading Level) (Cont.)

	Always	Sometimes	Never
E. Is able to use appropriate reference books in the content areas of social studies and science	❑	❑	❑
F. Is able to use the library card catalog at least to some extent	❑	❑	❑
G. Is able to use such parts of an encyclopedia as the key words, volume numbers, guide words, entry words, and cross-references	❑	❑	❑
H. Is able to use a study technique such as Survey Q3R, Survey Q4R, or PQRST at least to some extent	❑	❑	❑
I. Understands such paragraph patterns of organization as sequence, enumeration, cause-effect, comparison-contrast, and question and answer	❑	❑	❑
J. Is able to outline a content textbook chapter using the main ideas and subordinate headings	❑	❑	❑
K. Is able to take acceptable notes from a content textbook at the appropriate reading level	❑	❑	❑
L. Is a <u>flexible reader</u> (able to adjust reading rate to satisfy his/her purpose for reading and the difficulty of the material) at least at a beginning level	❑	❑	❑
M. Is able to skim the reading material to gain an overall impression of it	❑	❑	❑
N. Is able to scan the related material to locate a specific fact, name, or date	❑	❑	❑

CHECKLIST FOR ASSESSING VOCABULARY, COMPREHENSION, THE BASIC STUDY SKILLS, AND SILENT READING
(Intermediate-Grade Reading Level) (Cont.)

	Always	**Sometimes**	**Never**
V. Silent Reading			
A. Seems to enjoy reading silently as evidenced from reactions while reading silently	❑	❑	❑
B. Uses all of the word identification techniques (sight word identification, graphophonic analysis, structural analysis, and semantic analysis) to decode unknown words met in narrative and content reading	❑	❑	❑
C. Seems to understand material that is read silently	❑	❑	❑
D. Reads silently about twice as rapidly as orally	❑	❑	❑
E. Adjusts his/her reading rate to the reading material (shows reading flexibility)	❑	❑	❑
F. Is able to select appropriate reading material for pleasure reading	❑	❑	❑
G. Chooses to read for pleasure as a recreational activity	❑	❑	❑
H. Demonstrates correct posture and book position while reading silently	❑	❑	❑
I. Avoids inhibiting factors, such as lip movements, subvocalization, head movement, and fingerpointing, while reading silently	❑	❑	❑
J. Appears to be a more competent silent reader than oral reader	❑	❑	❑

Name _____ Grade _____ Teacher _____ Date _____

CHECKLIST FOR ASSESSING VOCABULARY, COMPREHENSION, THE BASIC STUDY SKILLS, AND SILENT READING*
(Middle/Upper-Grade Reading Level)

	Always	**Sometimes**	**Never**
I. Vocabulary			
A. Uses vocabulary appropriate for his/her level of maturity	❏	❏	❏
B. Uses interesting, varied, precise, complex vocabulary terms in speaking and writing	❏	❏	❏
C. Is able to understand the vocabulary while reading narrative materials on the appropriate reading level	❏	❏	❏
D. Is able to understand the specialized vocabulary terms contained in content materials such as social studies, science, and mathematics on the appropriate reading level	❏	❏	❏
E. Uses prediction strategies and activates prior knowledge before reading narrative and content material to improve his/her vocabulary	❏	❏	❏
F. Is able to learn new general and specialized vocabulary terms easily from various kinds of experiences and reading	❏	❏	❏
G. Uses newly learned vocabulary terms in his/her speaking and/or writing	❏	❏	❏
H. Understands figurative language such as the <u>metaphor</u> (When my mother passed away last summer, my grandmother shouldered the heavy burden of raising my three brothers and sisters and me), the <u>simile</u> (That old man unfortunately is as deaf as a doorpost), and <u>hyperbole</u> (My automobile is so decrepit that it makes a dinosaur look young)	❏	❏	❏

*This checklist overlaps considerably with the intermediate-grade reading level checklist. However, there are enough differences between the two reading levels to warrant a separate checklist for the middle-upper reading level.

	Always	Sometimes	Never
I. Is able to distinguish between and understand various regional and ethnic group dialects	❑	❑	❑
J. Is able to interpret such figurative language as the following:	❑	❑	❑

That English final exam was <u>duck soup</u>.

Most musicians certainly have <u>music in their blood</u>.

That boy <u>is not playing with a full deck</u>.

II. Some Elements of *Overall* Comprehension Ability

A. Use of Prior Knowledge

	Always	Sometimes	Never
1. Has adequate prior knowledge to interpret most narrative material at the appropriate reading level	❑	❑	❑
2. Has adequate prior knowledge to interpret most expository (content) material at the appropriate reading level	❑	❑	❑
3. Usually activates prior knowledge possessed before reading narrative or expository (content) material	❑	❑	❑
4. Usually contributes useful, accurate information to group or class discussions prior to reading narrative or expository (content) material	❑	❑	❑

B. Use of Prequestioning Skills

	Always	Sometimes	Never
1. Is able to formulate his/her own explicit (literal) comprehension questions prior to reading a narrative or expository (content) selection at the appropriate reading level	❑	❑	❑

CHECKLIST FOR ASSESSING VOCABULARY, COMPREHENSION, THE BASIC STUDY SKILLS, AND SILENT READING
(Middle/Upper-Grade Reading Level) (Cont.)

	Always	Sometimes	Never
2. Is able to formulate his/her own implicit (interpretive) comprehension questions prior to reading a narrative or expository (content) selection at the appropriate reading level	❑	❑	❑
3. Is able to formulate his/her own purposes for reading narrative or expository (content) selection at the appropriate reading level	❑	❑	❑

C. Use of Prediction Strategies

	Always	Sometimes	Never
1. Is able to predict the content of narrative or expository (content) material from its title or main heading	❑	❑	❑
2. At appropriate pausing points in a narrative story is able to accurately hypothesize (predict) what may occur next	❑	❑	❑
3. Is able to determine if his/her hypotheses (predictions) were accurate upon completing the reading material	❑	❑	❑
4. Is able to use the Directed Reading-Thinking Activity (DR-TA) effectively with both narrative and expository (content) material at the appropriate reading level	❑	❑	❑
5. Is able to formulate hypotheses (predictions) prior to reading narrative or expository (content) material that were determined to be accurate following the reading	❑	❑	❑

CHECKLIST FOR ASSESSING VOCABULARY, COMPREHENSION, THE BASIC STUDY SKILLS, AND SILENT READING
(Middle/Upper-Grade Reading Level) (Cont.)

	Always	Sometimes	Never
D. Use of Self-Monitoring (Metacognitive) Skills			
1. Has a positive attitude toward reading and high self-esteem about his/her reading skills in both narrative and expository (content) material	❑	❑	❑
2. Is able to understand the purpose of reading both complex narrative and expository (content) material	❑	❑	❑
3. Is able to generate his/her own questions and theories while reading both narrative and expository (content) material	❑	❑	❑
4. Usually self-corrects while reading narrative and expository (content) material	❑	❑	❑
5. Employs semantic cues effectively while reading narrative and expository (content) material	❑	❑	❑
6. Is able to alter reading strategies for different purposes	❑	❑	❑
7. Knows which fix-up strategies to employ when he/she does not understand complex narrative or expository (content) material well	❑	❑	❑
8. Is able to determine how new information gained from reading relates to what is already known	❑	❑	❑
9. Is able to determine the important information in a narrative or expository (content) selection	❑	❑	❑

CHECKLIST FOR ASSESSING VOCABULARY, COMPREHENSION, THE BASIC STUDY SKILLS, AND SILENT READING
(Middle/Upper-Grade Reading Level) (Cont.)

	Always	Sometimes	Never
E. Several Other Important Elements of Comprehension			
1. Understands the purpose of semantic networking	❑	❑	❑
2. Is able to formulate a semantic map from narrative or expository (content) material at the appropriate reading level	❑	❑	❑
3. Understands that a semantic map can be used effectively as a pre-reading strategy	❑	❑	❑
4. Is able to use K-W-L Plus to aid in summary and report writing	❑	❑	❑
5. Is able to use visual imagery as a comprehension strategy while reading narrative or expository (content) material at the appropriate reading level	❑	❑	❑
6. Observes such punctuation marks as periods, commas, exclamation points, semicolons, and colons while reading	❑	❑	❑
7. Is able to understand such elements of <u>story grammar</u> as the setting, the characters, the theme or plot, a few episodes in the plot, and the resolution of the plot that motivated the characters to action	❑	❑	❑
8. Is competent in using such guide words as <u>because, if, so, as, for, when, until, meanwhile, before, after, during, following,</u> and <u>always</u>	❑	❑	❑

CHECKLIST FOR ASSESSING VOCABULARY, COMPREHENSION, THE BASIC STUDY SKILLS, AND SILENT READING
(Middle/Upper-Grade Reading Level) (Cont.)

	Always	Sometimes	Never
9. Understands such anaphoric relationships as: The high school football player and <u>his</u> younger sister, who also is athletic, both received college scholarships since both <u>he</u> and <u>she</u> are very talented. Who received college scholarships? Answer: the football player and his younger sister	❏	❏	❏
10. Is able to complete such different variations of the cloze procedure as traditional cloze, random deletion cloze, and cloze procedures emphasizing deleting nouns, verbs, adjectives, and adverbs at the appropriate reading level	❏	❏	❏

III. Comprehension Skills

A. Explicit (Literal or Factual) Comprehension

	Always	Sometimes	Never
1. Is able to answer explicit (literal) comprehension questions from narrative and expository (content) material at the appropriate reading level	❏	❏	❏
2. Is able to understand the purpose of <u>who, what, when, where,</u> and <u>why</u> questions at the appropriate reading level	❏	❏	❏
3. Is able to competently use retelling or narrative and expository (content) material at the appropriate reading level	❏	❏	❏

CHECKLIST FOR ASSESSING VOCABULARY, COMPREHENSION, THE BASIC STUDY SKILLS, AND SILENT READING
(Middle/Upper-Grade Reading Level) (Cont.)

	Always	Sometimes	Never
4. In narrative material includes these elements in a story retelling:			
a. setting	❑	❑	❑
b. theme	❑	❑	❑
c. plot episodes	❑	❑	❑
d. resolution	❑	❑	❑
5. Is able to locate the directly stated main idea and/or topic sentence in a narrative or expository paragraph at the appropriate reading level	❑	❑	❑
6. Is able to write a statement of the main idea of a longer narrative or expository selection at the appropriate reading level	❑	❑	❑
7. Is able to read and carry out fairly complex directions	❑	❑	❑
8. Is able to place a significant number of items in correct sequence	❑	❑	❑
9. Is able to locate the significant details in a narrative or expository paragraph at the appropriate reading level	❑	❑	❑
10. Is able to locate the irrelevant details in a narrative or expository paragraph at the appropriate reading level	❑	❑	❑

B. Implicit (Interpretive) Comprehension

| 1. Is able to answer implicit (interpretive) comprehension questions from narrative or expository (content) material at the appropriate reading level. These questions require predicting outcomes, interpreting, inferring, drawing conclusions and generalizations, and summarizing | ❑ | ❑ | ❑ |

CHECKLIST FOR ASSESSING VOCABULARY, COMPREHENSION, THE BASIC STUDY SKILLS, AND SILENT READING
(Middle/Upper-Grade Reading Level) (Cont.)

	Always	Sometimes	Never
2. Is able to summarize in writing longer narrative or expository (content) selection at the appropriate reading level	❏	❏	❏
3. Is able to apply complex cause-effect relationships	❏	❏	❏
4. Is able to apply fairly complex comparison-contrast relationships	❏	❏	❏
5. Is able to determine an author's purpose for writing a narrative or expository (content) selection at the appropriate reading level	❏	❏	❏
6. Is able to verify in writing hypotheses (predictions) about a narrative or expository (content) selection at the appropriate reading level that were made before reading it	❏	❏	❏
7. Is able to locate the implied main idea in a narrative or expository (content) paragraph at the appropriate reading level	❏	❏	❏
8. Understands that sometimes a question can have multiple acceptable responses that make sense	❏	❏	❏
9. Is equally competent in implicit and explicit comprehension	❏	❏	❏
10. Seems competent in comprehending various types of literary genres	❏	❏	❏

C. Critical (Implicit) Comprehension

	Always	Sometimes	Never
1. Is able to answer questions that require critical (implicit or evaluative) responses from narrative or expository material at the appropriate reading level	❏	❏	❏

CHECKLIST FOR ASSESSING VOCABULARY, COMPREHENSION, THE BASIC STUDY SKILLS, AND SILENT READING
(Middle/Upper-Grade Reading Level) (Cont.)

	Always	Sometimes	Never
2. Is able to distinguish between fact and opinion at an advanced level	❏	❏	❏
3. Is able to read critically parts of local and out-of-area newspapers, such as the editorials and letters to the editor	❏	❏	❏
4. Is able to read critically all kinds of advertisements found in various types of reading material	❏	❏	❏
5. Is able to recognize such common propaganda techniques as testimonials, the bandwagon effect, glittering generalities, the halo effect, and emotionally charged words	❏	❏	❏
6. Is able to compare material from several different sources, such as an encyclopedia, a content textbook, a tradebook, or computer software	❏	❏	❏
7. Is able to evaluate the actions of the characters in narrative materials at the appropriate reading level	❏	❏	❏
8. Is able to determine an author's biases while reading any type of narrative or expository (content) selection	❏	❏	❏
9. Is able to estimate the answer to a verbal problem in mathematics	❏	❏	❏
10. Does equally well with this element of implicit comprehension as with explicit comprehension	❏	❏	❏

CHECKLIST FOR ASSESSING VOCABULARY, COMPREHENSION, THE BASIC STUDY SKILLS, AND SILENT READING
(Middle/Upper-Grade Reading Level) (Cont.)

	Always	Sometimes	Never
D. Creative (Script or Schema Implicit) Comprehension			
1. Is able to combine his/her own prior knowledge (experiences or scripts) with the printed material in the understanding and application of what is read to form new insights, attitudes, and concepts	❑	❑	❑
2. Is able to relate what he/she has read in some way that contributes to his/her personal improvement or to the improvement of society	❑	❑	❑
3. Is able to relate reading and writing activities in a creative manner, such as by writing poetry, prose, or drama	❑	❑	❑
4. Is able to follow up reading in a problem-solving manner, such as by fairly complex cooking or baking activities, art activities, construction activities, creative dramatics, sociodrama, storytelling, and pantomiming	❑	❑	❑
IV. Study Skills			
A. Is able to use such textbook aids as the table of contents, index, glossary, appendices, subheadings, headnotes, footnotes, italicized words, and typographical aids in narrative and expository (content) material of all type at the appropriate reading level	❑	❑	❑
B. Is able to interpret various kinds of maps, charts, diagrams, pictures, tables, graphs, and schedules found in narrative and expository (content) material of various types at the appropriate reading level	❑	❑	❑

CHECKLIST FOR ASSESSING VOCABULARY, COMPREHENSION, THE BASIC STUDY SKILLS, AND SILENT READING
(Middle/Upper-Grade Reading Level) (Cont.)

	Always	Sometimes	Never
C. Is able to use all of the elements of a dictionary at the appropriate reading level to locate the pronunciation and meaning of unknown words that are met in narrative or expository (content) reading. Such elements are alphabetical sequence, pronunciation key, guide words, diacritical marks, and, most important, selecting the correct definition for use in context	❑	❑	❑
D. Is able to use a thesaurus effectively	❑	❑	❑
E. Is able to use appropriate reference books in the content areas of social studies and science	❑	❑	❑
F. Is able to use effectively a library card catalog or on-line computer system in the library	❑	❑	❑
G. Is able to use such parts of an encyclopedia as the key words, volume numbers, guide words, entry words, and cross-references	❑	❑	❑
H. Is able to use a study technique such as Survey Q3R, Survey Q4R, or PQRST	❑	❑	❑
I. Is able to use a study strategy such as K-W-L or K-W-L Plus	❑	❑	❑
J. Understands such paragraph patterns of organization as sequence, enumeration, cause-effect, comparison-contrast, and question and answer	❑	❑	❑
K. Is able to outline a content textbook chapter using the main idea and subordinate headings	❑	❑	❑
L. Is able to take acceptable notes from a content textbook at the appropriate reading level	❑	❑	❑

CHECKLIST FOR ASSESSING VOCABULARY, COMPREHENSION, THE BASIC STUDY SKILLS, AND SILENT READING
(Middle/Upper-Grade Reading Level) (Cont.)

	Always	Sometimes	Never
M. Is able to take acceptable notes from a classroom lecture	❑	❑	❑
N. Is able to apply some effective test-taking strategies	❑	❑	❑
O. Is able to highlight the important points in a content textbook	❑	❑	❑
P. Makes effective use of his/her study time	❑	❑	❑
Q. Is able to use effectively various types of media, such as computer software and videotapes, in his/her study of expository (content) material	❑	❑	❑
R. Is a <u>flexible reader</u> (able to adjust reading rate to satisfy his/her purposes for reading and the difficulty of the material)	❑	❑	❑
S. Is able to skim the reading material to gain an overall impression of it	❑	❑	❑
T. Is able to scan the reading material to locate a specific fact, name, or date	❑	❑	❑

V. Silent Reading

	Always	Sometimes	Never
A. Seems to enjoy reading narrative and expository (content) material at the appropriate reading level as evidenced from reactions while reading silently	❑	❑	❑
B. Uses any of the word identification techniques when appropriate to decode unknown words met in narrative and expository (content) reading at the appropriate reading level	❑	❑	❑
C. Comprehends material that is read silently	❑	❑	❑
D. Reads silently about twice as rapidly as orally	❑	❑	❑

CHECKLIST FOR ASSESSING VOCABULARY, COMPREHENSION, THE BASIC STUDY SKILLS, AND SILENT READING
(Middle/Upper-Grade Reading Level) (Cont.)

	Always	Sometimes	Never
E. Reads fiction at a rate of about 200-250 words per minute with good comprehension	❏	❏	❏
F. Reads in thought units or phrases	❏	❏	❏
G. Adjusts his/her reading rate to the reading material (shows reading flexibility)	❏	❏	❏
H. Is able to select appropriate reading material for pleasure reading	❏	❏	❏
I. Chooses to read for pleasure as a recreational activity	❏	❏	❏
J. Demonstrates correct posture and book position while reading silently	❏	❏	❏
K. Avoids inhibiting factors while reading silently, such as lip movements, subvocalization, head movement, and fingerpointing	❏	❏	❏
L. Is a much more competent silent reader than oral reader	❏	❏	❏

on what happened first, second, and so forth. If the goal is to teach or assess the ability to integrate information and make inferences from text, a child should be told to think of things that have happened to him or her like those that happened to characters in the story (book). Props such as puppets, felt-board characters, or the pictures in the material can be used to help a child retell a story (book).

After the child has heard or read a story or book, you can ask questions such as these:

- What was this story (book) about?
- Can you tell me all that you remember about this story (book)?
- What do you remember about the story (book) that you just have read?

You also can ask the child to retell the story (book) in this way:

"A little while ago, I read the book _____
to you. Would you retell the book (story) as if you were telling it to a friend who has never heard the story?"

You can use prompts such as these if they seem necessary:

- "Once upon a time"
- Who was this book (story) about?
- When did this book (story) happen?
- Where did this book (story) happen?
- Who was the main character in this book (story) and what problem did he or she have?
- How did (the main character) in this book (story) try to solve the problem?
- How was the problem finally solved?
- How did the book (story) end?

EVALUATING A BOOK OR STORY RETELLING

If you plan to evaluate a book (story) retelling using the reproducible assessment device included in this handbook, during the introduction of the book (story) tell the child that he or she will be asked to retell it after listening to it or reading it. During evaluative retelling, do not give prompts beyond general ones such as:

- What happened next?
- Can you think of anything else about the story?

To assess the child's retelling for sense of story structure, you first should divide the events of the story into these four categories—*setting, theme, plot episodes,* and *resolution*. The retelling assessment device and the outline of the divided material then are used to record the number of ideas and details that the child includes within each category in the retelling. This device indicates which elements the teacher should stress in teaching about *setting, theme, plot episodes,* and *resolution.* Comparing analyses of several retellings over a year indicates a child's progress in understanding story structure.

Here is an outline of the picture storybook *Our Teacher's Having a Baby* by Eve Bunting (New York: Clarion Books, 1992). This book is about a teacher named Mrs. Neal who has a baby during the year her class is in first grade. When Mrs. Neal finally has a baby girl named Isabel and the class subsequently gets a substitute teacher, they become very worried that Mrs. Neal will no longer be able to be their first-grade teacher. The book ends by Mrs. Neal's telling the class during a visit to the school that she will be returning as their teacher soon, and that a mother can be a teacher too.

Here is a divided outline that can be used to help analyze a child's retelling of this book. It is included here for illustrative purposes.

DIVIDED STORY

Our Teacher's Having a Baby by Eve Bunting, illustrations by Diane deGroot. New York: Clarion Books, 1992.

Setting

1. A first-grade teacher named Mrs. Neal is going to have a baby.
2. Characters: Mrs. Neal (main character), Samantha, Polly, Janice, Mike, the baby who is named Isabel, and the substitute teacher Mrs. Boskie.

Theme

Mrs. Neal, a first-grade teacher, tells her class that she is going to have a baby. Later she has a baby girl who is named Isabel.

Plot Episodes

FIRST EPISODE: One day Mrs. Neal tells her first-grade class that she will be having a baby after a little while.

SECOND EPISODE: The first-grade class studies about baby animals of various kinds and how they are born.

THIRD EPISODE: The first-grade class writes letters to the baby, which its mother will give to it later. The children suggest names for Mrs. Neal's baby when it is born.

FOURTH EPISODE: One day Mrs. Neal has a baby girl whom she names Isabel. The first-grade class gets a substitute teacher for awhile.

FIFTH EPISODE: Mrs. Neal brings her baby Isabel to the first-grade class to visit.

Resolution

1. Mrs. Neal tells the first-grade class that she will be coming back to be their teacher again after a little while.

2. The first-grade class is relieved as they had been worried that a mother never could be a teacher too.

VERBATIM TRANSCRIPTION

Here is a verbatim transcription of Kristi's (aged six) retelling of *Our Teacher's Having a Baby*.

Mrs. Neal was a teacher and she told her class she was having a baby. And the class talked about it. The class learned about baby animals and they made up names for the baby. And they marched around the room one day. Then Mrs. Neal really had a baby, a baby girl Isabel. Then the class had another teacher but they wanted Mrs. Neal back. She came back for a visit with the baby. She told them she would be their teacher again. And they all were very happy.

Kristi's Book-Retelling Ability Checklist

Here is a "Retelling Ability Checklist" that has been completed for Kristi's retelling of the picture storybook *Our Teacher's Having a Baby*. (See page 116.) By examining it, you should easily be able to complete the reproducible model of this assessment device for any child's retelling of a book or story.

NOTE: In many instances, a reading teacher simply can complete the reproducible model of this checklist by using checks instead of numbers. These checks can be used to gain a general sense of the elements of a book or story that a child includes and his or her progress over a period of time.

REPRODUCIBLE STORY (BOOK) RETELLING ABILITY CHECKLIST

This is a ready-to-duplicate story (book) retelling ability checklist. (See page 117.) You can use it in its present form or modify it in any way you want. As stated earlier, checks can be used instead of numbers to gain a general sense of the story or book elements that a child includes and his or her progress over a period of time. A quantitative analysis is optional.

Checklist in Self-Monitoring of Reading Comprehension

It is very important that children monitor or evaluate their own comprehension ability. They should be aware of when they are not understanding what they are reading. Good readers normally are adept at self-monitoring, while poor readers are not. Students also should be able to determine the causes of their comprehension difficulty when they do not understand what they are reading. They also should know how to correct their comprehension difficulties by applying the appropriate fix-up strategies.

Name _____ Grade _____ Teacher _____ Date _____

STORY (BOOK) RETELLING ABILITY CHECKLIST*
(Primary-Grade Reading Level)

Title of Story (Book) Our Teacher's Having a Baby _____

Directions for the Teacher: Score *1* point for each element the child included. Give *1* point for each character named as well as for generic words such as *boy, girl, dog,* or *cat.* Credit plurals (for example, the word *friends)* with *2* points under characters.

SENSE OF STORY STRUCTURE

Setting:

1. Begins story with some type of introduction — 1
2. Names the main character — 1
3. Number of other characters named — 2
4. Actual number of other characters in the story (book) — 6
5. Score for the element of "other characters" in the story (book) retelling (#3 divided by #4) — .3
6. Includes a statement about the time and place in the story (book) — 0

Theme:

1. Refers to the goal of the main character or the problem to be solved in the story (book) — 1

Plot Episodes:

1. Number of episodes or plot events recalled — 5
2. Number of episodes or plot events included in the story (book) — 5
3. Score for the number of plot episodes remembered for the retelling (#1 divided by #2) — 1

Resolution:

1. Includes the solution to the problem in the attainment of the goal — 1
2. Provides an ending to the story (book) — 1

Sequence:

1. Retells the story (book) in the proper sequence illustrating an understanding of *story structure*: setting, theme, plot episodes, and resolution. (Score *2* for completely correct, *1* for partially correct, or *0* for no evidence of sequence used.) — 2

Best possible score: — 10

Child's score: — 8.3

© 1995 by John Wiley & Sons, Inc.

---

*Checks can be used instead of numbers to gain a general sense of the elements a child includes and his or her progress over a period of time. A quantitative analysis is optional.

Name _____ Grade _____ Teacher _____ Date _____

STORY (BOOK) RETELLING ABILITY CHECKLIST*
(Primary-Grade Reading Level)

Title of Story (Book) _____

Directions for the Teacher: Score *1* point for each element the child included. Give *1* point for each character named as well as for generic words such as *boy, girl, dog,* or *cat.* Credit plurals (for example, the word *friends)* with *2* points under characters.

SENSE OF STORY STRUCTURE

Setting:

1. Begins story with some type of introduction _____

2. Names the main character _____

3. Number of other characters named _____

4. Actual number of other characters in the story (book) _____

5. Score for the element of "other characters" in the story (book) retelling (#3 divided by #4) _____

6. Includes a statement about the time and place in the story (book) _____

Theme:

1. Refers to the goal of the main character or the problem to be solved in the story (book) _____

Plot Episodes:

1. Number of episodes or plot events recalled _____

2. Number of episodes or plot events included in the story (book) _____

3. Score for the number of plot episodes remembered for the retelling (#1 divided by #2) _____

Resolution:

1. Includes the solution to the problem in the attainment of the goal _____

2. Provides an ending to the story (book) _____

Sequence:

1. Retells the story (book) in the proper sequence illustrating an understanding of *story structure*: setting, theme, plot episodes, and resolution. (Score *2* for completely correct, *1* for partially correct, or *0* for no evidence of sequence used.) _____

Best possible score: __10__

Child's score: _____

---

*Checks can be used instead of numbers to gain a general sense of the elements a child includes and his or her progress over a period of time. A quantitative analysis is optional.

The self-monitoring checklist of reading comprehension on page 119 can help a student be more aware of his or her reading strategies and fix-up strategies. You can duplicate and use it in its present form or use it as a model for constructing your own checklist of this kind.

Checklist for Evaluating Reading Competencies in an Intermediate-Grade Whole Language Classroom

This reproducible checklist (see page 120) should enable the reading teacher to make an overall assessment of an intermediate-grade student's reading competencies. It encompasses some of the most important reading skills included in several of the more detailed checklists contained earlier in this chapter. Although it can be used in any intermediate-grade or middle-school classroom, it perhaps should be especially useful in a whole language classroom. You can duplicate and use this checklist in its present form or modify it in any way you wish.

Checklist for Pleasure Reading

Here is a brief checklist for assessing a student's attitudes toward reading for pleasure or recreation. (See page 121.) It probably is most appropriate at the intermediate-grade or middle-school levels. You can duplicate and use it in its present form or modify it in any way you wish.

Name _____ Grade _____ Teacher _____ Date _____

SELF-MONITORING CHECKLIST OF READING COMPREHENSION
(Upper Primary-Grade
or Intermediate-Grade Reading Level)

	Yes	No
1. Do I already know something about what this material is going to be about?	❑	❑
2. Should I predict what the material is going to be about before I begin to read it?	❑	❑
3. Should I ask myself some questions about what this material could be about before I begin to read it?	❑	❑
4. Do I know why I am going to read this material?	❑	❑
5. Should I read every word of this material?	❑	❑
6. Is it all right if I skip some of the words while I am reading this material?	❑	❑
7. Do I know how fast I should read this material?	❑	❑
8. Should I read all of the material more than once to be sure that I understand it?	❑	❑
9. Do I need to read the first sentence of each paragraph more than once?	❑	❑
10. Do I know what I should do if I meet a word in the material that I do not understand?	❑	❑
11. Can I answer most of my teacher's questions after I have finished reading the material?	❑	❑
12. Can I remember what I have read well enough to retell it after I have finished reading?	❑	❑
13. Can I remember what I have read well enough to answer most of the questions on a test about the material?	❑	❑
14. Do I know what information in the material is important and what information is not important?	❑	❑
15. Can I state the most important idea in the material after I have finished reading it?	❑	❑

Name _____ Grade _____ Teacher _____ Date _____

CHECKLIST FOR EVALUATING READING COMPETENCIES IN AN INTERMEDIATE-GRADE WHOLE LANGUAGE CLASSROOM
(Intermediate-Grade Reading Level)

	Always	Sometimes	Never
1. Shows a positive attitude toward all reading attitudes	❑	❑	❑
2. Borrows books from the school library to read for pleasure and information	❑	❑	❑
3. Understands the major purpose of reading—comprehending what is read	❑	❑	❑
4. Is able to read for a sustained period of time	❑	❑	❑
5. Is able to select a book appropriate to his/her reading ability	❑	❑	❑
6. Chooses reading material of various types and genres	❑	❑	❑
7. Understands the difference between acceptable and unacceptable miscues	❑	❑	❑
8. Predicts meaning while reading texts by using the appropriate cues (graphophonic [phonic], semantic [meaning], or syntactic [word order])	❑	❑	❑
9. Applies appropriate fix-up strategies while reading (rereading, looking back through the material, suspending judgment, or visual imagery)	❑	❑	❑
10. Can describe the development of story line in a novel in order: setting, problem, climax, and ending	❑	❑	❑
11. Can identify characters and describe their character traits	❑	❑	❑
12. Can classify books in terms of their genre: fiction, nonfiction, or fantasy	❑	❑	❑
13. Can summarize material including all of the major points	❑	❑	❑
14. Can read a long selection of narrative or expository (content) text	❑	❑	❑
15. Can skim material to obtain the needed information	❑	❑	❑
16. Can use appropriate reference skills when needed	❑	❑	❑

Name _____ Grade _____ Teacher _____ Date _____

CHECKLIST FOR PLEASURE READING

	Always	Sometimes	Never
1. Chooses to read during free time	❏	❏	❏
2. Has books to read during free time	❏	❏	❏
3. Visits the school library during free time	❏	❏	❏
4. Reads during library (or sustained silent reading) time	❏	❏	❏
5. Reads until required to stop	❏	❏	❏
6. Discards a book if it is not satisfactory or appropriate	❏	❏	❏
7. Begins reading quickly without wasting time	❏	❏	❏
8. Talks with classmates about books	❏	❏	❏
9. Recommends books to classmates	❏	❏	❏
10. Asks for recommendations about books from his/her teacher, librarian, or classmates	❏	❏	❏
11. Reads without pausing (looking around the classroom, talking to classmates, or wasting time in other ways)	❏	❏	❏

Comments:

_____

_____

_____

_____

_____

_____

_____

CHAPTER FOUR

Using Miscue Analysis
in Assessing Competencies
and Weaknesses in Reading

Have you ever taught a student who, while reading, substituted half or more of the actual words with words that made sense but were not correct? In addition, this type of student often can answer most of the comprehension questions that are asked or can retell the material effectively. If you have, you are a typical reading teacher.

Do you believe that it is as important to correct such a student's errors as it is to correct a child's errors who consistently substitutes words while reading that do not make sense? If you answered "No," I think you are correct. Of course, usually a student should not miscall an excessive amount of words. If he or she does so, the student may well profit from instruction and/or practice in sight word identification and/or graphophonic (phonic) analysis.

After reading and studying this chapter carefully, the literacy teacher should feel very competent in implementing miscue analysis in his or her program. Miscue analysis is an excellent informal assessment tool that should be part of every literacy teacher's repertoire.

Description of Miscue Analysis

The concept of *miscue analysis* is mainly credited to the work of Kenneth and Yetta Goodman of the University of Arizona and to some of their associates.

Miscue analysis is based upon the study of *psycholinguistics*. It is a method of analyzing how a student approaches the reading process and for determining how he or she views it. Stated simply, this theory maintains that deviations from the printed material are not truly *errors* but instead are *miscues* that may or may not interfere with comprehension.

Miscues usually are classified into some variation of the following:

- *graphophonic (graphonic or graphic) miscues*—those deviations in which there is a graphic charge in the deviation (the substitution of *walk* for *wall*)
- *semantic miscues*—those deviations in which there is a meaning change in the deviation (the substitution of *hop* for *hope*)
- *syntactic miscues*—those deviations in which there is a substitution in the grammatical structure of the sentence (for example, turning a question into a statement)

It is obvious that graphophonic miscues are concerned with whether a student's miscues are mainly found in the knowledge of sight words or with graphophonic (phonic) analysis which deals with the beginnings, middles, or endings of words. The semantic clues deal with whether or not the miscue interferes significantly with comprehension. Miscues that alter the meaning of the material significantly usually are called *major miscues*, while those that do not are called *minor miscues*. The syntactic miscues are concerned with whether or not the miscues are grammatically correct. Miscue analysis also considers the extent to which a student self-corrects while reading orally. Obviously, a student should be concerned with understanding what he or she is reading and therefore should self-correct when this is appropriate.

Thus, the use of miscue analysis can help a reading teacher much better understand the characteristics of a student's reading that impact upon his or her comprehension and subsequently improve reading instruction for that student.

ADVANTAGES OF USING MISCUE ANALYSIS

The following are the major advantages of using miscue analysis in an informal literacy assessment program. These are the reasons why every reading teacher should learn at least one system of miscue analysis.

- The reading teacher can learn a great deal about how a student understands or views the purpose and content of the reading process.
- The reading teacher can learn whether or not a student's miscues usually interfere significantly with comprehension. As stated earlier, those that do are considered much more relevant than those that do not.
- The reading teacher can learn if a student has difficulty with graphophonic (phonic) analysis and specifically with *word beginnings, middles, or endings*.
- The reading teacher can learn if a student usually self-corrects while reading.
- The reading teacher can learn if a student's deviation from the printed text results in the following:

    graphic change
    meaning change
    grammatical change

- Miscue analysis is an excellent way in which to observe informally a student's reading. This can help a teacher to teach reading much more effectively.

- Miscue analysis is a fairly accurate way to assess reading competencies and weaknesses when done by an experienced, well-trained reading teacher (as in the Reading Recovery Program described and illustrated later in the chapter).

LIMITATIONS OF MISCUE ANALYSIS

The following are the major limitations of using miscue analysis:

- An experienced well-trained reading teacher is needed to implement effectively any system of miscue analysis. Effective miscue analysis cannot be done by an untrained reading teacher as it requires a considerable amount of judgment in the evaluation of a student's performance.

- It can be very time consuming to implement successfully. This is especially true with some miscue analysis systems described later in this chapter.

- It requires considerable instruction and practice to become competent enough to implement any system of miscue analysis. However, some systems require more instruction and practice than others as is explained later.

- Miscue analysis must always be done on an *individual basis*. Therefore, it may not always be entirely practical in a classroom setting, especially if the reading teacher has a large class. It usually is easier to implement in a special reading program of some kind such as the Reading Recovery™ Program or a Chapter I program.

- The reading teacher must use considerable judgment in implementing any system of miscue analysis. Therefore, the evaluation of any student's performance using miscue analysis can vary greatly when made by different teachers.

IN SUMMARY

Despite its limitations, every reading teacher should be competent in several systems of miscue analysis. The chapter now describes and illustrates a number of different systems that can be used in informal assessment of reading abilities.

Description of Miscue Analysis as Used in the Individual Reading Inventory in This Handbook

Chapter 5 of this handbook contains two forms of a complete reproducible Individual Reading Inventory that can be duplicated and used with students from the primer through the twelfth-grade reading levels. Detailed directions for administering and evaluating this Inventory are included in Chapter 5.

However, the miscue analysis used in this Inventory can easily be adapted and used to assess any student's oral reading of either narrative or content material. Although this system of miscue analysis is briefly described again in Chapter 5, it is explained and illustrated in this chapter also. After reading the description and illustration of this miscue analysis system, you should be able to quite easily use it with any type of reading material.

Since it takes considerable practice to become adept at marking oral reading miscues while a child is reading, I recommend that you tape record his or her reading and mark the miscues later while playing back the tape recording. You can mark a child's oral reading miscues by a variety of systems. Here is the one I use, but any system with which you are familiar is equally useful.

- **Omission**—Circle the entire word or letter sound.

- **Addition**—Insert with a caret.

pretty

- **Substitutions/Mispronunciations**—Draw a line through the word and write in the substituted word.

flecks

~~flocks~~

- **Reversals**—Use the transposition symbol.

down from

- **Repetitions**—Use a wavy line to indicate a repetition of more than two words.

breaking the air waves

- **Words Aided**—If a child says nothing after about five seconds, provide the word and cross it out.

~~fascinating~~

Here are the guidelines you must consider when using this system of miscue analysis:

1. Count as a *major oral reading miscue* and deduct *one point* for any error that interferes with comprehension. Some examples are <u>make</u> for <u>man</u>, <u>pretty</u> for <u>parade</u>, <u>love</u> for <u>live</u>, or <u>house</u> for <u>horse</u>.

2. Count as a *minor oral reading miscue* and deduct *one-half point* for any deviation from the printed text that does *not* seem to interfere significantly with comprehension. Some examples are <u>happy</u> for <u>glad</u>, <u>fast</u> for <u>rapid</u>, <u>house</u> for <u>home</u>, or <u>lady</u> for <u>woman</u>.

3. Count an *addition* as *half an oral reading miscue* if it does not significantly change the meaning of the material. Usually an addition or insertion is a minor oral reading miscue since it does not significantly alter the meaning of the material.

4. Do *not* count a *self-correction* as a miscue if it occurs within a short period of time such as five seconds. A self-correction usually indicates that a student is *monitoring* his or her own reading and attempting to read for meaning.

5. Count a *repetition* as *half an oral reading miscue* if it occurs on *two or more words*. A repetition of a single word may indicate that the student is trying to monitor his or her own reading or correcting the miscue.

6. Do not count more than *one oral reading miscue* on the same word in any one passage. For example, if the child mispronounces the same word more than once while reading a passage, count it as a miscue only once.

7. Do not count an oral reading miscue on any *proper noun* found in a passage.

8. Deduct *one point* for any word that a student cannot pronounce after about five seconds *if that word interferes with comprehension*. Deduct *one-half point* for any word that a student cannot pronounce after about five seconds *if that word does not seem to interfere with comprehension*.

9. Do not count oral reading miscues that seem to exemplify a child's *cultural and regional dialect*. To consider this point, you must be quite familiar with the basic characteristics of the child's speech patterns such as in the African-American dialect or the Hispanic dialect.

When you have marked all of the miscues from the material the child has read, you can use the information just presented to determine the child's appropriate *independent, instructional,* and *frustration reading levels*.

The characteristics of the three major reading levels are usually similar to these:

- *Independent reading level*—The point at which a child is about 99 percent accurate in word identification and has about 95 percent or better comprehension.

- *Instructional reading level*—The point at which a student is about 90 percent accurate in word identification and has about 75 percent or better comprehension.

- *Frustration reading level*—The point at which a student is less than about 90 percent accurate in word identification and has less than 50 percent accuracy in comprehension.

From using this system of miscue analysis with hundreds of children over a period of many years, adding several other reading levels to the three basic levels can be helpful in placing children in reading materials. You also can use the following three subcategories of reading levels:

- *Low-independent reading level*
- *High-instructional reading level*
- *Low-instructional reading level*

It may be helpful at this point to indicate how the preceding information about this system of miscue analysis can be applied to determine a child's *appropriate reading level* in an actual situation. (The "Canada Geese" passage is taken from Wilma H. Miller's *Complete Reading Disabilities Handbook* [West Nyack, NY: The Center for Applied Research in Education, 1993, p. 80.])

See page 128. The child made the following ten major miscues, each of which result in a deduction of one point. These miscues included substitutions, omissions, and words aided. The substitutions and omissions were considered major miscues since the meaning of the material was altered significantly. The omission of the word *imprinted* and the teacher's providing the word *advantage* were considered major miscues because their inclusions were considered significant to the true understanding of the passage. Here is a list of the major miscues in this passage:

flocks
scientists
imprinted
route
advantage
updrafts
oval
average
gear
mate

In addition, the child made the following seventeen minor miscues, each of which resulted in a deduction of one-half point. These miscues included omissions, substitutions, repetitions, and an addition. The substitutions, omissions, and addition were considered to be minor miscues since the meaning of the material was not changed significantly. As stated earlier in this section, a repetition of two or more words results in a deduction of one-half point.

among
fascinating
in the world
migration
really
exactly

CANADA GEESE
(Fourth-Grade Reading Level)

Canada geese are (among) the most ~~fascinating~~ and amazing of any of the birds in
the world. Most of us have seen large ~~flocks~~ *flecks* of Canada geese flying in a V outline high
in the sky in the spring and fall.

~~Scientists~~ have studied the ~~migration~~ *travel* of Canada geese for many years. Although
they still do not (really) understand how Canada geese know (exactly) where to fly, they
are ~~beginning~~ *starting* to figure out something about it. Scientists now ~~believe~~ *think* that each Canada
goose is born (imprinted) with a ~~route~~ *room* that follows the stars. This can be called a "star
map" that shows each Canada goose (exactly) where to fly.

Canada geese always fly in a V outline. The leader of the outline becomes very
tired from breaking the air waves. That is why a flock of geese changes its leader many
times on each ~~migration~~ *trip* north or south. The rest of the flock flies in the V outline to
take ~~advantage~~ of the ~~updrafts~~ *upside* made by the wings of the bird in front of it. These
updrafts make it ~~easier~~ *easy* for each Canada goose to fly.

A Canada goose has a shining black head and neck with an ~~oval~~ *oven* patch of white. It
has a (pale) gray chest and a ~~gray-brown~~ *gray* body and wings. It also has a white *pretty* belly and
black tail feathers. The ~~average~~ goose weighs about ten pounds. Canada geese use their
legs as a landing ~~gear~~ *gone* when they come down from flying, much as an airplane uses landing gears when landing in an airport.

All baby Canada geese are born in the summer in Canada when it is safe for them.
However, they each ~~mate~~ *met* for life in the winter (somewhere) in the south.

Number of words in this selection   288

beginning
believe
breaking the air waves
in the V outline
easier
shining black head
pale
gray-brown
pretty
for life
somewhere

NOTE: Any major or minor miscue that occurred on the same word in this passage was counted only once as was explained earlier in point number 7.

The child made a total of 18 1/2 miscues (10 points and 8 1/2 points). Subtract 18 1/2 from 288 (the total number of words in this passage) to determine how many words the student pronounced correctly—**269.5**. Divide 288 (words in this passage) into 269.5 (total words that the student pronounced correctly) to obtain the percentage of correct words. This results in approximately **94 percent accuracy in word identification**, which is approximately the **high-instructional reading level**. The student would have had to attain about 259 words correctly pronounced to read at the low-instructional reading level (90 percent accuracy in word identification).

Remember to use your judgment in determining the low-independent, high-instructional, and low-instructional reading levels. This system of miscue analysis is designed to provide only an *approximation* of a student's actual reading levels, and the results from using it must be verified by careful teacher observation, other systems of miscue analysis, or various kinds of Individual Reading Inventories.

SAMPLE RECORD SHEET FOR MISCUE ANALYSIS

Page 130 is a sample completed record sheet for miscue analysis that is based on the child's performance on the passage "Canada Geese." It should prove very helpful in understanding the material just presented.

It is followed by a ready-to-duplicate record sheet (see page 132) you can use to record a student's performance using the miscue analysis system just explained. This record sheet can be copied as many times as needed.

INTERPRETING THE CHILD'S RESPONSES ON THIS TYPE OF MISCUE ANALYSIS

It is obvious that the major purpose of using this type of miscue analysis is to determine a student's instructional reading level and specific reading strengths and weaknesses so that appropriate reading instruction can then be provided for him or her.

Since the passage about "Canada Geese" is on approximately the fourth-grade reading level and Ben could read it at about the high-instructional reading level, a teacher can infer that he is reading at least at grade level. Many of Ben's omissions and

Name _Ben Berry_ Grade _4_ Teacher _Krista Brock_ Date _3/22/95_

RECORD SHEET FOR MISCUE ANALYSIS*+#

Text	Miscue	Omission	Addition	Substitution/Mispronunciation	Reversal	Repetition	Word Aided
among	—	½					½
fascinating	—						
in the world	—		1			½	
flecks	flecks			1			1
Scientists	—						
migration	travel	½		½			
really	—	½					
exactly	—						
beginning	starting			½		½	
believe	think			½		½	
imprinted	—	1		1			
route	room						
breaking the airwaves	—					½	
in the V outline	—					½	
advantage	—			½			
updrafts	upside			½			1
easier	easy						
shining black head	—					½	
oval	oven	½		1			
pale	—						
gray-brown	gray			½			

© 1995 by John Wiley & Sons, Inc.

130

Name _Ben Berry_ Grade _4_ Teacher _Krista Brock_ Date _3/22/95_

RECORD SHEET FOR MISCUE ANALYSIS*+# (CONT.)

Text	Miscue	Omission	Addition	Substitution/ Mispronunciation	Reversal	Repetition	Word Aided
pretty	—		½				
average	—						1
gear	gone						
mate	met			1			
for life	—			1			
Somewhere	—	½				½	
	Total ½	**Total** 3½	**Total** ½	**Total** 8½	**Total** 0	**Total** 2½	**Total** 3½

Total number of words in passage _288_

Total number of major miscues _10_

Total number of minor miscues _8½_

Total number of major and minor miscues _18½_

Percent of words correctly supplied _94%_

Approximate reading level _high instructional_

Independent reading level approx. 99%

Instructional reading level approx. 90%

Frustration reading level less than 90%

*Major miscue—deduct one point

+Minor miscue—deduct one-half point

#Repetition of two or more words—deduct one-half point

131

Name _____ Grade _____ Teacher _____ Date _____

RECORD SHEET FOR MISCUE ANALYSIS*+#

Text	Miscue	Omission	Addition	Substitution/ Mispronunciation	Reversal	Repetition	Word Aided
|||| ||||	|||| ||||	| | | | | | | |	| | | | | | | |	| | | | | | | |	| | | | | | | |	| | | | | | | |	| | | | | | | |

Name _____ Grade _____ Teacher _____ Date _____

RECORD SHEET FOR MISCUE ANALYSIS *+# (CONT.)

Text	Miscue	Omission	Addition	Substitution/ Mispronunciation	Reversal	Repetition	Word Aided
_____	_____	_____	_____	_____	_____	_____	_____
_____	_____	_____	_____	_____	_____	_____	_____
_____	_____	_____	_____	_____	_____	_____	_____
_____	_____	_____	_____	_____	_____	_____	_____
_____	_____	_____	_____	_____	_____	_____	_____
_____	_____	_____	_____	_____	_____	_____	_____
	Total	Total	Total	Total	Total	Total	Total
	_____	_____	_____	_____	_____	_____	_____

Total number of words in passage _____
Total number of major miscues _____
Total number of minor miscues _____
Total number of major and minor miscues _____
Percent of words correctly supplied _____
Approximate reading level _____
Independent reading level approx. 99%
Instructional reading level approx. 90%
Frustration reading level less than 90%

*Major miscue—deduct one point
+Minor miscue—deduct one-half point
#Repetition of two or more words—deduct one-half point

substitutions did not interfere significantly with comprehension and were therefore considered to be minor miscues. He did not repeat very often, and his teacher had to provide only four words after giving him sufficient time to determine the words himself. Ben did not have any reversals. It appears that Ben does not have one specific area of reading in which he demonstrates significant difficulties.

In summary, here are some of Ben's reading strengths:

- reading at grade level
- adequate comprehension (many of the miscues were minor)
- fair oral reading fluency

Here are some probable reading weaknesses:

- could make better use of semantic (context) cues in some instances
- could make better use of graphophonic (phonic) cues in some instances
- could take a few more risks while reading, thus avoiding the need to have his teacher supply any words

However, Ben could be considered to be a fairly good reader who should not need any reading help such as that provided in a pull-out program like Chapter I. However, he could profit from instruction and practice in the importance of using semantic (context) clues and risk-taking while reading. He also could be encouraged to notice graphophonic (phonic) elements when appropriate. In any case, at the fourth-grade reading level graphophonic elements should not receive undue emphasis. Ben mainly needs opportunities to read narrative and content materials on his instructional reading level and to be provided with many useful strategies for improving his interpretive (implicit) comprehension skills and study skills.

Description of Another System of Miscue Analysis

One useful, fairly simple system for coding reading miscues that you might consider using was developed by Susan B. Argyle and is described in her article "Miscue Analysis for Classroom Use" *(Reading Horizons*, 29, Winter 1989, pp. 93-102).[7] Very simply, this coding system attempts to determine if the miscue caused a meaning change, a graphic change, or was a self-correction. If the student's miscues resulted in few meaning changes, they usually are not very significant since they probably would not interfere with comprehension. If the student made a number of miscues that resulted in graphic changes, he or she possibly may need additional instruction or reinforcement in graphophonic (phonic) analysis or structural analysis depending upon their frequency or whether they interfered significantly with comprehension. If the student made a number of self-corrections, he or she probably does not have a very significant reading problem as compared with a student who does not recognize his or her miscues and, therefore, does not attempt to correct them.

---

[7]Used by permission of the Reading Center & Clinic at Western Michigan University.

In general, Argyle recommends the following steps for using this system of miscue analysis:

1. Choose reading material that is unfamiliar to your students. This may be part of a basal reader story or tradebook or a passage from a content textbook. Usually even adept readers make some miscues with totally unfamiliar material.
2. Copy the reading selection.
3. If you want to administer this material on an individual basis, tell the student that it is not a test in order to reduce his or her anxiety about reading it.
4. Have the student read the passage orally without any preparation. Tape recording helps you to code all of the miscues but may not be completely practical in a noisy setting. It is possible to code the miscues while the student reads, but it is fairly difficult.
5. Place the miscues on a summary sheet so that they can be analyzed.

Here is a very brief example of how Argyle's coding system may work:

- **Omission**   most (wild) animals

- **Addition**   *young*
                                     most wild animals
                                     ∧

- **Pause**   most / wild animals

- **Substitution**   *white*
                                     most ~~wild~~ animals

- **Repetition**   most <u>wild</u> animals

- **Reversal**   most wild animals

- **Self-Correction**   most wild <u>animals</u>

- **Word Supplied by Teacher**   T
                                     most wild animals

ILLUSTRATION OF THIS MISCUE ANALYSIS CODING SYSTEM

An oral reading passage entitled "Most Animals Don't Want Trouble" was written on the second-grade reading level and was taken from Wilma Miller's *Complete Reading Disabilities Handbook* (West Nyack, NY: The Center for Applied Research in Education, 1993, pp. 75-76). It was given to Tanya, a second-grade child who had evidenced reading problems. The passage was tape recorded, and Tanya's teacher coded her miscues using the system just described. The coded copy of this reading passage is included on page 137.

Tanya's teacher then transferred her miscues to a brief summary sheet that she had constructed. The summary sheet contains a list of all of Tanya's oral reading miscues. For each miscue the correct word is written first. Then as close a presentation as possible of the child's response is written in each instance. If the miscue resulted in a complete meaning change, the word *yes* is written, while if only a partial meaning change occurred, the word *partial* is written. If no meaning change resulted from the miscue, the word *no* is written. Next, each miscue is analyzed in terms of a graphic change in either the *beginning, middle,* or *end of the word*. In either instance, a — is normally written for a miscue in that part of the word, while a ✓ is written for a correct response in that part of the word. If the child self-corrects a miscue, the self-correction also is noted.

After coding Tanya's responses on the summary sheet, her teacher attempts to analyze some of her reading strengths and weaknesses mainly in terms of patterns that can be detected. You will find that it takes considerable time and effort to become adept in the interpretation of oral reading miscues and to develop an in-depth understanding of the reading process.

You will notice that Tanya made seventeen miscues that significantly interfered with comprehension and nine miscues that partially interfered with comprehension. In addition, she made four miscues that did not seem to interfere significantly with comprehension.

The percentages of graphic miscues that Tanya made were also coded by her teacher. From this analysis Tanya's teacher tried to notice if Tanya appeared to be more competent in identifying the *beginnings, middles*, or *endings* of the miscued words. Tanya's teacher noticed that she had the most difficulty with word middles, the next most difficulty with word endings, and the least difficulty with word beginnings. This is a very typical pattern of graphic miscues for a disabled reader. It is quite common for a child to have the most difficulty with word middles because they typically contain the vowel sounds that are the most difficult for nearly all children to discriminate and identify. Most children also are competent in identifying word beginnings, which was the case with Tanya. Tanya's teacher also noticed that she made no self-corrections, also indicative of a child with significant oral reading miscues who does not *monitor* his or her reading comprehension to see if reading makes sense.

You will also notice that Tanya made a total of **38** oral reading miscues on this passage out of a total of **167** words. This indicates that she mispronounced about **18%** of the words and correctly pronounced about **82%** of them. This percentage is well below the 90 to 95 percent level that ordinarily comprises the *instructional reading level*. Thus, this passage probably is on Tanya's **frustration reading level.**

Since the slash marks in the coding of Tanya's reading behavior indicate pauses in her oral reading, it appears that, although she may not have good oral reading fluency, there are not as many pauses as are typical of students who truly read in a word-by-word manner. In addition, she did not have an excessive number of repetitions while reading this passage.

Name _____ Grade _____ Teacher _____ Date _____

MOST ANIMALS DON'T WANT TROUBLE
(Second-Grade Reading Level)

Did you (know) that most (wild) animals try to // avoid ~~trouble~~ *terrible* if they can? Jenny

didn't (learn) that ~~until~~ *unless* she // spent the summer in the North Woods with her ~~grandfather~~ *grandpa*

and grandmother.

Jenny (first) ~~found~~ *find* that out about wild animals when she <u>was walking</u> on a road in

the woods ~~one~~ *once* day. She saw a porcupine way down the road coming ~~toward~~ *by* her. Jenny

~~could~~ *would* tell that the porcupine didn't seem to see her. As she and the porcupine came

closer (and) (closer), Jenny (really) ~~wondered~~ *wanted* what it would do. Finally, as they met on the

road, the porcupine saw her. As soon as it saw her, the porcupine ~~turned~~ *talked* and walked

<u>into</u> the <u>woods</u> as quickly as it could. Even ~~though~~ *through* the porcupine had (sharp) ~~quills~~ *quick*, it

didn't want ~~trouble~~ *terrible*.

~~Another~~ *One* time Jenny met a (large) black bear <u>when she</u> was walking on the road.

The bear looked at Jenny for awhile. Then it walked ~~across~~ *around* the road into the woods. It

also didn't // want trouble.

Number of words in this selection _____167_____

In summary, here are some of Tanya's reading strengths:

- fair, not good, oral reading fluency
- fairly good knowledge of word beginnings

Here are some of her reading weaknesses:

- comprehension
- making meaning changes that have semantic acceptability (make sense in sentence context)
- ability to identify word middles
- ability to identify word endings
- the use of self-correction or monitoring her own reading

Tanya's program of reading improvement should contain a number of different elements to ensure her optimum reading progress. She must be given reading materials that are on her own instructional or independent reading level even if that is below the second-grade level. Additional analysis should be done to determine these levels with some degree of accuracy. One way of doing this is with an Individual Reading Inventory (described and included in the next chapter of this handbook). She also must receive extensive instruction and practice in the importance of using semantic (context) cues to determine the meaning of unknown words and of monitoring her own reading carefully by making self-corrections when necessary. In addition, she needs instruction and reinforcement in graphophonic (phonic) elements, especially word middles and word endings. The important vowel elements probably should receive some stress in Tanya's reading program. She certainly must have extensive instruction and reinforcement in the various elements of reading comprehension and metacognition (monitoring her own reading to ensure that she is understanding).

In summary, the preceding is just one way in which a variation of oral reading miscue analysis can be used to determine a student's reading strengths and weaknesses. You will notice that although it is fairly simple to implement and modify—as it is an *informal* device—it requires considerable experience and knowledge of the reading process to administer. This technique, therefore, would have to be used judiciously by an inexperienced reading teacher. You may, in any case, wish to use another system of miscue analysis as a supplement to this one in some instances.

SAMPLE SUMMARY SHEET OF ORAL READING MISCUES

Page 139 is a sample completed summary sheet of oral reading miscues as described by Susan B. Argyle that is based on the child's performance on the passage "Most Animals Don't Want Trouble." It should prove very helpful in understanding the material just presented.

It is followed on page 140 by a ready-to-duplicate summary sheet you can use to record a student's performance using the miscue analysis system as described by Susan B. Argyle. This summary sheet can be copied as many times as needed or modified to fit your particular needs.

SUMMARY SHEET OF ORAL READING MISCUES

TEXT	MISCUE	MEANING CHANGE	GRAPHIC			SELF-CORR.
			B	M	E	
1. know	_____	yes	—	—	—	
2. wild	_____	partial	—	—	—	
3. trouble	terrible	yes	✓	—	✓	
4. learn	_____	yes	—	—	—	
5. until	unless	yes	✓	—	—	
6. grandfather	grandpa	no	✓	—	—	
7. first	_____	partial	—	—	—	
8. found	first	partial	✓	—	✓	
9. wild	_____	partial	—	—	—	
10. one	once	yes	✓	✓	—	
11. porcupine	_____	yes	—	—	—	
12. toward	by	partial	—	—	—	
13. could	would	yes	—	✓	✓	
14. porcupine	_____	yes	—	—	—	
15. porcupine	_____	yes	—	—	—	
16. and	_____	no	—	—	—	
17. closer	_____	no	—	—	—	
18. really	_____	no	—	—	—	
19. wondered	wanted	yes	✓	—	—	
20. Finally	_____	partial	—	—	—	
21. turned	talked	yes	✓	—	—	
22. quickly	_____	yes	—	—	—	
23. though	through	yes	✓	—	✓	
24. sharp	_____	partial	—	—	—	
25. quills	quick	yes	✓	—	—	
26. trouble	terrible	yes	✓	—	✓	
27. Another	One	partial	—	—	—	
28. large	_____	partial	—	—	—	
29. awhile	_____	yes	—	—	—	
30. across	around	yes	✓	—	—	
			11/	2/	5/	

Total 100%/ 37%/ 7%/ 17%

Name _____ Date _____

SUMMARY SHEET OF ORAL READING MISCUES

TEXT	MISCUE	MEANING CHANGE	GRAPHIC			SELF- CORR.
			B	M	E	

Variations of the Individual Reading Inventory

For many years, my teacher-trainees and graduate students have used an Individual Reading Inventory to assess the reading levels and specific reading strengths and weaknesses of the students whom they subsequently were going to tutor. Although these informal assessment devices have been very helpful in reading improvement programs, they always have had several limitations.

This chapter contains two comparable forms of a completely new classroom-tested informal reading inventory that incorporates contemporary research findings in an effort to make it more useful and to overcome the limitations inherent in previous inventories. This inventory assesses schema (prior knowledge) development and predictions before reading and uses a more contemporary way of evaluating comprehension ability. In addition, this inventory evaluates a child's self-monitoring ability while reading the passages.

Although the Individual Reading Inventory continues to be a subject of controversy in reading instruction, it remains a very useful, but certainly *not infallible*, way of determining a student's reading levels and specific reading strengths and weaknesses. Perhaps the modifications to the traditional inventory may make it a more useful means of assessment. Despite its limitations, it is an assessment tool in which classroom reading teachers, reading specialists, and learning disability teachers should be competent.

Description of a Typical Individual Reading Inventory

The *Individual Reading Inventory* may also be called an *informal reading inventory*. It is an informal device in contrast to a standardized assessment device. The Individual

Reading Inventory as it is known today probably originated with the late Emmett A. Betts and his doctoral student Patsy A. Kilgallon. Kilgallon established criteria for accuracy in word identification and comprehension that were then tested with forty-one students.[8] In the informal test the students read each passage silently and then orally, a very different procedure than normally is used today when giving such an inventory. Although they are not used in this handbook, these still are the most commonly used criteria. In any case, Betts spelled out his own definitions of the independent (easy), instructional (learning), and frustration (hard) levels and the listening comprehension level in a textbook that was published in 1946.[9]

An Individual Reading Inventory (IRI) is very pragmatic and classroom-oriented. Its main purposes include the following:

- determine a student's *approximate* independent (easy), instructional (learning), and frustration (hard) reading levels
- estimate a student's potential or capacity (listening comprehension) level
- place a student in appropriate groups
- help the teacher select appropriate reading material for a child
- appraise a child's progress in word identification (use of the three main cuing systems), oral reading fluency, and comprehension
- permit the teacher to make up-close observations of children operating under a variety of reading tasks and levels of demand

The IRI varies somewhat in format depending upon the different reading specialists who give it. The version presented in this handbook can be used by any classroom reading teacher, reading specialist, or learning disability teacher. If you are an elementary school teacher you may want to give an IRI to disabled readers during the first few months of the school year. If you are a reading specialist, you can give an IRI at the beginning of a remedial reading program after you have established rapport with a student. If you are a teacher of learning-handicapped students, you can give an IRI near the beginning of the school year.

> **NOTE:** You should not use too many assessment devices near the beginning of a remedial reading program. To do so may overwhelm the child and contribute significantly to his or her dislike of reading activities. Most reading specialists believe that assessment and remediation always should be a continuous, interwoven process.

Here are the main parts of a typical IRI:

---

[8]Patsy A. Kilgallon, "A Study of Relationships Among Certain Pupil Adjustments in Language Situations," doctoral dissertation, Pennsylvania State College, 1942.

[9]Emmett A. Betts, *Foundations of Reading Instruction.* (NY: American Book Company, 1946), pp. 438–485.

- *Establish rapport with the child.* It is necessary to establish rapport with a child before giving an IRI especially if you do not know the student well. Ask the child questions about his or her interests, hobbies, reading preferences, view of reading ability, and reading strengths and weaknesses. Ask the child questions about family *only* if this is pertinent to the assessment and can be done tactfully and sensitively.

- *Give a sight word test.* Give a child a sight-word test such as the Dolch Basic Sight Word Test, Fry's Instant Words, or Hillerich's 240 Starter Words. (A copy of the Dolch Basic Sight Word Test is found in Chapter 2, and a copy of Fry's Instant Words is found in Chapter 6.) A sight-word test usually should be given only to students who are severely or moderately disabled readers and who have evidenced a clear weakness in sight-word recognition by teacher observation. **You normally do not give a child both a sight-word test and the graded word lists on an Individual Reading Inventory as they may replicate each other.**

- *Give the graded word lists.* The graded word lists of an IRI are lists of words that begin at the preprimer or primer level and usually end at the twelfth-grade reading level. There normally are about twenty to twenty-five words on each graded word list. The child is to read each word aloud and continue until he or she misses about 5 words out of 25 words (20% level or greater) or reaches the obvious frustration level. The major purpose of giving the sight-word lists is to determine how well a child can identify words in isolation in comparison to in (sentence) context, to observe which cues a child uses to identify words, and to determine at about what level to have him or her begin to read the oral reading passages.

NOTE: A learning-handicapped child may be able to pronounce words in isolation more effectively than in (sentence) context, while a disabled reader may be able to use meaning (semantic) cues more effectively.

- *Give the graded oral (silent) reading passages.* The graded oral (silent) reading passages are a series of narrative and expository (content) passages that begin at the preprimer or primer level and often continue through the twelfth-grade reading level. Some of the passages can be used for evaluation of silent reading or as a listening comprehension test. Usually there are two or more comparable forms of the passages so that they can be used both for pre-testing and post-testing or for evaluating both oral and silent reading ability. Obviously, students do not read all of the passages either orally or silently. Students usually begin reading aloud a passage that is two or more grade levels below their estimated instructional reading level. This estimation can be made from the word lists or from teacher observation of previous classroom reading experience (if feasible).

Advantages and Limitations of Using an IRI

The following are the main *advantages* of using an Individual Reading Inventory:

- The reading levels as determined from an IRI usually are much more accurate than are those from a group-administered standardized survey reading or reading achievement test. For example, if a student receives a reading score of 5.2 on a standardized reading test, his or her actual instructional reading level may be about 4.0 or less. That partially is the result of group-administered standardized reading tests allowing students to randomly guess at answers. I once taught a second-grade child who was a nonreader yet was able to earn a grade-equivalent score of 2.5 in reading on the Stanford Achievement Test.

- An IRI permits the reading teacher to observe a child's reading behaviors while he or she is reading orally and to a lesser extent while reading silently. You can notice if a child makes good use of meaning cues, visual (graphophonic) cues, and structure cues, and cross-checks the three different cuing systems. You also can notice other elements of his or her reading performance, such as one-to-one correspondence (fingerpointing), signs of frustration, partially correct answers to comprehension questions, comprehension questions that are answered correctly after teacher prompts, distractibility, oral reading fluency, or word-by-word reading. None of these reading behaviors can be noticed while a child is taking a group-administered test.

- The graded oral (silent) reading passages on an IRI are a very good measure of the potential or capacity level (listening comprehension level). Using them in this way helps a teacher make an estimate of a child's probable reading improvement with very good instruction.

- Most of the commercially available IRIs have been classroom-tested, at least to some extent, and may have been evaluated for reliability and validity. Since they have been written by experienced reading specialists, in most cases they are very well designed.

- Most of the commercially available IRIs have comprehension questions at both the literal (explicit) and implicit (interpretive, critical, and creative) levels. In most cases a child is given credit for answers to the implicit comprehension questions which make sense even though they may not be the answers suggested by the inventory. Although some standardized reading tests attempt to allow children to provide divergent answers to implicit comprehension questions, it is very difficult for them to do so since the tests usually are computer scored.

- An IRI allows a reading teacher to determine a child's pattern of errors. It allows you to see clearly if a child has made an excessive number of omissions, substitutions, repetitions, reversals, pauses, or words supplied by the teacher. Some commercial inventories also enable you to determine if a child's miscues are mainly major (interfering significantly with comprehension) or minor (not interfering significantly with comprehension). However, not all commercial IRIs do this. The IRI included in this handbook enables a reading teacher to evaluate both major and minor miscues.

- Some commercial inventories reflect the actual narrative and expository (content) materials a child is reading better than do many standardized tests. Certainly, if you construct your own IRI, it can be formulated to exactly reflect the materials the child is reading. The expository (content) material in a number of standardized tests is quite dated because it is so expensive to revise such tests due to the required field-testing. However, most commercial inventories are revised quite often, and the material is kept up to date.

- Some of the more contemporary IRIs, such as the one contained in this handbook, use activation of prior knowledge and prediction which cannot be assessed in a group-administered reading test. Since these are very important elements of reading, they should be evaluated, and a few IRIs make the assessment fairly well.

However, here are some of the major *limitations* of using an IRI:

- Since an IRI is individually administered, it is quite time-consuming to give and evaluate. Although it would be helpful to give a number of children in elementary school an IRI, this usually is not practical because of the time involved. Thus, usually only moderately and severely disabled readers and learning-handicapped students with reading disabilities are given an Individual Reading Inventory.

- It is somewhat difficult to learn how to evaluate an Individual Reading Inventory. Each of them differs considerably on how to count and evaluate miscues, and each has a different scoring system. The reading teacher must spend considerable time learning how to evaluate an IRI before giving it, and usually this knowledge is not completely transferable to different IRIs. Some IRIs do not consider dialectal differences, errors that may or may not interfere significantly with comprehension, and self-corrections. You must study each IRI to determine what that inventory emphasizes. It is essential not to count dialectal miscues as errors, not to count self-corrections as errors since a student is trying to read for meaning, and to weigh more heavily those miscues that interfere with comprehension than those that do not.

- A student's performance on an IRI does not always "stair-step" in the way in which you think it should. For example, here is the way in which one may predict a student's performance:

> Independent reading level—Second grade
> Instructional reading level—Third grade
> Frustration reading level—Fourth grade

However, here is an actual student's performance levels on an IRI one of my teacher-trainees gave:

> Independent reading level—Second grade
> Instructional reading level—None
> Frustration reading level—Third grade

- A student's performance can vary greatly because of his or her prior knowledge and interest in any specific passage. Although most commercial inventories attempt to have both narrative and expository (content) passages that should interest both boys and girls, in practice this does not always happen. However, some IRIs have somewhat more relevant, interesting materials than others. You have to examine all of the passages on any IRI very carefully to determine how free from culture and gender bias they are and how interesting they may be.

- Some of the IRIs have excerpts in which the readability level is not accurate. Even if a passage does have the correct readability for that grade according to a readability formula, a student's prior knowledge and interest in a particular passage may not make it accurate for that particular child.

- Some IRIs have questions accompanying the passages that are not *passage dependent*. This indicates that a child might be able to answer some of the comprehension questions without reading a passage since he or she can answer them on the basis of prior knowledge.

- According to a research study by Duffelmeyer and Duffelmeyer, nearly 50% of the graded passages on the IRIs they studied did not have explicitly stated main ideas.[10] Therefore, you should ensure that each passage in any IRI you plan to use has a clearly stated main idea.

- Reading specialists do not agree on the criteria for determining the independent, instructional, and frustration reading levels. Some of the standards are set much higher than others, and one of them has been verified by a sufficient amount of research.

> **IMPORTANT:** In summary, the Individual Reading Inventory is a useful informal assessment device for determining a student's approximate reading levels and specific reading strengths and weaknesses. However, the findings from an IRI always should be interpreted very cautiously and should not be thought of as completely accurate. Instead, these findings should be regarded as only very tentative indicators of a child's reading levels and competencies and should be modified when necessary in a reading program. For, example, if you have found that a student has a fourth-grade instructional reading level yet has great difficulty with materials at this level, you should have the child read third-grade material instead.

Constructing the Word Lists and Graded Reading Passages of an IRI

Although most teachers probably will want to give the two comparable forms of the Individual Reading Inventory included in this handbook or one of the commercial IRIs listed and described later in this chapter, a few reading teachers may wish to construct their own IRI. However, before you decide to do so, you should be aware that this will take a considerable amount of time and effort. The major advantage of constructing your own IRI is that this informal assessment device will more closely parallel the actual narrative or content materials you are using in your classroom or clinic. Thus, you may gain a more accurate estimate of a child's actual independent (easy), instructional (learning), or frustration (hard) reading levels.

In constructing your own IRI, use reading materials that have been assigned reading levels (such as graded basal readers or content textbooks), or apply a valid readability formula to children's literature. Even with graded basal readers and content

---

[10]Frederick Duffelmeyer and Barbara Duffelmeyer, "Are IRI Passages Suitable for Assessing Main Idea Comprehension?" *The Reading Teacher,* 42 (February 1989), pp. 358–363.

textbooks, it may be very wise to use a readability formula since reading materials are not always graded accurately. You may want to use the Fry Readability found in the following source:

Wilma H. Miller, *Reading Teacher's Complete Diagnosis & Correction Manual.* West Nyack, NY: The Center for Applied Research in Education, 1988, pp. 282–283.

You also can use one of the readability formulae that has been placed on a computer program to make this determination.

To formulate the *graded word lists* of your own IRI, turn to the vocabulary list or glossary near the end of the basal reader or content textbook. Then randomly select every *n*th word (fifth word, eighth word, tenth word, etc.) so that you have a total of about *25* or *30 words* for each list. If you are using children's tradebooks, you can turn to several places near the beginning, middle, and end of the tradebook and select words randomly. On each selected page try to choose a few words at random until you have chosen about 25 to 30 words for that tradebook.

Then type the words using a word processor or computer. With primary-grade children or learning-disabled children, it is preferable to print each word on a separate 3 x 5 index card. Such children often become overwhelmed when they see an entire list of words all at once. If a word list is used, the teacher should have a copy of each word list on which to mark the student's correct or incorrect response. If word cards are used, the recognized and unrecognized words can be placed in two separate piles.

Then construct each of the graded reading passages from the selected basal reader series, content textbooks, or children's tradebooks. For each passage, you should attempt to use mainly the vocabulary representative of that book. You can attempt to condense an actual story although you also can formulate your own story from the appropriate words if you wish to do so.

After you have formulated a passage, you then must evaluate its readability level by using *at least one* of the formulae mentioned earlier. However, it is very important that you also consider the *interest level of a passage* since this obviously is not evaluated by any readability formula.

Normally the graded reading passages are fairly short in the early grades and then progress in length. Some reading specialists believe that such passages should be at least *50 words in length* at the preprimer level; *100 words in length* at the primer and first-reader level; and *200 words or more in length* at the second-reader level and above. However, other reading specialists recommend that a minimum of about *200 words* for any passage must be used to obtain a true sample of a student's reading.

You should be sure that each of the passages has a *very clearly stated main idea,* and that the comprehension questions are *passage dependent* (prior knowledge is not evaluated by these questions). The latter is often quite difficult to assure. Most reading specialists believe that the upper reading levels cannot be differentiated completely so they recommend that the upper-level passage encompass either grades 9-12 or 10-12.

You then formulate one question for each passage that assesses prior knowledge and one question that attempts to determine a student's interest in reading or listening to the passage. You also construct two or more explicit (literal or reading-the-lines) questions, implicit (interpretive or reading-between-the-lines) questions, and critical or creative (reading-beyond-the lines) questions for each passage. You also formulate one question for each passage to help the student assess how well he or she answered the comprehension questions.

Then type each of the passages on a sheet of paper with a word processor or computer so that the student can read from this copy. If possible, use a large font for typing the passages at the primary-grade reading level. Then glue or paste each passage onto a piece of posterboard. A number of reading specialists laminate the student's copies of the passages to make them more durable; then they can be used many times. Obviously, the student's copy of each passage does not contain the reading grade levels, the provision for assessing activation of schema, the assessment of self-monitoring, or the evaluation system. "Ben and the Porcupine" illustrates a graded reading passage for the second grade typed and glued on a sheet of posterboard.

Ben and the Porcupine

Ben is a brown and white dog that lives in the North Woods with his family. He likes to play in the woods whenever he can. One day last summer Ben met a porcupine in the woods.

Ben is a friendly dog who doesn't want trouble. When he met the porcupine, he just wanted to play with it. He ran over to the porcupine and touched it with his nose. The porcupine didn't understand that Ben just wanted to play. He was afraid of Ben and raised his very sharp quills.

Poor Ben! He ran home howling with porcupine quills all over his head and body. His owners tried to pull out the quills, but this hurt him too much. They had to take Ben to the vet who made him sleep while he was pulling out all of those quills. Ben had eighty-one quills all over his head and body! He even had one quill sticking out of his nose.

Today Ben is just fine, but he stays away from porcupines!

You can also type each of the graded reading passages on a word processor or computer so that you can mark each student's oral reading miscues on a separate copy.

A later part of this chapter includes two comparable sets of graded word lists and graded reading passages from the primer level through the twelfth-grade reading level. These are called Forms L and M, and they can be duplicated and used in their present form if you do not want to construct your own IRI.

Directions for Administering the Word Lists and Graded Reading Passages of an IRI

When administering the words lists on an Individual Reading Inventory, have the student begin pronouncing the words aloud on a word list that is *at least two reading levels* below his or her estimated instruction reading level. Have the student continue pronouncing the words on the graded word lists until he or she reaches the point when he or she is able to pronounce fewer than *90%* of the words on the list. Although this percentage is a commonly used place at which to stop, there is logic to instead using an *80%* accuracy level so that the student can begin reading at an easier passage.

Before the student begins reading the first appropriate oral reading passage, ask him or her the questions to ascertain prior knowledge and interest in the passage. Then have the student begin reading the graded oral reading passage which corresponds to the level at which *80–90%* of the words on a list were recognized. The beginning passage corresponds to the basal passage in an oral reading test. **It is very important to have the student begin reading at a low enough level so that he or she will experience success from the beginning and not become discouraged.** A few years ago I taught a teacher-trainee who was going to tutor a fifth-grade disabled reader. She had him start reading the third-grade word lists and passages. However, she quickly found that this level probably was his frustration reading level and had to change to the first-grade word list and passage. However, since he had become frustrated and discouraged at the beginning of the tutoring sessions, it was very difficult for her to encourage him to continue and do his best on the IRI.

As the student reads each of the passages aloud, mark his or her oral reading miscues on your copies of the passage.

You should carefully review the material in Chapter 4 about marking miscues in an IRI at this point. Very briefly, here is the marking system described and illustrated in Chapter 4:

- **Omission**—Circle the entire word or letter sound

- **Addition**—Insert with a caret

- **Substitution/Mispronunciation**—Draw a line through a substitution/mispronunci-ation and write it in

- **Reversal**—Use the transposition symbol

- **Repetition**—Use a wavy line to indicate a repetition *of two or more words*

a brown puppy

- **Word Aided**—If a student gives no response after about five seconds, give him or her the word and cross it out

NOTE: When you first try marking a student's oral reading miscues, you probably will find it very difficult to do. Since you must first focus so much on the marking system, you may well fall behind in the marking of a student's miscues and also may not be able to observe many other characteristics of the student's reading. Therefore, it may be helpful to tape record a student's read-ing of the passages. Then you can mark each student's miscues when you later play back the tape recording. You may have to replay some of the passages several times to locate all of the reading miscues. Even when you attain pro-ficiency in the marking system, you may want to tape record a student's read-ing of the passages. A student often is more self-conscious about his or her oral reading if he or she sees you marking miscues as he or she reads aloud.

As the child completes reading each passage aloud, you then ask him or her the comprehension questions which accompany that passage. Each of the answers can be scored at that time or during a later playback of the tape recording. (The next section of this chapter provides detailed directions on how to evaluate a child's responses to the questions.) After the child has answered the comprehension questions, you can ask the child to assess how well he or she did as is illustrated in the next section. As an alternative to asking the comprehension questions, you can have the child retell the important points of the passage. You should *not* ask the comprehension questions and use retelling also.

Have the child stop reading the graded passages when he or she reaches the frus-tration (hard) reading level. The frustration reading level is similar to the *ceiling level* on an oral reading test. This is the point at which the student makes many miscues, has poor comprehension, appears tense and nervous, and does not want to continue.

When a student reaches the frustration (hard) reading level, you can use the remaining reading passages as a *listening comprehension test* to establish his or her *potential or capacity level.* To do so, read several passages that follow the passage at which the student stopped reading and ask him or her the comprehension questions accompanying those passages. The level at which a student can answer about 75% of the questions correctly is called the *potential or capacity level.* This level corresponds to the potential reading level that can be measured by a listening comprehension test. It is the level to which a student *may be able to learn to read with excellent individually prescribed corrective or remedial reading instruction **if he or she has adequate prior knowledge.*** This level, however, should be considered only as a *very tentative indicator of reading potential* along with a number of others such as intelligence, prior knowledge, and motivation.

As stated earlier, the word lists and passages on any IRI can be used for several different purposes. For example, the word lists and passages contained in Form L and Form M of the IRI can be used for pre-testing and post-testing in a corrective or remedial reading program. The passages from these forms also can be used for oral-silent reading, silent-oral reading, oral-silent-oral reading, or silent-oral-silent reading.

Directions for Evaluating the Word Lists and Graded Reading Passages of an IRI

The major purpose for giving the graded word lists and reading passages of an IRI are to determine a student's *approximate* reading levels; to determine his or her *pattern* of oral reading miscues; to compare how well a student pronounces words in isolation and in context; to observe a student's self-corrections and assessment of comprehension ability; and to observe his or her various characteristics, strengths, and weaknesses in reading.

As the child pronounces each of the words on a word list, his or her response can be scored by placing a + for each correct word and a – or 0 for each incorrect response. If the child pronounces a word phonetically, in addition to the – or 0 you can write the phonetic spelling of that word. If you have printed the list words on individual cards, put them into two different piles as stated earlier. If you want, the word lists can be scored from replaying the tape recording.

You then can determine the child's reading levels on each of the word lists. This indicates his or her performance on words in isolation. You can use the following *approximate percentages* in making this determination:

- *99%* or more of the words on a list recognized—**independent reading level**
- *90%–98%* of the words on a list recognized—**instructional reading level**
- fewer than about *89%* of the words on a list recognized—**frustration reading level**

You can assess a student's prior knowledge and interest in reading a passage *informally* by asking yourself questions such as these:

- Did the student have very good, good, or poor prior knowledge for reading this passage?
- Was the student probably able to access his or her prior knowledge before reading the passage?
- Did the student probably have sufficient interest in reading the passage so that a lack of interest did not interfere significantly with his or her comprehension?

NOTE: These parts of the IRI necessarily are evaluated in an informal manner. This is consistent with the concept of an IRI being an informal assessment device.

Although you should refer back to Chapter 4 for a detailed discussion of evaluating the oral reading miscues on the passages, here briefly are the recommendations from that chapter:

1. Count any error that interferes significantly with comprehension as a *major oral reading miscue* and deduct one point.
2. Count any deviation from the printed text that does not seem to interfere significantly with comprehension as a *minor oral reading miscue* and deduct one-half point.
3. Count an addition as half a miscue if it does not significantly change the meaning of the material. Most often, it does not.
4. Do not count a self-correction as an error if it occurs within a short period of time, such as five seconds.
5. Count a repetition as half a miscue only if it occurs on *two or more words.*
6. Do not count more than one miscue on the same word within any passage.
7. Do not count a miscue on any *proper noun* found in a passage.
8. Deduct one point for any word a student cannot pronounce after about five seconds *if that word interferes significantly with comprehension.* Deduct one-half point for any word a student cannot pronounce after about five seconds *if that word does not interfere significantly with comprehension.*
9. Do not count miscues that seem to exemplify a student's cultural or regional dialect. To consider this point, you must be quite familiar with the basic characteristics of the child's speech patterns, as in the African-American, Hispanic, or Native American dialect.

Then evaluate the student's responses to the comprehension questions. On the first line by each question under the word *Score,* write the number *1* for a correct answer and the number *0* for an incorrect answer. On the second line by each answer under the word *Appropriateness,* write a + for a detailed or insightful answer or a ✓ for a completely irrelevant response. You do not have to place either of these marks if they are not pertinent. If more than one-third of the child's answers have been marked with a ✓, the child probably does not have a true idea of the purpose of the passage and certainly does not understand it adequately. If a child has a number of +'s, he or she has a high level of understanding of the material.

Then determine the student's comprehension score on each of the passages. If there are *six* comprehension questions accompanying a passage, the following scores are needed to attain the various reading levels:

- **Independent—6 correct**
- **Instructional—4–5 correct**
- **Frustration—3 or fewer correct**

If there are *eight* comprehension questions accompanying a passage, the following scores are needed to attain the various reading levels:

- **Independent—8 correct**
- **Instructional—5–7 correct**
- **Frustration—4 or fewer correct**

Instead of the comprehension questions, you can use *retelling* to assess comprehension ability. Consult Chapter 3 for a detailed description about how to quantitatively assess a child's retelling. If you use retelling instead of the comprehension questions in determining a student's reading levels, you will have to use considerable judgment in determining his or her reading levels. This is certainly acceptable for an experienced reading teacher since the IRI is necessarily an informal assessment device.

After you have evaluated a student's oral reading miscues and comprehension scores, you can determine his or her *approximate independent (easy), instructional (learning),* and *frustration (hard) levels.* There are a number of different classification schemes for determining these levels. Various IRIs use slightly different classification schemes for determining these levels. The percentages used in this handbook were selected from a careful examination of the fairly limited research in this area, logical analysis, and the reactions of thousands of reading teachers, undergraduate and graduate students, and children who have used the graded reading passages found in my three previous publications in this same area:

Wilma H. Miller, *Complete Reading Disabilities Handbook.* West Nyack, NY: The Center for Applied Research in Education, 1993.

Wilma H. Miller, *Reading Diagnosis Kit.* West Nyack, NY: The Center for Applied Research in Education, 1986.

Wilma H. Miller, *Reading Teacher's Complete Diagnosis & Correction Manual.* West Nyack, NY: The Center for Applied Research in Education, 1988.

The characteristics of the three *major reading levels* used in the IRIs included in this handbook are as follows:

- **Independent (Easy) Level**—the point at which a child is about *99%* accurate in word identification and has about *95%* or better comprehension

- **Instructional (Learning) Level**—the point at which a child is about *90%* accurate in word identification and has about *75%* or better comprehension
- **Frustration (Hard) Level**—the point at which a child is less than about *90%* accurate in word identification and has less than about *50%* accuracy in comprehension

From using the graded reading passages with thousands of children over many years, adding several other sublevels to these three basic levels can be useful in accurately placing these children in reading materials. Therefore, you also can use the following three subcategories:

- **Low Independent Level**
- **High Instructional Level**
- **Low Instructional Level**

This handbook uses these three subcategories of reading levels in addition to the three basic ones. Since any IRI necessarily is an informal assessment device, you must use your own judgment in arriving at these reading levels, and you should take a child's word identification miscues and comprehension score into account together. **I usually weigh the child's performance on comprehension more highly than I weigh his or her performance on word identification since comprehension obviously is much more important.** As you know, comprehension is the capstone of the reading process. Using the three additional approximate reading levels is justified since the graded oral reading passages always are *informal assessment devices and never should be thought of as infallible indicators of a child's completely accurate reading levels*.

In addition, you can assess the child's self-monitoring of his or her comprehension informally by noticing his or her responses to the questions following the comprehension questions for each passage. As you will notice from the passages in Form L and Form M, here is how self-monitoring of comprehension is assessed in this handbook:

How well do you think you answered these questions?
very well _____
all right _____
not so well _____

You then can make an informal comparison between each child's responses on these questions to his or her actual score on the comprehension questions. It appears that the following would be the most comparable responses:

Child's Response	*Comprehension Score on the Passage*	
	6 total questions	*8 total questions*
very well	6	8
all right	4–5	5–7
not so well	3 or fewer	4 or fewer

Any significant deviation from this pattern of response *may be evidence* that the child does not monitor his or her comprehension as effectively as possible.

The Word Lists and Graded Reading Passages for Form L and Form M

The chapter now includes the word lists and graded reading passages that comprise Form L and Form M of the Individual Reading Inventory. They are designed for use at the preprimer through the twelfth-grade reading levels. One of the word lists should be duplicated for the student to pronounce, and another set should be duplicated on which to record the scores. One set of graded reading passages at the appropriate reading levels should be duplicated without the questions to assess prior knowledge and interest in the passage, the comprehension questions, or the self-monitoring question. This is the set from which the student reads aloud. The other set contains the questions and the formula for scoring and is the set you evaluate. The child's set (both the word lists and graded reading passages) can be laminated for durability.

The following code has been placed on each of the word lists and graded reading passages so that the student cannot determine the levels of the word lists and passages he or she is asked to read.

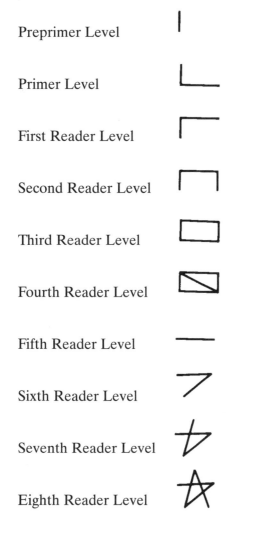

Preprimer Level

Primer Level

First Reader Level

Second Reader Level

Third Reader Level

Fourth Reader Level

Fifth Reader Level

Sixth Reader Level

Seventh Reader Level

Eighth Reader Level

Ninth Reader Level

Tenth-Twelfth Reader Level

Additional sets of graded word lists and graded reading passages can be found in the following sources:

Wilma H. Miller, *Complete Reading Disabilities Handbook.* West Nyack, NY: The Center for Applied Research in Education, 1993, pp. 64–95.

Wilma H. Miller, *Reading Diagnosis Kit.* West Nyack, NY: The Center for Applied Research in Education, 1986, pp. 198–259.

Wilma H. Miller, *Reading Teacher's Complete Diagnosis & Correction Manual.* West Nyack, NY: The Center for Applied Research in Education, 1988, pp. 69–59.

These additional word lists and passages can be used for pre-testing and post-testing or for different kinds of administration such as oral-silent-oral, silent-oral, oral-silent, and silent-oral-silent.

It is very difficult to discriminate between Ninth Reader Level and Twelfth Reader Level. Therefore, the reading level determined from these word lists and passages always should be considered *very tentative.*

FORM
L

Graded

Word

Lists

WORD LISTS

I	L	⌐
1. can	1. mother	1. around
2. green	2. thank	2. can't
3. see	3. two	3. father
4. ride	4. what	4. could
5. red	5. good	5. drop
6. big	6. where	6. many
7. saw	7. yellow	7. paint
8. three	8. cake	8. tell
9. make	9. out	9. why
10. book	10. please	10. every
11. play	11. find	11. cold
12. said	12. one	12. give
13. look	13. she	13. snow
14. an	14. into	14. found
15. help	15. laugh	15. once
16. funny	16. they	16. much
17. black	17. have	17. ball
18. and	18. came	18. walk
19. this	19. was	19. children
20. to	20. now	20. brown
21. in	21. that	21. again
22. blue	22. all	22. just
23. me	23. fly	23. never
24. get	24. away	24. men
25. down	25. your	25. street

Independent—24–25 correct on a word list

Instructional—22–23 correct on a word list

Frustration—21 or fewer correct on a word list

WORD LISTS

⌐	☐	⊠
1. together	1. eight	1. experience
2. write	2. escape	2. theater
3. pick	3. though	3. parachute
4. keep	4. planet	4. canoe
5. breakfast	5. magic	5. imitate
6. myself	6. thankful	6. pollute
7. carry	7. unusual	7. knowledge
8. which	8. decide	8. dignity
9. everyone	9. earth	9. enormous
10. hold	10. remember	10. prefer
11. these	11. close	11. decorate
12. always	12. mountain	12. vicious
13. friend	13. idea	13. original
14. today	14. several	14. protection
15. save	15. soup	15. island
16. light	16. special	16. design
17. been	17. ocean	17. weight
18. until	18. country	18. contradict
19. their	19. travel	19. predict
20. should	20. enough	20. force
21. buy	21. protect	21. modern
22. better	22. decide	22. critical
23. hurt	23. mystery	23. machine
24. does	24. built	24. legend
25. grow	25. strange	25. coward

Independent—**24–25 correct on a word list**
Instructional—**22–23 correct on a word list**
Frustration—**21 or fewer correct on a word list**

WORD LISTS

1. international	1. competition	1. boulevard
2. surgery	2. loathe	2. ambitious
3. merchant	3. liberty	3. scaffold
4. scientist	4. privacy	4. collapse
5. organize	5. transparent	5. horizontal
6. territory	6. conviction	6. progressive
7. photograph	7. applause	7. tolerate
8. value	8. contrary	8. independent
9. manage	9. antibiotic	9. warden
10. grief	10. microphone	10. domestic
11. telegram	11. pounce	11. implication
12. responsible	12. sensitive	12. conceive
13. plateau	13. helicopter	13. elusive
14. apparent	14. moisture	14. sculpture
15. intense	15. technical	15. famine
16. horizon	16. depression	16. neutral
17. image	17. symbol	17. radius
18. qualify	18. transfusion	18. exaggerate
19. argument	19. surf	19. ecstasy
20. ceremony	20. particle	20. terrain
21. amount	21. coyote	21. algebra
22. burden	22. subconscious	22. monarch
23. navigate	23. associate	23. exception
24. gentle	24. request	24. belligerent
25. region	25. wreath	25. alliance

Independent—24–25 correct on a word list

Instructional—22–23 correct on a word list

Frustration—21 or fewer correct on a word list

WORD LISTS

1. prescription	1. undergraduate	1. devastate
2. discipline	2. aggressive	2. philanthropy
3. intrigue	3. priority	3. assimilate
4. apex	4. arduous	4. atrocious
5. buffet	5. indispensable	5. exhilarate
6. miscellaneous	6. insignia	6. heirloom
7. universal	7. aquatic	7. malinger
8. arrogant	8. enviable	8. proprietor
9. discipline	9. malicious	9. legacy
10. competent	10. countenance	10. malign
11. conservative	11. judicial	11. memoir
12. triumphant	12. nutritional	12. inaudible
13. adjacent	13. desolation	13. callous
14. inconceivable	14. environment	14. nautical
15. politician	15. ornate	15. contemplate
16. docile	16. partisan	16. legacy
17. juvenile	17. brazen	17. kinetic
18. rebuke	18. disobedient	18. gregarious
19. oppressive	19. suffice	19. consecrate
20. rehearsal	20. ventilator	20. prolific
21. yacht	21. premature	21. obtuse
22. browse	22. legitimate	22. fictitious
23. masquerade	23. lucrative	23. hypothesis
24. embankment	24. industrialist	24. fallacy
25. quota	25. regime	25. charlatan

Independent—24–25 correct on a word list

Instructional—22–23 correct on a word list

Frustration—21 or fewer correct on a word list

ORAL READING PASSAGE

DICK'S BIG DOG* |

Dick has a big dog.

The dog's name is Sam.

Sam is a big, black dog.

Dick and Sam like to run.

Sam has a red ball.

He likes to run after the ball.

Sam likes to jump too.

He likes to eat dog food.

Dick likes to play with Sam.

Dick and Sam have fun.

*The readability level of this passage was computed by the Spache Readability Formula.

DICK'S BIG DOG

BEFORE READING

Assessing Prior Knowledge and Interest

1. What are some of the ways a boy and a big dog could have fun together?
2. Do you think you will like reading this story? Why? Why not?

AFTER READING

Number of words in this selection ___56___

Number of word identification miscues _____

Word Identification Miscues

    Independent reading level ___0–1___

    Low independent reading level approx. ___2___

    High instructional reading level approx. ___3–4___

    Instructional reading level approx. ___5–6___

    Low instructional reading level approx. ___7___

    Frustration reading level ___8+___

Assessing Comprehension

    Score <u>1</u> for a correct response and <u>0</u> for an incorrect response in the appropriate column. Score ✓ for any answers that are clearly illogical or + for any answers that are very good, detailed, or insightful.

	Score	*Appropriateness*
Reading the Lines		
1. What is the dog's name (**Sam**)	_____	_____
2. What does Sam like to eat? (**dog food**)	_____	_____
Reading Between the Lines		
3. Why do you think Dick and Sam like to run? (**it's fun; it's good for them; they like to be together; they like the out-of-doors**)	_____	_____
4. Why do you think Sam likes to jump? (**he's happy; he likes people; it's fun for him**)	_____	_____
Reading Beyond the Lines		
5. If you had a dog, what could the two of you do together? (**any logical answer—some examples: take a walk; play with a ball; play with a frisbee**)	_____	_____
6. Why do you think a dog is a good pet for a child? (**any logical answer—some examples: the dog could be the child's best friend; the child and the dog could take a walk together; the child and the dog could play together; the dog could protect the child**)	_____	_____

Number of comprehension questions correct _____

Comprehension Score

    Independent reading level ___6___

    Instructional reading level ___4–5___

    Frustration reading level ___3 or fewer___

SELF-MONITORING OF COMPREHENSION

    How well do you think you answered these questions?

    very well _____

    all right _____

    not so well _____

ORAL READING PASSAGE

THE NINE PUPPIES* ⌐

We have a large tan dog. She had nine puppies in the fall. The puppies were little and could not see. The mother dog fed them milk. The puppies got bigger.

Then the puppies walked and ran. They played too. The puppies liked to eat. They ate and ate all the time! The puppies got bigger and bigger. They played and played.

One day a boy came and took a puppy home. A girl came and took a puppy home too. Boys and girls all were happy. The puppies all were happy too. I was not happy. I liked the nine puppies. I wanted them all at my house!

*The readability level of this passage was computed by the Spache Readability Formula.

THE NINE PUPPIES

BEFORE READING

Assessing Prior Knowledge and Interest
1. What are some of the things nine puppies could do?
2. Do you think you will like reading this story? Why? Why not?

AFTER READING

Number of words in this selection __118__
Number of word identification miscues _____

Word Identification Miscues

Independent reading level __0–1__
Low independent reading level approx. __2–3__
High instructional reading level approx. __4–6__
Instructional reading level approx. __7–11__
Low instructional reading level approx. __12–13__
Frustration reading level __14+__

Assessing Comprehension

Score <u>1</u> for a correct response and <u>0</u> for an incorrect response in the appropriate column. Score
✓ for any answers that are clearly illogical or + for any answers that are very good, detailed, or insightful.

	Score	*Appropriateness*
Reading the Lines		
1. How many puppies did the child's family have? **(nine)**	_____	_____
2. When the puppies were little, what did the mother dog feed them? **(milk)**	_____	_____
Reading Between the Lines		
3. As they grew older, what do you think the puppies probably ate? **(puppy food; dog food; food they liked)**	_____	_____
4. Why do you think the child in the story wanted to keep all of the puppies? **(he/she liked (loved) them; they were fun to play with; they were cute)**	_____	_____
Reading Beyond the Lines		
5. If you had a puppy, how would you take care of it?**(any logical answer—some examples: feed it; give it water; take it outside to go to the bathroom; teach it to walk on a leash; put it in its bed to sleep when it was tired)**	_____	_____
6. If you had a puppy, how could you play with it? **(any logical answer—some examples: teach it to run after a ball and bring it back to me; play tug-of-war with it; let it chew a rawhide bone while I hold it; let it run and jump with me)**	_____	_____

Number of comprehension questions correct _____

Comprehension Score

Independent reading level __6__
Instructional reading level __4–5__
Frustration reading level __3 or fewer__

SELF-MONITORING OF COMPREHENSION

How well do you think you answered these questions?
very well _____
all right _____
not so well _____

ORAL READING PASSAGE

STOP FOR TURTLES* ⌐

Have you ever stopped for a turtle? Many men and women do just that when they are driving in the big woods.

In the summer turtles walk from one side of roads to the other side. The turtles are dark green and can be big or little. Some of them are as little as a little dish. Some of them are as big as the top of a big, big basket. The turtles walk on the busy roads where there are many cars and trucks. Some of them want to lay eggs on the other side of the road.

Most men and women who live in the big woods like turtles. That is why they stop when they see a turtle and wait for it if they can. They may get out of the car or truck and stop other cars and trucks. Then the turtle can walk to the other side of the road. A turtle may bite. That is why a man or woman will stay away from them.

_____

*The readability level of this passage was computed by the Spache Readability Formula.

STOP FOR TURTLES

BEFORE READING

Assessing Prior Knowledge and Interest
  1. What do you know about the turtles that live in the big woods?
  2. Do you think you will like reading this story? Why? Why not?

AFTER READING

Number of words in this selection __171__
Number of word identification miscues _____

Word Identification Miscues

  Independent reading level __0–3__
  Low independent reading level approx. __4–6__
  High instructional reading level approx. __7–11__
  Instructional reading level approx. __12–17__
  Low instructional reading level approx. __18–19__
  Frustration reading level __20+__

Assessing Comprehension

  Score <u>1</u> for a correct response and <u>0</u> for an incorrect response in the appropriate column. Score ✓ for any answers that are clearly illogical or + for any answers that are very good, detailed, or insightful.

	Score	Appropriateness

Reading the Lines
  1. What color are the turtles in this story? (**[dark] green**) _____ _____
  2. Why do some of the turtles cross the roads? (**to lay eggs [on the other side]**) _____ _____

Reading Between the Lines
  3. Why do you think some people get out of their car or truck to stop the traffic when they see a turtle on the road? (**otherwise other drivers might not see the turtle and kill it; otherwise other drivers might be driving too fast to be able to stop in time; a driver could not stop other drivers if he/she stayed inside his/her car or truck**) _____ _____
  4. Why do you think a turtle might bite a person who is trying to help it? (**it may be afraid of the person; it doesn't know that the person is trying to help it; it may try to protect itself**) _____ _____

Reading Beyond the Lines
  5. How might you help a turtle go across a road if it just stopped in the middle? (**any logical answer—some examples: push it gently with a stick; yell at it to go across; tell it to go across; stand behind it and tell it to go across**) _____ _____
  6. Why do you think a big turtle probably is more dangerous than a little turtle? (**any logical answer—some examples: a big turtle could bite harder than a little turtle; if a car or truck hit a big turtle, the car or truck might get damaged; a big turtle has a longer neck than a little turtle and could reach further to bite a person**) _____ _____

Number of comprehension questions correct _____

Comprehension Score

  Independent reading level __6__
  Instructional reading level __4–5__
  Frustration reading level __3 or fewer__

SELF-MONITORING OF COMPREHENSION

  How well do you think you answered these questions?
  very well _____
  all right _____
  not so well _____

ORAL READING PASSAGE

BEN AND THE PORCUPINE*#

Ben is a brown and white dog that lives in the North Woods with his family. He likes to run and play in the woods whenever he can. One day last summer Ben met a porcupine in the woods.

Ben is a friendly dog who doesn't want trouble. When he met the porcupine, he just wanted to play with it. He ran over to the porcupine and touched it with his nose. The porcupine didn't understand that Ben just wanted to play. He was afraid of Ben and raised his very sharp quills.

Poor Ben! He ran home howling with porcupine quills all over his head and body. His owners tried to pull out the quills, but this hurt him too much. They had to take Ben to the vet who made him sleep while he pulled out all of those quills. Ben had eighty-one quills all over his head and body! He even had one quill sticking out of his nose.

Today Ben is just fine, but he stays away from porcupines!

*The readability level of this passage was computed by the Spache Readability Formula.
#This is a true story.

BEN AND THE PORCUPINE

BEFORE READING

Assessing Prior Knowledge and Interest
1. What do you know about porcupines?
2. Do you think you will like reading this story? Why? Why not?

AFTER READING

Number of words in this selection ___173___
Number of word identification miscues _____

Word Identification Miscues

      Independent reading level __0–3__
      Low independent reading level approx. __4–6__
      High instructional reading level approx. __7–11__
      Instructional reading level approx. _12–17_
      Low instructional reading level approx. _18–19_
      Frustration reading level __20+__

Assessing Comprehension

Score <u>1</u> for a correct response and <u>0</u> for an incorrect response in the appropriate column. Score ✓ for any answers that are clearly illogical or + for any answers that are very good, detailed, or insightful.

	Score	*Appropriateness*

Reading the Lines
1. What did Ben want to do with the porcupine? (**play**)
2. What did the vet have to do to Ben before he could pull out the quills? (**make him sleep**)

Reading Between the Lines
3. Why do you think the porcupine was afraid of Ben? (**Ben ran up to it and touched it with his nose; a porcupine would be afraid of any animal that touched it; it may have never seen a dog before**)
4. How did Ben's owners know that it hurt him too much for them to pull out the quills? (**he howled; he ran away from them; he wouldn't let them touch him**)

Reading Beyond the Lines
5. What would you do if you met a porcupine while you were walking in the woods? (**any logical answer—some examples: stay away from it; walk the other way; run away from it**)
6. If your dog met a porcupine and got quills in its body from it, what would you do? (**any logical answer—some examples: ask my father or mother what to do; try to pull them out; have my father or mother try to pull them out; have my father or mother take it to the vet**)

Number of comprehension questions correct _____

Comprehension Score

      Independent reading level___6___
      Instructional reading level__4–5__
      Frustration reading level_3 or fewer_

SELF-MONITORING OF COMPREHENSION

      How well do you think you answered these questions?
      very well _____
      all right _____
      not so well _____

Name _____ Grade _____ Teacher _____ Date _____

ORAL READING PASSAGE

THE BEAGLE BRIGADE* ☐

If you go to an airport in a large city in our country, you may be surprised to see a small, friendly dog there. This small Beagle may be wearing a green coat and walking around the baggage.

One such Beagle is named Jackpot, and he works at an airport in New York City. His job is to check luggage and packages that are being brought into this country. When Jackpot picks up the scent of food or plants that cannot be brought here, he is trained to sit down by it.

Many kinds of foods, plants, and animal products cannot be brought here because they may carry insects or other things that could infect our crops or animals. In his work at the airport Jackpot has found many different kinds of foods, plants, and even birds.

Jackpot was trained by first putting a little piece of meat into an empty box. When he found the box with the meat, Jackpot was trained to sit down by it and was given a reward. Next meat was hidden with other things such as clothes, shoes, bread, and candy. Later the trainer left out the meat and used fruits like oranges, lemons, and limes. Now instead of a reward Jackpot is given praise or a pat on the head when he finds something that cannot come into this country.

Dogs like Jackpot are better at smelling than any machine that could ever be used.

© 1995 by John Wiley & Sons, Inc.

---

*The readability level of this passage was computed by the Spache Readability Formula.

THE BEAGLE BRIGADE

BEFORE READING

Assessing Prior Knowledge and Interest

1. What do you know about dogs that are used to find things that are not legal?
2. Do you think you will like reading this story? Why? Why not?

AFTER READING

Number of words in this selection __242__
Number of word identification miscues _____

Word Identification Miscues

Independent reading level __0–4__
Low independent reading level approx. __5–9__
High instructional reading level approx. __10–14__
Instructional reading level approx. __15–22__
Low instructional reading level approx. __23–26__
Frustration reading level __27+__

Assessing Comprehension

Score <u>1</u> for a correct response and <u>0</u> for an incorrect response in the appropriate column. Score ✓ for any answers that are clearly illogical or + for any answers that are very good, detailed, or insightful.

	Score	Appropriateness

Reading the Lines

1. Where does Jackpot work? (**an airport; an airport in New York City; New York City**) _____ _____
2. When Jackpot was being trained, what was the first item hidden? (**meat**) _____ _____

Reading Between the Lines

3. Why do you think the trainers use small, friendly dogs for this kind of work? (**this kind of dog won't scare people; it doesn't take as much space for a small dog to sit down by an object as it would take for a big dog; he/she has to be near many people all the time and is trustworthy**) _____ _____
4. Why do you think Jackpot is now given only praise instead of food reward? (**he would get too fat if he ate all those treats; he could get sick from eating all of those treats; it would be too expensive to buy all of the treats that would be needed for all of the dogs that do this kind of work**) _____ _____

Reading Beyond the Lines

5. If you saw a dog like Jackpot at an airport, do you think you should pet it? Why? Why not? (**any logical answer—some examples: YES it would be fun; he is friendly and would like it; NO he has a job to do and you could keep him from doing it; you should never pet a working dog like a seeing eye dog or a hearing ear dog**) _____ _____
6. Do you think you could train your dog to do a job like Jackpot's *if* you have a dog? (**any logical answer—some examples: YES my dog is smart; he/she is a good dog; he/she can smell real well; NO my dog isn't smart enough; my dog is too old; my dog can't smell that well; I don't have the time to train him/her**) _____ _____

Number of comprehension questions correct _____

Comprehension Score

Independent reading level __6__
Instructional reading level __4–5__
Frustration reading level __3 or fewer__

SELF-MONITORING OF COMPREHENSION

How well do you think you answered these questions?
very well _____
all right _____
not so well _____

ORAL READING PASSAGE

PRESIDENT CLINTON'S CHILDHOOD*

As everyone probably knows, Bill Clinton is the forty-second president of the United States. However, you may not be aware of how his childhood has shaped him into the man that he now has become.

President Clinton was born Billy Blythe in Hope, Arkansas, in 1946. Unfortunately, his father was killed in an automobile accident several months before his birth. Since Billy's mother needed to go to nursing school so that she could support him, Billy spent much of his first four years living with his grandparents. His grandparents taught him to read and to do arithmetic when he was only three years old. His grandfather owned a small grocery store in a mostly black neighborhood in Hope. He taught Billy the importance of respecting all people no matter what race they were.

When Billy was four years old, his mother married Roger Clinton, and the family moved to a farm near Hot Springs, Arkansas. Billy was a highly intelligent child who could read the newspaper when he was in first grade. Everyone who knew Billy liked him very much since he treated each person with respect.

When Bill was ten years old, his mother had a baby, and Bill then had a new stepbrother named Roger Jr. Unfortunately, Bill's stepfather was an alcoholic who sometimes flew into rages and slapped and punched Bill's mother. Once he fired a gun into the living room wall and had to go to jail.

When Bill was fourteen, he told his stepfather that the violence had to stop. Although it did stop, the drinking continued. To make his mother happy, Bill Blythe legally changed his name to Bill Clinton in 1960. In spite of the turmoil in his childhood, Bill continued to be an excellent, ambitious student.

---

*The readability level of this passage was computed by the Dale-Chall Readability Formula.

PRESIDENT CLINTON'S CHILDHOOD

BEFORE READING

Assessing Prior Knowledge and Interest

    1. What do you know about President Clinton's childhood?

    2. Do you think you will like reading this story? Why? Why not?

AFTER READING

Number of words in this selection ___294___

Number of word identification miscues _____

Word Identification Miscues

    Independent reading level ___0–5___

    Low independent reading level approx. ___6–10___

    High instructional reading level approx. ___11–16___

    Instructional reading level approx. _17–25_

    Low instructional reading level approx. _26–31_

    Frustration reading level ___32+___

Assessing Comprehension

Score 1 for a correct response and 0 for an incorrect response in the appropriate column. Score ✓ for any answers that are clearly illogical or + for any answers that are very good, detailed, or insightful.

                                  Score   *Appropriateness*

Reading the Lines

    1. In what town in Arkansas was Bill Clinton born in 1946? (**Hope**) _____ _____

    2. Throughout his childhood what kind of student was Bill Clinton? (**excellent; very good; good; ambitious**)

Reading Between the Lines

    3. How do you think Billy probably felt when he could not live with his mother when he was a little boy? (**unhappy; sad; lonely; he missed her**) _____ _____

    4. How do you think Bill may have felt when he saw his stepfather hit his mother? (**angry; mad; unhappy; sad; afraid**) _____ _____

Reading Beyond the Lines

    5. If you could meet President Clinton, what would you tell him that you thought about his childhood? (**any logical answer— some examples: that I felt sorry for him; that I admire him for becoming president anyway; that I think he was a brave boy**) _____ _____

    6. Would you like to grow up to become president of the United States? Why? Why not? (**any logical answer—some examples: YES it's an important job; everyone would admire me then; I could live in the White House; I could fly in a private plane; I would make a lot of money; NO it's too much work; it's not a safe job; the president makes many enemies; the president doesn't have any privacy**) _____ _____

Number of comprehension questions correct _____

Comprehension Score

    Independent reading level ___6___

    Instructional reading level ___4–5___

    Frustration reading level _3 or fewer_

SELF-MONITORING OF COMPREHENSION

    How well do you think you answered these questions?

    very well _____

    all right _____

    not so well _____

ORAL READING PASSAGE

TROPICAL RAIN FORESTS OF THE WORLD* ⸺

A tropical rain forest is a beautiful, emerald-green forest that is warm, moist, and quiet. It essentially looks like it did millions of years ago. In a rain forest the trees grow tall and close together blocking out the sunshine to the forest floor below. It is so quiet since the wind cannot move the dense top leaves.

Over two hundred million people live in the world's tropical rain forests. People in a tropical rain forest live mainly by hunting, fishing, and eating wild fruits. In some rain forests the people live in houses made of poles and palm leaves, while in other forests the houses may be built of wood. Some children who live there do not go to school but instead learn what they need to survive from their parents and other adults. They may learn to hunt deer, wild pigs, and other animals. They also may learn to grow vegetables.

Many of the foods that you eat were first grown in a rain forest. Some of these foods are corn, sweet potatoes, rice, oranges, and chocolate. Today coffee beans, vanilla, and cinnamon are only grown in tropical rain forests. These forests also are very important to doctors and medical research. Many of the drugs that are now sold in drug stores first came from plants in a rain forest. Many waxes, flavorings, and dyes also come from the tropical rain forests of the world.

However, the tropical rain forests of the world are now in danger. . People are cutting down the trees for firewood or lumber. More than <u>40%</u> of the world's tropical rain forests have already been destroyed. The clearing and burning of the forests is called <u>deforestation</u>, and many scientists believe that it must be stopped.

---

*The readability level of this passage was computed by the Dale-Chall Readability Formula.

TROPICAL RAIN FORESTS OF THE WORLD

BEFORE READING

Assessing Prior Knowledge and Interest
1. What do you know about the tropical rain forests of the world?
2. Do you think you will like reading this story? Why? Why not?

AFTER READING

Number of words in this selection ___291___
Number of word identification miscues _____

Word Identification Miscues

Independent reading level ___0–5___
Low independent reading level approx. ___6–10___
High instructional reading level approx. ___11–16___
Instructional reading level approx. __17–25__
Low instructional reading level approx. __26–31__
Frustration reading level ___32+___

Assessing Comprehension

Score <u>1</u> for a correct response and <u>0</u> for an incorrect response in the appropriate column. Score ✓ for any answers that are clearly illogical or + for any answers that are very good, detailed, or insightful.

	Score	Appropriateness

Reading the Lines
1. What is the usual temperature in a tropical rain forest? (**warm; hot**)   _____   _____
2. About how many people live in the world's tropical rain forests? (**over two hundred million; about two hundred million**)   _____   _____
3. What is deforestation? (**the cutting [and burning] of the rain forests**)   _____   _____

Reading Between the Lines
4. Why do you think houses made of wood probably are built in some tropical rain forests? (**the trees are plentiful in the rain forests; trees can easily be cut down in a rain forest**)
5. Why do you think some children in the tropical rain forests don't go to school? (**there are no schools in that rain forest; children in the rain forest don't need to know how to read, write, and do arithmetic to survive; the tropical rain forests are primitive societies**)   _____   _____
6. Why do you think it will take many, many years to renew a tropical rain forest that was destroyed by deforestation? (**it takes a long time for large trees to grow again; it would take hundreds of years for trees to grow that tall**)

Reading Beyond the Lines
7. Would you like to visit a tropical rain forest somewhere in the world someday? Why? Why not? (**any logical answer—some examples: YES it would be beautiful to see; I would like to see the animals and birds that live there; I would like to see the plants that grow there; NO I would have to travel too far to get there; some of the animals there could be dangerous; it would be too hot there**)   _____   _____
8. How could you work toward stopping the deforestation of the tropical rain forests? (**any logical answer—some examples: write letters to the leaders of the countries that have a tropical rain forest; become a scientist who works toward preventing the deforestation of the tropical rain forests**)   _____   _____

Number of comprehension questions correct _____

Comprehension Score

Independent reading level ___8___
Instructional reading level __5-7__
Frustration reading level __4 or fewer__

SELF-MONITORING OF COMPREHENSION

How well do you think you answered these questions?
very well _____
all right _____
not so well _____

Name _____ Grade _____ Teacher _____ Date _____

ORAL READING PASSAGE

THE MOST FAMOUS STEAMBOAT RACE*

Have you ever seen a steamboat traveling up or down a river? Recently I had the unique opportunity to take a steamboat cruise on the Mississippi River and found it to be fascinating.

The Mississippi River has been famous as a waterway since the adventuresome bargemen first carried goods on it in the early nineteenth century. Shortly thereafter the Mississippi River was opened to steamboat navigation. Undoubtedly the most famous steamboat race of all time was the race between the Robert E. Lee and the Natchez that began on June 30, 1870.

On that day the two steamboats just happened to be leaving New Orleans at about five in the afternoon. The race occurred because the Natchez had steamed up the river from New Orleans to St. Louis in three days, twenty-one hours, and fifty-eight minutes. She was thought to be the fastest steamboat on the Mississippi by everyone except the captain and crew of the Lee.

When Captain John Cannon heard of the remarkable record set by the Natchez, he determined that his steamboat would smash it. He stripped the Lee of all of the upper works that might catch the wind and arranged for coal to be supplied by coal flatboats that could be carried alongside the Lee while his crew transferred it. He refused to carry any goods or passengers on this trip fearing that they would slow the Lee down.

Since the Lee and the Natchez were leaving New Orleans at the same time, a race commenced although the Natchez was carrying passengers. Over $1,000,000 was wagered on this race. Near the end of the race both steamboats ran into heavy fog, but the Lee kept steaming through the murk while the Natchez tied up for four hours.

The Robert E. Lee easily won the race, arriving at St. Louis at 11:25 A.M. July 4, 1870. The Lee had made the journey in three days, eighteen hours, and fourteen minutes and had shattered the old record by thirty-three minutes.

*The readability level of this passage was computed by the Dale-Chall Readability Formula.

THE MOST FAMOUS STEAMBOAT RACE

BEFORE READING

Assessing Prior Knowledge and Interest
1. What do you know about river steamboats?
2. Do you think you will like reading this story? Why? Why not?

AFTER READING

Number of words in this selection __333__
Number of word identification miscues _____

Word Identification Miscues

Independent reading level __0–6__
Low independent reading level approx. __7–12__
High instructional reading level approx. __13–19__
Instructional reading level approx. __20–31__
Low instructional reading level approx. __32–38__
Frustration reading level __39+__

Assessing Comprehension

Score <u>1</u> for a correct response and <u>0</u> for an incorrect response in the appropriate column. Score ✓ for any answers that are clearly illogical or + for any answers that are very good, detailed, or insightful.

	Score	Appropriateness

Reading the Lines
1. In what year did the famous steamboat race between the <u>Robert E. Lee</u> and the <u>Natchez</u> take place? (**1870**)
2. How much money was wagered on the race between the <u>Robert E. Lee</u> and the <u>Natchez</u>? (**over one million dollars; $1,000,000**)
3. Which of the two steamboats won the race? (**the <u>Lee</u>; the <u>Robert E. Lee</u>**)

Reading Between the Lines
4. Why do you think Captain Cannon of the <u>Robert E. Lee</u> arranged for coal flatboats to be carried alongside it to supply it with coal? (**it would save time; the <u>Lee</u> wouldn't have to take the time to tie up at a dock to take on coal**)
5. Why do you think it probably was dangerous for the <u>Natchez</u> to carry passengers during the race? (**there could have been a collision with the <u>Lee</u>; the <u>Natchez</u> could have exploded due to the speed of the race; the passengers might have gotten sick from the speed of the race**)
6. Why do you think the <u>Natchez</u> probably tied up during the heavy fog? (**it had passengers on board; the captain thought it would be too dangerous to continue in the heavy fog**)

Reading Beyond the Lines
7. Would you like to take a steamboat trip on a river sometimes in the future? Why? Why not? (**any logical answer—some examples: YES it would be interesting; I would like to see all of the barges on the river; I like boats; I would like to see the paddlewheel; NO I don't like water; I'm afraid of water; I don't like to travel**)
8. Would you have liked to have been a passenger on the <u>Natchez</u> during the famous steamboat race? Why? Why not? (**any logical answer—some examples: YES it would have been very exciting; I like to go fast; NO it could have been very dangerous; there could have been an accident**)

Number of comprehension questions correct _____

Comprehension Score

Independent reading level __8__
Instructional reading level __5-7__
Frustration reading level __4 or fewer__

SELF-MONITORING OF COMPREHENSION

How well do you think you answered these questions?
very well _____
all right _____
not so well _____

Name _____ Grade _____ Teacher _____ Date _____

ORAL READING PASSAGE

LEARNING ABOUT THE COLORS IN LIGHT*

Did you know that the scientific discoveries upon which radio waves, microwaves, radar, and lasers are based originated in a rudimentary form in 1665? In that year a twenty-three-year-old scientist named Isaac Newton first experimented with light.

Since Newton's experiment was conducted on a sunny day, he pulled the curtain shut in his room, allowing the light to come through only a little chink that was cut out. The beam of sunlight then passed through a triangular piece of glass known as a <u>prism</u>. The light beam bent in its path as it passed through the prism, and this bending is known as <u>refraction</u>. Since the glass prism was there, the beam of light spread out and formed a rainbow on the wall. The light appeared to be colored red, orange, yellow, green, blue (indigo), and violet. When white light passes through a prism and is refracted, the different colors are refracted by different amounts. The refraction separates the colors and spreads them out in a strip instead of putting them in a circle.

Then Newton conducted a second experiment in which he let the light pass through the prism, but before it could reach the wall, he let it pass through a second prism with the point of the triangle facing the opposite way from the first prism. Now the light bent the opposite way as it went through the second prism. Therefore, the colors separated as they went through the first prism but came together again as they passed through the second prism. That is why only one circle of white light appeared on the wall after it had traveled through both prisms.

Since no one in Newton's time understood what comprised light, there were two different theories at that time. It was possible that the light might consist of a stream of tiny particles all moving rapidly in a straight line. It also was possible that light might be made up of very tiny waves all traveling very quickly in a straight line. It was later discovered that light did indeed consist of very tiny waves moving extremely rapidly. The average wavelength of light is about 1/50,000 of an inch long. This means that if you had a beam of light only one inch long, it would consist of about 50,000 waves.

Of course, scientists have had to conduct many sophisticated experiments to progress from Newton's original experiments to translate his findings into radio waves, microwaves, radar, and lasers. However, you can replicate Newton's original experiments quite easily to see how it all began.

---

*The readability level of this passage was computed by the Dale-Chall Readability Formula.

LEARNING ABOUT THE COLORS IN LIGHT

BEFORE READING

Assessing Prior Knowledge and Interest
1. What do you know about the colors in light?
2. Do you think you will like reading this story? Why? Why not?

AFTER READING

Number of words in this selection __430__
Number of word identification miscues _____

Word Identification Miscues

Independent reading level __0–7__
Low independent reading level approx. __8–16__
High instructional reading level approx. __17–26__
Instructional reading level approx. __27–37__
Low instructional reading level approx. __38–47__
Frustration reading level __48+__

Assessing Comprehension

Score <u>1</u> for a correct response and <u>0</u> for an incorrect response in the appropriate column. Score ✓ for any answers that are clearly illogical or + for any answers that are very good, detailed, or insightful.

	Score	Appropriateness

Reading the Lines
1. What was the name of the scientist who first experimented with light? (**Isaac Newton; Newton**) _____ _____
2. What was the piece of glass called through which the beam of light passed? (**prism**) _____ _____
3. What is a beam of light composed of? (**waves**) _____ _____

Reading Between the Lines
4. Why do you think Newton drew the curtains in his room nearly shut when he conducted his experiments with light? (**it was a sunny day and the colors of light would not have shown up well otherwise; it would have been too bright for the colors of the light to show up well otherwise**) _____ _____
5. Why do you think no one can see the waves in a beam of light with his/her naked eyes? (**they are much too tiny; they move too rapidly**) _____ _____
6. Which of the inventions mentioned in this passage makes you think that some waves must be very hot? (**microwave [oven] lasers**) _____ _____

Reading Beyond the Lines
7. Do you think you will duplicate Newton's experiments with light? Why? Why not? (**any logical answer—some examples: YES it would be very interesting; I could prove to myself that what the passage said about the colors of light is true; I like science; NO I don't like scientific experiments; I couldn't find two prisms**) _____ _____
8. How could you learn more about how waves of light are used in a microwave oven? (**any logical answer—some examples: read an encyclopedia article about microwave [ovens]; watch an article about microwaves on a CD-Rom computer disc; read a chapter about microwaves from a science textbook; read the owner's manual of a microwave oven**) _____ _____

Number of comprehension questions correct _____

Comprehension Score

Independent reading level __8__
Instructional reading level __5-7__
Frustration reading level __4 or fewer__

SELF-MONITORING OF COMPREHENSION

How well do you think you answered these questions?
very well _____
all right _____
not so well _____

© 1995 by John Wiley & Sons, Inc.

Name _____ Grade _____ Teacher _____ Date _____

ORAL READING PASSAGE

SOJOURNER TRUTH, AFRICAN-AMERICAN HEROINE*

It is unfortunate that so few Americans are aware of the unique contributions that a former slave has made through her eloquence in promoting equality and dignity for both African-Americans and women. Although this woman was born Isabella (Belle) Hardenbergh in New York in 1797, at the age of forty-six she took the name <u>Sojourner Truth</u>, which meant a <u>traveler</u> for her master whom she considered to be God or the "Truth."

Certainly Belle's early life as a slave was extremely harsh. She was first sold at the young age of nine and later was sold several times to other masters, often suffering cruel treatment, such as whippings, from them. However, she always fought for her rights ferociously, once taking a white man to court who had not given her son the freedom that was due him. Although this was unheard of in 1827, Belle believed that her faith would overcome all odds, and it certainly did.

By 1843 Belle believed that her Lord wanted her to travel across the country speaking out for equality for both African-Americans and women. Thus, Belle became <u>Sojourner Truth</u>, the name she retained throughout her life. Although she was illiterate, she was a very eloquent speaker as well as a very courageous woman. She always preached respect for all people regardless of their race or gender. This angered many white men who believed that both African-Americans and women should be subservient. Indeed, she was unafraid of anyone and was an imposing woman who stood over six feet tall, usually wearing a gray dress, white shawl, and white turban. To help support her travels for justice, in 1850 Sojourner dictated a book about her life entitled <u>The Narrative of Sojourner Truth</u>. At the age of sixty-four, she traveled to Washington, D.C. to advise President Lincoln and was warmly received and highly respected by him. At this time she worked for the National Freedmen's Relief Association in Washington, D.C., helping African-Americans to achieve economic and moral freedom. She also tried to teach them to demand dignity and take control of their own lives.

Sojourner left Washington, D.C. after several years and continued to speak eloquently about equality for African-Americans and women for the remainder of her life. Over the years she traveled to twenty-one states, often making the journey on foot. She died in 1883 at the age of eighty-six and is remembered for her determination and self-assertion by a memorial in Battle Creek, Michigan, where she is buried. She can be remembered as a unique role model even today more than a hundred years after her death.

© 1995 by John Wiley & Sons, Inc.

---

*The readability level of this passage was computed by the Dale-Chall Readability Formula.

SOJOURNER TRUTH, AFRICAN-AMERICAN HEROINE

BEFORE READING

Assessing Prior Knowledge and Interest

1. What do you know about an African-American woman named Sojourner Truth?
2. Do you think you will like reading this story? Why? Why not?

AFTER READING

Number of words in this selection __434__

Number of word identification miscues _____

Word Identification Miscues

Independent reading level approx. __0–7__
Low independent reading level approx. __8–16__
High instructional reading level approx. __17–26__
Instructional reading level approx. __27–37__
Low instructional reading level approx. __38–47__
Frustration reading level __48+__

Assessing Comprehension

Score 1 for a correct response and 0 for an incorrect response in the appropriate column. Score ✓ for any answers that are clearly illogical or + for any answers that are very good, detailed, or insightful.

	Score	Appropriateness

Reading the Lines

1. How old was Belle when she was first sold as a slave? (**nine**) _____ _____
2. Which president did Sojourner advise about the needs of African-Americans? (**President Lincoln; Lincoln**) _____ _____
3. How did Sojourner often travel? (**on foot; by walking**) _____ _____

Reading Between the Lines

4. What do you think gave Sojourner the courage to do all of the difficult things she did? (**her religious faith; her faith in God; her belief that they were the right things to do**) _____ _____
5. Why do you think Sojourner's height probably was an advantage for her? (**she stood as tall as most men; she appeared to be a very strong woman; she did not appear to be intimidated by a man**) _____ _____
6. Why do you think Sojourner was so warmly received by President Lincoln? (**he believed that slavery was wrong and had already freed the slaves; he respected a woman of great courage; he did not judge people by their skin color or gender**) _____ _____

Reading Beyond the Lines

7. How could you demonstrate Sojourner's beliefs in your own life? (**any logical answer—some examples: not judge anyone by his/her skin color or gender; think of each person as an individual; respect each person as a unique individual; stand up for your beliefs if you think they are right**) _____ _____
8. How could you learn more about other famous African-Americans in American history? (**any logical answer—some examples: ask your teacher to recommend some appropriate reading materials; look up African-Americans in an encyclopedia; ask a librarian to recommend some appropriate reading materials**) _____ _____

Number of comprehension questions correct _____

Comprehension Score

Independent reading level __8__
Instructional reading level __5-7__
Frustration reading level __4 or fewer__

SELF-MONITORING OF COMPREHENSION

How well do you think you answered these questions?
very well _____
all right _____
not so well _____

Name _____ Grade _____ Teacher _____ Date _____

ORAL READING PASSAGE

THE NORTHERN LIGHTS* ✦

Those people who have witnessed a spectacular display of the northern lights or <u>aurora borealis</u> say that it is a sight that they will always remember. The northern lights may appear at dusk and then for several hours blend into various glowing colors, weaving graceful forms. When they first appear, they may color a graying sky with a yellowish or greenish white light in the form of a huge arc. Suddenly after a few hours, the lower edge grows intense and bright, and the arc separates into fanlike rays that blaze into pink, red, and purple. In the climax of the display, the lights fill the entire sky. However, the climax lasts only a few minutes, and the intense colors quickly fade leaving the sky with only a faint glowing light.

Very briefly, the colorful display of northern lights occurs when solar wind particles, which are charged particles of electrons or protons, are first caught up in the Earth's magnetic field. Since the entire Earth is a giant magnet, it has both north and south magnetic poles, and the entire magnetic force field is called the <u>magnetosphere</u>. The solar wind then is speeded up by the Van Allen radiation belts, which are huge doughnut-shaped rings that surround the Earth and are part of the magnetosphere.

The solar wind particles are then hurled into the Earth's upper atmosphere where they collide with atoms and molecules formed mostly of oxygen and nitrogen. Each time an oxygen or nitrogen atom is struck, it loses one or more electrons. However, almost immediately it finds one or more loose electrons and replaces the lost one. As it does so, the atom gives off a little burst of energy that is seen as light.

When oxygen atoms regain lost electrons, they give off bursts of green or red light. So it is the energy bursts of oxygen atoms that account for the reddish, pink, or green colors of the northern lights. When nitrogen molecules regain the lost electrons, they give off bursts of violet or blue light.

Although the northern lights may be seen occasionally throughout the year, they are especially frequent and bright when there is much activity on the sun, which occurs about every eleven years. Since the last period of activity was in 1990, the next period should be in 2001. One of the most spectacular auroras ever seen occurred on the night of February 11, 1958, following a strong solar flare two days earlier.

© 1995 by John Wiley & Sons, Inc.

*The readability level of this passage was computed by the Dale-Chall Readability Formula.

THE NORTHERN LIGHTS

BEFORE READING

Assessing Prior Knowledge and Interest

1. What do you know about the northern lights or aurora borealis?
2. Do you think you will like reading this story? Why? Why not?

AFTER READING

Number of words in this selection ___412___
Number of word identification miscues _____

Word Identification Miscues

Independent reading level ___0–7___
Low independent reading level approx. ___8–16___
High instructional reading level approx. ___17–26___
Instructional reading level approx. _27–37_
Low instructional reading level approx. _38–47_
Frustration reading level ___48+___

Assessing Comprehension

Score <u>1</u> for a correct response and <u>0</u> for an incorrect response in the appropriate column. Score ✓ for any answers that are clearly illogical or + for any answers that are very good, detailed, or insightful.

	Score	*Appropriateness*

Reading the Lines

1. What is the other common name for the northern lights? (**aurora borealis**) _____ _____
2. How long does the climax of the northern lights last? (**a few minutes; several minutes**) _____ _____
3. In what year will the next period of especially bright and frequent display of northern lights occur? (**2001**) _____ _____

Reading Between the Lines

4. Why do you think a display of the northern lights impresses people so much? (**it is so beautiful; the colors are so beautiful; the northern lights may light up the entire sky**) _____ _____
5. What kind of weather do you think is necessary for the best display of the northern lights? (**clear weather; clear, cold weather; a clear sky**) _____ _____
6. Why do you think the northern lights are the most frequent and bright when there is much activity on the sun? (**the sun would be giving off many solar wind particles**) _____ _____

Reading Beyond the Lines

7. Would you like to see a display of the northern lights in 2001? Why? Why not? (**any logical answer—some examples: YES   it would be beautiful to see; it would be exciting to see; it would be interesting to see;   NO   I'm not interested in astronomy**) _____ _____
8. Would you ever be interested in studying astronomy? Why? Why not? (**any logical answer—some examples: YES   I like to learn about the sun, planets, and moon; I like to use a telescope; it would be interesting;   NO   I don't like to study about the sun, planets, or moon; I don't like science at all**) _____ _____

Number of comprehension questions correct _____

Comprehension Score

Independent reading level ___8___
Instructional reading level _5-7_
Frustration reading level _4 or fewer_

SELF-MONITORING OF COMPREHENSION

How well do you think you answered these questions?
very well _____
all right _____
not so well _____

Name _____ Grade _____ Teacher _____ Date _____

ORAL READING PASSAGE

WHAT ARE ALLERGIES?* ==

Allergies are associated with the working of the body's immune system which is designed to keep a person from harm. However, when a person develops allergies, the immune system goes out of control in a manner that can be very annoying and even potentially dangerous.

One of the body's primary line of defense against foreign invaders and potentially harmful substances within it is a type of white blood cells called <u>lymphocytes</u>. The <u>T-lymphocytes</u> specialize in recognizing those substances that belong in the body and those that do not. T-lymphocytes send out chemical messages to summon white blood cells called <u>macrophages</u> to destroy foreign invaders. The major job of the B-lymphocytes is to produce substances called <u>antibodies</u>. When antibodies have been matched up with the invading chemicals called <u>antigens</u>, the body can keep copies of these antibodies on hand as patterns, which is an efficient way a person can develop immunity to a disease.

The antibodies form a class of body chemicals called <u>immunoglobulins</u>. One of the immunoglobulins called <u>IgE</u> is the globulin responsible for allergic reactions. An IgE molecule is shaped like a Y, and the tail of the Y can attach to particular spots on the surface of special cells called <u>mast cells</u>. The arms of the two Y-shaped IgE molecules next to each other can share in holding the antigen, forming a bridge. When the IgE bridge is formed, tiny chemical packets inside the mast cells are stimulated to spill out their contents which pass out of the mast cells.

One of the main chemicals that the mast cells release is called <u>histamine</u>. Histamine, which is an allergy mediator, can act on the cells around them, producing a number of different effects such as the dilation (widening) of the capillaries and their becoming sieve-like so that fluid from the blood can leak into the tissues. If this occurs in the nose, the nasal membranes become swollen and watery, while if this occurs in the eyes, the eyes become itchy and produce excessive tears. An allergic reaction in the skin causes it to swell up with hives, while an allergic reaction deep in the breathing passages causes the air pipes to contract while their linings swell, making it difficult to breathe. Allergic reactions in the stomach and intestines can produce painful cramps and diarrhea, while allergic reactions in the circulatory system can cause the blood vessels to leak.

© 1995 by John Wiley & Sons, Inc.

---

*The readability level of this passage was computed by the Dale-Chall Readability Formula.

BEFORE READING

Assessing Prior Knowledge and Interest
1. What do you know about the causes of allergies?
2. Do you think you will like reading this story? Why? Why not?

AFTER READING

Number of words in this selection __409__
Number of word identification miscues _____

Word Identification Miscues

Independent reading level __0–7__
Low independent reading level approx. __8–16__
High instructional reading level approx. __17–26__
Instructional reading level approx. __27–37__
Low instructional reading level approx. __38–47__
Frustration reading level __48+__

Assessing Comprehension

Score 1 for a correct response and 0 for an incorrect response in the appropriate column. Score ✓ for any answers that are clearly illogical or + for any answers that are very good, detailed, or insightful.

	Score	Appropriateness

Reading the Lines
1. What type of white blood cells is one of the body's primary defenses against dangerous substances? (**lymphocytes**) _____ _____
2. What immunoglobulin is responsible for allergic reactions? (**IgE**) _____ _____
3. What is the main chemical that mast cells release? (**histamine**) _____ _____

Reading Between the Lines
4. Why do you think a person with many allergies should have complete allergy tests from a doctor who specializes in the diagnosis and treatment of allergies? (**the person could then avoid the allergy-causing agents that the doctor located; if the allergy-causing agents were avoided, the allergies would get much better or go away entirely**) _____ _____
5. Why do you think many allergies are treated with various kinds of antihistamines? (**they would counteract the damaging effects caused by histamine; they would stop the damaging effects caused by histamine**) _____ _____
6. Why do you think hives are the allergic reaction in the skin? (**histamine causes the capillaries in the skin to dilate [become wider], thus causing the hive; thus the capillaries in the skin dilate [become wider], the skin swells, causing the hive**) _____ _____

Reading Beyond the Lines
7. As far as you know, are you allergic to any substance? If you are, what are you allergic to? (**any logical answer—some examples: YES strawberries; cat fur; chocolate; sugar; dust**) _____ _____
8. If you are found to be allergic to some specific substance, what do you think you should do? (**any logical answer—some examples: avoid eating it; avoid coming in contact with it; find another home for my cat; try to avoid it**) _____ _____

Number of comprehension questions correct _____

Comprehension Score

Independent reading level __8__
Instructional reading level __5-7__
Frustration reading level __4 or fewer__

SELF-MONITORING OF COMPREHENSION

How well do you think you answered these questions?
very well _____
all right _____
not so well _____

FORM M

Graded

Word

Lists

WORD LISTS

I

1. play
2. funny
3. green
4. big
5. said
6. and
7. three
8. me
9. it
10. black
11. look
12. not
13. jump
14. come
15. see
16. can
17. up
18. in
19. book
20. to
21. little
22. help
23. you
24. play
25. I

⌐

1. good
2. please
3. laugh
4. then
5. find
6. have
7. cake
8. where
9. eat
10. mother
11. came
12. out
13. some
14. into
15. thank
16. white
17. two
18. where
19. yellow
20. away
21. was
22. what
23. all
24. but
25. too

¬

1. snow
2. father
3. every
4. many
5. once
6. ball
7. walk
8. can't
9. children
10. after
11. around
12. gave
13. must
14. old
15. why
16. could
17. from
18. again
19. her
20. give
21. far
22. ask
23. may
24. drop
25. fly

Independent—24–25 correct on a word list

Instructional—22–23 correct on a word list

Frustration—21 or fewer correct on a word list

WORD LISTS

⌐┐	▭	⬓
1. beautiful	1. escape	1. knowledge
2. hurt	2. thought	2. interrupt
3. strong	3. inventor	3. graduation
4. instead	4. wander	4. decorate
5. always	5. bush	5. balance
6. friend	6. eight	6. original
7. save	7. young	7. theater
8. night	8. reason	8. patient
9. together	9. planet	9. design
10. would	10. remember	10. contradict
11. breakfast	11. diamond	11. dignity
12. done	12. special	12. prefer
13. should	13. unusual	13. experience
14. does	14. decide	14. protection
15. surprise	15. close	15. parachute
16. which	16. strange	16. ancient
17. clean	17. mountain	17. exercise
18. eyes	18. hours	18. island
19. those	19. country	19. canoe
20. small	20. protect	20. weight
21. been	21. enough	21. pollute
22. their	22. mystery	22. predict
23. goes	23. several	23. vicious
24. buy	24. built	24. force
25. grow	25. fright	25. machine

Independent—24–25 correct on a word list

Instructional—22–23 correct on a word list

Frustration—21 or fewer correct on a word list

WORD LISTS

—

1. merchant
2. gentle
3. international
4. telegram
5. plateau
6. opponent
7. intense
8. horizon
9. image
10. qualify
11. argument
12. ceremony
13. amount
14. grief
15. gentle
16. responsible
17. manager
18. scientist
19. organize
20. territory
21. photograph
22. burden
23. parallel
24. considerable
25. intestines

7

1. transparent
2. particle
3. contrary
4. loathe
5. symbol
6. antibiotic
7. privacy
8. microphone
9. depression
10. associate
11. sensitive
12. applause
13. coyote
14. helicopter
15. surf
16. moisture
17. technical
18. wreath
19. pounce
20. subconscious
21. request
22. liberty
23. transfusion
24. midstream
25. hearth

⊅

1. terrain
2. tolerate
3. boulevard
4. conceive
5. scaffold
6. predator
7. perpetual
8. horizontal
9. ambitious
10. collapse
11. ecstasy
12. monarch
13. warden
14. elusive
15. notable
16. neutral
17. progressive
18. independent
19. exception
20. belligerent
21. alliance
22. species
23. famine
24. humidity
25. geological

Independent—24–25 correct on a word list
Instructional—22–23 correct on a word list
Frustration—21 or fewer correct on a word list

WORD LISTS

1. arrogant	1. aquatic	1. bereaved
2. competent	2. indispensable	2. exhilarated
3. apex	3. malicious	3. prolific
4. embankment	4. countenance	4. amethyst
5. quota	5. avalanche	5. devastate
6. juvenile	6. insignia	6. rhapsody
7. masquerade	7. harmonize	7. atrocious
8. discipline	8. undergraduate	8. assimilate
9. adjacent	9. arduous	9. contemporary
10. sequence	10. aggressive	10. unobtrusively
11. intrigue	11. enviable	11. proprietor
12. prescription	12. judicial	12. mediocre
13. extension	13. nutritional	13. gregarious
14. conservative	14. desolation	14. malign
15. inconceivable	15. partisan	15. memoir
16. torture	16. disposition	16. consecrate
17. politician	17. lucrative	17. fallacy
18. obsolete	18. suffice	18. eloquent
19. docile	19. ornate	19. callous
20. rebuke	20. premature	20. kinetic
21. congregation	21. environment	21. nautical
22. rehearsal	22. ventilator	22. inaudible
23. currency	23. legitimate	23. heirloom
24. triumphant	24. industrialist	24. obtuse
25. yacht	25. formidable	25. fictitious

Independent—24–25 correct on a word list

Instructional—22–23 correct on a word list

Frustration—21 or fewer correct on a word list

ORAL READING PASSAGE

PAT'S WHITE CAT* |

Pat has a white cat.

The cat's name is Muff.

Muff is a big, white cat.

Muff likes to play.

He likes to jump up on the bed too.

Muff eats cat food.

He likes to eat it.

Pat likes to play with Muff.

Pat and Muff have fun.

Pat likes Muff.

Muff likes Pat too.

*The readability level of this passage was computed by the Spache Readability Formula.

PAT'S WHITE CAT

BEFORE READING

Assessing Prior Knowledge and Interest
1. What are some of the reasons a child might like to have a cat?
2. Do you think you will like reading this story? Why? Why not?

AFTER READING

Number of words in this selection ___56___
Number of word-identification miscues _____

Word Identification Miscues

Independent reading level __0–1__
Low independent reading level approx. __2__
High instructional reading level approx. __3–4__
Instructional reading level approx. __5–6__
Low instructional reading level approx. __7__
Frustration reading level __8+__

Assessing Comprehension

Score 1 for a correct response and 0 for an incorrect response in the appropriate column. Score ✓ for any answers that are clearly illogical or + for any answers that are very good, detailed, or insightful.

	Score	*Appropriateness*

Reading the Lines
1. What is the cat's name? (**Muff**) ___ ___
2. Where does Muff like to jump? (**[on] the bed**) ___ ___

Reading Between the Lines
3. What kind of things do Pat and Muff do when they're playing? (**play with a ball of yarn; play with a toy for cats, like a toy mouse**) ___ ___
4. Why do you think Muff jumps up on the bed? (**he wants to sleep with Pat; he likes sleeping in the bed; he wants to take a nap in the bed**) ___ ___

Reading Beyond the Lines
5. If you had a cat, what could the two of you do together? (**any logical answer—some examples: you could pet the cat; it could sleep in your bed; you and the cat could play together with a ball of yarn**) ___ ___
6. Why do you think a cat is a good pet for a child? (**any logical answer—some examples: it could be the child's best friend; the child could pet it; it could sleep with the child; the cat and the child could play together**) ___ ___

Number of comprehension questions correct _____

Comprehension Score

Independent reading level __6__
Instructional reading level __4–5__
Frustration reading level __3 or fewer__

SELF-MONITORING OF COMPREHENSION

How well do you think you answered these questions?
very well _____
all right _____
not so well _____

ORAL READING PASSAGE

THE BABY PIGS*

I saw six baby pigs at a farm. They were little and fat. They were funny to look at.

I held a baby pig and looked at it. The baby pig was white and fat. It didn't want me to hold it. The baby pig wanted to jump down. It was happy then. The mother pig did not see me hold the baby pig. She would not be happy to see me hold it.

I named the baby pig Jim. I wanted to take it home with me. A baby pig would not be happy in a house. I will get a dog for a pet. A baby pig is not a pet for a boy.

*The readability level of this passage was computed by the Spache Readability Formula.

THE BABY PIGS

BEFORE READING

Assessing Prior Knowledge and Interest
1. What do you know about baby pigs?
2. Do you think you will like reading this story? Why? Why not?

AFTER READING

Number of words in this selection __129__
Number of word-identification miscues _____

Word Identification Miscues

Independent reading level __0–1__
Low independent reading level approx. __2–3__
High instructional reading level approx. __4–7__
Instructional reading level approx. __8–12__
Low instructional reading level approx. __13–14__
Frustration reading level __15+__

Assessing Comprehension

Score <u>1</u> for a correct response and <u>0</u> for an incorrect response in the appropriate column. Score ✓ for any answers that are clearly illogical or + for any answers that are very good, detailed, or insightful.

	Score	Appropriateness

Reading the Lines
1. How many baby pigs did the boy see at the farm? (**six**) _____ _____
2. What pet is the child going to get instead of a baby pig? (**dog**) _____ _____

Reading Between the Lines
3. Why do you think the baby pig didn't want the boy to hold it? (**it was afraid; it had never been held by a person before; it didn't know what was going to happen to it**) _____ _____
4. Why do you think a baby pig would not be happy in a house? (**it is a farm animal, not a pet; it would miss the other baby pigs; it was not born to be a pet**) _____ _____

Reading Beyond the Lines
5. If you could, would you ever want to hold a baby pig at a farm? Why? Why not? (**any logical answer—some examples: YES baby pigs are cute; I like animals; baby pigs are funny; baby pigs are fat; NO the mother pig might get mad; the baby pig would be scared; I might drop it since it would wiggle**) _____ _____
6. Would you want to have a baby pig for a pet? Why? Why not? (**any logical answer—some examples: YES they're cute; I like pigs; they're fat and cuddly; NO baby pigs are not pets; it would go to the bathroom in the house; I wouldn't know what to feed it; it wouldn't be happy in a house**) _____ _____

Number of comprehension questions correct _____

Comprehension Score

Independent reading level __6__
Instructional reading level __4–5__
Frustration reading level __3 or fewer__

SELF-MONITORING OF COMPREHENSION

How well do you think you answered these questions?
very well _____
all right _____
not so well _____

© 1995 by John Wiley & Sons, Inc.

195

Name _____ Grade _____ Teacher _____ Date _____

ORAL READING PASSAGE

FIVE DOGS IN A HOUSE*#

Would you like to live in a house with five dogs? A while ago I went to a house in the woods to buy a picture from a woman.

When I walked into the house I saw five dogs looking at me. There were three very big dogs and two little dogs. The five dogs were barking and barking at me. They were walking and running all over the house.

The woman's house was very big and pretty. It was very clean too. I don't know how the house stayed so clean with five dogs there.

The woman told me that she just liked dogs. She said that she had no children. Her dogs were her children. I like dogs very much too. I don't want to have five dogs in my house! One dog in my house is fine for me. How many dogs would you like to have?

---

*The readability level of this passage was computed by the Spache Readability Formula.
#This true story occurred during the summer of 1993 in northern Wisconsin.

FIVE DOGS IN A HOUSE

BEFORE READING

Assessing Prior Knowledge and Interest
1. What do you think a house with five dogs would be like?
2. Do you think you will like reading this story? Why? Why not?

AFTER READING

Number of words in this selection ___151___
Number of word-identification miscues _____

Word Identification Miscues

Independent reading level ___0–3___
Low independent reading level approx. ___4–6___
High instructional reading level approx. ___7–9___
Instructional reading level approx. ___10–15___
Low instructional reading level approx. ___16–17___
Frustration reading level ___18+___

Assessing Comprehension

Score 1 for a correct response and 0 for an incorrect response in the appropriate column. Score ✓ for any answers that are clearly illogical or + for any answers that are very good, detailed, or insightful.

	Score	*Appropriateness*

Reading the Lines
1. How many big dogs did the woman have? (**three**)   _____ _____
2. What did the woman say were her children? (**her dogs**)   _____ _____

Reading Between the Lines
3. Why do you think it is good that the woman has a very big house? (**it gives the dogs more space to move around; the dogs don't have to be near each other all the time; the woman can put the dogs in different rooms sometimes if they are bad**)   _____ _____
4. Why do you think the woman said that her five dogs are her children? (**they keep her from being lonely; she can take care of them like she would her children if she had children; dogs are like children in a lot of ways**)   _____ _____

Reading Beyond the Lines
5. Would you like to live in a house with five dogs? Why? Why not? (**any logical answer—some examples: YES I like dogs; it would be fun to play with five dogs; they would keep me from getting lonely; I would like to take care of five dogs; NO it would be too noisy; the dogs might break things in the house; it would take too much time to take care of five dogs; it would cost too much**)   _____ _____
6. If you had to live with five dogs, where would be a good place to live? (**any logical answer—some examples: a farm; the country; the woods; an island**)   _____ _____

Number of comprehension questions correct _____

Comprehension Score

Independent reading level ___6___
Instructional reading level ___4–5___
Frustration reading level ___3 or fewer___

SELF-MONITORING OF COMPREHENSION

How well do you think you answered these questions?
very well _____
all right _____
not so well _____

ORAL READING PASSAGE

LOONS*

Do you know what loons are? Loons are birds that look like ducks, but they are very different.

Loons live near the lakes up North. They are black with white markings. A loon has a sharp beak that helps it catch fish. It also has red eyes which makes it look different from a duck. Loons make a screaming sound that is very strange and pretty.

A loon is a very good fisherman. It dives under the water in a lake and swims a long way looking for a fish. It comes up far away. Sometimes it catches a fish, and sometimes it doesn't.

A mother loon often lays only a few eggs. That is one reason why there are not many loons today. Most lakes have only one or two pair of loons. Sometimes people in boats bother them. A person should never get too near a loon.

Maybe you will be able to see and hear loons someday. I know that you would like them very much.

*The readability level of this passage was computed by the Spache Readability Formula.

BEFORE READING

Assessing Prior Knowledge and Interest
1. What do you know about loons?
2. Do you think you will like reading this story? Why? Why not?

AFTER READING

Number of words in this selection ___169___
Number of word-identification miscues _____

Word Identification Miscues

Independent reading level __0–3__
Low independent reading level approx. __4–6__
High instructional reading level approx. __7–11__
Instructional reading level approx. __12–17__
Low instructional reading level approx. __18–19__
Frustration reading level __20+__

Assessing Comprehension

Score 1 for a correct response and 0 for an incorrect response in the appropriate column. Score ✓ for any answers that are clearly illogical or + for any answers that are very good, detailed, or insightful.

	Score	Appropriateness

Reading the Lines
1. What color eyes does a loon have? (**red**)   _____ _____
2. What kind of sound does a loon make? (**screaming [strange, pretty]**)   _____ _____

Reading Between the Lines
3. Why do you think a loon would have to live near a lake? (**it eats fish; it needs to be where fish are; fish are what it eats**)   _____ _____
4. How do you think people in a boat could bother a loon? (**they could scare it; they could make it lose a fish it was eating**)   _____ _____

Reading Beyond the Lines
5. Would you like to see a loon someday? Why? Why not? (**any logical answer—some examples: YES   it makes an interesting sound; it looks pretty; I'd like to be by a lake; it sounds nice;   NO   I don't like to leave home**)   _____ _____
6. How could you learn more about loons? (**any logical answer— some examples: read a book; ask my teacher; ask my father or mother; watch a TV program about them**)   _____ _____

Number of comprehension questions correct _____

Comprehension Score

Independent reading level ___6___
Instructional reading level ___4–5___
Frustration reading level _3 or fewer_

SELF-MONITORING OF COMPREHENSION

How well do you think you answered these questions?
very well _____
all right _____
not so well _____

ORAL READING PASSAGE

SEARCH AND RESCUE DOGS* ☐

There are many dogs that have been trained to search for and rescue people. These dogs are the most common in the states that have many campers, hikers, mountain climbers, and skiers.

Search and rescue dogs are taught to trail or air scent or to do both. When trailing, a dog follows a person's scent on the ground. Sometimes a good trailing dog can follow a scent that is as much as two days old. However, a good trailing dog will also use air scent. Air scent is carried on air currents from the cone-shaped aura of scent that a person gives off.

A good search and rescue dog must be friendly and like people. The dog must really like people to want to go to the work of finding them. The dogs all live in their trainers' homes just like most pets do.

Some search and rescue dogs wear a red harness with a bell on it. The harness tells the dog that it is working. The harness and bell also make the dog seem more friendly to the person that it finds.

It takes hundreds of hours to train a dog to be a search and rescue dog. However, the dog is only being asked to do what it can do anyway so well— smell. Dogs have noses that are very well built for scenting. Search and rescue dogs have saved the lives of many, many thankful people in the past.

*The readability level of this passage was computed by the Spache Readability Formula.

BEFORE READING

Assessing Prior Knowledge and Interest
1. What do you know about search and rescue dogs?
2. Do you think you will like reading this story? Why? Why not?

AFTER READING

Number of words in this selection __242__
Number of word-identification miscues _____

Word Identification Miscues

Independent reading level __0–4__
Low independent reading level approx. __5–9__
High instructional reading level approx. __10–14__
Instructional reading level approx. __15–22__
Low instructional reading level approx. __23–26__
Frustration reading level __27+__

Assessing Comprehension

Score 1 for a correct response and 0 for an incorrect response in the appropriate column. Score ✓ for any answers that are clearly illogical or + for any answers that are very good, detailed, or insightful.

	Score	Appropriateness

Reading the Lines
1. When a dog is trailing, where does it follow a person's scent? (**the ground**) _____ _____
2. What does wearing a harness tell a search and rescue dog? (**that it's working**) _____ _____

Reading Between the Lines
3. Why do you think a search and rescue dog must not be a mean, vicious dog? (**it might bite a person that it had found; it might scare a person that it had found**) _____ _____
4. Do you think it is cruel to make a dog spend hundreds of hours in training to be a search and rescue dog? Why? Why not? (**any logical answer—some examples:** YES **the dog might get tired of it; the dog would rather be playing than training; it's too hard for them;** NO **the dog is just doing what it can do well—smelling; a dog likes people; a dog likes to please its owner/trainer**) _____ _____

Reading Beyond the Lines
5. If you had a dog, would you want to train it to be a search and rescue dog? Why? Why not? (**any logical answer—some examples:** YES **I would like teaching my dog new things; I would like to help find lost people; my dog and I would like to walk [run] together;** NO **it would be too hard; it would take too much time and work; it could be dangerous**) _____ _____
6. If you were lost in the woods, would you rather be found by only people or by a person and a dog? Why? (**any logical answer— some examples:** ONLY PEOPLE **I don't like dogs; I'm afraid of all dogs; I don't want to be licked by a dog;** DOG AND A PERSON **I like dogs; the dog might help me get found quicker; I would like to see a dog come running toward me if I were lost**) _____ _____

Number of comprehension questions correct _____

Comprehension Score

Independent reading level __6__
Instructional reading level __4–5__
Frustration reading level __3 or fewer__

SELF-MONITORING OF COMPREHENSION

How well do you think you answered these questions?
very well _____
all right _____
not so well _____

Name _____ Grade _____ Teacher _____ Date _____

ORAL READING PASSAGE

CHRISTA McAULIFFE, TEACHER IN SPACE* ▨

Have you studied about Christa McAuliffe, the woman who was chosen to be the first teacher in space? Tragically, she died shortly after liftoff when the space shuttle <u>Challenger</u> exploded.

Christa was a middle school social studies teacher in New Hampshire when she entered a contest to choose the first teacher who would travel in space. This contest was held to honor all teachers since they are so important in the life of the United States.

Christa entered the contest along with ten thousand other teachers. To her surprise she was finally chosen as one of the ten finalists. She had taken many different kinds of tests and had gone to many different kinds of meetings to become a finalist. To her amazement she was chosen the winning teacher who would travel in a space shuttle with six other astronauts.

After Christa was chosen as the winning teacher, she had very extensive, difficult training at the Johnson Space Center in Texas. She was going to fly on the space shuttle <u>Challenger</u> with six experienced astronauts. She was very well liked and respected by the other astronauts. Christa planned to present several lessons from space to the school children of the United States who would watch her on television. Later she planned to travel around the country speaking to schoolchildren about the future of space travel. The <u>Challenger's</u> liftoff took place from the Kennedy Space Center in Florida on January 28, 1986. Only a minute into its flight, the <u>Challenger</u> exploded, and all the crew members were killed. Although Christa did not live to present her lessons from space, she has remained as a lasting tribute to all teachers everywhere.

---

*The readability level of this passage was computed by the Dale-Chall Readability Formula.

© 1995 by John Wiley & Sons, Inc.

CHRISTA McAULIFFE, TEACHER IN SPACE

BEFORE READING

Assessing Prior Knowledge and Interest

1. What do you know about Christa McAuliffe, the first teacher in space?
2. Do you think you will like reading this story? Why? Why not?

AFTER READING

Number of words in this selection __279__
Number of word-identification miscues _____

Word Identification Miscues

Independent reading level __0–5__
Low independent reading level approx. __6–9__
High instructional reading level approx. __10–15__
Instructional reading level approx. __16–26__
Low instructional reading level approx. __27–30__
Frustration reading level __31+__

Assessing Comprehension

Score 1 for a correct response and 0 for an incorrect response in the appropriate column. Score ✓ for any answers that are clearly illogical or + for any answers that are very good, detailed, or insightful.

                                     Score   *Appropriateness*

Reading the Lines

1. What was the name of the space shuttle on which Christa flew? (**Challenger**) _____ _____
2. In what state is the Kennedy Space Center located? (**Florida**) _____ _____

Reading Between the Lines

3. Why do you think Christa wanted to be the first school teacher to travel in space? (**she liked adventure; she wanted to be able to later share her experiences in space with schoolchildren; she liked science; she wanted to be well known**) _____ _____
4. Why do you think the other astronauts liked and respected Christa? (**she was friendly; she tried hard to learn; she wanted to be a good astronaut**) _____ _____

Reading Beyond the Lines

5. Would you ever like to travel in space? Why? Why not? (**any logical answer—some examples: YES it would be very exciting; it would be an adventure; it could help our country; it would be thrilling; NO it is too dangerous; it would take too much time; it would be too hard**) _____ _____
6. Do you think other teachers should travel in space in the future? Why? Why not? (**any logical answer—some examples: YES it would honor all teachers; teachers deserve special honor [recognition]; the teachers could tell children about their space travel; NO it is too dangerous; they would not be so well trained as the other astronauts; they aren't so experienced as the other astronauts**) _____ _____

Number of comprehension questions correct _____

Comprehension Score

Independent reading level __6__
Instructional reading level __4–5__
Frustration reading level __3 or fewer__

SELF-MONITORING OF COMPREHENSION

How well do you think you answered these questions?
very well _____
all right _____
not so well _____

ORAL READING PASSAGE

THE GREAT FLOOD OF 1993* ——

Some weather forecasters have called the flood of 1993 the flood of the century, while other forecasters have called it a flood that would occur only once every five hundred years. In either case, it was a very disastrous flood.

During the summer of 1993 incredible amounts of rain fell on the Midwest. At times as much as one inch of rain fell every six minutes! The consequences of such heavy rain were devastating all up and down the basin of the Mississippi River. The states of Missouri, Illinois, and Iowa received the most damage.

To attempt to prevent damage to homes, businesses, and cropland, the Army Corps of Engineers distributed 26 million plastic bags throughout the region. Volunteers then filled each of them with thirty-five pounds of sand and stacked them to create makeshift barriers, called <u>levees</u>, against the floodwaters. Sometimes these levees constructed from sandbags held, and much damage was prevented. However, some of the levees broke and thousands of homes and other buildings were damaged. Thousands of acres of valuable cropland also were flooded.

During the flood thousands of families were forced to leave their homes, and more than eight billion dollars of property was damaged. Fortunately, modern weather forecasting techniques provided plenty of warning that the floodwaters were rising. Therefore, people usually had enough time to get themselves and their possessions to higher ground. However, some people were able to make the best of a bad situation and traveled around their town in a motorboat or canoe. People hope that never again will the United States have so disastrous a flood. However, since most people usually have great courage, they have tried hard to go on with their lives.

————

*The readability level of this passage was computed by the Dale-Chall Readability Formula.

THE GREAT FLOOD OF 1993

BEFORE READING

Assessing Prior Knowledge and Interest

1. What do you know about the great flood of 1993?
2. Do you think you will like reading this story? Why? Why not?

AFTER READING

Number of words in this selection ___283___
Number of word-identification miscues _____

Word Identification Miscues

Independent reading level __0–5__
Low independent reading level approx. __6–10__
High instructional reading level approx. __11–16__
Instructional reading level approx. _17–25_
Low instructional reading level approx. _26–31_
Frustration reading level __32+__

Assessing Comprehension

Score <u>1</u> for a correct response and <u>0</u> for an incorrect response in the appropriate column. Score ✓ for any answers that are clearly illogical or + for any answers that are very good, detailed, or insightful.

	Score	*Appropriateness*

Reading the Lines

1. During the very hardest rainstorms, about how much rain fell in only six minutes? (**one inch**) _____ _____
2. About how many pounds of sand did the volunteers put in each of the plastic bags? (**thirty-five**) _____ _____
3. What is a levee designed to do? (**keep the floodwaters back**) _____ _____

Reading Between the Lines

4. Why do you think the volunteers took their time to fill all of the sand bags? (**they may have been friends of some of the people who were affected by the flood; they may have been neighbors of some of the people who were affected by the flood; they may have felt sorry for the people whose property was in the path of the flood; they may have thought it was the right thing to do**) _____ _____
5. Why do you think some of the levees may have broken? (**the water washed against them too hard; the water seeped underneath them; the water went over the top of them**) _____ _____
6. Why do you think some of the people traveled around their town in a motorboat or a canoe during the flood of 1993? (**that was the only way to travel at that time; they thought it was fun; they could not drive on any of the streets**) _____ _____

Reading Beyond the Lines

7. Would you have wanted to be a volunteer filling sandbags during the flood of 1993? Why? Why not? (**any logical answer—some examples: YES it would make me feel good to help those people; it would have been exciting; I like to work with other people; NO it would be too hard work; I couldn't shovel that much sand; it would have been discouraging when a levee broke anyway**) _____ _____
8. If your family's house had been damaged by the flood of 1993, would you want to move back there again after the water had gone down? Why? Why not? (**any logical answer—some examples: YES I would want to go home; I would be used to it there; NO it would be too much work cleaning up the house; a flood could happen again sometime**) _____ _____

Number of comprehension questions correct _____

Comprehension Score

Independent reading level ___8___
Instructional reading level __5–7__
Frustration reading level _4 or fewer_

SELF-MONITORING OF COMPREHENSION

How well do you think you answered these questions?
very well _____
all right _____
not so well _____

Name _____ Grade _____ Teacher _____ Date _____

ORAL READING PASSAGE

THE ALCATRAZ LIGHTHOUSE* 7

If you ever have been to the seashore, you may have seen a lighthouse since it is as much a part of the scene as are the sand and water, the seashells, and the sea gulls wheeling and dipping overhead. However, in the darkness of night or when fog or a severe storm blocks out all sight of sand or water, a beacon's flashing light or sound of warning can mean the difference between life or death for the crew of a ship that has lost its way.

The oldest lighthouse in California is Alcatraz Lighthouse, which was erected in 1854 close against the great gray fortress of Alcatraz prison. Alcatraz, familiarly known to criminals as the "Rock," was built by the Spaniards on an island in the bay. Originally a fort and then a military jail, Alcatraz was turned into a prison for civilians in 1933. Although it was thought that no prisoner could ever escape from Alcatraz, in 1937 two prisoners crawled through drain pipes and ventilators, dropped through a small window to the rocks below, and disappeared into the fog. Although it was believed that they were drowned in the icy waters, no one is positive since their bodies were never found.

In 1958 two prisoners attempted to escape from the "Rock" but both were killed in their unsuccessful attempt. In June of 1962 three more men disappeared from the "Rock," leaving no trace except a waterproof plastic bag containing some personal effects. The final attempt to escape occurred six months later when two men, using makeshift water wings made out of inflated surgeon's gloves and the sleeves of prison shirts, tried to escape. However, both were returned to Alcatraz to complete their sentences. Therefore, it was extremely difficult, if not impossible, to escape from Alcatraz prison.

Since repairs and maintenance at Alcatraz became very expensive, in 1963 the government moved the inmates elsewhere and abandoned the prison, leaving the island and its lighthouse to a caretaker and his wife, the sea gulls, and the beautiful wild flowers that bloom in profusion around the crumbling walls of the once terrifying "Rock."

© 1995 by John Wiley & Sons, Inc.

---

*The readability level of this passage was computed by the Dale-Chall Readability Formula.

THE ALCATRAZ LIGHTHOUSE

BEFORE READING

Assessing Prior Knowledge and Interest

1. What do you know about the Alcatraz lighthouse?
2. Do you think you will like reading this story? Why? Why not?

AFTER READING

Number of words in this selection ___354___
Number of word-identification miscues _____

Word Identification Miscues

Independent reading level ___0–6___
Low independent reading level approx. ___7–12___
High instructional reading level approx. ___13–19___
Instructional reading level approx. ___20–31___
Low instructional reading level approx. ___39+___

Assessing Comprehension

Score 1 for a correct response and 0 for an incorrect response in the appropriate column. Score ✓ for any answers that are clearly illogical or + for any answers that are very good, detailed, or insightful.

	Score	*Appropriateness*

Reading the Lines

1. What is the oldest lighthouse in California? (**the Alcatraz [lighthouse]**) _____ _____
2. What was the nickname of the Alcatraz prison? (**the "Rock"**) _____ _____
3. Who are the only people now living on the island of Alcatraz? (**the caretaker and his wife; the caretaker of the lighthouse and his wife**) _____ _____

Reading Between the Lines

4. Why do you think the island of Alcatraz received the nickname of the "Rock"? (**it may have appeared like a rock when it was approached by a boat or ship; it may have been dark in color; life in the prison was as "hard as a rock"**) _____ _____
5. Why do you think before the first escape attempt it was thought that no one could escape from the Alcatraz prison? (**the prison was on an island; the prison was very well built; the prison seemed to be very secure**) _____ _____
6. Why do you think a caretaker is still living at the Alcatraz lighthouse? (**he is needed to repair the lighthouse which is still operating; he is needed to clean the lighthouse beacon which is still operating**) _____ _____

Reading Beyond the Lines

7. Would you ever like to visit the old Alcatraz prison? Why? Why not? (**any logical answer—some examples: YES it is very historic; it would be interesting; it would be fun; NO it could be dangerous since the prison is in poor repair; it is too far away from my house; I don't like to go on a boat or ship**) _____ _____
8. Would you like to be a lighthousekeeper some day? Why? Why not? (**any logical answer—some examples: YES I like the ocean; I could then save people's lives; I like the out-of-doors; it would be interesting; NO it would be much too lonely; I like to live in a town or city**) _____ _____

Number of comprehension questions correct _____

Comprehension Score

Independent reading level ___8___
Instructional reading level ___5–7___
Frustration reading level ___4 or fewer___

SELF-MONITORING OF COMPREHENSION

How well do you think you answered these questions?
very well _____
all right _____
not so well _____

ORAL READING PASSAGE

HOW FAST IS FAST?*

The question posed in this title is relative. Speed, of course, differs greatly whether it is the speed of a glacier, an animal, an athlete, a bird, a hydroplane, a racing car, an aircraft, the wind in a tornado, sound, the Earth, or light.

One of the slowest objects in the universe is a glacier, which is a frozen river of snow and ice that moves less than one foot in an entire day. However, a snail, one of the slowest creatures, can travel that far in three minutes. A box turtle, which is thought of as a very slow animal, can travel about ten feet in a minute while a snail can travel only four inches.

Although a champion runner can travel an entire mile in less than four minutes, a speed of about fifteen miles an hour, a race horse can travel a mile in about ninety seconds, a speed of nearly forty miles an hour. However, a fish called a wahoo that lives in the Caribbean Sea and along the eastern coast of South America can swim about fifty miles per hour. A faster creature, however, is the cheetah which can run up to seventy miles per hour. An even faster creature is a bird called a chimney swift which can fly almost ninety miles per hour. This is the fastest speed recorded for any living creature.

A motorboat called a hydroplane skims across the top of the water at nearly 300 miles an hour, while some types of racing cars can travel more than 500 miles per hour. The wind in a tornado may have a speed of 600 miles per hour, but sound waves can travel through the air on a dry winter day at a speed of up to 740 miles per hour. However, some jet aircraft, satellites, and spaceships can travel much more rapidly than this at speeds of several thousands of miles per hour or more.

The Earth moves around the sun extremely rapidly at a speed of about 67,000 miles per hour. However, light travels 186,000 miles in only one second, meaning that light from the moon, which is 240,000 miles away, takes a little more than one second to reach the Earth, while light from the sun, which is 93,000,000 miles away, takes about 8 minutes to reach the Earth. No material thing in our universe can travel faster than the speed of light.

---

*The readability level of this passage was computed by the Dale-Chall Readability Formula.

HOW FAST IS FAST?

BEFORE READING

Assessing Prior Knowledge and Interest
1. What do you know about the speed of various animals, machines, and light?
2. Do you think you will like reading this story? Why? Why not?

AFTER READING

Number of words in this selection __404__
Number of word-identification miscues _____

Word Identification Miscues

Independent reading level __0–7__
Low independent reading level approx. __8–15__
High instructional reading level approx. __16–24__
Instructional reading level approx. __25–36__
Low instructional reading level approx. __37–45__
Frustration reading level __46+__

Assessing Comprehension

Score 1 for a correct response and 0 for an incorrect response in the appropriate column. Score ✓ for any answers that are clearly illogical or + for any answers that are very good, detailed, or insightful.

	Score	Appropriateness

Reading the Lines
1. What is the slowest object mentioned in this passage? (**a glacier**) _____ _____
2. What is the fastest material thing in our universe? (**light**) _____ _____
3. How fast can a champion runner run in four minutes? (**one mile; a mile**) _____ _____

Reading Between the Lines
4. Why do you think a glacier moves so slowly? (**it digs up earth as it moves; it is so huge that it couldn't move fast; it is so thick that it couldn't move fast**) _____ _____
5. What does a chimney swift probably have that makes it able to fly so quickly? (**long wings; a lightweight body; a small size**) _____ _____
6. Why do you think a hydroplane can travel so fast? (**it does not go into the water like a regular motorboat does; it is light weight in comparison to a regular motorboat**) _____ _____

Reading Beyond the Lines
7. How could you determine that the information given in this passage about the speed of a glacier is correct? (**any logical answer—some examples: visit an actual glacier and measure its progress from day to day; check the information in the encyclopedia; check the information on the CD-ROM disc; check the information in a science textbook**) _____ _____
8. Would you like to try to measure the speed of light? Why? Why not? (**any logical answer—some examples:** YES **it would be interesting; I like astronomy; I like science;** NO **I would not know how to do it; I don't like science**) _____ _____

Number of comprehension questions correct _____

Comprehension Score

Independent reading level __8__
Instructional reading level __5–7__
Frustration reading level __4 or fewer__

SELF-MONITORING OF COMPREHENSION

How well do you think you answered these questions?
very well _____
all right _____
not so well _____

© 1995 by John Wiley & Sons, Inc.

Name _____ Grade _____ Teacher _____ Date _____

ORAL READING PASSAGE

CARL SAGAN, EXTRAORDINARY SCIENTIST*

Most adults have not heard of any very famous scientists with the possible exception of Madame Curie, Albert Einstein, or Jonas Salk. However, most Americans have heard of an exceptional scientist named Carl Sagan because of his consistent exposure on such television programs as <u>The Tonight Show</u> and his own popular series <u>Cosmos</u> which appeared in the late 1970s and early 1980s. Perhaps more than any other scientist, Sagan is identified with his interest in UFOs (unidentified flying objects) and the exploration of Mars. Indeed Sagan is so well known that in one of his classes at Cornell University a student used to shout out "Heeere's Carl" in imitation of the opening line of <u>The Tonight Show</u>. Sagan clearly is "The Scientist Superstar."

Sagan was born in 1934 in New York, the son of an immigrant Russian garment cutter. Even as a child he was fascinated by the stars and the planets— the science of astronomy. He also was engrossed in science fiction, especially that emphasizing life on the planet of Mars. Indeed, the study of astronomy at The University of Chicago was an obvious choice for Sagan since Chicago had an outstanding astronomy department with many well-known professors. He eventually completed his doctorate degree at Chicago in astronomy and astrophysics.

Sagan has spent most of his entire adult life in the academic world and has played a role in a number of space expeditions to various plants for which he has received numerous awards. He also has been a prolific writer of articles for scientific journals and <u>Parade</u>, the Sunday supplement to many newspapers, as well as scientific books and a novel entitled <u>Contact</u>. He has always been fascinated with the idea that there might be different forms of life in space.

One of Sagan's more interesting projects was that of attaching a small golden plaque to the <u>Pioneer 10</u> spacecraft in 1977, which was first bound for Jupiter and then to become the first man-made object ever to leave the solar system. This plaque contained a message that might possibly be interpreted by an extraterrestrial being. It was written in the symbolic language of science and contained drawings of a man and woman done by Sagan's wife.

Sagan undoubtedly received his most fame through the television series <u>Cosmos</u>. This series covered the scientific exploration of everything in the world from the atom to the edge of the universe. It took three years to film the thirteen episodes of <u>Cosmos</u> and became the most popular show ever broadcast by PBS.

Through his television appearances and writing, Sagan has become the only "superstar" in the world of science, a model for any student who loves science and wants to study it further.

---

*The readability level of this passage was computed by the Dale-Chall Readability Formula.

BEFORE READING

Assessing Prior Knowledge and Interest

1. What do you know about a famous scientist named Carl Sagan?
2. Do you think you will like reading this story? Why? Why not?

AFTER READING

Number of words in this selection   __470__

Number of word-identification miscues _____

Word Identification Miscues

    Independent reading level __0–7__

    Low independent reading level approx. __8–16__

    High instructional reading level approx. __17–26__

    Low instructional reading level approx. __27–47__

    Frustration reading level __48+__

Assessing Comprehension

Score 1 for a correct response and 0 for an incorrect response in the appropriate column. Score ✓ for any answers that are clearly illogical or + for any answers that are very good, detailed, or insightful.

                                                      Score   *Appropriateness*

Reading the Lines

1. What was the name of Carl Sagan's own television series in the late 1970s and early 1980s? (**Cosmos**)   _____   _____

2. With what planet was Sagan especially fascinated? (**Mars**)   _____   _____

3. From what university did Sagan receive his doctoral degree? (**University of Chicago**)   _____   _____

Reading Between the Lines

4. Why do you think the most famous scientists are not well known by most people? (**they have not appeared on television; their work is mainly read only by other scientists; their work is hard for most people to understand**)   _____   _____

5. Why do you think the small golden plaque on the Pioneer 10 spacecraft contained drawings of a man and a woman? (**to show extraterrestrials what human beings look like; so that extraterrestrials might know who sent the plaque to them**)   _____   _____

6. Why do you think it took three years to film the thirteen episodes of the television series Cosmos? (**they contained very complicated, scientific material; they were filmed in many different locations**)   _____   _____

Reading Beyond the Lines

7. Would you like to become a famous scientist someday? Why? Why not? (**any logical answer—some examples:** YES **I like to study science; I might be able to help people in many different ways; I would like to make a lot of money;** NO **I don't like to study science; I don't understand science very well**)   _____   _____

8. Would you like to travel to the planet Mars some day? Why? Why not? (**any logical answer—some examples:** YES **it would be exciting; I would like to see if anyone lives there;** NO **it would be too dangerous; no human being could survive on Mars**)   _____   _____

Number of comprehension questions correct _____

Comprehension Score

    Independent reading level __8__

    Instructional reading level __5–7__

    Frustration reading level __4 or fewer__

SELF-MONITORING OF COMPREHENSION

    How well do you think you answered these questions?

    very well _____

    all right _____

    not so well _____

ORAL READING PASSAGE

THE EARLY HISTORY OF THE WHEEL*

It is a certainty that while <u>fire</u> is the greatest <u>discovery</u> ever made by humans, the <u>wheel</u> is the greatest <u>invention</u> ever made. The invention of the wheel has been credited to people who lived in the Tigris-Euphrates River Valley at least 5,000 years ago.

Humans became civilized by finding simpler means of doing tasks; for example, people realized after a time that oxen and horses could carry burdens that people could not. After the Spaniards brought horses to America, Native Americans began dragging heavy objects with two long poles lashed together across a horse's back at one end and trailing the ground on the other in what was called a <u>travois</u>.

Long before the invention of the wheel, an early vehicle may have been a <u>sledge</u> made from a naturally forked tree limb with the branches serving as runners. The entire sledge was hitched to oxen using a rawhide thong. Later, someone thought of moving a heavy loaded sledge on rollers, placing them on the ground ahead of the load, picking them up from behind after the sledge has been passed over them, and quickly moving them around to the front again.

Later it occurred to someone to use rollers for light loads also. Pins put through the runners would still allow them to turn. The rollers turning under the sledge would wear notches in the runners, and the runners would groove the rollers. However, as the grooves wore deeper, the middle part of the roller would begin to rub on the bottom of the sledge. Then the roller was made thinner between the runners, at which time the roller was not a roller anymore but rather two wheels connected by an axle tree, and the sledge became a cart or wagon. Since an axle tree would require that both wheels turn at the same time, the wheels were forced to rotate at the same speed and simply skidded around the turn. Later wheels were perfected that could turn while their axles were held still.

The first true wheels were circular chunks of wood cut or burned from the end of tree trunks with a hole near the middle for the axle to go through. The end of the axle stuck out beyond the wheel and had a pin through it called the <u>linchpin</u> to keep the wheel from coming off. Thus, the predecessor of the modern wheel had been invented—a tribute to the ingenuity and intelligence of humans.

*The readability level of this passage was computed by the Dale-Chall Readability Formula.

THE EARLY HISTORY OF THE WHEEL

BEFORE READING

Assessing Prior Knowledge and Interest

    1. What do you know about how the wheel was invented?

    2. Do you think you will like reading this story? Why? Why not?

AFTER READING

Number of words in this selection ___412___

Number of word-identification miscues _____

Word Identification Miscues

    Independent reading level ___0–7___

    Low independent reading level approx. ___8–16___

    High instructional reading level approx. ___17–26___

    Instructional reading level approx. ___27–37___

    Low instructional reading level approx. ___38–47___

    Frustration reading level ___48+___

Assessing Comprehension

Score <u>1</u> for a correct response and <u>0</u> for an incorrect response in the appropriate column. Score ✓ for any answers that are clearly illogical or + for any answers that are very good, detailed, or insightful.

	Score	*Appropriateness*

Reading the Lines

    1. About how many years ago is the wheel supposed to have been invented? (**5,000 years ago**) _____ _____

    2. What early vehicle was probably made from a naturally forked tree limb? (**the sledge**) _____ _____

    3. From what material were the first true wheels probably made? (**wood; tree trunks**) _____ _____

Reading Between the Lines

    4. Why do you think it was easier for oxen and horses to carry heavy burdens than it was for humans? (**they are stronger; they are larger**) _____ _____

    5. Why do you think it was not very convenient to move a heavily loaded sledge on rollers? (**it would take a long time to move the rollers to the front of the sledge as it was moving; it would have been very heavy to get the rollers under a loaded sledge; the rollers might slip out from under the sledge**) _____ _____

    6. Why do you think the very first wheels were made of wood? (**tree trunks probably were plentiful at that time; tree trunks would not have cost anything to get; a tree trunk is very nearly circular**) _____ _____

Reading Beyond the Lines

    7. Where do you think you might be able to see an example of a very old wheel? (**any logical answer—some examples: a museum; an automobile museum**) _____ _____

    8. What kind of material could you use to construct your own version of a wheel today? (**any logical response—some examples: wood; wire**) _____ _____

Number of comprehension questions correct _____

Comprehension Score

    Independent reading level ___8___

    Instructional reading level ___5–7___

    Frustration reading level ___4 or fewer___

SELF-MONITORING OF COMPREHENSION

    How well do you think you answered these questions?

    very well _____

    all right _____

    not so well _____

ORAL READING PASSAGE

THE HIGHER BRAIN*

The higher brain is composed of several different parts, each of which has a unique function. The outermost part of the <u>cerebrum</u>, which is called the <u>cerebral cortex</u>, contains the centers of sight, hearing, taste, smell, and touch as well as thinking and memory.

No other animal has a cerebrum that is comparable to that possessed by humans. For example, the cerebrum of an adult man would fit snugly inside a one-and-a-half quart container. It is the cerebral cortex that is concerned with thinking, learning, remembering, and dreaming—all the things that make us human beings.

The outside of the human cerebrum is marked by many wrinkles and deep furrows and looks rather like the meat of a walnut. These wrinkles are called <u>convolutions</u>, and the human brain has far more convolutions than are found in any other animal. Since the human cerebral cortex is convoluted, it can contain significantly more cells than would fit into the same space if it were smooth as is the case in the many lower animals.

Although the brain is the most important structure in the entire body, it also is rather delicate but is wrapped in three membranes called <u>meninges</u> to protect it. A liquid that fills the space between the inner meninges helps to cushion the brain from bumps and jars. The <u>cranium</u>, which is the bony skull in which the brain is nestled, helps to protect it from injury caused by blows to the head.

Twelve pairs of nerves branch out from the brain to various parts of the head and body. These are called <u>cranial nerves</u>, and some of them bring messages from the eyes, ears, and other sense organs, while others control the action of various muscles and glands.

A large furrow which runs along the middle of the brain divides the cerebrum into two halves or <u>hemispheres</u>, the left and the right. Curiously, the nerves that connect the brain with the rest of the body cross over so that the right hemisphere receives messages and controls the actions of the left side of the body, while the right hemisphere is concerned with the left side. Thus, if you are right-handed, the left hemisphere of your brain is the more highly developed, while if you are left-handed, the right hemisphere is better developed.

*The readability level of this passage was computed by the Dale-Chall Readability Formula.

THE HIGHER BRAIN

BEFORE READING

Assessing Prior Knowledge and Interest

1. What do you know about the higher brain in human beings?
2. Do you think you will like reading this story? Why? Why not?

AFTER READING

Number of words in this selection ___388___

Number of word-identification miscues _____

Word Identification Miscues

Independent reading level ___0–6___
Low independent reading level approx. ___7–15___
High instructional reading level approx. ___16–25___
Instructional reading level approx. ___26–36___
Low instructional reading level approx. ___37–45___
Frustration reading level ___46+___

Assessing Comprehension

Score 1 for a correct response and 0 for an incorrect response in the appropriate column. Score ✓ for any answers that are clearly illogical or + for any answers that are very good, detailed, or insightful.

	Score	*Appropriateness*

Reading the Lines

1. What is the outermost part of the cerebrum called? (**the cerebral cortex**) _____ _____
2. What are the wrinkles in the outside of the cerebrum called? (**convolutions**) _____ _____
3. What are the twelve pairs of nerves that branch out from the brain to various parts of the body called? (**cranial nerves**) _____ _____

Reading Between the Lines

4. Why do you think the human brain is carefully protected by the cranium and the meninges? (**it is so delicate that it could easily become damaged otherwise; the cranium is so hard that it can protect the brain from injury due to blows to the head; without this protection, brain injury might be fairly common, as everyone hits his/her head once in a while**) _____ _____
5. Why do you think the nerves that branch out from the brain to various parts of the body are called <u>cranial nerves</u>? (**they come out of the brain; the word "cranial" is related to the word "cranium"; they are controlled by the brain**) _____ _____
6. If a person's brain had both hemispheres developed to a fairly similar level, what might you expect that person to be able to do? (**use both the right and left hands equally well; be nearly ambidextrous**) _____ _____

Reading Beyond the Lines

7. Would you ever want to study to become a neurologist (medical specialist in the brain)? Why? Why not? (**any logical response—some examples: YES then I could help many people who really need it; I would probably make a lot of money; it would be very interesting and challenging; NO it would be very difficult to learn and practice; I don't like to study anything about the human body; I don't like to study science**) _____ _____
8. Would you ever like to see an actual human brain? Why? Why not? (**any logical response—some examples: YES I could learn a great deal; it would be very interesting; I like to study about the human body; NO it might make me feel ill; I just wouldn't want to learn on an actual human brain; I would rather study a model of the brain; I don't like to study about the human body**) _____ _____

Number of comprehension questions correct _____

Comprehension Score

Independent reading level ___8___
Instructional reading level ___5–7___
Frustration reading level ___4 or fewer___

SELF-MONITORING OF COMPREHENSION

How well do you think you answered these questions?
very well _____
all right _____
not so well _____

List of Commercial Individual Reading Inventories

Here is a fairly comprehensive listing of commercially available Individual Reading Inventories.

Analytical Reading Inventory

(Woods and Moe, Merrill Publishing Company, 1989). Each of the three forms contains seven graded 20-word lists (primer—grade 6) and ten graded passages (primer—grade 9). It contains six comprehension questions at primer and first-reader levels and eight comprehension questions at the other levels. The following questioning types are included: literal, terminology, cause-effect, interpretive, and drawing conclusions. Two expository subtests consisting of graded social studies and science passages (nine each, grades 1–9) are also included. This inventory also contains a class record summary sheet and is designed for grades 1–9.

Basic Reading Inventory

(Johns, Kendall/Hunt Publishing Company, 1991). Each of the three forms consists of ten graded 20-word lists (preprimer—grade 8) and ten graded passages (preprimer—grade 8). Words on the lists are first shown quickly and unknown words are presented again untimed. It contains four comprehension questions and one vocabulary question at the preprimer level and the following ten questions at the other levels: one main idea, five literal, two interpretive, one vocabulary, and one critical. This inventory contains various kinds of miscue analysis and comprehension summary sheets. It is designed for grades 1–8.

Burns–Roe Informal Reading Inventory

(Burns and Roe, Houghton Mifflin Company, 1993). This inventory contains two graded word lists (preprimer—grade 12) and four sets of graded passages (preprimer—grade 12). There are eight questions at the preprimer—second reader level; ten questions at the other levels (with six types on each passage: main idea, detail, sequence, cause-effect, interpretive, and vocabulary). The silent reading measure and the listening tests are optional. This inventory is designed for grades 1–12.

Classroom Reading Inventory

(Silvaroli, William C. Brown Publishing Company, 1994). Each form has eight graded 20-word lists and eight to ten graded passages (preprimer—grade 8 or grades 1–8). Each passage is followed by five comprehension questions that are literal, interpretive, or vocabulary. There is an optional spelling test. Forms A and B are for grades 1–6; Form C is for junior high school; and Form D is for senior high school and the adult level. This inventory is designed for grades 1–adult level.

Ekwall–Shanker Reading Inventory

(Ekwall and Shanker, Allyn and Bacon, 1993). This inventory consists of the San Diego Quick Assessment or Graded Word List for grades preprimer—grade 9 and four forms each of which contains nine graded passages (preprimer—grade 8). There are five comprehension questions at the preprimer level and ten at the other reading levels. They consist of the following: literal, interpretive, and vocabulary. This inventory also contains supplementary tests in letter knowledge, phonics, structural analysis, contractions, and the El Paso Phonics Survey. It is designed for grades 1–9.

Flynt–Cooter Reading Inventory for the Classroom

(Flynt and Cooter, Gorsuch Scarisbrick, Publishers, 1993). This inventory contains an interest/attitude questionnaire and three equivalent forms–Forms A, B, and C. Each of the three forms is divided into three sections: sentences to determine initial passage selection (this inventory contains no word lists), reading passages, and accompanying assessment protocols. Forms A and B are narrative (story) passages, while Form C passages are expository (content). The comprehension check for each passage is in the form of retellings with questions only asked after the retelling is finished. This inventory contains the following elements: high interest, longer passages, the questions related to either story grammar elements/level of comprehension or expository grammar elements/level of comprehension, and a miscue analysis grid designed to analyze pattern of performance in mispronunciations, substitutions, self-corrections, insertions, teacher assistance, omissions, or meaning disruptions. This inventory also contains a development performance summary and is designed for grades 1–9.

New Sucher–Allred Reading Placement Inventory

(Sucher and Allred, McGraw-Hill, 1986). This inventory consists of two forms, each of which contains twelve word lists and twelve oral reading passages. There are five comprehension questions for each passage (literal, interpretive, cause-effect, and main idea). This inventory is designed for grades 1–9.

The Interest Inventory

The interest inventory is a helpful *informal assessment device* that can be used in any developmental, corrective, or remedial reading program. It is a technique that can enable a reading teacher to ascertain a student's specific interests. An interest inventory can be given either on an individual or group basis, depending on the reading and writing ability of the student who is to complete it. Since children in the early primary grades normally cannot complete an interest inventory by themselves, reading teachers usually must administer this assessment device on an individual basis. This also may be the case with a disabled reader in an intermediate grade or middle school. However, most students at this level can complete an interest inventory in a group setting.

You then can use the results of the interest inventory in selecting and recommending books that a child can read independently for pleasure or information. Usually a student will put forth much more effort to read a trade book, magazine article, or newspaper article if it reflects his or her special interests. For example, a disabled reader in an intermediate grade who is interested in playing soccer often will attempt to read material about soccer or soccer players even if he or she usually is not interested in reading. The use of a child's interests in selecting and recommending materials in any reading program has proved to be very important in motivating him or her to make reading improvement in the thousands of tutoring situations I have supervised over many years.

I also have found it helpful to administer the interest inventory near the beginning of the tutoring sessions *in a creative manner.* My teacher-trainees have given an interest inventory in a puzzle situation with the questions on the inventory printed on puzzle pieces and blank puzzle pieces on which the child's answers can be written. The other side of the completed puzzle pieces have formed Garfield the cat, Snoopy the dog, Charlie Brown, a heart for Valentine's Day, and a snowman, among many others. Other teacher-trainees have printed the questions from the interest inventory on homemade or commercial fish, placed a paper clip on each fish, and had the child select each fish from a bowl with a stick to which string and a magnet were attached. The child then answered that question. It also is important for the child to ask the tutor many of the same questions so that he or she can become better acquainted with his or her tutor early in the tutoring session.

> **REMEMBER:** Give an interest inventory in a creative and motivating manner since this can help set the tone of the entire tutoring sessions. The creative administration of an interest inventory is important in creating good rapport between the reading tutor and the tutee.

As can be seen from the following two sample interest inventories, the typical interest inventory attempts to determine a child's specific interests in such areas as favorite kinds of books, favorite television programs, favorite foods, hobbies, favorite after-school and weekend activities, favorite vacation places, and favorite parts of the newspaper. After determining the child's interests, the reading teacher then should try to locate reading material that capitalizes on those interests. This material can be teacher-constructed games or activity sheets (often very motivating since it is specifically designed for the child), can be in the form of appropriate trade books, or can be in the form of supplementary materials. In any case, the materials always should be on the student's independent reading level or low instructional reading level and should be designed to improve his or her specific reading skill weaknesses. It is important that the material be very easy for the student to read as well as interesting if it is to help him or her make the optimum amount of reading progress.

SAMPLE INTEREST INVENTORIES

Here are two sample interest inventories. The one on page 219 is designed for use in the primary grades, while the other on page 220 is designed for use in the intermediate grades or middle school. You can duplicate and use either of them in their present form or modify them in any way you would like. They mainly are samples of the kinds of items that can be included in any useful interest inventory.

INTEREST INVENTORY (Primary-Grade Level)
Oral or Written Form

1. What is the name of one of your favorite books that someone has read aloud to you?

2. What is the name of one of your favorite books that you have read for yourself?

3. What kind of books and stories do you like to hear read aloud?

4. Do you have a library card?

5. Have you ever gone to the library and picked out a book to take home and have someone read to you or read for yourself?

6. What are the names of your two favorite television programs?

7. What is your favorite color?

8. What is your favorite food to eat?

9. What do you like to do the best after school?

10. What do you like to do the best on the weekends?

11. What kinds of games do you like to play?

12. Do you like to read the comics in the newspaper?

13. Do you like to read comic books? If you do, what is the name of your favorite comic book?

14. Do you collect anything? If you do, what kinds of things do you like to collect?

15. Do you enjoy reading for fun?

16. Where does your family like to go for vacations?

17. What do you like to do best with your mother? (father) (brother) (sister)

18. What do you like to do the best in school?

19. What don't you like to do in school very well?

20. What is the name of the best movie you have ever seen?

INTEREST INVENTORY (Intermediate-Grade Level)
Written Form

1. How much do you like to read?

   very much _____   not very much _____

   quite a bit _____   not at all _____

2. What are the titles of several of the books you really have enjoyed reading?

3. What are the titles of some of the books in your home?

4. Do you have a library card?

5. What are the names of some of the books you have checked out from the school library or public library during the past month or so?

6. What part of the newspaper do you like to read?

   sports section _____   letters to the editor _____

   comics section _____   classified ads _____

   news section _____   editorials _____

   advice column like "Dear Abby" or "Ann Landers" _____

7. What are the names of the magazines you read quite often?

8. What are the names of some of the comic books you enjoy reading?

9. What are the names of your three favorite television programs?

10. What sports do you like to watch on television?

11. What is your favorite subject in school? Why is it your favorite? What is your hardest subject in school? Why do you think that it is hard for you?

12. What do you like the best about school?

13. What do you like the least about school?

14. What do you like to do the best after school?

15. What do you like to do the best on the weekends?

16. What kinds of hobbies do you have?

17. Do you have any collections? If you do, what do you collect?

18. What do you want to be when you grow up?

19. Where do you usually go on vacation with your family?

20. Have you ever gone to camp in the summer? If you have, what did you enjoy the most about camp?

Content Reading Inventories

A number of students in the intermediate grades and middle school have much difficulty in comprehending and studying their social studies and science textbooks. You can use a variation of a group reading inventory to determine if your students have the ability to comprehend any selected content textbook effectively. Although lower-level textbooks in these content areas should be provided, if possible, for the moderately and severely disabled readers in the intermediate grades and middle school, many other students need to be taught comprehension strategies such as DR-TA, story impressions, the herringbone technique, semantic mapping, K-W-L, and K-W-L Plus as well as the reading–study skills that are needed for successful comprehension in these content areas. Descriptions and examples of these strategies are found in the following sources among others:

> Wilma H. Miller, *Complete Reading Disabilities Handbook.* West Nyack, NY: The Center for Applied Research in Education, 1993, pp. 342–377.

> Wilma H. Miller, *Reading Comprehension Activities Kit.* West Nyack, NY: The Center for Applied Research in Education, 1990.

A *content reading inventory* can help you determine the unique reading skills that should be presented in the different content areas. There are several variations of content reading inventories. One such variation tries to determine if a group of students can use the *various aids* that are included in the selected content textbook. This informal inventory is usually given at the beginning of a course or semester. To formulate such an inventory, construct about twenty questions on the use of textbook aids such as the table of contents, the index, the diagrams, the maps, the italicized words, the tables, and the graphs. The students try to complete this inventory by using their textbook to answer the questions.

Another version of a content reading inventory is designed to determine if students can successfully understand and study a selected content textbook. To construct this type of inventory, the teacher chooses a passage of about one thousand to two thousand words from the middle of the content textbook. The students then silently read the passage from their textbook. Each student then answers an open-ended question, such as the following: *What was this passage about?* Each student also answers some objective questions about the passage. These questions can evaluate a student's competency in such reading skills as explicit (literal) comprehension, implicit (interpretive) comprehension, critical reading, specialized vocabulary, the directly stated main idea, significant details, irrelevant details, and the implied main idea.

Another version of a content reading inventory is based on *one specific chapter* of the selected content textbook. This also is an open-book test that is given at the beginning of a class or semester. It is designed to determine if a student possesses the unique reading skills that are required to effectively comprehend the selected content textbook. This content inventory includes a matching vocabulary exercise composed of some of the specialized vocabulary terms contained in the chapter. It also can consist of explicit (literal), implicit (interpretive), critical, and creative questions as well as questions about the main ideas and important details from the chapter.

MODELS OF TWO CONTENT INVENTORIES

Beginning on page 223 are two models of content inventories that were constructed from intermediate-grade science textbooks. Since any content inventory must necessarily be based on the content textbook you are actually going to use, these two models are mainly designed to be examples. Additional models of all of the variations of content reading inventories are found in the following source:

Wilma H. Miller, *Reading Diagnosis Kit.* West Nyack, NY: The Center for Applied Research in Education, 1986, pp. 307–310.

MODEL OF A CONTENT INVENTORY
ON USING TEXTBOOK AIDS*

1. On what page does the chapter "Electricity" begin?

2. On what page does the unit EARTH SCIENCE begin?

3. According to the glossary of the textbook, what is the definition of the word alveoli?

4. According to the index of the textbook, on what pages does the materials on "pulsars" appear?

5. According to the glossary of the textbook, what is the definition of the word scrubber?

6. What is the name of Table 1 on page 302 of this book?

7. How many units does the textbook contain?

8. In what year was this textbook published?

9. According to the picture on page 452 of this textbook, what items are included in the dairy products?

10. As indicated in the picture on page 412 of this textbook, to what bone are all of the ribs connected?

11. How many lessons does Chapter 11 in this textbook contain?

12. According to the picture on page 46 of this textbook, what is the chemical formula of hydrogen peroxide?

13. According to the glossary of the textbook, what is the definition of the word bacteria?

14. According to the picture on page 440 of the textbook, how many kidneys does a human being have?

15. How many lessons does Chapter 28 in this textbook contain?

16. On what page does Lesson 1 Digestion, Chapter 17 begin?

17. On page 160 of this textbook, what type of lever is illustrated?

18. According to the index of this textbook, on what pages are there illustrations of "arteries"?

19. According to the glossary of the textbook, what is the definition of the word vaccine?

20. On page 282 of the textbook, what career is described?

*Formulated from an intermediate-grade science textbook for a model of this type of inventory.

MODEL OF A GROUP READING INVENTORY

Source of Reading Selection

Dean Hurd, Charles William McLaughlin, Susan M. Johnson, Edward Benjamin Snyder, George F. Matthias, and Jill D. Wright, General Science: A Voyage of Discovery. Englewood Cliffs, NJ: Prentice Hall, 1992.

Length of Reading Selection

About 1400 words

Subject Area

Science–Digestion

Grade Level

Intermediate

Brief Summary

This selection discusses the beginning stages of digestion in human beings.

Part One

What did the author say about digestion being necessary to sustain life in humans?

Part Two

A. It is important to select the significant details in what you read. Here are statements of details in the selection you have read. If the statement is true, put a T on the line before the statement. If the statement is false, put an F on the line before the statement.

_____ 1. Saliva contains a chemical substance called ptyalin.

_____ 2. Incisors are the back teeth in humans.

_____ 3. The epiglottis automatically closes over your windpipe as you swallow.

B. It is important to get main ideas from your reading. Put an X in front of each statement below that represents a main idea in this passage.

_____ 1. Food is necessary to sustain life in humans for a number of reasons.

_____ 2. The digestion of food by enzymes is called mechanical digestion.

_____ 3. The word "esophagus" comes from a Greek word meaning to carry what is eaten.

MODEL OF A GROUP READING INVENTORY (Cont.)

C. It is important for you to draw conclusions and generalizations from what you have read. Put an X in front of each of the following conclusions and generalizations that can be correctly drawn from this passage.

_____ 1. Foods are required to replace the cells that are constantly wearing out.

_____ 2. It would be very difficult for good digestion to occur if humans did not have teeth.

_____ 3. Peristalsis is not necessary for digestion in humans.

D. It is important to know the exact meaning of words you read. Below are sentences with a word underlined in each. Under each sentence are four choices. Put the correct letter on the line in front of each sentence.

_____ 1. Ptyalin is but one of the many <u>enzymes</u> in the human body.

    a. chemicals

    b. ingredients

    c. organs

    d. bones

_____ 2. The <u>molars</u> grind and crush the food as a human eats.

    a. tongue

    b. teeth

    c. mouth

    d. gum

_____ 3. <u>Peristalsis</u> helps food move through the esophagus into the stomach.

    a. gravity

    b. power

    c. wave-like motions

    d. work

E. Write about how you went about reading this material. What did you do to get the main ideas? What did you do to get the details? What did you do when you came to a word that you didn't know?

CHAPTER SIX

Using Informal Inventories and Other Informal Assessment Devices in the Word Identification Techniques

During this past school year, one of my teacher-trainees tutored a second-grade child in reading named Amber. Amber was recommended for help because she was reading below grade level. Although Amber's sight word vocabulary was nearly on grade level, she still was experiencing considerable difficulty in both pronouncing words and comprehension. When Amber was reading and came to a word she did not immediately recognize, she replaced the unknown word with a word that sometimes began with the same letter but that did not make sense. Therefore, after a short time it was apparent to her tutor that Amber did not have a good method of word attack. She especially needed help in graphophonic (phonic) analysis so that she could effectively sound out unknown words. It was important for her tutor to precisely determine in which subskills of graphophonic analysis Amber needed appropriate instruction and reinforcement. Her tutor made this precise determination by using a graphophonic analysis inventory at the second-grade reading level.

This chapter contains numerous classroom-tested informal inventories and other informal assessment devices in the various important word identification techniques. Since all of these informal assessment devices can be duplicated and used in their present form, their use should save the reading teacher countless time. In addition, a reading teacher should be able to determine with precision a student's exact weaknesses in the various word identification techniques that need to be presented and practiced.

Any reading teacher should find this chapter extremely useful in assessing a student's competencies and weaknesses in the various elements of the very important word identification techniques. Most disabled readers in the primary grades, especially at the emergent literacy level and later in first and second grades, have difficulties with either sight words or the very important elements of graphophonic analysis. If these difficulties are corrected and the child subsequently can identify more sight words and can understand and apply the most important skills, he or she often then can read at grade level. Thus, this chapter is designed to help the reading teacher locate and subsequently teach the important word identification techniques that are prerequisites to successful comprehension.

Description of Letter-Name Knowledge

Letter-name knowledge has been found by many research studies to be very predictive of primary-grade reading achievement. Although it is probable that a child could learn to read without knowledge of the letter names, it is important for all children to learn both the capital and lower-case letter names near the beginning of reading instruction.

Letter-name knowledge really consists of two discrete elements: *letter recognition and letter identification*. The latter is much more difficult for most children since it is usually easier for a child to select a letter from several options than it is for him or her to name that same letter. In tutoring children at the emergent literacy level, my teacher-trainees usually stress letter matching first, then letter recognition, and finally identification of all the capital and lower-case letter names. However, *letter identification* always is the ultimate goal.

Research has not discovered a preferred order for teaching the letter names. My teacher-trainees usually teach the letters in the child's own name first since the child's name is very important to him or her. Although many children enter kindergarten printing their first name in all capital letters, we try to teach it the proper way: **Allison**. After the child has learned to recognize and identify the letters in his or her first name, we usually teach the more useful letters next. You can choose to teach the easier letters instead if you wish.

It is very important for a child at the emergent literacy level to learn the difference between a *letter* and a *word*. You may be surprised that a number of kindergarten children are not aware of the difference and say that the word **father** has *six words in it*. It also is important for a child to learn to use the proper terms. For example, the letter **B** can be called either a *capital* or an *upper-case letter*. The terms "big" and "little" should *not* be used as the letter **k** may well be thought of as "big" by a child.

At the emergent literacy stage, it is important to determine which capital and lower-case letter names a child knows. We normally do this at the beginning of kindergarten or early first-grade tutoring with the children who are recommended for special help in emergent literacy by their teachers. After the teacher-trainees have made the informal assessment, we attempt to teach the child the letter names that he or she needs to know. This often is a very difficult task for the children with whom we work since a number of these children later will be classified as learning disabled. It may take as long as ten 30-minute tutoring sessions for the child to learn up to three or four letter names. The various tracing techniques have been found to be the most effective in teaching letter names to this type of child.

A useful resource that contains many strategies for teaching the capital and lower-case letter names to children at the emergent literacy level is the following:

Wilma H. Miller, *Complete Reading Disabilities Handbook*. West Nyack, NY: The Center for Applied Research in Education, 1993, pp. 214–238.

STRATEGIES FOR ASSESSING LETTER-NAME KNOWLEDGE

There are several strategies the reading teacher can use for informally assessing a child's letter-matching, letter-recognition, and letter-identification ability. Usually the following easy-to-difficult sequence should be used for these purposes:

- letter matching
- letter recognition
- letter identification

As an initial assessment technique, ask the child to write the alphabet in both capital and lower-case letters. After the child finishes, you can ask the child to write any omitted letters or write any letters that seemed to give him or her special difficulty.

We often use some kind of word puzzle to see if a child can *match* each capital letter name to its lower-case counterpart. To construct a series of puzzles, cut oaktag or posterboard into pieces about 5 or 6 inches wide. Then print each capital letter and its matching lower-case letter on the piece of oaktag with a marking pen and cut each puzzle apart using different types of cuts. Here are some examples.

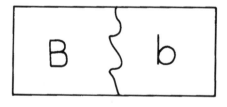

Put all of the puzzle parts into a large brown envelope. Then have the child try to put each puzzle together by matching each capital letter with its lower-case counterpart. Have the child pronounce each capital and lower-case letter name as the puzzle is assembled and state whether it is a capital or lower-case letter.

Another *matching activity* is to put out five upper-case letters and five matching lower-case letters and ask the child to match them. If the child is relatively successful, you can continue through the alphabet.

There are group-administered assessment sheets that can be used to assess ability in *letter recognition*. You simply pronounce a capital or lower-case letter name and have the child locate it on the assessment sheet. Reproducible examples of this type of assessment device are found later in this section. This type of assessment can be in the form of either letter-name recognition *in isolation or in context*.

> **NOTE:** Although the *whole-language philosophy* prefers that letter-name knowledge be assessed and presented in word and sentence context, the letter names must be taught and practiced in isolation some of the time, especially with children who have a very difficult time with them and with learning-disabled children. The assessment sheets included in this section assess letter-recognition ability in both isolation and in context.

When possible, letter-name identification is best evaluated in isolation by using *individual letter cards*. Simply print each capital and lower-case letter name on a separate small card (about 2 or 3 inches square) with a marking pen.

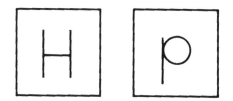

Then present the capital and lower-case letter names in random order and have the child identify each of them. If you wish to stress the lower-case letter names first, do not assess the child's ability in the capital letter names until later. Most disabled readers prefer to use flash cards since they become very frustrated when all of the letters are printed in a line. Do not present the letter names in alphabetical order but always in random order and tape record the testing if possible. The tape can be played back later to compare the child's responses to a prepared record sheet that lists the letters in the same order as they were presented to the child.

If a child has a great deal of difficulty identifying many of the letters, you can proceed to a little easier task. This involves having the child identify the letters as you call them. The 2 x 2 or 3 x 3 cards will work well for this, or you may wish to arrange the flash cards so the child can see at least five to ten of them at a time. With children who have extreme difficulty with letter identification, you can use one of the matching activities which were described earlier.

ASSESSMENT SHEETS FOR EVALUATING LETTER-NAME RECOGNITION IN ISOLATION

Here are several assessment sheets (see pages 230–233) you can use to help determine a child's ability in *letter recognition in isolation*. You can duplicate and use the sheets in their present form or modify them in any wish you wish.

ASSESSING LETTER RECOGNITION IN ISOLATION
(Emergent Literacy Level)

Upper-Case Letter Recognition in Isolation

1.   Put your finger on the line that begins with the sun.
In that line put an X on the capital **C**.

     C   F   R   P   Q

2.   Put your finger on the line that begins with the moon.
In that line put an X on the capital **F**.

     B   E   O   F   S

3.   Put your finger on the line that begins with the apple.
In that line put an X on the capital **S**.

     T   S   Z   U   A

4.   Put your finger on the line that begins with the flower.
In that line put an X on the capital **A**.

     A   D   Y   W   E

5.   Put your finger on the line that begins with the tree.
In that line put an X on the capital **Y**.

     W   X   Y   C   T

6.   Put your finger on the line that begins with the man.
In that line put an X on the capital **O**.

     C   Q   O   R   B

7.   Put your finger on the line that begins with the cat.
In that line put an X on the capital **P**.

     P   R   X   B   C

8.   Put your finger on the line that begins with the dog.
In that line put an X on the capital **E**.

     E   O   F   R   U

9.   Put your finger on the line that begins with the mitten.
In that line put an X on the capital **U**.

     U   O   Z   P   M

10.   Put your finger on the line that begins with the shoe.
In that line put an X on the capital **K**.

     R   S   K   P   E

Child's Copy
ASSESSING LETTER RECOGNITION IN ISOLATION

Upper-Case Letter Recognition in Isolation

C F R P Q

B E O F S

T S Z U A

A D Y W E

W X Y C T

C Q O R B

P R X B C

E O F R U

U O Z P M

R S K P E

ASSESSING LETTER RECOGNITION IN ISOLATION
(Emergent Literacy Level)

Lower-Case Letter Recognition in Isolation

1. Put your finger on the line that begins with the woman.
   In that line put an X on the lower-case **f**.

   g   f   e   l   i

2. Put your finger on the line that begins with the sock.
   In that line put an X on the lower-case **m**.

   m   o   n   h   p

3. Put your finger on the line that begins with the flag.
   In that line put an X on the lower-case **p**.

   p   r   q   h   b

4. Put your finger on the line that begins with the plate.
   In that line put an X on the lower-case **d**.

   p   b   r   d   h

5. Put your finger on the line that begins with the airplane.
   In that line put an X on the lower-case **a**.

   c   o   a   b   e

6. Put your finger on the line that begins with the car.
   In that line put an X on the lower-case **i**.

   j   l   i   e   t

7. Put your finger on the line that begins with the star.
   In that line put an X on the lower-case **e**.

   o   e   r   s   c

8. Put your finger on the line that begins with the pig.
   In that line put an X on the lower-case **k**.

   k   l   h   p   b

9. Put your finger on the line that begins with the rake.
   In that line put an X on the lower-case **r**.

   r   t   s   b   v

10. Put your finger on the line that begins with the snake.
    In that line put an X on the lower-case **w**.

    v   u   r   s   w

Child's Copy
ASSESSING LETTER RECOGNITION IN ISOLATION

Lower-Case Letter Recognition in Isolation

g   f   e   l   i

m   o   n   h   p

p   r   q   h   b

p   b   r   d   h

c   o   a   b   e

j   l   i   e   t

o   e   r   s   c

k   l   h   p   b

r   t   s   b   v

v   u   r   s   w

Assessing Letter-Name Knowledge in Context

As stated earlier, letter-name knowledge can be assessed and taught in context as well as in isolation. According to the proponents of the whole language philosophy, letter-name knowledge is best assessed and presented in context of words and sentences.

Proponents of whole language correctly believe that letter-name knowledge is most meaningful for children when letter names are identified in their own dictated or written language-experience stories, in predictable books, or in easy-to-read tradebooks. For example, the letter **s** probably is more meaningful to a child when he or she sees it in dictated or written language-experience stories or in a predictable book he or she either has read or listened to in comparison to seeing the letter in an activity sheet.

NOTE: However, I still believe it is necessary to assess and present the letter names in isolation at times and especially to learning-disabled children.

Assessment Sheet for Recognizing Upper-Case and Lower-Case Letter Names in Context

Here is a ready-to-reproduce sheet (see pages 235 and 236) to help assess a child's emergent reading ability to recognize the upper-case and lower-case letter names in context. You can duplicate and use this activity sheet in its present form or modify it in any way you wish.

ASSESSING LETTER RECOGNITION IN CONTEXT
(Emergent Literacy Level)

1. Put your finger on the line that begins with the duck.

   Circle all of the capital and lower-case **a's** you can find in the sentence on that line.

   Ann ate an apple.

2. Put your finger on the line that begins with a turtle.

   Circle all of the capital and lower-case **d's** you can find in the sentence on that line.

   Dick's dog dug a hole.

3. Put your finger on the line that begins with a triangle.

   Circle all of the capital and lower-case **s's** you can find in the sentence on that line.

   Sally saw some shoes at the store.

4. Put your finger on the line that begins with a square.

   Circle all of the capital and lower-case **t's** you can find in the sentence on that line.

   Tim and Tom are tall twins.

5. Put your finger on the line that begins with a television set.

   Circle all of the capital and lower-case **b's** you can find in the sentence on that line.

   Bobby and Billy can both buy bikes.

6. Put your finger on the line that begins with a spoon.

   Circle all of the capital and lower-case **m's** you can find in the sentence on that line.

   My mother made my dress.

7. Put your finger on the line that begins with a cow.

   Circle all of the capital and lower-case **p's** you can find in the sentence on that line.

   Patty put a pail on the porch.

8. Put your finger on the line that begins with a frog.

   Circle all of the capital and lower-case **r's** you can find in the sentence on that line.

   Ray rode his red sled.

9. Put your finger on the line that begins with a bird.

   Circle all of the capital and lower-case **w's** you can find in the sentence on that line.

   Wes went to the wide window.

10. Put your finger on the line that begins with a mouse.

    Circle all of the capital and lower-case **g's** you can find in the sentence on that line.

    A goat is a good pet.

Child's Copy
ASSESSING LETTER RECOGNITION IN CONTEXT

 Ann ate an apple.

 Dick's dog dug a hole.

 Sally saw some shoes at the store.

 Tim and Tom are tall twins.

 Bobby and Billy can both buy bikes.

 My mother made my dress.

 Patty put a pail on the porch.

 Ray rode his red sled.

 Wes went to the wide window.

 A goat is a good pet.

© 1995 by John Wiley & Sons, Inc.

CONSTRUCTING AND GIVING THE INFORMAL LETTER-ASSESSMENT DEVICE

To prepare for administering this informal letter assessment device, make enough copies of the answer sheet on page 238 so that you will have one for each student who is to be assessed. Then duplicate the "Letter Assessment Sheet" on page 239 and attach it to a piece of posterboard. You also may want to laminate the sheet and posterboard so that it can be used again and again.

Before you administer the actual device, you may want to have the child write all of the letters in both capitals and lower-case. When this is completed, you can record the child's performance on *Subtest 1* of the answer sheet.

To assess competency in *letter matching*, show the child the "Letter-Assessment Sheet" and have him or her match the capital letters with the lower-case letters. For example, point to the letter **w** in the lower-case letters portion and have the child point to the capital **W** in the capital letters part of this sheet. You can alternate this assessment by first pointing to a capital letter and then having the child point to its corresponding lower-case letter. Be sure to do all of them so that you are certain the child can match all of the capital and lower-case letter pairs. Record the child's performance on *Subtest 2* of the assessment device.

To assess ability in *letter recognition*, have the child point to the letters as you name them. Present them in random order from the lower-case letters and then present them in random order from the capital letters. Be sure to assess competency in all of them so that you are certain the child can recognize all of the letters when they are named. If the child can do this, record his or her performance on *Subtest 3* of this informal assessment device.

To assess ability in *letter identification*, have the child identify (read) all of the letters in each of the rows. You can have him or her identify the lower-case letter names first and then the capital letter names. If they are identified correctly, place a plus or a check mark on the appropriate line. If they are not identified correctly, write the answer given by the child in each blank. Then record the child's performance on *Subtest 4* of the letter-assessment device.

Name _____ Grade _____ Teacher _____ Date _____

INFORMAL LETTER-ASSESSMENT DEVICE ANSWER SHEET

Subtest 1

_____ Child can write all of the lower-case letters correctly.

_____ Child can write all of the capital letters correctly.

Comments _____

_____

Subtest 2

_____ Child can match all capital and lower-case letters.

_____ Child cannot match all capital and lower-case letters.

Comments _____

_____

Subtest 3

_____ Child can recognize all of the capital letters.

_____ Child cannot recognize all of the capital letters.

_____ Child can recognize all of the lower-case letters.

_____ Child cannot recognize all of the lower-case letters.

Comments _____

_____

Subtest 4

_____ Child can identify all of the capital letters.

_____ Child cannot identify all of the capital letters.

_____ Child can identify all of the lower-case letters.

_____ Child cannot identify all of the lower-case letters.

_____H _____A_____L_____O_____K_____Q

_____N_____G_____B_____F_____C

_____D_____J_____E_____M_____S

_____T_____P_____V_____Z_____U

_____I_____W_____Y_____R_____X

_____u_____a_____i_____h_____o_____q

_____b_____d_____h_____j_____n

_____c_____e_____k_____r_____x

_____m_____s_____v_____z_____g

_____t_____w_____y_____p_____f

LETTER ASSESSMENT SHEET

1. H A L O K Q

2. N G B F C

3. D J E M S

4. T P V Z U

5. I W Y R X

---

1. u a i l o q

2 b d h j n

3. c e k r x

4. m s v z g

5. t w y p f

Brief Description of Sight Word Knowledge

Since *sight word knowledge* was described in detail in Chapter 2, it is only very briefly discussed in this chapter. Chapter 2 also presented a number of strategies for improving competency in this important word identification technique.

Sight word knowledge consists of two different elements: *sight word recognition* and *sight word identification*. The latter is the more difficult of the two since a child must be able to *identify* a word while reading, not merely just be able to *recognize* it. However, sight word recognition, the less relevant skill, is still commonly assessed and practiced in elementary reading instruction. Although it may be helpful to assess ability in sight word recognition as a starting point, it is more useful to provide assessment and instruction in *sight word identification* in any reading program.

In any case, *sight words* can be described in a number of different ways. They are those words that a reader recognizes immediately upon seeing. A reader does not have to stop and analyze a sight word by using such word identification techniques as graphophonic (phonic) analysis or structural analysis. Any competent reader must have a large sight word bank. Many of the disabled readers whom my teacher-trainees tutor in first and second grades need to learn to immediately identify many more sight words in order to be able to read at grade level.

However, sight words also can be described as those words that do not have a regular sound-symbol relationship. Therefore, such words cannot be analyzed effectively but are most effectively recognized as a total unit or word. Some examples of sight words are **love, mother, of, some, once, one, said, dog,** and **would**.

Environmental print now also is thought of as an important concept in both emergent literacy and sight word knowledge. These words are commonly found in the environment of preschool and kindergarten children, who learn to recognize and identify them by noticing them and asking an adult or older sibling what the word is. Some common examples of environment print are: **STOP, McDonalds, Aladdin, Kmart, Crest, Pizza Hut, Alpha-Bits,** and **Cheerios**.

As stated in Chapter 2, there are several different sight word lists all of which are about equally useful. Probably the best known is the *Dolch Basic Sight Word List* which was included in Chapter 2 of this resource. The 220 words on this list are said to make up about *70* percent of the words found in most first-grade readers and about *65* percent of the words contained in most second-grade and third-grade readers. As with all sight word lists, the majority of the words contained in this list are **structure or function words**, meaning that they have no referent. An inventory constructed from the Dolch Basic Sight-Word List is contained later in this chapter.

Another very useful sight word list that was updated fairly recently is *Fry's Instant Words*. Edward Fry, Professor Emeritus of Rutgers University, has graciously given all textbook authors permission to reprint his Instant Words in the hope that this may help to improve reading instruction. The first *100* words make up half of all written materials, and the *300* words make up about *85* percent of all written matrials. A copy of *Fry's Instant Words* is now included for your use; the chapter also contains an inventory constructed from this useful recent sight word list.

FRY'S INSTANT WORDS*

FIRST HUNDRED

Words 1-25	Words 26-50	Words 51-75	Words 76-100
the	or	will	number
of	one	up	no
and	had	other	way
a	by	about	could
to	word	out	people
in	but	many	my
is	not	then	than
you	what	them	first
that	all	these	water
it	were	so	been
he	we	some	call
was	when	her	who
for	your	would	oil
on	can	make	its
are	said	like	now
as	there	him	find
with	use	into	long
his	an	time	down
they	each	has	day
I	which	look	did
be	do	more	get
this	how	write	made
have	their	go	may
from	if	see	part

Common suffixes: -s, -ing, -ed, -er, -ly, -est

© 1995 by John Wiley & Sons, Inc.

* If you want more than the three hundred sight words, the following is a list of three thousand sight words: Elizabeth Sakiey and Edward B. Fry, *3000 Instant Words* (West Providence, RI: Jamestown Publishers, 1984).

FRY'S INSTANT WORDS

SECOND HUNDRED

Words 101-125	Words 126-150	Words 151-175	Words 176-200
over	say	set	try
new	great	put	kind
sound	where	end	hand
take	help	does	picture
only	through	another	again
little	much	well	change
work	before	large	off
know	line	must	play
place	right	big	spell
year	too	even	air
live	mean	such	away
me	old	because	animal
back	any	turn	house
give	same	here	point
most	tell	why	page
very	boy	ask	letter
thing	came	men	answer
our	want	read	found
just	show	need	study
name	also	land	still
good	around	different	learn
sentence	home	form	should
man	three	us	America
think	same	move	world

Common suffixes: -s, -ing, -ed, -er, -ly, -est

FRY'S INSTANT WORDS

THIRD HUNDRED

Words 201-225	Words 226-250	Words 251-275	Words 276-300
high	saw	important	miss
every	left	until	idea
near	don't	children	enough
add	few	side	eat
food	while	feet	face
between	along	car	watch
own	might	mile	far
below	chose	night	Indian
country	something	walk	really
plant	seem	white	almost
last	next	sea	let
school	hard	began	above
father	open	grow	girl
keep	example	took	sometimes
tree	begin	river	mountain
never	life	four	cut
start	always	carry	young
city	those	state	talk
earth	both	once	soon
eye	paper	book	list
light	together	hear	song
thought	got	stop	being
head	group	without	leave
under	often	second	family
story	run	late	it's

Common suffixes: -s, -ing, -er, -ly, -est

STRATEGIES FOR ASSESSING SIGHT-WORD IDENTIFICATION IN ISOLATION

Sight word identification can be assessed in isolation by placing a random sampling of words from a sight word list such as the *Dolch Basic Sight-Word List* or *Fry's Instant Words* either on individual word cards or by printing or typing them in very short lists.

However, it is important to place each selected sight word on an individual word card for children who are reading at the early primary-grade level. These often are children in first grade, disabled readers who are functioning at about that reading level, or learning-disabled children. Many disabled readers and learning-disabled children become frustrated just from seeing all of the words on such a list, and subsequently may not make much of an effort to pronounce them.

To construct such word cards, randomly select about *twenty to thirty words* from the level of the sight word list you wish to use. Then print each word on a separate small card (about 2 or 3 inches square) with a marking pen. Here are several examples.

Then tape record the actual assessment so that it can be evaluated accurately when the tape is played back later. Present one or two cards per second since the sight-words should be identified immediately to be considered truly mastered. Do *not* separate the cards into right and wrong piles since to do so may well confuse you and distract the child. When the child cannot respond to four or five consecutive words, you probably should not continue the assessment further.

You need to make an answer sheet so that the child's responses can be recorded later. Here is an example of an answer sheet, which is found in a reproducible assessment device included later in this chapter, that was constructed from the first twenty words on the Dolch List.

_____ the
_____ to
_____ and
_____ he
_____ a
_____ I
_____ you
_____ it
_____ of
_____ in
_____ was
_____ said
_____ his

_____ that
_____ she
_____ for
_____ on
_____ they
_____ but

You can also place sight word phrases on individual word cards and present them to the child. This is in keeping with the *whole language philosophy* which states that sight word identification should be assessed and practiced in the context of phrases, sentences, paragraphs, and passages. Here is an example of an answer sheet for selected phrases constructed from the Dolch List:

_____ I had to
_____ he said that
_____ it is
_____ to the
_____ and they said
_____ of a
_____ for his
_____ of that
_____ that was in
_____ on a

You also can evaluate a child's sight word recognition in a group setting by using an assessment device for this purpose such as those included later in this chapter. However, you should understand that such a device does not evaluate ability in *sight word identification*. As you know, sight word identification, *not* sight word recognition, is required in actual reading. Even though such a device saves considerable time and may therefore be more practical, it is not quite as accurate as an individually administered device. Therefore, a group-administered device may be more beneficial for less disabled readers.

Name _____ Grade _____ Teacher _____ Date _____

INDIVIDUAL ASSESSMENT OF DOLCH SIGHT WORDS

(Listed in Descending Order of Frequency of Use)[11]

List 1	List 2	List 3	List 4
1. _____the	1. _____at	1. _____do	1. _____big
2. _____to	2. _____him	2. _____can	2. _____went
3. _____and	3. _____with	3. _____are	3. _____are
4. _____he	4. _____up	4. _____when	4. _____come
5. _____a	5. _____all	5. _____if	5. _____around
6. _____I	6. _____look	6. _____now	6. _____want
7. _____you	7. _____is	7. _____long	7. _____don't
8. _____it	8. _____her	8. _____see	8. _____no
9. _____of	9. _____there	9. _____not	9. _____came
10. _____in	10. _____some	10. _____were	10. _____ask
11. _____was	11. _____out	11. _____get	11. _____very
12. _____said	12. _____as	12. _____them	12. _____an
13. _____his	13. _____be	13. _____like	13. _____over
14. _____that	14. _____have	14. _____one	14. _____your
15. _____she	15. _____go	15. _____this	15. _____its
16. _____for	16. _____we	16. _____my	16. _____ride
17. _____on	17. _____am	17. _____would	17. _____into
18. _____they	18. _____then	18. _____me	18. _____just
19. _____but	19. _____little	19. _____will	19. _____blue
20. _____had	20. _____down	20. _____yes	20. _____red
/20	/20	/20	/20

© 1995 by John Wiley & Sons, Inc.

---

[11] Adapted from "Computer study of high frequency words in popular trade juveniles," William K. Durr, *The Reading Teacher*, October 1973. Copyright by the International Reading Association.

INDIVIDUAL ASSESSMENT OF DOLCH SIGHT WORDS (Cont.)

List 5	List 6	List 7	List 8
1. _____from	1. _____away	1. _____walk	1. _____tell
2. _____good	2. _____old	2. _____two	2. _____much
3. _____any	3. _____by	3. _____or	3. _____keep
4. _____about	4. _____their	4. _____before	4. _____give
5. _____around	5. _____here	5. _____eat	5. _____work
6. _____want	6. _____saw	6. _____again	6. _____first
7. _____don't	7. _____call	7. _____play	7. _____try
8. _____how	8. _____after	8. _____who	8. _____new
9. _____know	9. _____well	9. _____been	9. _____must
10. _____right	10. _____think	10. _____may	10. _____start
11. _____put	11. _____ran	11. _____stop	11. _____black
12. _____too	12. _____let	12. _____off	12. _____white
13. _____got	13. _____help	13. _____never	13. _____ten
14. _____take	14. _____make	14. _____seven	14. _____does
15. _____where	15. _____going	15. _____eight	15. _____bring
16. _____every	16. _____sleep	16. _____cold	16. _____goes
17. _____pretty	17. _____brown	17. _____today	17. _____write
18. _____jump	18. _____yellow	18. _____fly	18. _____always
19. _____green	19. _____five	19. _____myself	19. _____drink
20. _____four	20. _____six	20. _____round	20. _____once
/20	/20	/20	/20

INDIVIDUAL ASSESSMENT OF DOLCH SIGHT-WORDS (Cont.)

List 9	List 10	List 11
1. _____soon	1. _____use	1. _____wash
2. _____made	2. _____fast	2. _____show
3. _____run	3. _____say	3. _____hot
4. _____gave	4. _____light	4. _____because
5. _____open	5. _____pick	5. _____far
6. _____has	6. _____hurt	6. _____live
7. _____find	7. _____pull	7. _____draw
8. _____only	8. _____cut	8. _____clean
9. _____us	9. _____kind	9. _____grow
10. _____three	10. _____both	10. _____best
11. _____out	11. _____sit	11. _____upon
12. _____better	12. _____which	12. _____these
13. _____hold	13. _____fall	13. _____sing
14. _____buy	14. _____carry	14. _____together
15. _____funny	15. _____small	15. _____please
16. _____warm	16. _____under	16. _____thank
17. _____ate	17. _____read	17. _____wish
18. _____full	18. _____why	18. _____many
19. _____those	19. _____own	19. _____shall
20. _____done	20. _____found	20. _____laugh
/20	/20	/20

Activity Sheets for Assessing Sight Word Recognition in Isolation

The chapter now includes reproducible devices (see pages 250-252) for assessing a child's sight word recognition in isolation on the first-, second-, and third-grade reading levels. The words were taken from the first hundred, second hundred, and third hundred of Fry's Instant Word List. You can duplicate them in their present form or modify them in any way you wish.

These are the words you should pronounce from each sheet:

First-Grade Level	Second-Grade Level	Third-Grade Level
1. as	1. new	1. food
2. the	2. name	2. below
3. one	3. help	3. never
4. said	4. through	4. school
5. use	5. same	5. something
6. each	6. around	6. life
7. about	7. large	7. example
8. many	8. does	8. group
9. some	9. even	9. always
10. more	10. turn	10. together
11. like	11. why	11. important
12. number	12. land	12. until
13. find	13. kind	13. carry
14. down	14. again	14. four
15. made	15. animal	15. enough
	16. answer	16. watch
	17. page	17. sometimes
	18. still	18. song
	19. three	19. family
	20. house	20. second

ASSESSING SIGHT WORD RECOGNITION
IN ISOLATION

(First-Grade Level)

In each line <u>circle</u> the <u>word</u> that your teacher pronounces.

1. had	as	will	that
2. the	but	your	people
3. an	one	some	could
4. into	my	said	first
5. use	about	now	no
6. like	do	each	number
7. about	how	this	their
8. would	many	so	been
9. some	as	are	out
10. could	use	do	more
11. time	like	have	from
12. I	be	number	up
13. from	find	them	if
14. if	will	up	down
15. see	has	made	who

Name _____ Grade _____ Teacher _____ Date _____

ASSESSING SIGHT WORD RECOGNITION
IN ISOLATION

(Second-Grade Level)

In each line <u>circle</u> the <u>word</u> that your teacher pronounces.

1. set	new	try	only
2. live	too	name	back
3. our	help	just	say
4. sentence	man	through	picture
5. same	also	went	point
6. think	around	know	much
7. large	page	follow	boy
8. form	small	another	does
9. want	land	even	try
10. turn	thing	set	put
11. change	set	why	where
12. land	change	letter	mother
13. good	think	small	kind
14. ask	again	out	small
15. such	hand	animal	me
16. answer	after	great	help
17. page	old	any	try
18. very	tell	because	still
19. large	well	end	three
20. house	before	line	work

Name _____ Grade _____ Teacher _____ Date _____

ASSESSING SIGHT WORD RECOGNITION
IN ISOLATION

(Third-Grade Level)

In each line circle the word that your teacher pronounces.

1. food	high	every	between
2. white	sea	below	really
3. never	country	plant	below
4. own	school	miss	idea
5. far	almost	let	something
6. mountain	begin	life	keep
7. tree	example	earth	city
8. saw	left	group	young
9. always	light	thought	head
10. above	together	father	last
11. important	story	under	often
12. never	seem	chose	until
13. soon	leave	it's	carry
14. four	paper	group	both
15. enough	eye	start	last
16. idea	face	girl	watch
17. being	got	sometimes	walk
18. until	children	song	light
19. family	hard	open	important
20. second	side	feet	car

ASSESSING SIGHT WORD RECOGNITION IN CONTEXT

As stated earlier, *sight word recognition* can be assessed in context as well as in isolation. Assessment of sight word recognition in the context of phrases, sentences, paragraphs, and passages is in keeping with the *whole language philosophy*. However, it may not be especially useful with learning-disabled children. In a number of instances their assessment can be made more effectively in isolation.

However, as you know it is much more time-consuming to make an effective assessment of sight word identification than it is of sight word recognition. Therefore, assessing ability in sight word recognition may be of some use with mildly and moderately disabled readers.

Activity Sheets for Assessing Sight Word Recognition in Context

The chapter now contains several reproducible devices (see pages 255-257) you can use to assess a child's sight word recognition in context. You can duplicate them in their present form or modify them in any way you wish.

NOTE: The same sight words from Fry's Instant Words are used at the first-grade, second-grade, and third-grade levels in the devices to assess sight word recognition in isolation and context. Thus, the reading teacher can make a direct comparison between a child's ability in sight word recognition in isolation and context.

Although this certainly is not always the case, I have found that a learning-disabled child sometimes does better in sight word recognition in isolation than in context. On the other hand, some disabled readers do better in sight word recognition in context than in isolation.

These are the words you should pronounce from each sheet:

First-Grade Level	**Second-Grade Level**	**Third-Grade Level**
1. as	1. new	1. food
2. the	2. name	2. below
3. one	3. help	3. never
4. said	4. through	4. school
5. use	5. same	5. something
6. each	6. around	6. life
7. about	7. large	7. example
8. many	8. does	8. group
9. some	9. even	9. always
10. more	10. turn	10. together
11. like	11. why	11. important
12. number	12. land	12. until

First-Grade Level	Second-Grade Level	Third-Grade Level
13. find	13. kind	13. carry
14. down	14. again	14. four
15. made	15. animal	15. enough
	16. answer	16. watch
	17. page	17. sometimes
	18. still	18. song
	19. three	19. family
	20. house	20. second

ASSESSING SIGHT WORD RECOGNITION
IN CONTEXT

(First-Grade Level)

In each sentence <u>circle</u> the <u>word</u> that your teacher pronounces.

1. Jim is as old as I.

2. I saw the boy playing ball.

3. My baby sister is one year old.

4. My mother said that I had to go to school today.

5. Can you use some help today?

6. I hope that each one of them can come to the party.

7. My dog is about five years old.

8. Sam has many brothers and sisters.

9. Jim would like to have some candy.

10. My father would like to have some more ice cream.

11. I like to play in the snow.

12. Sally knows her telephone number.

13. Pat would like to find some money.

14. Ellen fell down in the snow.

15. My mother made a cake today.

ASSESSING SIGHT WORD RECOGNITION
IN CONTEXT

(Second-Grade Level)

In each sentence <u>circle</u> the <u>word</u> that your teacher pronounces.

1. Mary got a new puppy for her birthday last week.

2. My teacher's name is Mr. Jones.

3. I wish that you would help me with this work.

4. I wonder when I will get through with this.

5. My bike looks the same as yours does.

6. Joan's father is going to travel around the world.

7. That is a very large piece of pie.

8. I wonder if Amy knows why she does those things all the time.

9. It may even be hot by tomorrow.

10. I think that you had better turn around right now.

11. I wonder why Ann has to stay after school today.

12. Jack's father owns a lot of land in the country.

13. I am always kind to all animals.

14. I hope that my brother doesn't play that song again.

15. A tiger is a very pretty animal.

16. Jill couldn't answer the teacher's question today.

17. Please turn to page 29 in your book.

18. It is still raining this afternoon.

19. That lady has three dogs in her house.

20. Sue's house is painted brown with white trim.

ASSESSING SIGHT WORD RECOGNITION
IN CONTEXT

(Third-Grade Level)

In each sentence <u>circle</u> the <u>word</u> that your teacher pronounces.

1. My favorite food certainly is pizza.

2. Put the meat in the refrigerator on the shelf below the milk.

3. Sarah has never been late for school in her life.

4. I have always liked school very, very much.

5. I really hope that I receive something nice for my birthday.

6. Jimmy's dog certainly has a very good life.

7. That model is a very good example of a dinosaur that lived many, many years ago.

8. My sister belongs to the youth group at our church.

9. My mother and I have always been very good friends.

10. My dog and I walk a long way together every day.

11. Bill's father is a very important person.

12. I can't wait until Christmas Eve so that I can get all of my presents.

13. My mother can never carry all of the groceries that she buys at the store.

14. Bob's dog had four puppies about two weeks ago.

15. That coat is not big enough for me.

16. Tara's dog is a very good watch dog.

17. I wish that sometimes I would get to go to the movies.

18. That is a very beautiful song.

19. I have a very wonderful family.

20. That is the second time we have driven around looking for Jeff.

SAN DIEGO QUICK ASSESSMENT LIST

The *San Diego Quick Assessment List* is a very useful, quick way to determine a child's *approximate instructional reading level*. It certainly is *not* a substitute for giving an Individual Reading Inventory with its graded word lists and graded reading passages. However, if a reading teacher merely wants a *very easy, quick estimation of a child's approximate instructional reading level*, we have found it to be fairly useful for that purpose.

> **NOTE:** The San Diego Quick Assessment List never should be thought of as a substitute for an Individual Reading Inventory, but it can be useful for the purpose for which it was designed.

Administration

1. Type out each list of words on index cards.
2. Begin with a card that is at least two years below the child's grade-level assignment.
3. Ask the child to read the words aloud to you. If he or she misreads any on the list, drop to easier lists until he or she makes no errors. This indicates the *base level*.
4. Write down all incorrect responses, or use diacritical marks on your copy of the list. For example, *acrid* might be read and recorded as *acid. Molecule* might be recorded as *mōle ′cūle*.
5. Encourage the child to read words that he or she does not know so that you can identify the techniques he or she uses for word identification.
6. Have the child read from increasingly difficult lists until he or she misses at least three words.

Analysis

1. The list in which the child misses no more than *one of the ten words* is the level at which he or she can read *independently*. Two errors indicate the *instructional reading level*. Three or more errors indicate material that *may be too difficult (frustration reading level)*.
2. An analysis of the child's errors is useful. Among those that occur with greatest frequency are the following:

Error	Example
reversal	*how* for *who*
consonant	*book* for *look*
consonant blend	*string* for *spring*
short vowel	*note* for *not*
long vowel	*rod* for *road*
prefix	*protest* for *pretext*
suffix	*entering* for *entered*
miscellaneous	(omission of accent, etc.)

3. As with other reading-assessment devices, teacher observation of student behavior is very important. Such things are posture, facial expression, and voice quality may signal nervousness, lack of confidence, or frustration while reading.

SAN DIEGO QUICK ASSESSMENT LIST[12]

Preprimer	Primer	One	Two
see	you	road	our
play	come	live	please
me	not	thank	myself
at	with	when	town
run	jump	bigger	early
go	help	how	send
and	is	always	wide
look	work	night	believe
can	are	spring	quietly
here	this	today	carefully

Three	Four	Five	Six
city	decided	scanty	bridge
middle	served	business	commercial
moment	develop	amazed	abolish
frightened	silent	considered	trucker
exclaimed	wrecked	discussed	apparatus
several	improve	behaved	elementary
lonely	certainly	splendid	comment
drew	entered	acquainted	necessity
since	realized	escaped	gallery
straight	interrupted	grim	relativity

[12]Word list and excerpt from "The graded word list: Quick gauge of reading ability," Margaret LaPray and Ramon Ross, *Journal of Reading*, January 1969. Reprinted with permission of Margaret LaPray and the International Reading Association.

SAN DIEGO QUICK ASSESSMENT LIST (Cont.)

Seven	**Eight**	**Nine**
amber	capacious	conscientious
dominion	limitation	isolation
sundry	pretext	molecule
capillary	intrigue	ritual
impetuous	delusion	momentous
blight	immaculate	vulnerable
wrest	ascent	kinship
enumerate	acrid	conservatism
daunted	binocular	jaunty
condescend	embankment	inventive

Ten	**Eleven**
zany	galore
jerkin	rotunda
nausea	capitalism
gratuitous	prevaricate
linear	risible
inept	exonerate
legality	superannuate
aspen	luxuriate
amnesty	piebald
barometer	crunch

Brief Description of Graphophonic (Phonic) Analysis

Since *graphophonic (phonic) analysis* was described in detail in Chapter 2, it is only very briefly discussed in this chapter. Chapter 2 also presented a number of useful strategies for improving competency in this very important word identification technique.

Graphophonic (phonic) analysis can be defined as using the phonic elements found in a word to determine its pronunciation and meaning. Since a number of reading teachers believe that competency in graphophonic analysis is absolutely necessary for success in beginning reading, it undoubtedly has received more stress in beginning reading programs in the past than has any other word identification technique.

In any case, graphophonic analysis is a very important technique of word identification that should be presented to all children *who have the requisite auditory discrimination skills to be able to profit from it.* However, a number of reading teachers probably have presented too many phonic elements and rules in isolation to too many students at too young an age in the past. As you know, the *whole language philosophy* recommends that graphophonic elements be presented to children in the context of words, phrases, sentences, and passages.

> **NOTE:** One possible exception to this statement is the learning-disabled child who *may* profit from a structured program of graphophonic analysis with much concrete repetition *if he or she has the requisite auditory discrimination ability.* Some learning-disabled children may need the structure of some type of formal phonic program.

However, graphophonic analysis is rarely used by good readers in the intermediate grades and above. For example, most adult readers rarely, if ever, use phonic skills when they meet an unknown word while reading. Most of the most common graphophonic elements and rules have been taught to the typical child by the end of the third-grade reading level. Thus, graphophonic analysis can be very useful for identifying unknown words at the primary-grade level. However, it is a less useful technique at the middle–upper and adult reading levels.

Certainly at the middle–upper and adult reading levels semantic (meaning) clues and structural clues are much more effective. I have found in testing the graphophonic skills of many students at the middle–upper level that although they cannot provide the definition of graphophonic elements or rules, they usually can apply them effectively. Therefore, when my teacher-trainees tutor older disabled readers at the middle–upper levels, they stress only the important phonic elements—such as long and short vowel sounds, consonants, consonant blends, and phonograms (word families) if these have not been previously mastered.

It also is helpful to realize that graphophonic analysis usually is the most valuable when it is combined with semantic (meaning) clues. As an example, note how the addition of the beginning consonant in this sentence immeasurably helps the reader to deduce the omitted word:

I am going on a p_____ tomorrow.
> vacation
>
> picnic
>
> trip

It certainly is possible for a person to be a competent reader with no graphophonic ability at all. This obviously is illustrated by a hearing-impaired person. If a child has truly failed to learn the graphophonic elements and rules after some exposure to them, he or she probably should have most of the emphasis in his or her reading program placed upon sight words, semantic clues, and syntactical (grammatical) clues with some emphasis possibly being placed on tracing strategies. Again, the possible exception to this statement is the learning-disabled child if he or she has an adequate auditory channel.

Since graphophonic analysis is extremely complicated, you can refer to Chapter 2 of this resource or the following resources for much more detail:

Edward B. Fry, Jacqueline Kress, and Dona Fountoukidis, *The Reading Teacher's Book of Lists*, Third Edition. Englewood Cliffs, NJ: Prentice-Hall, 1993.

Ken Goodman, *Phonics Phacts*. Portsmouth, NH: Heinemann, 1993.

Arthur Heilman, *Phonics in Proper Perspective*. Columbus, OH: Merrill Publishing Company, 1989.

Marion A. Hull, *Phonics for the Teacher of Reading*. Columbus, OH: Merrill Publishing Company, 1989.

Lee Ann Rinsky, *Teaching Word Attack Skills*. Dubuque, IA: Scarisbrick, Gorusch Publishers, 1993.

REPRODUCIBLE GRAPHOPHONIC (PHONIC) ANALYSIS INVENTORIES

Here are reproducible graphophonic analysis inventories at the first-grade, second-grade, third-grade, and intermediate-grade reading levels. (See pages 266–269.) You can duplicate and use them in their present form or modify them in any way you like. Their use should help you to determine with precision the exact graphophonic skills in which a child lacks competence and therefore should receive instruction and/or reinforcement.

The answers to these inventories are:

Second-Grade Reading Level

Note: No answer key is provided for items 1, 2, and 3 as the answers are self-evident.

4. shall mile bent brave light stick box middle happy fiddle plug write saddle save steed held plop cube rung bright smoke

5. <u>ch</u>in <u>th</u>ose <u>sh</u>ould <u>th</u>ink ri<u>ng</u> rou<u>gh</u> <u>wh</u>ite

6. s<u>oi</u>l c<u>ou</u>ch pl<u>ow</u> t<u>oy</u>

7. shoot hook foot moose

8. wrote name gnome great mean knee tie page write dream gnat sneeze

9. h<u>ur</u>t sk<u>ir</u>t h<u>er</u>d c<u>a</u>re h<u>ar</u>m f<u>or</u>t c<u>a</u>r f<u>ur</u> sh<u>ir</u>t f<u>ar</u>m b<u>ur</u>st m<u>a</u>re

10. fot drick dute sprete vold lote sprut prup zet pred cade

Third-Grade Reading Level

Note: No answer key is provided for items 1, 2, and 3 as the answers are self-evident.

4. high battle strange copper mope matter state children web bleed fret strip scrub socks pity fact screen plop fake might

5. <u>ch</u>ute <u>th</u>ough <u>ch</u>ipmunk <u>th</u>imble <u>wh</u>isper cou<u>gh</u> fi<u>ng</u>er <u>sh</u>iver

6. fl<u>ew</u> tr<u>ou</u>t f<u>oi</u>l h<u>ow</u>l <u>oy</u>ster

7. hoof loop hooves brook

8. wrestle complete reason bright gnash dread joke either thief height wriggle range break breeze pleasure

9. <u>ur</u>ge f<u>a</u>re invent<u>or</u> wand<u>er</u> st<u>ar</u>t st<u>or</u>y c<u>ur</u>dle d<u>ir</u>ty h<u>er</u>d b<u>a</u>rely h<u>ar</u>m f<u>ur</u>l

10. bri vot strigh crale dreat spleam plet tway sprill croat

11. bin|dle bum|ple ri|gle splot|ter su|ley crum|key sack|et ho|ger en|dle mim|mer

Intermediate-Grade Reading Level

NOTE: No answer key is provided for items 1, 2, and 3 as the answers are self-evident.

4. dēmon* īsland† ghōst lŭll desīgn blĕss dĕprĕss ŭnhăppy̆ rēlăx ĭmpăct vīŏlĭn hy̆mn shrĭll knīght

5. <u>ch</u>ampion <u>th</u>eater <u>ph</u>otograph <u>th</u>ou lin<u>g</u>er <u>sh</u>ea<u>th</u>e <u>ch</u>iffon <u>ch</u>aracter <u>wh</u>irlwind

6. <u>j</u>e<u>w</u>el <u>p</u>o<u>u</u>nce ro<u>y</u>alty h<u>oi</u>st <u>ow</u>lish

7. harpōon chĭldhood marōon hookwŏrm

8. lettuc͢e dispos͢e ẃrea͢th veng͢eful ravin͢g concentrat͢e imag͢e ree͢f navigat͢e gri͢ef valu͢e ǵnarl ẃrench univers͢e ḱnothol͢e

9. dist<u>u</u>rb op<u>e</u>rator regist<u>e</u>r th<u>e</u>rmomet<u>e</u>r mockingb<u>i</u>rd nostr<u>i</u>ls m<u>a</u>rsh settl<u>e</u>r mission<u>a</u>ry transp<u>a</u>rent

10. oig sā|gl͢e chĕtch glĭn|dĕt strīgh tū|vĭt͢e bree͢t thāme͢ dī|ger lēa|cher scrȳ stăd|der stŏn|der wŭt|ter proint

11. wealthy   proclaim   hinder   skeleton

    sickle   innocent   moment   twinkle

    peasant   explode   prickle   velvet

---

*o in demon is a ə; omit if you think it would be too confusing
†a in island is a ; omit if you think it would be too confusing

ORAL GRAPHOPHONIC (PHONIC) ANALYSIS INVENTORY
(First-Grade Reading Level, Second Semester)

1. Tell me what letter each of these words <u>begins</u> with (assessing competency in initial consonants):

   boy came duck fun goat hat jump kitten lake man now pay rain say table vine water yellow zoo

2. Tell me what letter each of these words <u>ends</u> with (assessing competency in final consonants):

   land huff dog fill ham sun hop her miss rent try

3. Tell me what <u>two letters</u> each of these words begin with (assessing competency in initial consonant blends):

   black flag please sled stop glass tree snow

4. Tell me what <u>letter</u> in each of these words makes the <u>long vowel sound</u> (assessing competency in long vowel sounds):

   cake jeep ice rope use

5. Tell me what <u>letter</u> in each of these words makes the <u>short vowel sound</u> (assessing competency in short vowel sounds):

   apple met till top duck

OPTIONAL ORAL GRAPHOPHONIC INVENTORY

Note: The following four examples do *not* meet the requirements of the whole language philosophy that states sounds should *not* be stated in isolation. However, their use may be of some value with severely disabled readers or learning-disabled children.

6. Pronounce each of these words and then say the <u>sound of the first letter</u> (assessing competency in initial consonant sounds):

   big candy dig fan get help jet kite like my new pan ran sit toy very wet yes zoo

7. Pronounce each of these words and then say the <u>sounds of the first two letters</u> (assessing competency in initial consonant blends):

   blue fly play slide stay glad try snake

8. Pronounce each of these words and then give the <u>long vowel sound</u> found in the middle of it (assessing competency in long vowel sounds):

   make feet kite hope mule

9. Pronounce each of these words and then give the <u>short vowel sound</u> found in the middle of it (assessing competency in short vowel sounds):

   cat bed pig not nut

Name _____ Grade _____ Teacher _____ Date _____

ORAL GRAPHOPHONIC (PHONIC)
ANALYSIS INVENTORY
(Second-Grade Reading Level)

1. Pronounce each of these words and then <u>underline the initial consonant</u> in that word.

   bicycle carry dirt finish gold held jelly kept learn middle none people reach surprise together vine window yourself zebra

2. Pronounce each of these words and then <u>underline the final consonant</u> in that word.

   should cuff log kick beautiful plum learn flop their kiss kept box

3. Pronounce each of these words and then <u>underline the two-letter or three-letter consonant blend</u> in that word.

   blew brick clown crew drank flour fright glue grope pleasant pretty scare skate slippery smile snail spun stood swan trouble scream shrink splash spring squirrel string throw

4. Pronounce each of these words and <u>mark the vowels in its middle either long — or short ∪</u>.

   shall mile bent brave light stick box middle happy fiddle plug write saddle save steed held plop cube rung fright smoke

5. Pronounce each of these words and then <u>underline the consonant digraph</u> that it contains.

   chin those should think ring rough white

6. Pronounce each of these words and then <u>underline the diphthong</u> it contains.

   soil couch plow toy

7. Pronounce each of these words and then <u>mark the double oo's either long — or short ∪</u>.

   shoot hook foot moose

8. Pronounce each of these words and <u>mark the silent letter or letters with a slash mark /</u>.

   wrote name gnome great mean knee tie page write dream gnat sneeze

9. Pronounce each of these words and then <u>underline the r-controlled vowel</u>.

   hurt skirt her care harm fort car fur shirt farm burst mare

10. Pronounce each of these <u>nonsense words using the correct phonic rules</u>.

   fot drick dute sprete vold lote sprut prup zet pred cade

ORAL GRAPHOPHONIC (PHONIC) ANALYSIS INVENTORY
(Third-Grade Reading Level)

1. Pronounce each of these words and then <u>underline the initial consonant</u> in that word.

   business   copper   city   diamond   face   gamble   humble   journey kitchen   leave   magic   nobody   paper   river   soup   terrible   victory wiggle   xylophone   youth   zipper

2. Pronounce each of these words and then <u>underline the final consonant</u> in that word.

   magic   tread   bluff   plug   unusual   swamp   remember   precious planet   ax

3. Pronounce each of these words and then <u>underline the two-letter or three-letter consonant blend</u> in that word.

   blueberry   bramble   clippers   crumb   dread   fleet   fright   glow grumble   plantation   precious   scribble   skipper   slumber   smoke snipe   spike   stationery   strength   swamp   through   tremble   twelve

4. Pronounce each of these words and <u>mark the vowels in its middle either long —</u> or short ∪.

   high   battle   strange   copper   mope   matter   state   children   web bleed   fret   strip   scrub   socks   pity   fact   screen   plop   fake   might

5. Pronounce each of these words and then <u>underline the consonant digraph</u> it contains.

   chute   though   chipmunk   thimble   whisper   cough   finger   shiver

6. Pronounce each of these words and then <u>underline the diphthong</u> it contains.

   flew   trout   foil   howl   oyster

7. Pronounce each of these words and then <u>mark the double oo's either long — or</u> short ∪.

   hoof   loop   hooves   brook

8. Pronounce each of these words and mark <u>the silent letter or letters with a slash mark /</u>.

   wrestle   complete   reason   bright   gnash   dread   joke   either   thief height   wriggle   range   break   breeze   pleasure

9. Pronounce each of these words and then <u>underline the r-controlled vowel</u>.

   urge   fare   inventor   wander   start   story   curdle   dirty   herd   barely harm   furl

10. Pronounce each of these <u>nonsense words using the correct phonic rules</u>.

    bri   vot   strigh   crale   dreat   spleam   plet   tway   sprill   croat

11. Pronounce each of these words correctly <u>which have been spelled phonetically for you</u>.

    bĭn|dle   bŭm|ple   rī|gle   splŏt|ter   sū|lēy   crŭm|key   săck|et   hō|ger ĕn|dle   mĭm|mer

© 1995 by John Wiley & Sons, Inc.

Name _____ Grade _____ Teacher _____ Date _____

ORAL GRAPHOPHONIC (PHONIC) ANALYSIS INVENTORY

(Intermediate-Grade Reading Level)

1. Pronounce each of these words and then <u>underline the initial consonant</u> in that word.
   burro compass celery dazzle fiction geology harpoon jungle kindle landscape microphone navigate pollution responsibility survivor tempest vicious windshield youngster zone

2. Pronounce each of these words and then <u>underline the final consonant</u> in that word.
   antibiotic orchard surf chug wick international telegram transfusion develop ancestor subconscious ornament phlox

3. Pronounce each of these words and then <u>underline the two-letter or three-letter consonant blend</u> in that word.
   blight bribery clipboard critical drama flounder friction glimpse graduation plaster prairie scalpel skulk slough smolder snorkel spectacle stamen stringent swindle threshold triplicate twilight

4. Pronounce each of these words and <u>mark the vowels either long — or short ∪</u>.
   demon island ghost lull design bless depress unhappy relax impact violin hymn shrill knight

5. Pronounce each of these words and then <u>underline the consonant digraph(s)</u> it contains.
   champion theater photograph thou linger sheathe chiffon character whirlwind

6. Pronounce each of these words and then <u>underline the diphthong</u> it contains.
   jewel pounce royalty hoist owlish

7. Pronounce each of these words and then <u>mark the double oo's either long — or short ∪</u>.
   harpoon childhood maroon hookworm

8. Pronounce each of these words and <u>mark the silent letter or letters with a slash mark /</u>.
   lettuce dispose wreath vengeful ravine concentrate image reef navigate grief value gnarl wrench universe knothole

9. Pronounce each of these words and then <u>underline the r-controlled vowel</u>.
   disturb operator register thermometer mockingbird nostrils marsh settler missionary transparent

10. Pronounce each of these <u>nonsense words using the correct phonic rules</u>.
    oig sagle chetch glindet strigh tuvite breet thame diger leach-er scry stadder stonder wutter proint

11. Pronounce each of these words correctly <u>which have been spelled phonetically for you</u>.

'wel-thē	prō-'klām	'hin-dər	'skel-ə-tən
'sik-əl	'in-ə-sənt	'mō-mənt	'twin-kəl
'pez-nt	ik-splōd	'prik-əl	vel-vət

269

QUICK SURVEY WORD LIST

To **construct** the *Quick Survey Word List*, reproduce it and glue it to a 5 x 8 card. After fastening it to the card, you may want to laminate it so that it will be more durable. The *Quick Survey Word List* is designed to enable a reading teacher to quickly ascertain if a student has the necessary word attack skills to successfully read material written at the *adult level*. Therefore, it can be given to students at about the fourth-grade reading level or above to determine if it is necessary to give the more comprehensive and time-consuming *El Paso Phonics Survey*.

To **administer** the test simply give the student the word list and ask him or her to pronounce each word. Tell the student that the words he or she is going to pronounce are *nonsense words* or words that are not real words. Tell the student that these words are difficult, but that you need to know if he or she is able to pronounce them correctly. If the student can pronounce each of the words correctly, it is not necessary to administer the *El Paso Phonics Survey* since the purpose of learning phonic analysis is to enable the student to successfully attack unknown words. However, if it becomes obvious after one or two words that the student is not able to complete the test successfully, it should be discontinued, and the *El Paso Phonics Survey* given instead.

The correct pronunciation of the words on the *Quick Survey Word List* is provided below. This key shows the correct pronunciation as well as the part of each word that should be stressed. However, you should remember that accent rules or generalizations in the English language are not consistent. Therefore, if the student pronounces the words correctly except for the accent or stress shown on certain syllables, they should be considered correct.

NOTE: The *Quick Survey Word List* is also designed to test a student's knowledge of such phonic and structural skills as syllabication, vowel rules, rules for *c, g, and y*, and accent generalizations. Remember, if students do not perform well on the first two or three words, the test should be discontinued. Only if a student is able to pronounce all of the words correctly should you continue through the entire test.

PRONUNCIATION OF THE QUICK SURVEY WORDS[13]

rat´-bel-ing

däs´-nit

pram´-min-cil-ing

hwet´-split-tər

jin´-kyool

crin´-gāl

slat´-run-gəl

tw̄a´-fräl

sprēn´-plit

gōn´-bāt

strē´-gran

glam´-mər-tick-ly

gran´-tel-lēn

āp´sid

PRONUNCIATION KEY

l—litt<u>le</u>

ə —<u>a</u>bout

ä—f<u>a</u>ther

ə —tamp<u>e</u>r

hw—<u>wh</u>at

kyoo—c<u>u</u>te

---

[13]Reprinted by permission of Allyn and Bacon, Inc., from Eldon E. Ekwall, *Teacher's Handbook on Diagnosis and Remediation in Reading*, Second Edition. (Boston: Allyn and Bacon, 1986).

QUICK SURVEY WORD LIST[14]

wratbeling

dawsnite

pramminciling

whetsplitter

gincule

cringale

slatrungle

twayfrall

spreanplit

goanbate

streegran

glammertickly

grantellean

aipcid

---

[14]Reprinted by permission of Allyn and Bacon, Inc. from Eldon E. Ekwall, *Teacher's Handbook on Diagnosis and Remediation in Reading*, Second Edition (Boston: Allyn and Bacon, 1986).

EL PASO PHONICS SURVEY[15]

To **construct** the *El Paso Phonics Survey*, reproduce pages 275 and 276 and glue to 5 x 8 cards, and then laminate them for durability. You should also make multiple copies of the Answer Key so that you can mark each student's responses on a separate copy. There are both *general directions and specific directions* for administering this survey, which should be followed carefully.

General Directions

Here are the general directions for administering the *El Paso Phonics Survey.*

1. Before beginning the test, make sure the child has instant recognition of the test words (**in, up, am**) that appear in the box at the top of the first page of the survey. These words should be known instantly by the child. If they are not immediately recognized, the test should be given later when the child has been taught and has mastered them.

2. Give the student the copy of the *El Paso Phonics Survey.*

3. Point to the letter in the first column and have the child say the name of that letter (not the sound that it represents). Then point to the word in the middle column and have the child pronounce it. Then point to the nonsense word in the third column and have the child pronounce it.

4. If the child can give the name of the letter, the word in the middle column, and the nonsense word in the third column, mark the answer sheet with a **plus (+)**.

5. If the child cannot pronounce the nonsense word after giving the name of the letter and the word in the middle column, mark the answer sheet with a **minus (–)**; or you may wish to write the word phonetically as the student pronounced it. If the student can tell you the name of the letter and the small word in the middle column but cannot pronounce the nonsense word, you may wish to have him or her give the letter sound in isolation. If the child can give the sound in isolation, either the child is unable to *blend* or does not know the letter well enough to give its sound and blend it at the same time.

6. Whenever an asterisk appears on the answer sheet, refer to the *Special Directions* sheet.

7. To the right of each blank on the answer sheet is a *grade-level designation.* This number represents the point by which most basal reader series have taught that sound. By that point, you should expect it to be known. As an example, the designation **1.9** means the ninth month of the first year.

8. When the child comes to two- or three-letter consonant digraphs or blends, as with the **qu** in item 22, he or she is to say **"q-u"** as with the single letters. The student never is to give letter sounds in isolation while doing actual reading.

---

[15]*Ibid.*

9. When the child comes to the vowels (item 59), he or she is to say **"short a"** and so forth and then explain what this means. The same is to be done with the long vowels when the **macron** (–) appears.

10. All vowels and vowel combinations are put with only one or two of the first eight consonants. If any of the first eight consonants are not known, they should be taught before you attempt to test for vowel knowledge. You will probably find that a child who does not know the first eight consonant sounds rarely knows the vowel sounds anyway.

11. You will notice that words appear to the right of some of the blanks on the answer sheet. These words illustrate the correct consonant or vowel sound that should be heard when the child answers.

12. Included are phonic elements that have a high enough utility to make them worthwhile learning. For example, the vowel pair **ui** is very rare, and when it does appear, it may stand for the short **i** sound in **build** or the long **oo** sound in **fruit**. Therefore, there really is no reason to teach it as a sound. However, some letters such as **oe** may represent several different sounds, but most often represent one particular sound. In the case of **oe** the long **o** sound should be used. In such cases, the most common sound is illustrated by a word to the right of the blank on the answer sheet. If the child gives another correct sound for the letter(s), you can say, "Yes, that's right, but what is another way you could pronounce this nonsense word?" The child must then say it as illustrated in the small word to the right of the blank on the answer sheet. Otherwise, the answer should be counted as wrong.

13. Discontinue the test after **five consecutive misses** or if the child appears frustrated from missing a number of items even though he or she has not missed five consecutive items.

Specific Directions

Here are the specific directions for administering and evaluating the *El Paso Phonics Survey*:

3. If the child uses another **s** sound as in **sugar (sh)** in saying the nonsense word **sup**, ask, "What is another **s** sound?" The child must use the **s** as in the word **soap**.

15. If the child uses the **soft c** sound as in **city** in saying the nonsense word **cam**, ask, "What is another **c** sound?" The child must use the **hard c** as in the word **cat**.

16. If the child uses the **soft g** sound as in **gem** in saying the nonsense word **gup**, ask, "What is another **g** sound?" The child must use the hard **g** sound as in the word **gate**.

17. Ask, "What is the **y** sound when it comes at the beginning of a word?"

23. The child must use the **ks** sound of **x**, and the nonsense word **mox** must rhyme with **fox**.

35. If the child uses the **th** sound heard in **that**, ask, "What is another **th** sound?" The child must use the **th** sound as in the word **thin**.

44. If the child uses the **hoo** sound of **wh** in saying the nonsense word **whup**, ask, "What is another **wh** sound?" The child must use the **wh** sound as in the word **white**.

72. The child may either give the **ea** sound heard in **head** or the **ea** sound heard in **meat**. Be sure to indicate on the answer sheet which one the child said.

73. If the same **ea** sound is given this time as was given for item 72, say, "Yes, that's right, but what is another way you could pronounce this nonsense word?" Whichever sound was **not** used in item 72 must be used here. Otherwise, this item should be recorded as incorrect.

81. The child may give either the **ow** sound heard in the word **now** or the **ow** sound heard in the word **blow**. Be sure to indicate on the answer sheet which sound was used.

82. If the same **ow** sound is given this time as was given for item 81, say, "Yes, that's right, but what is another way you could pronounce this nonsense word?" Whichever sound was not used in item 81 must be used here. Otherwise, this item should be recorded as incorrect.

88. The child may give either the **oo** sound heard in **look** or the **oo** sound heard in **goose**. Be sure to indicate on the answer sheet which sound was used.

89. If the same **oo** sound is given this time as was given for item 88, say, "Yes, that's right, but what is another way that you could pronounce this nonsense word?" Whichever sound was not used in item 88 must be used here. Otherwise, this item should be recorded as incorrect.

EL PASO PHONICS SURVEY

in	up	am

1. p	am	pam	25. sl	in	slin
2. n	up	nup	26. pl	up	plup
3. s	up	sup	27. fl	in	flin
4. r	in	rin	28. st	am	stam
5. t	up	tup	29. fr	in	frin
6. m	up	mup	30. bl	am	blam
7. b	up	bup	31. gr	up	grup
8. d	up	dup	32. br	in	brin
9. w	am	wam	33. tr	am	tram
10. h	up	hup	34. sh	up	shup
11. f	am	fam	35. th	up	thup
12. j	up	jup	36. ch	am	cham
13. k	am	kam	37. dr	up	drup
14. l	in	lin	38. cl	in	clin
15. c	am	cam	39. gl	am	glam
16. g	up	gup	40. sk	up	skup
17. y	in	yin	41. cr	in	crin
18. v	am	vam	42. sw	up	swup
19. z	up	zup	43. sm	in	smin
20. c	in	cin	44. wh	up	whup
21. g	in	gin	45. sp	up	spup
22. qu	am	quam	46. sc	up	scup
23. m	ox	mox	47. str	am	stram
24. pr	am	pram	48. thr	up	thrup

49. scr	in	scrin	77. ar	arb	
50. spr	am	spram	78. er	ert	
51. spl	in	splin	79. ir	irt	
52. squ	am	squam	80. oe	poe	
53. sn	up	snup	81. ow	owd	
54. tw	am	twam	82. ow	fow	
55. wr	in	wrin	83. or	orm	
56. shr	up	shrup	84. ur	urd	
57. dw	in	dwin	85. oy	moy	
58. sch	am	scham	86. ew	bew	
59. ă		tam	87. aw	awp	
60. ĭ		rin	88. oo	oot	
61. ĕ		nep	89. oo	oop	
62. ŏ		sot	90. au	dau	
63. ŭ		tum			
64. a̲		sape			
65. o̲		pote			
66. i̲		tipe			
67. e̲		rete			
68. u̲		pune			
69. ee	eem				
70. oa	oan				
71. ai	ait				
72. ea	eam				
73. ea	eap				
74. ay	tay				
75. oi	doi				
76. ou	tou				

Name _____ Sex _____ Date _____

School _____Examiner_____

EL PASO PHONICS SURVEY
Answer Sheet

Mark answers as follows:
Pass +
Fail – (or write word as pronounced)

PEK = point at which phonic element is expected to be known

			PEK				PEK
Initial Consonants				**Ending Consonant** _____			
1.	p	pam	_____ 1.3	*23.	m	mox	_____1.3
2.	n	nup	_____ 1.3	**Initial Consonant Clusters**			
*3.	s	sup	_____1.3	24.	pr	pram	_____1.3
4.	r	rin	_____1.3	25.	sl	slin	_____1.6
5.	t	tup	_____1.3	26.	pl	plup	_____1.6
6.	m	mup	_____1.3	27.	fl	flin	_____1.6
7.	b	bup	_____1.3	28.	st	stam	_____1.6
8.	d	dup	_____1.3	29.	fr	frin	_____1.6
9.	w	wam	_____1.3	30.	bl	blam	_____1.6
10.	h	hup	_____1.3	31.	gr	grup	_____1.6
11.	f	fam	_____1.3	32.	br	brin	_____1.9
12.	j	jup	_____1.3	33.	tr	tram	_____1.9
13.	k	kam	_____1.3	34.	sh	shup	_____1.9
14.	l	lin	_____1.3	*35.	th	thup	_____1.9
*15.	c	cam	_____1.3			thin	
*16.	g	gup	_____1.3	36.	ch	cham	_____1.9
*17.	y	yin	_____1.3			chin	
18.	v	vam	_____1.3	37.	dr	drup	_____1.9
19.	z	zup	_____1.3	38.	cl	clin	_____1.9
20.	c	cin	_____1.3	39.	gl	glam	_____1.9
21.	g	gin	_____1.3	40.	sk	skup	_____1.9
22.	qu	quam	_____1.3	41.	cr	crin	_____1.9
				42.	sw	swup	_____1.9

277

EL PASO PHONICS SURVEY
Answer Sheet (Cont.)

			PEK					PEK
43.	sm	smin	2.5	66.	i	tipe	1.9	
*44.	wh	whup	2.5	67.	e	rete	1.9	
45.	sp	spup	2.5	68.	u	pune	1.9	
46.	sc	scup	2.5	69.	ee	eem	1.9 (heed)	
47.	str	stram	2.5	70.	oa	oan	1.9 (soap)	
48.	thr	thrup	2.5	71.	ai	ait	1.9 (ape)	
49.	scr	scrin	2.5	*72.	ea	eam	1.9 (meat)	
50.	spr	spram	2.5	*73.	ea	eap	2.5 (head)	
51.	spl	splin	2.5	74.	ay	tay	2.5 (hay)	
52.	squ	squam	2.9	75.	oi	doi	2.5 (boy)	
53.	sn	snup	2.9	76.	ou	tou	2.5 (cow)	
54.	tw	twam	2.9	77.	ar	arb	2.5 (harp)	
55.	wr	wrin	2.9	78.	er	ert	2.5 (her)	
56.	shr	shrup	3.5	79.	ir	irt	2.5 (hurt)	
57.	dw	dwin	3.5	80.	oe	poe	2.9 (hoe)	
58.	sch	scham	3.9	*81.	ow	owd	2.9 (blow or now)	

Vowels, Vowel Teams, and Special Letter Combinations

			PEK					PEK
				*82.	ow	fow	2.9 (blow or now)	
				83.	or	orm	2.9 (corn)	
59.	a	tam	1.6	84.	ur	urd	2.9 (hurt)	
60.	i	rin	1.6	85.	oy	moy	2.9 (boy)	
61.	e	nep	1.6	86.	ew	bew	2.9 (few)	
62.	o	sot	1.6	87.	aw	awp	2.9 (paw)	
63.	u	tum	1.6	*88.	oo	oot	2.9 (book or goose)	
64.	a	sape	1.6	*89.	oo	oop	3.5 (book or goose)	
65.	o	pote	1.6	90.	au	dau	3.5 (paw)	

© 1995 by John Wiley & Sons, Inc.

THE NAME TEST[16]

In an article in *The Reading Teacher*, Patricia Cunningham proposed a new, brief, informal assessment device in decoding. This device assesses a child's ability to decode names. The use of names may have some advantages over conventional word lists and nonsense words (pseudo words). In some instances, names may encourage a child to put forth a better effort while decoding than do nonsense words. Although there are no specific norms for this test at this time, the *Name Test* has been found to be very reliable (.98 reliability coefficient).

Constructing the Name Test

1. Type or print the 25 names on a piece of paper or posterboard. Make sure that the print size is appropriate for the age or grade level of the child being tested.
2. If you think it would be helpful, type or print each of the names on index cards so that they can be read individually. I recommend this procedure for any disabled reader.
3. Prepare a scoring sheet. Type the list of names in a column and, following each name, draw a blank line on which you can record a child's responses.

Administering the Name Test

1. Administer the *Name Test* on an individual basis. Choose a quiet, distraction-free environment.
2. Explain to the child that he or she is to pretend to be a teacher who must read a list of the names of the children in his or her class. Have the child read the names as if he or she were taking attendance.
3. Have the child read the entire list. Tell the child that you will not be able to help him or her with difficult names, but to make a guess at each name if possible.
4. Place a check on the answer sheet for each name the child reads correctly. Write phonetic spellings for each name that is not pronounced correctly.

Scoring and Evaluating the Name Test

1. Count a name as correct if all of the syllables are pronounced correctly regardless of where the child placed the accent. As an example, the name **Westmoreland** is correct whether it is pronounced **'West more land; West 'more land;** or **West more land.'**
2. For words in which the vowel pronunciation depends on which syllable the consonant is placed with, count them correct for either pronunciation. For example, either **Ho/mer** or **Hom/er** is counted as correct.
3. Count the number of names read correctly, and analyze those mispronounced, looking for patterns indicative of decoding strengths and weaknesses.

---

[16]Adapted from the name test from "The Name Test: a quick assessment of decoding ability," Patricia Cunningham, *The Reading Teacher*, November 1990. Copyright by the International Reading Association.

THE NAME TEST

Jay Conway   _____

Tim Cornell   _____

Chuck Hoke   _____

Yolanda Clark   _____

Kimberly Blake   _____

Roberta Slade   _____

Homer Preston   _____

Gus Quincy   _____

Cindy Sampson   _____

Chester Wright   _____

Ginger Yale   _____

Patrick Tweed   _____

Stanley Shaw   _____

Wendy Swain   _____

Glen Spencer   _____

Fred Sherwood   _____

Flo Thornton   _____

Dee Skidmore   _____

Grace Brewster   _____

Ned Westmoreland   _____

Ron Smitherman   _____

Troy Whitlock   _____

Vance Middleton   _____

Zane Anderson   _____

Bernard Pendergraph   _____

Brief Description of Structural Analysis

Since *structural analysis* was described in detail in Chapter 2, it is only very briefly discussed in this chapter. Chapter 2 also presented a number of useful strategies for improving competency in this important word identification technique.

Structural analysis (morphemic analysis) can be defined as using *word structure* or *word parts* to determine the pronunciation and meaning of unknown words encountered while reading. This word identification technique is especially helpful in improving vocabulary by using the meanings of *prefixes, suffixes*, and *word roots*.

As explained in detail in Chapter 2, structural analysis is composed of a number of different subskills. One important subskill is the attaching of a *prefix* or *suffix (affix)* to a *base or root word* to form a *derivative*. This word identification technique also deals with *inflections*, changes in a word that are made for grammatical reasons. For example, an inflection occurs when the singular form of the word *mother* is made into the plural form *mothers* by adding the suffix *s*.

Structural analysis also deals with the term *morpheme* which is the smallest unit of meaning in a language. Some other subskills of structural analysis are the understanding and use of syllabication, compound words, stress, and word origins.

With the emphasis on *whole language*, structural analysis often should be assessed, taught, and practiced in the context of meaningful words, sentences, and passages. However, structural analysis skills also occasionally should be assessed, presented and reinforced in isolation, perhaps especially for some learning-disabled children. Structural analysis may be more useful than graphophonic analysis for some children since it deals with larger, more meaningful units of language. However, it continues to be important for graphophonic elements to be emphasized with some learning-disabled children.

Normally, structural analysis may be the most useful when used in conjunction with semantic analysis or graphophonic analysis. As an example, if a child is to attack a polysyllabic word structurally, he or she must be able to decode each of the syllables by the use of graphophonic analysis and then blend the syllables together into what should be a recognizable word (a word in the child's speaking vocabulary). After the word has been analyzed both structurally and phonetically, the child must determine whether it makes sense in sentence context.

REPRODUCIBLE STRUCTURAL ANALYSIS INVENTORIES

The chapter now includes reproducible structural analysis inventories (along with their answer keys) at the first-grade, second-grade, third-grade, fourth-grade, fifth-grade, sixth-grade, and middle–upper reading levels. You can duplicate and use them in their present form or modify them in any way you wish. Their use should help you to determine with precision the structural analysis skills in which a student lacks competence and therefore should receive instruction and/or reinforcement.

GROUP-ADMINISTERED
STRUCTURAL ANALYSIS INVENTORY
(First-Grade, Second Semester Reading Level)

1. <u>Underline the ending</u> in each word.

laughing	**farmer**	**jumping**	**wooden**
golden	**landed**	**apples**	**walking**
dogs	**gladly**	**sadly**	**fathers**

2. Divide each of these <u>compound words by drawing a /</u> <u>between the two small words</u>.

snowman	**playhouse**	**popcorn**
cowboy	**airplane**	**railroad**
blueberry	**cupcake**	**sailboat**
doghouse	**football**	**sunset**

3. Draw a <u>circle around each contraction your teacher</u> <u>pronounces</u>.

aren't	**I'll**	**it's**	**wasn't**
he'll	**let's**	**doesn't**	**what's**
don't	**he's**	**can't**	**you'll**
that's	**here's**	**haven't**	**didn't**
couldn't	**there'll**	**what's**	**who'll**
she's	**you'll**	**wouldn't**	**hadn't**

4. <u>Underline the beginning</u> in each word.

along	**unhappy**	**belong**
beside	**alike**	**undo**

ANSWER KEY

Since the answers for 1, 2, and 4 and self-evident, no answer key is provided. However, here are the contractions the teacher should pronounce for item 3 in each line:

aren't
doesn't
he's
haven't
there'll
hadn't

GROUP-ADMINISTERED
STRUCTURAL ANALYSIS INVENTORY
(Second-Grade, Second Semester Reading Level)

1. <u>Underline the base or root word</u> in each word.

kindly	**answered**	**unwise**	**following**
animals	**quickly**	**replay**	**smaller**
learned	**return**	**wooden**	**fastest**

2. <u>Underline</u> each word in this sentence that is a <u>base or root word</u>.

   Amy's two dogs ran very quickly after several chipmunks that they saw eating acorns.

3. <u>Underline the prefix</u> in each word.

rewind	**because**	**unwell**	**rework**
behind	**undone**	**recover**	**before**

4. <u>Underline</u> each word in this sentence that contains a <u>prefix</u>.

   Even though I'm unhappy about it, my mother says that I will have to return this shirt.

5. <u>Underline the suffix</u> in each word.

smaller	**happily**	**sleepy**	**waiting**
showed	**babies**	**teacher**	**runner**
hopping	**largest**	**making**	**sanded**

6. <u>Underline</u> each word in this sentence that contains a *suffix*.

   Several farmers were waiting unhappily in their trucks to sell their grain.

7. Add the <u>suffix **ing**</u> to each base or root word and write the new word on the line beside it.

   run _____   bite _____

   hop _____   make _____

   dig _____   hope _____

8. Add the <u>suffix **es**</u> to each base or root word and write the new word on the line beside it.

   lady _____   penny _____

   puppy _____   try _____

   baby _____   pony _____

9. Divide each of these compound words <u>by drawing a /</u> between each of the two small words that make it up.

flashlight	**scarecrow**	**firecracker**	**rattlesnake**
toothbrush	**silverware**	**daylight**	**windshield**
grasshopper	**nutcracker**	**headlight**	**nightgown**

10. <u>Underline</u> each <u>compound word</u> in this sentence.

    At midnight my grandfather used a flashlight to look in the fireplace where he had heard a strange noise.

ANSWER KEY

1. <u>kind</u>ly   <u>answer</u>ed   un<u>wise</u>   <u>follow</u>ing

   <u>animal</u>s   <u>quick</u>ly   re<u>play</u>   <u>small</u>er

   <u>learn</u>ed   re<u>turn</u>   <u>wood</u>en   <u>fast</u>est

2. Amy's two <u>dog</u>s ran very <u>quick</u>ly after several <u>chipmunk</u>s they saw <u>eat</u>ing <u>acorn</u>s.

3. <u>re</u>wind   <u>be</u>cause   <u>un</u>well   <u>re</u>work

   <u>be</u>hind   <u>un</u>done   <u>re</u>cover   <u>be</u>fore

4. Even though I'm <u>un</u>happy about it, my mother says that I will have to <u>re</u>turn this shirt.

5. small<u>er</u>   happi<u>ly</u>   sleep<u>y</u>   wait<u>ing</u>

   show<u>ed</u>   bab<u>ies</u>   teach<u>er</u>   runn<u>er</u>

   hopp<u>ing</u>   larg<u>est</u>   mak<u>ing</u>   sand<u>ed</u>

6. Several farm<u>er</u>s were wait<u>ing</u> unhappi<u>ly</u> in their truck<u>s</u> to sell their grain.

7. running   biting

   hopping   making

   digging   hoping

8. ladies   pennies

   puppies   tries

   babies   ponies

9. flash/light   scare/crow   fire/cracker   rattle/snake

   tooth/brush   silver/ware   day/light   wind/shield

   grass/hopper   nut/cracker   head/light   night/gown

10. At <u>midnight</u> my <u>grandfather</u> used a <u>flashlight</u> to look in the <u>fireplace</u> where he had heard a strange noise.

Name _____ Grade _____ Teacher _____ Date _____

GROUP-ADMINISTERED
STRUCTURAL ANALYSIS INVENTORY
(Third-Grade Reading Level)

1. Underline the base or root word in each word.

   thankful   remembering   thirteenth   honored
   unimportant   displace   escaped   attachment
   import   beware   goodness   frighten

2. Underline each word in this sentence that contains a base or root word.
   Jay hopes the directors will reopen both of the closed museums soon so that he can visit them again.

3. Underline the prefix in each word.

   befriend   exclaim   unclear   discover
   display   insight   remark   regroup

4. Underline each word in this sentence that contains a prefix.
   Sarah is unsure if her brother will ever completely recover from the experience that made him very unhappy.

5. Underline the suffix in each word.

   honorable   rapidly   crawled   vacation
   heavy   connection   gladden   kindness
   sixteenth   bushes   basement   unusually

6. Underline each word in this sentence that contains a suffix.
   Joe's brothers and sisters have always wanted to give a truly memorable birthday party for their mother.

7. Add the suffix **ing** or **es** to each base or root word and write the new word on the line beside it.

   escape _____   receive _____
   skip _____   wiggle _____
   country _____   decide _____
   carry _____   enemy _____
   bush _____   survive _____

8. Divide each of these compound words by drawing a / between each of the two small words that make it up.

   wiretap   copyright   fruitcake   headquarters
   screwdriver   ferryboat   headache   downpour
   thunderstorm   volleyball   classmate   textbook

9. Divide each of these words into syllables by drawing a / between each syllable.

   reason   begin   protect   country
   magic   music   decide   invent
   matter   ocean   until   silent

10. Optional Oral Test: Pronounce each of these contractions.

    he'd   they've   they're   I've
    we've   they'd   we'd   they'll
    I'd   we're   you'll   who'd

ANSWER KEY

1. <u>thank</u>ful   <u>remember</u>ing   <u>thirteen</u>th   <u>honor</u>ed
   un<u>import</u>ant   dis<u>place</u>   <u>escap</u>ed   <u>attach</u>ment
   im<u>port</u>   be<u>ware</u>   g<u>ood</u>ness   <u>frigh</u>ten

2. Jay <u>hope</u>s the <u>director</u>s will re<u>open</u> both of the <u>close</u>d <u>museum</u>s soon so that he can visit them again.

3. <u>be</u>friend   <u>ex</u>claim   <u>un</u>clear   <u>dis</u>cover
   <u>dis</u>play   <u>in</u>sight   <u>re</u>mark   <u>re</u>group

4. Sarah is <u>un</u>sure if her brother will ever completely <u>re</u>cover from the experience that made him very <u>un</u>happy.

5. honor<u>able</u>   rapid<u>ly</u>   crawl<u>ed</u>   vaca<u>tion</u>
   heav<u>y</u>   connec<u>tion</u>   gladd<u>en</u>   kind<u>ness</u>
   sixteen<u>th</u>   bush<u>es</u>   base<u>ment</u>   unusual<u>ly</u>

6. Joe's brother<u>s</u> and sister<u>s</u> have always want<u>ed</u> to give a tru<u>ly</u> memo-rable birthday party for their mother.

7. escaping (escapes)   receiving (receives)
   skipping   wiggling (wiggles)
   countries   deciding (decides)
   carries (carrying)   enemies
   bushes   surviving (survives)

8. wire/tap   copy/right   fruit/cake   head/quarters
   screw/driver   ferry/boat   head/ache   down/pour
   thunder/storm   volley/ball   class/mate   text/book

9. rea/son   be/gin   pro/tect   coun/try
   mag/ic   mu/sic   de/cide   in/vent
   mat/ter   o/cean   un/til   si/lent

GROUP-ADMINISTERED
STRUCTURAL ANALYSIS INVENTORY
(Fourth-Grade Reading Level)

1. <u>Underline the base or root word</u> in each word.

   ghostly   **deplane**   **intelligently**   **contribute**
   enclose   **parachutes**   **canoes**   **compile**
   developed   **preferred**   **champions**   **interrupted**

2. <u>Underline</u> each word in this sentence that contains a <u>base or root word</u>.
   When Mark graduated from college on a sunny day in May, he certainly felt very joyful.

3. <u>Underline the prefix</u> in each word.

   disbelief   **nonmetal**   **enclose**   **rewire**
   exchange   **intake**   **predawn**   **uncrate**
   misspell   **defrost**   **propane**   **retire**

4. <u>Underline</u> each word in this sentence that contains a <u>prefix</u>.
   I return to the woods each summer because they are so unspoiled.

5. <u>Underline the suffix</u> in each word.

   survivor   **blessing**   **slavish**   **personable**
   loneliest   **originally**   **friction**   **loveliest**
   loyalty   **pollution**   **fortieth**   **designer**

6. <u>Underline</u> each word in this sentence that contains a <u>suffix</u>.
   My grandparents have needed an extremely restful vacation for months.

7. <u>Write the plural of each noun</u> on the line beside it.

   goose _____   **country** _____
   ox _____   **valley** _____
   mouse _____   **moose** _____
   servant _____ **nephew** _____

8. Divide each of these words into syllables by <u>placing a / between each syllable</u>.

   invention   **terror**   **interrupt**   **stallion**
   metal   **prefer**   **minute**   **pavement**
   predict   **equal**   **planet**   **balance**
   pronounce   **alphabet**   **skeleton**   **honest**

9. <u>Mark the accented syllable</u> for each word in this way: **'peo ple**.

   en fold   **be side**
   whim per   **a round**
   trans late   **mon ster**
   mach ine   **em brace**
   ro bot   **ig loo**

ANSWER KEY

1. <u>gh</u>ostly   de<u>plane</u>   <u>intelligent</u>ly   con<u>tribute</u>

   en<u>close</u>   <u>parachut</u>es   <u>canoe</u>s   com<u>pile</u>

   <u>develop</u>ed   <u>prefer</u>red   <u>champion</u>s   inter<u>rupt</u>ed

2. When Mark <u>graduat</u>ed from college on a <u>sunn</u>y day in May, he <u>cer-tain</u>ly felt very <u>joy</u>ful.

3. <u>dis</u>belief   <u>non</u>metal   <u>en</u>close   <u>re</u>wire

   <u>ex</u>change   <u>in</u>take   <u>pre</u>dawn   <u>un</u>crate

   <u>mis</u>spell   <u>de</u>frost   <u>pro</u>pane   <u>re</u>tire

4. I <u>re</u>turn to the woods each summer <u>be</u>cause they are so <u>un</u>spoiled.

5. surviv<u>or</u>   bless<u>ing</u>   slav<u>ish</u>   person<u>able</u>

   loneli<u>est</u>   original<u>ly</u>   fric<u>tion</u>   loveli<u>est</u>

   loyal<u>ty</u>   pollu<u>tion</u>   fortie<u>th</u>   design<u>er</u>

6. My grandparent<u>s</u> have need<u>ed</u> an extreme<u>ly</u> rest<u>ful</u> vaca<u>tion</u> for months.

7. geese   countries

   oxen   valleys

   mice   moose

   servants   nephews

8. in/ven/tion   ter/ror   in/ter/rupt   stal/lion

   met/al   pre/fer   min/ute   pave/ment

   pre/dict   e/qual   plan/et   bal/ance

   pro/nounce   al/pha/bet   skel/e/ton   hon/est

9. en'fold   be'side

   'whim per   a'round

   'trans late   'mon ster

   'mach ine   em 'brace

   'ro bot   'ig loo

GROUP-ADMINISTERED
STRUCTURAL ANALYSIS INVENTORY
(Fifth-Grade Reading Level)

1. <u>Underline the base or root word</u> in each word.

fellowship	pronoun	embarrassed	welcoming
accountant	alcoholic	dispose	brotherhood
submarine	graceful	ambulance	registered

2. <u>Underline</u> each word in this sentence that contains a <u>base or root word</u>.
   Our society can effectively decrease traffic accidents by having more driver education.

3. <u>Underline the prefix</u> in each word.

midstream	nonunion	proponent	detract
progress	predate	misadventure	encourage
subway	transport	overheat	review

4. Underline each word in this sentence that contains a <u>prefix</u>.
   George returns to his home in the suburbs on the subway to avoid smelling the exhaust fumes of the buses.

5. <u>Underline the suffix</u> in each word.

responsible	priesthood	cultured	fiftieth
ceremonies	obtainable	strengthen	hoarsely
prairies	comical	cosmetic	amazement

6. <u>Underline</u> each word in this sentence that contains a <u>suffix</u>.
   There is something nearly magical about viewing an eclipse of the sun even though it may be damaging to the eyes if a person isn't careful.

7. Divide each of these words into syllables by <u>placing a / between each syllable</u>.

burden	investigate	legend	amount
orbit	concentrate	border	telegram
fascinate	ambulance	vinegar	argument
salmon	manager	intestines	plateau

8. <u>Mark the accented syllable</u> in each word in this way: **'mus cle**.

mer chant	sur gery
ex tinct	trans port
ho ri zon	en gage
val ue	un leash
gen tle	op po nent

ANSWER KEY

1. <u>fello</u>wship   pro<u>noun</u>   <u>em</u>bar<u>rass</u>ed   <u>welcoming</u>

    <u>accoun</u>tant   al<u>cohol</u>ic   dis<u>pose</u>   <u>brother</u>hood

    sub<u>marine</u>   <u>grace</u>ful   <u>ambu</u>lance   <u>register</u>ed

2. Our society can <u>effective</u>ly de<u>crease</u> traffic <u>accident</u>s by <u>having</u> more <u>driver</u> education.

3. <u>mid</u>stream   <u>non</u>union   <u>pro</u>ponent   <u>de</u>tract

    <u>pro</u>gress   <u>pre</u>date   <u>mis</u>adventure   <u>en</u>courage

    <u>sub</u>way   <u>trans</u>port   <u>over</u>heat   <u>re</u>view

4. George <u>re</u>turns to his home in the <u>sub</u>urbs on the <u>sub</u>way to avoid smelling the <u>ex</u>haust fumes of the buses.

5. respons<u>ible</u>   priest<u>hood</u>   cultur<u>ed</u>   fifti<u>eths</u>

    ceremon<u>ies</u>   obtain<u>able</u>   strength<u>en</u>   hoarse<u>ly</u>

    prairi<u>es</u>   comic<u>al</u>   cosmet<u>ic</u>   amaze<u>ment</u>

6. There is something near<u>ly</u> magic<u>al</u> about view<u>ing</u> an eclipse of the sun even though it may be damag<u>ing</u> to the eye<u>s</u> if a person isn't care<u>ful</u>.

7. bur/den   in/ves/ti/gate   leg/end   a/mount

    or/bit   con/cen/trate   bor/der   te/le/gram

    fas/ci/nate   am/bu/lance   vin/e/gar   ar/gu/ment

    sal/mon   man/ag/er   in/tes/tines   pla/teau

8. 'mer chant   'sur gery

    ex 'tinct   'trans port

    hor 'ri zon   en 'gage

    'val ue   un 'leash

    'gen tle   op 'po nent

GROUP-ADMINISTERED
STRUCTURAL ANALYSIS INVENTORY
(Sixth-Grade Reading Level)

1. Underline the base or root word in each word.

mispronounce	interlock	southward	radical
microphone	transatlantic	burros	auctioneer
pounced	subvert	poisonous	purplish

2. Underline each word in this sentence that contains a base or root word.

   Many of my friends disagree with me about the importance of protecting endangered wild animals.

3. Underline the prefix in each word.

exhale	disembark	insensitive	misjudge
midsection	reframe	antidote	prolong
prewar	interurban	imperfect	overactive

4. Underline each word in this sentence that contains a prefix.

   Unfortunately, Marsha belittled the prosecutor and made him feel unimportant since he had lost a case about a man's being deported.

5. Underline the suffix in each word.

charitable	callous	legislature	tolerance
worthless	conviction	windward	helicopters
department	masculinity	sensitivity	irksome

6. Underline each word in this sentence containing a suffix.

   The hapless elderly gentleman very nearly was injured when he collapsed at the department store.

7. Divide each of these words into syllables by placing a / between each syllable.

envelope	demon	symbol	technical
insurance	microscope	fantastic	combustion
applause	fossil	cathedral	dazzle
depression	quarry	elegant	instinct

8. Mark the accented syllable in each word in this way: **'dor sal**.

cus tom er	re sem ble
re quest	na tive
vi bra tion	reg u lar
re wind	a brupt
ob stin ate	spec i men

ANSWER KEY

1. mis<u>p</u>ro<u>noun</u>ce   inter<u>lock</u>   <u>south</u>ward   <u>rad</u>ical
   micro<u>phone</u>   trans<u>atlantic</u>   <u>burro</u>s   <u>auction</u>eer
   <u>poun</u>ced   sub<u>vert</u>   <u>poison</u>ous   <u>purpl</u>ish

2. Many of my <u>friend</u>s dis<u>agree</u> with me about the <u>import</u>ance of <u>pro-</u><u>tect</u>ing <u>endanger</u>ed wild <u>animal</u>s.

3. <u>ex</u>hale   <u>dis</u>embark   <u>in</u>sensitive   <u>mis</u>judge
   <u>mid</u>section   <u>re</u>frame   <u>anti</u>dote   <u>pro</u>long
   <u>pre</u>war   <u>inter</u>urban   <u>im</u>perfect   <u>over</u>active

4. <u>Un</u>fortunately, Marsha <u>be</u>littled the <u>pro</u>secutor and made him feel <u>un</u>important since he had lost a case about a man's being <u>de</u>ported.

5. charit<u>able</u>   call<u>ous</u>   legisla<u>ture</u>   toler<u>ance</u>
   worth<u>less</u>   convic<u>tion</u>   wind<u>ward</u>   helicopter<u>s</u>
   depart<u>ment</u>   masculin<u>ity</u>   sensitiv<u>ity</u>   irk<u>some</u>

6. The hap<u>less</u> elder<u>ly</u> gentleman very near<u>ly</u> was injur<u>ed</u> when he col-laps<u>ed</u> at the depart<u>ment</u> store.

7. en/ve/lope   de/mon   sym/bol   tech/ni/cal
   in/sur/ance   mi/cro/scope   fan/tas/tic   com/bus/tion
   ap/plause   fos/sil   ca/the/dral   daz/zle
   de/pres/sion   quar/ry   el/e/gant   in/stinct

8. 'cus tom er   re 'sem ble
   re 'quest   'na tive
   vi 'bra tion   'reg u lar
   re 'wind (or 're wind)   a 'brupt
   'ob stin ate   'spec i men

GROUP-ADMINISTERED
STRUCTURAL ANALYSIS INVENTORY
(Middle–Upper Grade Reading Level)

1. Underline the base or root word in each word.

autobiography	dehydrate	superintendent	extraordinary
tenacious	evangelist	aquarium	hyperactive
continuance	liquefy	enterprise	interstate

2. Underline each word in this sentence that contains a base or root word.
   Mr. Goodman, my teacher, has always seemed to be a highly introspective, extremely sensitive person.

3. Underline the prefix in each word.

enterprise	retroactive	beguile	counterclockwise
malnutrition	pentagon	bilingual	circumnavigate
instigate	phonograph	centimeter	milligram

4. Underline each word in this sentence that contains a prefix.
   Judi has always engaged in an extraordinary number of extracurricular activities in high school although she also has a part-time job.

5. Underline the suffix in each word.

profiteer	certitude	dictionary	malice
crystallize	exposure	bigoted	docile
sanitarium	blockade	patroness	invalidism

6. Underline each word in this sentence that contains a suffix.
   Since golden retrievers are a docile breed of dog, they have provided infinite happiness to humans for countless years.

7. Divide each of these words into syllables by placing a / between each syllable.

magistrate	ecology	amethyst	commute
competent	lucrative	consecrate	arduous
defiant	rancor	spectacle	conservative
apprehension	prolific	aggressive	galvanize

8. Mark the accented syllable in each word in this way: re 'vile.

cus to dy	zeal ot
be reave	a wry
ag i tate	ki net ic
ar ro gant	gul lible
seg ment	ma lign

© 1995 by John Wiley & Sons, Inc.

ANSWER KEY

1. auto<u>biography</u>   de<u>hydr</u>ate   <u>super</u>inten<u>d</u>ent   extra<u>ordinary</u>
<u>ten</u>acious   evange<u>l</u>ist   <u>aqu</u>arium   hyper<u>active</u>
<u>continu</u>ance   li<u>quef</u>y   enter<u>prise</u>   inter<u>state</u>

2. Mr. Goodman, my <u>teach</u>er, has al<u>ways</u> <u>seem</u>ed to be a <u>high</u>ly intro-<u>spective</u>, <u>extreme</u>ly <u>sens</u>itive person.

3. <u>enter</u>prise   <u>retro</u>active   <u>be</u>guile   <u>counter</u>clockwise
<u>mal</u>nutrition   <u>penta</u>gon   <u>bi</u>lingual   <u>circum</u>navigate
<u>in</u>stigate   <u>phono</u>graph   <u>centi</u>meter   <u>milli</u>gram

4. Judi has <u>always</u> <u>engaged</u> in an <u>extra</u>ordinary number of <u>extra</u>curricu-lar activities in high school <u>although</u> she also has a part-time job.

5. profit<u>eer</u>   certi<u>tude</u>   diction<u>ary</u>   mal<u>ice</u>
crystal<u>lize</u>   expos<u>ure</u>   bigot<u>ed</u>   doc<u>ile</u>
sanit<u>arium</u>   block<u>ade</u>   patron<u>ess</u>   invalid<u>ism</u>

6. Since golden retriever<u>s</u> are a doc<u>ile</u> breed of dog, they have provid<u>ed</u> infinite happ<u>iness</u> to human<u>s</u> for count<u>less</u> year<u>s</u>.

7. mag/is/trate   ecol/o/gy   am/e/thyst   com/mute
com/pe/tent   lu/cra/tive   con/se/crate   ar/du/ous
de/fi/ant   ran/cor   spec/ta/cle   con/ser/va/tive
ap/pre/hen/sion   pro/lif/ic   ag/gres/sive   gal/va/nize

8. 'cus to dy   'zeal ot
be 'reave   a 'wry
'ag i tate   ki 'net ic
'ar ro gant   'gull ible
'seg ment   ma 'lign

Brief Description of Semantic (Context) Cues

Since *semantic (context) cues* were described in some detail in Chapter 2, they are only very briefly described in this chapter. Chapter 2 also presented a number of useful strategies for improving competency in this very important word identification technique.

Semantic cues are a word identification technique in which the reader determines the meaning (and sometimes the pronunciation) of unknown words by examining the context in which they are found. That context may be the sentence, the adjacent sentences, that paragraph, or perhaps the entire passage. They also are somewhat related to syntactic or grammatical clues.

With the current emphasis on *whole language* and on reading as a *global, language-based process that stresses comprehension* of what is read from the initial stages of reading instruction, it is obvious that semantic cues are the single most useful and important word identification technique. Semantic cues also are most effective when used in conjunction with structural and graphophonic analysis and when there are not too many unknown words in the reading material. Usually there should not be more than about *1 in 50 unknown words* in the material if semantic cues are to be used most effectively.

Semantic cues can be presented as early as the *emergent literacy level* when the teacher orally gives a sentence with an omitted word. The teacher then asks the children to provide a word that makes sense in that sentence. At the primary-grade reading level, the importance of semantic cues should be explained to children, and they should be encouraged to use context to deduce the meaning of unknown words they meet while reading.

It is very important to ensure that children in both the primary and intermediate grades be encouraged to supply *words that make sense* while reading both silently and orally, even if the provided words are not those found in the reading material. Especially in the primary grades, children may well be discouraged from *risk-taking*, which in turn may hinder their reading since too much stress is then placed upon *word-perfect reading*. **However, the supplied words should always make sense in sentence context and should not be excessive in number.** Sometimes, my teacher-trainees tutor disabled readers who miscall up to one half of the words while reading and yet are able to effectively retell the material or to answer comprehension questions about the material. These students should continue to have instruction and/or practice in either sight word identification, structural analysis, or graphophonic analysis depending upon their weakness.

In summary, semantic cues are the one technique of word identification that best represents the concept that reading is a language-based process that emphasizes comprehension. It also best reflects the *whole language philosophy*. Therefore, all children in the elementary and middle school should be taught that semantic cues are not merely guessing at the meaning of unknown words but rather are a calculated estimate of the meaning of unknown words that demands interpretive thinking on the reader's part.

ASSESSING ABILITY IN SEMANTIC (CONTEXT) CUES

There are several ways in which you can assess a child's ability in the use of semantic cues. One of the simplest and most effective is simply to observe the student's reading to see if the supplied words make sense in context and to determine if he or she comprehends effectively. Such teacher observation probably can be made more effective by using a structural checklist such as that found in Chapter 2.

Oral reading miscue analysis also can be very helpful in determining a child's ability in the use of semantic cues. As described and illustrated in Chapter 4, Susan Argyle's coding system of oral reading miscues emphasizes whether or not the miscues significantly change the meaning of the material. In addition, the miscue analysis used in Reading Recovery™ also is useful for this purpose.

Obviously, one of the most effective ways to assess a child's competency in semantic cues is simply to observe his or her oral and silent reading in an informal manner. You can notice whether the child makes meaningful substitutions in oral reading. If he or she usually substitutes words that do not make sense in sentence context, he or she probably does not have a good command of semantic cues.

A child's *comprehension ability* also can be used to determine his or her ability in semantic cues to some extent. If a child has effective comprehension of material that has been read either silently or orally, he or she undoubtedly makes good use of semantic cues. On the other hand, the child who does not comprehend well often does not monitor his or her comprehension and is not very concerned whether or not the reading material makes sense.

In addition, you can make a comparison between a child's ability to identify words *in isolation* and *in context* as a measure of his or her competency in semantic cues. Many children are able to identify words *in context* better than they can identify words *in isolation* since they can make use of context while attempting to identify the unknown words. However, a possible exception to this statement may be learning-disabled children who sometimes seem able to identify words more effectively *in isolation* than *in context*.

USING THE CLOZE PROCEDURE AS AN ASSESSMENT DEVICE FOR SEMANTIC CUES

The *cloze procedure* was developed by Wilson L. Taylor[17] and is based upon the psychology theory of *closure*, which presumes that a person wishes to finish any incomplete pattern. The cloze procedure is therefore based upon the *prediction aspects* of reading, which indicates that a reader wants to predict the unknown words he or she may meet in a passage. Therefore, the cloze procedure makes use of both *semantic and syntactic cues* to help a reader deduce the unknown words he or she may meet in reading.

---

[17]Wilson L. Taylor, "Cloze Procedure: A New Tool for Measuring Readability," *Journalism Quarterly*, 30 (Fall 1953), pp. 415-433.

The cloze procedure has a number of different variations, each of which can be useful in improving a child's ability in both semantic analysis and comprehension skills. Since the construction, administration, and evaluation of the traditional cloze procedure are very well known, they are not described in this handbook. However, if you want detailed directions on how to construct, give, and evaluate many different variations of the cloze procedure, you are encouraged to consult any of the following resources. Each resource also contains a number of reproducible examples of the different variations of cloze.

> Wilma H. Miller, *Complete Reading Disabilities Handbook*. West Nyack, NY: The Center for Applied Research in Education, 1993, pp. 96–104.

> Wilma H. Miller, *Reading Diagnosis Kit*. West Nyack, NY: The Center for Applied Research in Education, 1986, pp. 311–326.

> Wilma H. Miller, *Reading Teacher's Complete Diagnosis & Correction Manual*. West Nyack, NY: The Center for Applied Research in Education, 1988, pp. 108–119.

REPRODUCIBLE SEMANTIC (CONTEXT) INVENTORIES AND CLOZE PROCEDURES

Here are reproducible semantic (context) inventories (and their answer keys) at the first-grade, second-grade, third-grade, fourth-grade, fifth-grade, sixth-grade, and middle–upper grade reading levels. Some of these reproducible assessment devices also include brief versions of variations of the traditional cloze procedure. However, you should remember that they are not true cloze procedures since they are not 250 words or more in length. Instead, they are just brief examples of how cloze can be used to make a partial assessment of ability in semantic cues. They should be used along with other types of assessment in this crucial word identification technique.

SEMANTIC INVENTORY
(First-Grade, Second Semester Reading Level)
Circle the one word that belongs in each sentence.

1. My mother said she will _____ a cake for my birthday.
   boat
   bake
   boy

2. Jim and Jill are going _____ their father to the store.
   with
   will
   wish

3. It is a very cold _____ today.
   doll
   day
   does

4. I _____ a horse at the farm.
   seven
   sail
   saw

5. How _____ you today?
   are
   am
   ant

6. _____ is that new boy in our school?
   When
   Who
   With

7. My teacher said that Bob _____ play ball now.
   can
   cow
   cane

8. There were many _____ at my house.
   pail
   people
   pile

9. I fell _____ on the way to school.
   does
   did
   down

10. Sammy must let his dog _____ now.
    out
    own
    one

MODIFIED CLOZE PROCEDURE

Read this story. Then write the one word from the words on the bottom so that the story makes sense.

Sal saw a turtle on the road today. He didn't want a car or truck to run _____ it. He didn't know what to do.

Sal stopped _____ truck from hitting the turtle by holding up his _____ when he saw a truck coming fast. Then he _____ a little stick to make the turtle move. He _____ hurt the turtle at all, but it walked off _____ road. Then it would not get hurt.

hand	**took**
over	**a**
didn't	**the**

ANSWER KEY

1. bake	6. Who
2. with	7. can
3. day	8. people
4. saw	9. down
5. are	10. out

Modified Cloze Procedure

over	took
a	didn't
hand	the

SEMANTIC INVENTORY

(Second-Grade Reading Level)

Circle the one word that belongs in each sentence.

1. Mrs. Tucker's class is supposed to _____ our class into the lunchroom.

    follow
    falling
    filled

2. A black bear is a very big _____ that likes to eat honey.

    always
    animal
    apple

3. Jake's mother took a _____ of him wearing his new jacket.

    palace
    picture
    pale

4. I had better write a _____ to my grandmother today.

    lettuce
    lamp
    letter

5. _____ are you going to play ball after school?

    Where
    Which
    Witch

6. I don't believe that a dog should ever be _____ and bite anyone.

    mile
    mine
    mean

7. A farmer needs to have good _____ so that he or she can plant crops.

    load
    land
    lead

8. Our teacher is a very _____ person who is always smiling.

    kite
    knot
    kind

9. Everyone in our class must do the work on _____ 43 of the book.

    page
    pane
    paint

10. The _____ seems very clear today.

    air
    ear
    aunt

11. That is a very good _____ for your story.

    sense
    sentence
    sent

12. Please turn to the _____ at the end of the hall.

    right
    ride
    road

MODIFIED CLOZE PROCEDURE

Read this story. Then write the one word from the words on the bottom so that the story makes sense.*

One morning this summer my neighbor was riding his bicycle on a road in the North Woods. His dog Ben was running with him.

_____ my neighbor and Ben saw a big

_____ bear on the road. Ben started running

_____the bear as fast as he could. _____

chased the bear right into the woods! _____ neighbor said

that he could hear the _____ running fast. He even

crashed into a _____ tree, knocking it down while he ran.

_____ neighbor said that the bear probably was

_____ of Ben. He really was a very _____

dog!

Later that morning my dog and _____ were walking

along the same road. Suddenly _____ dog stopped and

looked into the woods. _____ had stopped exactly where

the bear had _____ into the woods three hours earlier. I

_____ that she could still smell the bear's

_____. I didn't find out until later that

_____ about how Ben had chased the bear. I don't think

that my dog is as brave as Ben!

My	**She**	**black**
run	**after**	**My**
Suddenly	**dead**	**I**
bear	**afraid**	**guess**
He	**scent**	**my**
brave	**morning**	

⎯⎯⎯⎯

*This is a true story that happened in northern Wisconsin during the summer of 1994.

ANSWER KEY

1. follow	7. land
2. animal	8. kind
3. picture	9. page
4. letter	10. air
5. Where	11. sentence
6. mean	12. right

Modified Cloze Procedure

Suddenly	brave
black	I
after	my
He	She
My	run
bear	guess
dead	scent
My	morning
afraid	

Name _____ Grade _____ Teacher _____ Date _____

SEMANTIC INVENTORY

(Third-Grade Reading Level)

Circle the one word that belongs in each sentence.

1. When Chris went with his family on a trip to the West last summer, he saw many beautiful _____.

    monsters
    mountains
    mice

2. My older sister likes to listen to loud _____ all the time.

    music
    museum
    magic

3. Have you ever _____ in a jet airplane?

    trip
    tried
    traveled

4. Sue likes to read _____ books the best of all.

    mystery
    master
    miss

5. Mr. Goodman is a good _____ of a very nice man.

    except
    exit
    example

6. That is the _____ time your mother has told you to clean your room.

    second
    since
    sight

7. It is very important to protect our _____.

    earth
    either
    earring

8. Eddie would like to _____ on a spaceship someday.

        trip
        travel
        trial

9. My sister is two years _____ than I am.

        younger
        youth
        yellow

10. Our teacher is certainly a very _____ person.

        special
        speech
        speak

11. Karen _____ her dog was lost yesterday when he wandered away for a little while.

    through
    though
    thought

12. _____ in a while it is nice to play soccer and just have some fun.

    Once
    One
    Only

MODIFIED CLOZE PROCEDURE

**Read this story to yourself about a mother deer who had triplet fawns. The first letter or first two letters of each omitted word have been put on the blank space as a clue. Write each entire omitted word in the space. When you are done, read the story again to make sure that it all makes sense.*

Have you ever seen a fawn, which is a baby deer? I have seen many fawns, and they a_____ very beautiful. A fawn is brown with wh_____ spots all over its back. The spots h_____ to protect the fawn from danger while i_____ is waiting in the woods for its m_____ to return.

I have even seen twin f_____ although they are more unusual. However, I d_____ know that a mother deer could have tr_____ fawns!

One day several years ago two f_____ saw a fawn swimming across a large l_____ at dawn. Since they were afraid that th_____ fawn had lost its mother, the fishermen br_____ the fawn to a wildlife park. The f_____ was named Esther after the famous swimmer Esther Williams i_____ the movies long ago.

Esther the fawn gr_____ up and two years later had triplet f_____, which is very uncommon. I saw them, a_____ they were just so beautiful with their b_____ brown eyes, white spots, and long thin l_____. Since they will grow up and live at the wildlife park, they will always have plenty of food to eat and be safe.

_____

*This is a true story. The triplet fawns were born in northern Wisconsin during June, 1994.

ANSWER KEY

1. mountains
2. music
3. traveled
4. mystery
5. example
6. second

7. earth
8. travel
9. younger
10. special
11. thought
12. Once

Modified Cloze Procedure

are
white
help
it
mother
fawns
didn't
triplet
fishermen
lake

the
brought
fawn
in
grew
fawns
and
big
legs

SEMANTIC INVENTORY
(Fourth-Grade Reading Level)
Circle the one word that belongs in each sentence.

1. Jenny would very much like to learn to paddle a _____ this summer.

    canvas

    canoe

    coyote

2. I believe that I probably am my Aunt Sally's favorite _____.

    nephew

    nobody

    nonsense

3. It is fairly safe to _____ that Erin will become a doctor someday.

    property

    predict

    product

4. Birch Lake has one beautiful _____ right in the middle of it.

    island

    icicle

    imagine

5. I walk with my dog about six miles every day to get some _____.

    excerpt

    exercise

    extra

6. Pluto is supposed to be a small _____ in our universe that is far away from the Earth.

    plant

    planet

    plantation

7. Joey never wants anyone to think he is a _____.

    crowd

    coward

    cavern

8. We must be very careful not to _____ the environment.

      pollute
      platter
      pouch

9. Barbara would like to study to be a _____ forecaster when she goes to college.

      weather
      whisper
      whimper

10. I think my mother is a very _____ woman.

      intervene
      intelligent
      interpret

11. Juan is very good at fixing all types of _____.

      machines
      mustard
      moustache

12. It is not polite to _____ anyone while he or she is speaking.

      interrupt
      imperfect
      improbable

13. You look as though you have just seen a _____.

      guest
      ghost
      gnash

14. My neighbor seems to be an extremely _____ person.

      critical
      creak
      croak

15. He appeared to be in absolute _____ when he saw the tornado approaching.

      terrible
      terror
      tear

MODIFIED CLOZE PROCEDURE

Read this story to yourself about the moon. Each of the omitted words has been replaced by short lines indicating how many letters that word contains. Write each omitted word on the line putting one letter on each line.

When a person looks into the sky on a clear night, the moon usually is noticed first. A full moon seems to be the _ _ _ _ beautiful. The Earth's moon is much smaller _ _ _ _ are the moons of other planets in _ _ _ universe.

Astronomers have studied the moon for _ _ _ _ years using various types of telescopes. These _ _ _ _ _ _ _ _ _ _ _ _ found large craters, mountains, valleys, and plains _ _ the moon's surface.

It was very exciting _ _ _ _ some astronauts landed on the surface of _ _ _ moon in July, 1969. When a person _ _ _ _ _ at the moon at night, it is _ _ _ _ _ difficult to believe that men have actually _ _ _ _ _ _ on the moon. The astronauts collected rock _ _ _ _ _ _ _ from the surface of the moon so _ _ _ _ they could be studied by scientists on _ _ _ _ _. These rock samples also have been displayed _ _ many people. Perhaps you will also be able to see these rock samples from the moon someday if you already haven't.

ANSWER KEY

1. canoe
2. nephew
3. predict
4. island
5. exercise
6. planet
7. coward
8. pollute

9. weather
10. intelligent
11. machines
12. interrupt
13. ghost
14. critical
15. terror

Modified Cloze Procedure

most
than
our (the)
many
researchers
on
when
the

looks
still
walked
samples
that
Earth
to

SEMANTIC INVENTORY
(Fifth-Grade Reading Level)

Circle the one word that belongs in each sentence.

1. Mr. and Mrs. Lopez own a very profitable apple _____ and sell apples from a stand in the fall.

   orchard
   orchid
   orchestra

2. My hands can nearly stretch an _____ on the piano.

   octagon
   occupy
   octave

3. The southwestern part of this country is a fairly mountainous _____.

   region
   regime
   regard

4. Once when Jeff was walking, he very nearly fell into a _____.

   retreat
   ravine
   ranch

5. One of the most beautiful _____ in the world is located in Australia.

   reefs
   reaches
   recites

6. A ruby is a gem of unequaled _____.

   valid
   value
   vacant

7. My _____ came from the country of Sweden almost ninety years ago.

   ancestors
   ancient
   ancestral

8. _____ is the study of rocks, minerals, and fossils.

       George

       Geology

       Geographic

9. The _____ are an important part of the digestive system.

       intestines

       intake

       incisors

10. It is very difficult to dance to the _____ of this music.

       rhythm

       rift

       rote

11. When Sarah grows up, she would like to become a _____ and study the environment.

       scientist

       science

       scientific

12. Have you ever watched a fascinating Native American _____?

       celebrate

       ceremony

       celebrity

13. Susie has bought a Christmas _____ for her best friend.

       ornament

       ornate

       organ

14. Melissa is a very _____ young woman.

       response

       responsible

       responsibility

15. One of my students once gave me a very large _____ that her husband had caught.

       sandwich

       salmon

       saliva

MODIFIED CLOZE PROCEDURE

Read this story to yourself about hot air balloons. Write a word that makes sense in each blank. When you are finished, reread the story to make sure it sounds correct.

The hot air balloon was the first aircraft invented by man. The first balloon was sent into the _____ in 1783, and it was a large bag _____ of paper. This balloon was _____ with hot air and _____ from a fire made by burning straw.

Any _____ rises into the air _____ it is filled _____ a gas that is _____ than the air outside. For _____, the balloons that are _____ used at _____ parties are filled with helium, _____ them to stay up in _____ air.

Some balloons _____ engines that turn a propeller _____ pushes them through the air. This _____ of balloon can be guided _____ a pilot and may _____ called a dirigible or airship.

The radio _____ in the city in which I live _____ a large hot air balloon that is used _____ advertising. One day the principal _____ a local elementary school rode _____ the balloon wearing a penguin _____ because the children in his school _____ read many, many books. The "Penguins" is the name of all of the school's teams.

ANSWER KEY

1. orchard
2. octave
3. region
4. ravine
5. reefs
6. value
7. ancestors
8. Geology
9. intestines
10. rhythm
11. scientist
12. ceremony
13. ornament
14. responsible
15. salmon

Modified Cloze Procedure

Note: In this modified cloze procedure, any word that makes sense in sentence context should be considered correct. The following answers are just examples of words that can be written in each blank.

air
made
filled
smoke
balloon
because
with
lighter
example
often
birthday
causing
the

have
which
type
by
be
station
has
for
of
on
suit
had

SEMANTIC INVENTORY
(Sixth-Grade Reading Level)

Circle the one word that belongs in each sentence.

1. A stone _____ is a very fascinating place to visit.
   quarter
   quarry
   quartet

2. Cathy brought a very interesting rock _____ to show her class.
   specimen
   special
   spice

3. My father received two blood _____ after his motorcycle accident.
   transit
   transfusions
   translate

4. When I had strep throat last winter, the doctor gave me a very strong _____.
   antiquated
   antique
   antibiotic

5. When Mrs. Lindstrom gave a speech at the convention, she had to use a _____ to be heard.
   microphone
   microscope
   microwave

6. Have you ever ridden in a _____?
   heliport
   helicopter
   hurricane

7. My older sister is sorting and opening _____ as a summer job.
   envelopes
   enfold
   endanger

8. I would very much like to be an archaeologist so that I could examine _____.
   follows
   fellows
   fossils

9. My city is the home of one of the largest _____ companies in the world.

insert
interrupt
insurance

10. Most entertainers love to hear the sound of _____ after a performance.

applause
applied
application

11. We always have a _____ hanging on our door at Christmas time.

writhe
wreath
wring

12. Mrs. Powers seems to be a very _____ lady who always wears beautiful, expensive clothes.

elegant
elephant
embark

13. When he becomes angry, Mr. Smith always gets a very _____ look on his face.

menacing
meandering
meadow

14. Our church has sent a great many _____ to Africa in the past.

missiles
missionaries
missives

15. Although she still is an _____, Frannie is a truly superb pianist.

amber
ambitious
amateur

MODIFIED CLOZE PROCEDURE

Read this story to yourself about lizards. Write a word that makes sense in each blank. When you are finished, reread the story to make sure it sounds correct.

You may be surprised to learn that there are approximately 3,000 kinds of lizards that differ greatly in color, size, shape, and actions. Amazingly, the _____ types of lizards can _____ in size from two _____ to twelve feet in _____.

Although lizards may _____ have great appeal for some _____, only two _____ are probably truly poisonous. _____, most lizards are beneficial _____ they eat insects that _____ harmful to humans.

Although some _____ lay eggs that have a tough, leathery _____, others have young _____ are born alive.

Since lizards are cold-blooded _____, they cannot tolerate _____ variations in temperature. Usually in _____ desert area, if the _____ becomes very hot, lizards _____ to locate a shelter such as a _____ or a large rock. In a Mexican desert, _____ example, I recently saw a lizard attempting _____ escape the hot _____ sun by running under a _____.

Interestingly, today lizards seem_____ be becoming more popular_____ household pets. Some people even prefer them to traditional pets such as dogs or cats.

© 1995 by John Wiley & Sons, Inc.

ANSWER KEY

1. quarry
2. specimen
3. transfusions
4. antibiotic
5. microphone
6. helicopter
7. envelopes
8. fossils
9. insurance
10 applause
11. wreath
12. elegant
13. menacing
14. missionaries
15. amateur

Modified Cloze Procedure

Note: In this modified cloze procedure, any word that makes sense in sentence context should be considered correct. The following answers are just examples of words that can be written in each blank:

various	creatures
range	great
inches	a
length	sun
not	attempt
people	bush
types	for
Indeed	to
since	midday
are	bush
lizards	to
shell	as
that	

SEMANTIC INVENTORY
(Middle–Upper Grade Reading Level)

Circle the one word that belongs in each sentence.

1. When my sister received a scholarship to go to college, she was in sheer
   _____.

   ecstasy
   exuberant
   eloquent

2. Mr. and Mrs. Swanson have just been granted complete _____ of
   the baby they have been trying to adopt.

   callous
   custody
   consecutive

3. My aunt in California was completely _____ when the earthquake
   destroyed her home last year.

   devastated
   digression
   debacle

4. My mother is a truly _____, joyous person who loves everybody.

   gauntlet
   gist
   gregarious

5. The _____ today is very, very oppressive.

   humidity
   humidor
   harangue

6. The prosecuting attorney and defense attorney normally are
   _____.

   anniversaries
   adversaries
   adjunct

7. I have always found advanced mathematics to be very _____.

   obtuse
   obstinately
   oblong

8. That salesman may well be a _____ if a person is to believe
   all that has been said about him.

   chalet
   charlatan
   crypt

9. It often takes a long time to recover from the _____ of losing a loved one to death.

     bereavement
     berate
     bourgeois

10. That famous general is preparing to write his _____ at long last.

      malign
      malinger
      memoirs

11. Patti's fuchsia dress certainly seems very _____ to me.

      gauche
      gullible
      gravitate

12. Mr. Thompson is a very _____, pompous man.

      awry
      assimilate
      arrogant

13. That house is just a _____ of corridors and hallways.

      labyrinth
      legitimate
      libertarian

14. That barbershop quartet certainly can _____ very well.

      harmonious
      harmonize
      heathen

15. The project was a _____ waste of taxpayers' money.

      phlegm
      phenomenal
      phase

MODIFIED CLOZE PROCEDURE

Read this story to yourself about the ocean tides. Write a word that makes sense in each blank. When you are finished, reread the story to make sure it sounds correct.

One of the most fascinating aspects of the oceans found on our Earth may well be the moving tides. Interestingly, the tides in _____ ocean are governed_____ both the moon and the sun, _____ the moon is much more influential since _____ is so much nearer _____ the Earth.

The _____ flood tides and the lowest ebb _____ occur twice each _____ at the littlest or _____ phases of the moon. They _____ called the spring _____, and occur because the sun _____ moon are lined up _____ are pulling in the same _____, causing the surf to _____ high up on the _____ and then pushing _____ out again.

At the _____ and third quarters _____ the moon, the neap tides occur, _____ that there is the least difference _____ the deep and _____ water. This occurs because the _____ and the sun are pulling _____ different directions of each _____.

When you next visit the seashore, carefully consider the influences that cause the interesting ocean tides.

© 1995 by John Wiley & Sons, Inc.

ANSWER KEY

1. ecstasy
2. custody
3. devastated
4. gregarious
5. humidity
6. adversaries
7. obtuse
8. charlatan
9. bereavement
10. memoirs
11. gauche
12. arrogant
13. labyrinth
14. harmonize
15. phenomenal

Modified Cloze Procedure

Note: In this modified cloze procedure, any word that makes sense in sentence context should be considered correct. The following answers are just examples of words that can be written in each blank.

any
by
although
it
to
highest
tides
month
fullest
are
tides
and
and

direction
come
seashore
it
first
of
meaning
between
shallow
moon
in
other

CHAPTER SEVEN

Additional Alternative Ways of Assessing Reading Skills and Attitudes

Do you think all children monitor their reading comprehension equally well? If you are an experienced teacher, you are well aware that the answer to this question is a most definite "No." There are great differences between the self-monitoring of abilities of good readers and poor readers when they are reading either silently and orally. Obviously, the typical good reader is very well aware of whether or not he or she is understanding what is being read and the various "fix-up" strategies that can be applied if comprehension is inadequate. On the other hand, the typical below-average reader often does not care whether or not he or she is understanding what is being read and does not know the strategies to use to comprehend better. A number of the disabled readers we tutor mispronounce many words while reading orally and are unaware that their substitutions could not possibly make sense. Teaching children to *self-monitor their comprehension* is one of the most effective ways of improving reading comprehension. That is one of the important reading skills addressed in this chapter.

This chapter provides you with many classroom-tested alternative ways of assessing a child's reading skills and attitudes. Since a number of them directly relate to reading comprehension, this most important aspect of reading also is very briefly described. After reading the chapter, you will be aware of many useful ways of assessing reading skills and attitudes, and will be provided with numerous reproducible assessment devices whose use should save you immeasurable time and effort and also should enable you to teach reading to all children more effectively.

The reading teacher will find this chapter to be very comprehensive in providing useful alternative ways of determining a child's reading skills and attitudes. Although the strategies and reproducible devices included in this chapter also can be used in traditional reading programs, such as the basal reader approach and phonic approaches, *they may be the most useful in whole language programs.*

Description of Teacher-Pupil Reading Conferences

Teacher-pupil reading conferences are very commonly used in *whole language programs* both for *reading instruction* and *reading assessment.* They are very commonly used in a whole language program instead of the typical reading achievement groups, which are used in the basal reader approach. However, they also should be used on a regular basis even when basal readers are used as the major or supplementary reading approach. Teacher-pupil conferences can be used both to assess and to present or reinforce many different literacy concepts and skills.

Teacher-pupil reading conferences can take place as early as first grade as soon as a child can read a very simple trade book independently. However, they should be regularly scheduled one-on-one sessions from the second-grade through the sixth-grade levels. Each teacher should have a sheet a child can sign to request a conference when it is needed or wanted. In addition, each child should be scheduled to have individual reading conferences with his or her teacher on a regular basis.

When a teacher uses teacher-pupil reading conferences as part of a whole language program, he or she usually can meet with about ten children each day. The conferences usually last from several minutes to about fifteen minutes with most conferences lasting about five to ten minutes.

Recordkeeping is a very important part of any program of teacher-pupil reading conferences. The *teacher* can have a notebook with a section for each child. The child's records should include the dates of the conferences, the titles and authors of the books the child read, the specific reading skills in which the child is competent and weak, and observations about how the child feels about reading in general and about reading specific books. The *child* also should keep his or her own records. Often the child's records are kept on index cards. Have the child simply list the title and author of each book and his or her reaction to the book on a separate card. There also are many creative ways in which a child can keep reading records. Here is a very good source of creative ways of helping the child keep his or her records of reading:

Patricia Tyler Muncy, *Hooked on Books! Activities and Projects That Make Kids Love to Read.* West Nyack, NY: The Center for Applied Research in Education, 1995.

The child also can include some of his or her reading records in his or her portfolio.

Very briefly teacher-pupil reading conferences can be used for the following general purposes:

- to assess a child's competency in the various word-identification skills
- to evaluate a child's comprehension skills

- to help the child in finding more information on a topic
- to help the child obtain teacher feedback about his or her reading
- to share an enjoyable book
- to teach and/or reinforce a specific reading skill in which the child lacks competence

The typical teacher-pupil reading conference has the following parts:

- listening to the child speak
- talking with the child
- listening to the child read
- presenting and/or reinforcing a needed skill or skills

This is the format most teachers in a whole language program use when having teacher-pupil reading conferences:

- discussing the book the child has read with him or her, thus ensuring comprehension and helping the child to extend its meaning
- having the child read aloud and giving help or instruction as needed
- discussing additional activities or readings

NOTE: It is important to often let the child take the lead in teacher-pupil reading conferences if possible.

Here are some questions you can ask during a teacher-pupil reading conference to evaluate a child's reading comprehension in an effective way:

- How do you feel about the book you're reading?
- What are some of the interesting things you learned from reading this book?
- What was really exciting or funny about the book?
- What kind of people were the characters in this book?
- Would you ever like to meet people who are like some of the characters in the book? Which characters?
- What are the most important parts of the book?
- Will you please read your favorite part of the book aloud?

NOTE: As the child is reading his or her favorite portion of the book out loud, note the kind of miscues he or she makes. You also can note the word identification strategies he or she uses when meeting an unknown word. As explained in detail in Chapter 4, in most instances *semantic cues along with graphophonic cues* provide the best method of word identification. The child should always be encouraged to use *multiple cueing systems*.

SAMPLE TEACHER-PUPIL READING CONFERENCE AT THE THIRD-GRADE READING LEVEL

The chapter now contains a sample *teacher-pupil reading conference* at the approximate third-grade reading level. Although this is the type of reading conference that would most typically be used in a *whole language program* that employs much individual reading instruction and reinforcement, it also is very useful in a traditional reading program, such as the basal reader approach, whenever possible. It is very important for a reading teacher to meet on an individual basis with each child in his or her classroom as often as possible.

Mrs. Talbert: Well, Jennifer, what is the name of the book you've been reading this week?

Jennifer: It's called *Sarah, Plain and Tall.*

T: Can you tell me who Sarah is?

J: She's a lady who lived in this country a long time ago.

T: Why was she called "plain and tall"?

J: Because she thought she wasn't pretty, and she knew she was really tall.

T: What did Sarah do in this book?

J: She went West on the train to live with a man and his kids since their mother had died. She was going to be their new mother.

T: What was the problem in this book?

J: I think the problem was if the man and the kids would like her well enough so that she could stay. They liked her after a little while, and she married the man and did stay.

T: How do you think Sarah was like your mother?

J: Well, they're both nice, and they both like kids and flowers. My mother works in an office, but Sarah did lots of hard work at home.

T: Did you like this book?

J: I really liked it. I liked how the kids liked her at the end, and she stayed.

T: What was your favorite part of the book?

J: The part when Sarah first saw the man and the boy and girl and her new house.

T: Will you read that part aloud now? (*Jennifer read that portion of the book aloud, demonstrating good oral reading fluency and only a few miscues that did not interfere with comprehension. They were miscues that were semantically and syntactically correct.*)

T: You really read that very well, don't you think? I liked that you read it as though you really understood it very well. Is there any reading skill you would like me to help you with today?

J: I don't think so. I'm doing great. I really love reading books like this.

T: Then I bet you would really like to read the book *Little House on the Prairie* by Laura Ingalls Wilder. It's about a girl who lived in South Dakota a long time ago, and she was kind of like the children in *Sarah, Plain and Tall*.

J: I think I'll love it. May I go to the library right now and see if it's there so I can check it out?

T: Of course. Have fun reading it.

NOTE: If Jennifer had requested help on any specific reading skills or Mrs. Talbert had determined that she needed help in any subskill of sight-word identification, graphophonic analysis, structural analysis, semantic analysis, or comprehension, Mrs. Talbert would have provided instruction and/or reinforcement in that specific reading skill either on an individual basis right then or later, or otherwise in a small-group setting a short time later.

Description of Alternative Kinds of Teacher-Pupil Interviews

In addition to the teacher-pupil reading conference described earlier, there are alternative kinds of teacher-pupil interviews that can be very useful in obtaining information about a child's literacy skills. One of the most effective ways of doing this is simply to ask the child the right questions about literacy (reading and writing). Although interviewing has a long history in the field of *ethnography*, it is finally now considered a very effective way of gathering information about literacy skills and attitudes.

However, the *structured interview* with predetermined questions often does not work very well with children. In this setting they will often tell you what they think you want to hear. I can relate a personal experience that indicates this very clearly. A number of years ago one of my graduate students gave an "Incomplete Sentences Test" to one of the students in her eighth-grade remedial reading classes. As you may know, an "Incomplete Sentences Test" is an informal device to determine a student's attitudes toward family, school, and reading. Several examples of them are found in the following resource:

> Wilma H. Miller, *Reading Diagnosis Kit*. West Nyack, NY: The Center for Applied Research in Education, 1986, pp. 35–354.

In any case, I reviewed the boy's responses and determined that he probably was a normal eighth-grade boy. Imagine my amazement when I found out that he had recently been arrested for the rape of a young woman! I do not know why he was not in a correctional facility for boys at that time.

An *interview* is a social interaction that can be seen as conveying various messages. In interviewing children about literacy, *questions about use* can be helpful. As an example, ask a third-grade child: "If a second-grade child were having trouble telling the difference between *short e* and *short i*, what could you tell him or her that would help him or her to be able to hear the differences between them?"

It is important in a teacher-pupil interview to try to equalize the power differences between the teacher and student. Of course, this is very difficult to do since teachers intrinsically have more power than do children. Usually before a child will give you truly helpful information you have to provide an atmosphere of trust and develop an excellent rapport. You can do this best by being truly supportive and interested in what the child is saying. You must make the child believe that his or her views are as valid as yours. One way of doing this is having the child tell you about a book he or she has read recently but you have not. You then can share a different book you have read but that the child has not. In this way the child can be respected as an "expert" on his or her book and opinions. The child also should learn that interviews are the time when the child can talk to the teacher on an individual basis and *must* not be interrupted by other children.

Here are some sample questions that can be used in teacher-pupil interviews to gain information on reading skills and attitudes:

- What have you learned most recently in reading?
- What would you like to learn next in reading?
- Let's imagine that you have a younger brother or sister who is just entering first grade. What could you tell him or her about reading (literacy) that would help him or her become good at it?
- If you were giving advice about learning to read to a first-grade child, what would be the most helpful to tell him or her?
- What was your favorite part of the book? (Avoid saying: Tell me about the book.)
- You said that the book made you happy. Can you tell me more about that?
- What was it about the book that made you happy?
- What would be a good question to ask the author of this book?
- Can you tell me what it's like for you to read at school?
- What do you do when you read?
- Can you tell me some of the things that usually happen in your reading group?
- How do you use the classroom (school, public) library? When do you use it?
- Can you study the next chapter of your social studies (science) textbook and tell me just how you would go about it?
- What did you do in your reading time today?
- When you read this chapter of the book to me, could you tell me what you are thinking?
- Have you read any hard books lately? What was it about them that made them hard for you?
- What kinds of reading do you like the best? Can you give me some examples?

- Are you really good at some kinds of reading? Why do you think you are good at that kind of reading?
- Do you like some kinds of books better than others? What makes the good books so much better than the other books?
- Why did you select the book that you're reading now?
- Why did you not like the book that you said didn't appeal to you?
- What would you like to learn so that you could become a better reader?
- Are there different kinds of books? Can you tell me what some of them are?
- If I asked you to (give an activity in reading), just how could you go about doing it?
- If I asked (Beth) to (give an activity in reading), what do you think she would need to be able to do it?
- Can you tell me what you usually do in the evenings?
- Can you tell me what you usually do on the weekends?

Assessing and Activating Prior Knowledge

Prior knowledge is of the utmost importance to effective reading comprehension. Prior knowledge is all of the previous experiences a reader brings to his or her reading. In many cases prior knowledge is more important to the comprehension of the reading material than is the print itself. As an example, a child who lacks prior knowledge about kangaroos since he or she has never seen either a live kangaroo or a picture of one usually will have a great deal more difficulty comprehending a book or story about kangaroos than will a child who possesses such prior knowledge.

It also is important to understand that the more prior knowledge a child has, the less the printed material is needed. For example, a child who is very familiar with the Civil War usually will be able to skip more words while reading any type of material about the Civil War while retaining good comprehension than a child with limited prior knowledge about this period in American history.

It is exceedingly important both to assess and activate prior knowledge before reading to ensure the optimum comprehension possible of the material to be read. The teacher and/or child can use a number of different strategies to assess a child's prior knowledge. Some of the ways in which this assessment can be made are as follows: the Pre-Reading Procedure (PReP—illustrated later), noting a child's contributions to a class discussion about the topic to be read, the use of a semantic map or web, assessment of prior-knowledge activity sheets, questionnaire-inventories, the Anticipation Guide, and vocabulary overviews or advance organizers.

If children would assess and activate their prior knowledge before reading any type of narrative or expository (content) material, it would greatly improve their reading comprehension. Indeed, it is one of the very best ways of improving comprehension of what is read. Yet this requires no special material or cost, but rather just requires the child to have a "mind-set" to do so. **I cannot emphasize enough how very, very important this is.**

Description of the Pre-Reading Procedure (PReP)

The *Pre-Reading Procedure* can be used to assess and activate a child's prior knowledge before he or she reads a selection. It usually is the most effective with expository (content) reading material. Very briefly, here is how it can be used to assess prior knowledge:

1. The teacher chooses three major concepts from a 700- to 800-word content textbook passage. For example, from a passage about *weather,* the teacher might select the concepts: *jet stream, cold front,* and *warm front.*

2. The teacher then tells the children they will be using what they already know about the important ideas that will appear in the material they are going to read. The children are told that this prereading discussion will help the teacher to determine if any additional background discussion is needed before they read the material. They also are told that this discussion will help them activate their own prior knowledge of the material because readers comprehend new information most effectively by relating it to what they already know.

3. The children are to make associations with the first important concept. "Tell anything that comes to your mind when you hear the term *jet stream.*" The teacher then writes the children's responses in the form of a semantic map as illustrated here.

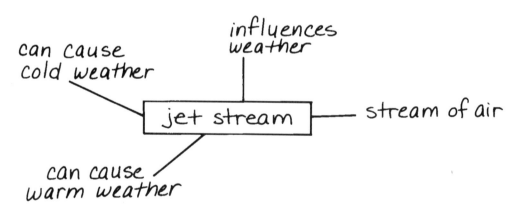

4. The next step is for the teacher to ask the children to think about their initial associations: "What do you think about _____?" This helps the children to better develop their associations with the concept being discussed.

5. The final step is to ask the children to rethink their knowledge about the concepts being discussed. The teacher can say: "Considering our discussion, do you have any new ideas about _____?" This step helps the children to understand new or modified associations formulated from the discussion. The procedure is repeated for each new concept.[18]

---

[18]Adapted from Judith A. Langer, "From Theory to Practice: A Prereading Plan," *Journal of Reading,* Volume 25 (November 1981), pp. 152–156.

This prereading discussion helps the teacher learn how much prior knowledge the child or children have about the topic to be read. If they have much prior knowledge, the responses will be in the form of a *superordinate concept. (The jet stream is often responsible for much of the weather in the Midwest.)* On the other hand, if the children lack prior knowledge in the topic, the responses are usually in the form of *examples.(The jet stream is a bunch of air.)*

Using Questionnaires and Inventories to Assess Prior Knowledge

Thomas G. Devine has described some indirect ways of assessing children's prior knowledge before reading. Most of them probably are the most relevant with expository (content material. Very briefly, here are some of the more useful ways:

1. *Simple questionnaires and inventories.* The teacher can have children complete a short 20- to 30-item questionnaire or inventory of questions that contains some true-false items, fill-in-the-blank items, and incomplete sentences items (only the first part of the statement is given).

2. *Open-ended inventories.* The children must write out responses to such questions as: *What do you now know about the continent of Australia?* or *The continent of Australia* _____

    _____

3. *Informal content checks.* These pretests help determine how much children know about an area before they have to study it.

4. *Informal concept checks.* The children list the words on the chalkboard that label the concept or the sentences containing the concepts. This technique helps the teacher locate children who have inaccurate schemata (prior knowledge) in that subject.

5. *Synonym and definition tests.* In these tests the teacher lists words and concepts on the chalkboard or an activity sheet with a parallel list of synonyms placed in correct order. The child must draw a line from each word to its synonym.[19]

A SAMPLE QUESTIONNAIRE-INVENTORY TO ASSESS PRIOR KNOWLEDGE

Page 336 is a sample questionnaire-inventory for assessing prior knowledge about the continent of Australia. It is on the approximate sixth-grade reading level. The questionnaire-inventory is followed by a brief inventory. This prereading device incorporates both structured and open-ended items. Although the reading teacher can reproduce and use it in its present form if it seems applicable, it is mainly designed to serve as a model for this type of device that reading teachers can construct.

---

[19]Adapted from Thomas G. Devine, *Teaching Reading Comprehension: From Theory to Practice.* Boston: Allyn and Bacon, 1986, pp. 79–81.

The answers are:

1. F
2. T
3. T
4. T
5. T
6. 1770
7. Sydney
8. difficult (hard)

9. many new immigrants to Australia
10. 600,000 new immigrants to Australia
11. wool
12. people to get much land for free and later become wealthy
13. pearls
14. outback (desert—not entirely correct but a good answer)
15. contributions

Name _____ Grade _____ Teacher _____ Date _____

QUESTIONNAIRE-INVENTORY FOR ASSESSING PRIOR KNOWLEDGE

(Approximate Sixth-Grade Reading Level)

In a few minutes you are going to read a story about the early history of the continent of Australia. The activity below tries to find out just how much you know about Australia before you read the story. Complete all of the items the best you can and then read the story to yourself. Then see how well you did on the items you marked.

1. **T** **F**   Captain James Cook was the first Englishman to set foot on Australian soil.

2. **T** **F**   The first English settlers to arrive in Australia were convicts and their guards.

3. **T** **F**   The original inhabitants of the continent of Australia were the aborigines.

4. **T** **F**   Australia experienced a Gold Rush similar to that in the United States and at about the same time.

5. **T** **F**   Cattle and wool made fortunes for some of the Australia immigrants.

6. Captain James Cook landed on the east coast of Australia in _____.

7. The first English settlers built a settlement named _____.

8. The first English settlers found life in Australia to be very _____.

9. In 1848 the Irish potato famine brought _____.

    _____.

10. In 1851 the discovery of gold in Australia brought _____.

    _____.

11. The raising of sheep made fortunes for some settlers who sold _____.

12. Squatting on uninhabited land in Australia allowed _____.

    _____.

13. Japanese came to Australia to dive for _____.

14. Camels were used for transportation in the Australian _____.

15. All of the immigrants to Australia made their own unique _____.

A BRIEF HISTORY OF AUSTRALIA

The continent of Australia has a most unique and colorful history unlike any other in the world. Although it is not well known, the buccaneer William Dampier was the first Englishman to set foot on Australian soil in 1688. He landed in the northwestern part of Western Australia. Although it is commonly thought that Captain James Cook was the first Englishman to land in Australia, he actually sailed into Botany Bay on the opposite east coast many years later in 1770.

At that time the British economy was very poor, and poverty and unemployment had overcrowded the jails with people whose crimes ranged from using bad language to murder. Since England needed a place to send inmates, Australia was chosen despite its immense distance.

The first shipment of prisoners arrived at what is now Port Jackson, near Botany Bay in 1788. At that time, Captain Arthur Phillip took possession of a large portion of eastern Australia, named it New South Wales, and enabled the first white settlers who were convicts and their prison guards to try to make a living from this harsh, alien land. Of course, the original inhabitants of Australia were the aborigines who had lived there for hundreds of years.

The new settlers eked out a hard life and built a settlement called Sydney. Extensive exploration of the continent of Australia occurred throughout the nineteenth century. The transportation of convicts to Australia ended in 1840, and the population of free settlers grew steadily. For example, during the Irish potato famine of 1848, thousands of poor Irish people emigrated to Australia.

The early part of the nineteenth century also brought German settlers to southern Australia and Italians to western Australia. However, the discovery of gold in Victoria and New South Wales in 1851 brought in about 600,000 new settlers. While prospectors were mining for gold, other new settlers cultivated the land and made fortunes in cattle and wool. Until about 1850, the practice of squatting (similar to the American idea of homesteading) turned poor farmers into wealthy landowners.

Later immigrants arrived to work in a variety of industries. For example, Chinese came to work in the gold fields; Pacific Islanders came to cut sugar cane; Japanese came to dive for pearls off the coast of western Australia; and Afghans arrived to wrangle camels in the Australian outback. All of these immigrants made their own unique contributions to the fascinating continent of Australia.

Reproducible Schema Assessment Device

Schema theory, which is related to prior knowledge, attempts to explain how a person stores information or knowledge in his or her mind, how the knowledge which is currently possessed is used, and how new knowledge is acquired. The term *schema* (the plural is *schemata*) deals with the structure of knowledge or information in the human mind. From the aspect of schema theory, reading can be defined as the following: an active search for meaning, a constructive process, an application of different kinds of knowledge, and a strategic process.

As one way of assessing a child's schema about a topic, you can put a list of terms on an activity sheet. Some of the terms should relate to the expository (content) material that is going to be read, while others should be unrelated. Have the child then place a check mark next to all of the terms on the list that he or she thinks are related to the material to be read. As an alternative, you can do this with a group of children by placing the terms on the chalkboard or a transparency. This section provides a reproducible schema assessment device at the intermediate-grade reading level that follows this format. You may duplicate this sheet, revise it in any way you want, or use it as a model for your own schema assessment device that your students can complete before they read any kind of expository (content) material.

The answers are:

gill nets	headdress
wall-eyed pike	balsam evergreens
birch-bark canoes	bow and arrows
fawn	harmony with nature
drums	forest
black bear	deerskin
moccasins	tribal

SCHEMA ASSESSMENT DEVICE

(Intermediate-Grade Reading Level)

Pretend that you are going to read a passage later about the **Chippewa band of Native Americans who live(d) in the states of Wisconsin and Minnesota**. Put a check mark in front of each term you believe probably would be included in the passage you will read.

_____ gill nets

_____ Pacific Ocean

_____ glacier

_____ wall-eyed pike

_____ birch-bark canoes

_____ fawn

_____ New York City

_____ drums

_____ black bear

_____ moccasins

_____ headdress

_____ desert

_____ balsam evergreens

_____ dragon

_____ bow and arrows

_____ harmony with nature

_____ Florida

_____ forest

_____ deerskin

_____ soybeans

_____ tribal

_____ diamonds

_____ plaid

_____ university

Brief Description of Reading Comprehension

Since *reading comprehension* is a very complex process, it is difficult to explain it simply. Very briefly, *comprehension is constructing and reconstructing meaning from the printed material.* It is an *interactive process* that requires the use of *prior knowledge* in combination with the *printed material.* When this definition is used, it is important to consider both the reader and the printed material. In the case of the reader, his or her prior knowledge about the material, interest in reading the material, purpose for reading the material, and ability to pronounce the words found in the material must be considered. In the case of the printed material, the number of difficult words, the syntax or sentence structure of the material, the length of the sentences in the material, and the format of the material must be taken into account.

Although both prior knowledge and the characteristics of the printed material must be considered, in most cases the reader's prior knowledge is the more important. In addition, the more prior knowledge a reader possesses, the less use he or she needs to make of the printed material. This is why a specialist in a particular area such as World War II history usually is able to read material in that area much more rapidly than is someone who does not have such extensive prior knowledge.

Contemporary research in comprehension also focuses on *schema theory,* which was described and illustrated earlier. Another recent focus of comprehension is *metacognition or self-monitoring,* which is concerned with the child's awareness of his or her own thinking as he or she is attempting to understand the printed material. It is important for a child to learn how to *monitor* his or her own comprehension. Research has shown that good readers are much better at monitoring their comprehension than are poor readers.

THE LEVELS OF READING COMPREHENSION

In the past comprehension skills often have been divided into three or four major categories: literal, interpretive, critical (can be considered an aspect of interpretive), and creative.

However, today comprehension is considered to be a language-based process that cannot really be divided into levels such as these. Instead, reading specialists state that there are two major categories of comprehension: **vocabulary knowledge (word meaning), and the understanding of the reading material.**

However, it is important to teach the most important elements of comprehension separately, at least sometimes, to all children, but perhaps especially to disabled readers and learning-disabled children. As an example, how can the reading teacher be sure that a child can answer interpretive ("Think and Search") questions if he or she does not make a concerted effort to ask this type of question?

Here are the different levels of comprehension and the more important subskills that comprise them.

Textually Explicit (Literal or Factual) Comprehension

- responding to "Right There" questions (found in the reading material)
- locating directly stated main ideas

- locating significant and irrelevant details
- placing a number of items in correct sequence or order
- reading and carrying out directions

Textually Implicit (Interpretive or Inferential) Comprehension

- responding to "Think and Search" questions (the reader has to deduce the answers from reading the material)
- drawing conclusions and generalizations
- predicting the outcomes
- summarizing what has been read
- sensing the author's mood and purpose
- locating implied main ideas

Critical (Textually Implicit or Evaluative) Reading

- responding to "Think and Search" questions (the reader has to evaluate the reading material)
- discriminating between real and make-believe (fact and fantasy)
- evaluating the accuracy or truthfulness of the reading material
- comparing information from several different printed sources
- sensing an author's biases
- recognizing such propaganda techniques as the bandwagon technique, testimonials, card-stacking, and emotionally toned words

Scriptually Implicit (Script Implicit, Schema Implicit, Creative, or Applied) Comprehension

- responding to "On My Own" questions (the reader has to combine prior knowledge with the printed material to arrive at new knowledges or actions)
- applying the knowledge gained from reading to one's own problem-solving
- bibliotherapy (solving a problem through reading about a similar problem)
- art activities as a follow-up to reading
- rhythm activities as a follow-up to reading
- cooking and baking activities as a follow-up to reading
- creative writing of prose and poetry (including the use of invented spelling if necessary)
- construction activities as a follow-up to reading
- creative dramatics and socio-drama
- puppetry
- scientific experiments
- creative book reports
- any reading that appeals to the emotions (affective aspect of reading)

Questioning Strategies or QARs

In several research studies, Taffy Raphael and P. David Pearson taught children three kinds of *question-answer relationships or questioning strategies* (**QARs**). QAR instruction encourages children to consider both the information found in their own prior knowledge and the reading material when answering questions. The relationship for questions with answers directly stated in the material in one sentence was called "Right There." The researchers encouraged the children to look for words in the questions and read the sentence containing the answer.

However, the relationship for questions with an answer in the story that required information from a number of sentences or paragraphs was called "Think and Search." The relationship for questions for which the answer had to come from the child's own prior knowledge was called "On My Own."

In the research studies *modeling the decision* about the type of QAR that a question constituted was an important part of teaching the children the concept of QARs. *Supervised practice* following the teacher modeling with immediate feedback of children's responses was also very important. The practice involved gradually increasing passage lengths, thus progressing from simpler to more difficult tasks. The children in the study who were taught the three types of QARs were able to answer questions more successfully than did the children in a control group. Average and below-average children had the greatest improvement after training in the use of QARs. However, primary-grade children needed more repetition to learn QARs than did intermediate-grade children.

Later, Raphael modified QAR instruction to include four categories, clustered under two different headings. The following diagram illustrates her modification:

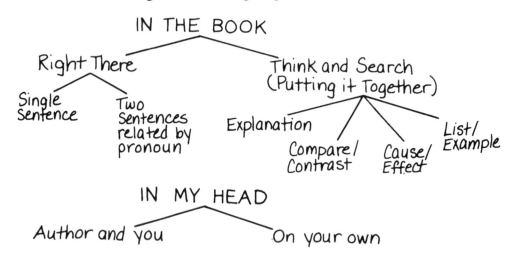

In the modified plan, the "In My Head" category is divided into questions that involve both the reader's prior knowledge (Author and You) and the text information and those that can be answered from the reader's experience without any information from the material (On My Own).

Discussing the use of QAR categorization to plan questioning strategies, Raphael stated: Questions asked prior to reading are usually On My Own

QARs. They are designed to help students think about what they already know and how it relates to the upcoming story or content text. In creating guided reading questions, it is important to balance text-based and inference questions. For these, Think and Search QARs should dominate, since they require integration of information and should build to the asking of Author and You QARs. Finally, for extension activities, teachers will want to create primarily On My Own or Author and You QARs focusing again on students' background information as it pertains to the text.[20]

It is very important for reading and learning disability teachers to be aware of the concept of three types of QARs or questioning strategies in both *assessing* and *improving* comprehension ability. In the past far too many teachers have asked a majority of the "Right There" questions that did not allow for inferencing or the use of the child's prior knowledge in combination with the printed material. If the child has not been asked many "Think and Search" or "On My Own" questions, it is not logical to assume he or she ever will become competent in answering these kinds of questions. Although contemporary reading teachers are asking more higher-level comprehension questions than in the past, we all should be very much aware of the importance of doing so on a regular basis for all children, including those with reading and learning disabilities.

Using Metacognition for Assessing Reading Comprehension

As explained earlier, *metacognitive strategies or self-monitoring of comprehension ability* have been stressed a great deal lately as one way of both assessing and improving comprehension skills. *Metacognition* means teaching children to think about or monitor their own comprehension. Often children with reading difficulties are unable to monitor their own comprehension as well as the typical good or average readers. For example, disabled readers often have difficulty with such reading skills as:

- Understanding the purpose for reading a selection
- Considering how new information relates to what is already known
- Modifying their reading strategies for different purposes and different types of reading
- Evaluating the reading material to see if it is complete and consistent
- Not knowing what *fix-up* strategies to use when not comprehending
- Determining the important and unimportant information in the material
- Deciding how well the material has been comprehended

Children in the primary grades can make a start in metacognition and self-monitoring that can be refined at the middle and upper reading levels. They should learn to

---

[20]Figure 1 from "Teaching Question-Answer Relationships, revisited," Taffy E. Raphael, *The Reading Teacher,* February 1986. Reprinted with permission of Taffy E. Raphael and the International Reading Association.

recognize what parts of reading may cause them comprehension difficulties and what to do when this occurs. They also should understand the great importance of always reading for meaning.

EXAMPLES OF A SELF-MONITORING (METACOGNITIVE) OR SELF-CORRECTION ASSESSMENT DEVICE AND A SAMPLE METACOGNITIVE CHECKLIST

The chapter now contains reproducible examples of both a self-monitoring (metacognitive) assessment device and a sample metacognitive checklist. You can duplicate either of them in their present form if they seem applicable or modify them in any way you wish.

The answers are:

1. c	9. a
2. a	10. a
3. a	11. a
4. a	12. a
5. b	13. d
6. d	14. c
7. a	15. a
8. b	

Name _____ Grade _____ Teacher _____ Date _____

SELF-MONITORING (METACOGNITIVE) OR SELF-CORRECTING ASSESSMENT DEVICE
(Intermediate-Grade Reading Level)

For each question choose the one statement that tells the best thing to do <u>before you read</u> a story, book, or content textbook to help you understand it the best. Then circle the letter in front of each of these statements.

1. Before I begin reading, it's very helpful to
    a. summarize the first part of the material
    b. count how many pages are found in the material
    c. make some predictions about what might happen in the material
    d. ask my best friend if the material is easy or hard to understand

2. Before I begin reading, I always should
    a. preview the material, looking at the main headings, subheadings, pictures, diagrams, graphs, and tables
    b. make a guess as to how long it will take me to read the material
    c. see if the material probably will make sense to me
    d. underline all of the hard words in the material

3. Before I begin reading, it's very helpful to
    a. read the title of the story, book or textbook chapter to myself
    b. reread the hardest part of the material
    c. look through the material to find all of the syllables
    d. use the dictionary or glossary to look up the meanings of the unknown words in the material

4. Before I begin reading, it's very helpful to
    a. ask myself some important questions I want to have answered from reading the material
    b. focus on learning only one very important concept about the material
    c. make sure that I know all of the words before I start
    d. up information about the copyright date of the book (when the book was published)

5. Before I begin reading, it's very helpful to know
    a. how rapidly I should read the material
    b. why I am supposed to read the material
    c. who the author or authors of the story or book are
    d. how many easy words are found in the material

For each question choose the one statement that tells the best thing to do <u>while you are reading</u> a story, book, or content textbook to help you understand it the best. Then circle the letter in front of each of these statements.

6. While I'm reading, it's very helpful to
    a. look at how many pages I have left to read
    b. skip the paragraphs that seem too boring
    c. ask my friend if he or she has read the material
    d. see if I can very briefly retell what has happened or what I have learned so far

7. While I'm reading, I should
    a. revise any predictions I made that were not right
    b. skip all of the hard words
    c. slowly read each word in the material
    d. read only the first sentence in each paragraph

8. While I'm reading, it's very helpful to
   a. look up all of the unknown words in the dictionary
   b. see if I can answer most of the questions I asked before I read the material
   c. read the title or heading another time
   d. read the material aloud to a friend

9. While I'm reading, it's very helpful to
   a. reread any parts of the material I couldn't understand
   b. skim all of the material
   c. decide what I haven't liked about reading the material
   d. count how many pages of the material I have already read

10. While I'm reading, it's very helpful to
    a. see if most of my predictions were right
    b. see how many pictures are found in the material
    c. ask my teacher why the material is so difficult to read
    d. think about the main reason for reading the material

For each question, choose the one statement that tells the best thing to help you understand a story, book, or content textbook <u>after you have finished reading it.</u> Then circle the letter in front of each of these statements.

11. When I've finished reading, it's very helpful to
    a. decide if my predictions were mostly correct or incorrect
    b. count how many pages there were in the material
    c. see if I liked the pictures in the material
    d. look up the meanings of the difficult words in the dictionary

12. When I've finished reading, it's very helpful to
    a. retell all of the main points to see if I've understood the material
    b. decide if the title or heading made sense
    c. reread the entire material silently
    d. count how many pictures were in the material

13. When I've finished reading, it's very helpful to
    a. count how many words I had to look up in the dictionary
    b. ask my friend if he or she understood the material
    c. read the first part of the material again
    d. tell a friend some of the most important things I learned from reading the material

14. When I've finished reading, it's very helpful to
    a. reread the title or heading
    b. make a list of the things I didn't understand
    c. summarize the material in my own mind or in writing
    d. make some new predictions

15. When I've finished reading, it's very helpful to
    a. review the major things I got out of reading the material
    b. find out who wrote the material
    c. find out the copyright date of the material (when it was published)
    d. reread the entire material silently

Name _____ Grade _____ Teacher _____ Date _____

SELF-MONITORING CHECKLIST
OF READING COMPREHENSION SKILLS

(Upper Primary-Grade or Intermediate-Grade Reading Level)

	Yes	No
1. Do I already know something about what this material may be about?	❏	❏
2. Do I need to ask myself some questions about what the material might be about before I read it?	❏	❏
3. Do I understand why I am going to read this material?	❏	❏
4. Do I need to predict what the material will be about before I read it?	❏	❏
5. Do I need to know how fast I should read the material?	❏	❏
6. Do I need to read every word of the material carefully or can I skip some of the words?	❏	❏
7. Do I need to read all of the material more than once to understand it?	❏	❏
8. Do I need to read the first sentence of each paragraph more than once?	❏	❏
9. Do I know what I should do if I meet a word that I don't understand?	❏	❏
10. Do I usually look up the meaning of unknown words either in the dictionary or in the glossary of the book?	❏	❏
11. Am I able to answer most of my teacher's questions after I have finished reading the material?	❏	❏
12. Am I able to remember what I have read well enough to retell it when I've finished reading?	❏	❏
13. Am I able to remember what I have read well enough to answer most of the questions on a test about the material?	❏	❏
14. Am I able to decide what information in the material is important and what is not important?	❏	❏
15. Am I able to state the main idea of the material after I have finished reading it?	❏	❏

Brief Description of "Think-Alouds"

"Think-alouds" are one strategy you can use to determine an intermediate-grade, middle-school, or secondary-school student's self-monitoring (metacognitive) or thinking processes while he or she is reading. "Think-alouds" mandate one-on-one interaction with the teacher and student although it is theoretically possible, but difficult, to tape record a child's responses as he or she is completing the reproducible "think-aloud" included in this chapter.

"Think-alouds" can be defined as the verbalization of a reader's processes *before, during, and after reading.* They can provide a framework for assessment that is integrated with instruction. To assess comprehension in process, children are asked to read a portion of material and then verbalize their thoughts. You can ask a child to report his or her thoughts as he or she gives a play-by-play account of where he or she is intellectually as he or she tries to figure out the reading.

"Think-alouds" have a long history in reading instruction dating back to Edmund Huey's 1908 research study on using *retrospection and introspection* to analyze college students' understanding of vocabulary terms. There recently has been some increase in using reader's "think-aloud" protocols while studying his or her behaviors. Myers and Lytle suggested the use of "think-aloud" protocols as part of what they called *process assessment,* a model for assessing children with learning problems. Their model evaluates the processes of learning by focusing on the task, the child, and the environment.[21]

Lytle also developed an interesting model that can be used in evaluating "think-alouds." Her *Types of Moves* contained six major categories and a *move* was defined as the "verbal response to readers to sentences in the text" or what readers do as they make their way through text.

The six major categories you can consider as you evaluate a child's "think-alouds" are as follows:

- *Monitoring*—"I don't understand that." "This just doesn't make sense to me." Demonstrated by statements or questions indicating the child doubts his or her understanding (including conflict).

- *Signaling*—"What do I understand?" Demonstrated by statements in which the child signals his or her current understanding of the reading material's meaning (agrees, paraphrases, summarizes).

- *Analyzing*—"Just how does this material work?" Demonstrated by statements in which the child viewing the reading material notices, describes, or comments on the features of the material (words, sentences, structure, style). Thus, for the purpose of observing a child's sense of text structure, the reader would expect to see this move within the "think aloud" process.

---

[21]From " Assessment of the learning process" by Joel Myers and Susan Lytle, *Exceptional Children,* 53, 1986, pp. 138–144. Copyright 1986 by The Council for Exceptional Children. Reprinted with permission.

- *Judging*—"How good is this?" Demonstrated by statements indicating the reader is evaluating the reading material (ideas or text features).

- *Reasoning*—"How can I figure this out?" "What might _____ mean?"Demonstrated by statements or questions indicating the reader is trying to resolve doubts, and interpret the reading material (hypothesis, prediction, question, use of evidence).

- *During the observation of a child's "think-aloud," you can use prompts such as these while the child verbalizes his or her responses while reading for the "think-aloud":*

  "Did you just figure out something?"

  "You look confused. Can you tell me what you're thinking?"

  "Just a minute. I don't know what you're thinking. How did you get from thinking about crops to thinking about cities?"

  "I think I may have gotten something wrong here. I wrote down _____, I don't think that's what you said, is it?"

However, you should always make it clear that it is *you* who is responsible for the misunderstanding, not the child. Once a child understands that you may have this kind of problem, he or she begins to elaborate statements for you even before you ask him or her to.

Although you may well think of many additional creative ways of using "think-alouds" with your students, here is one very good way to go about a "think-aloud" session focusing on a student's *understanding of text structure*. The text that the student is to read should be similar to the normal text he or she is required to read for your class. Tell the child he or she will be reading a story or text that is *mixed-up*. Ask the child to read each section of the text you have cut apart between paragraph boundaries and shuffled. It is helpful to have each section color coded. As an example, you might code the beginning red, the middle blue, and so on. That way, it will be relatively easy to relate students' "think-aloud" commentaries with various sections of the story. To prepare the material for a session, simply shuffle the text sections into random order as you would a deck of cards. It is also a good idea to tape record the session for later analysis.

You need to write a script to introduce a student to a "think-aloud" session so that the process will go well. The following script is adapted from Lytle.

I am going to give you a story (or text) to read and put together the way you, as an author, would write it. The story (or text) is divided into paragraph sections that are mixed up. Call each section by the colored dot on it.

Read each section to yourself silently. Tell me the color before you begin reading. Then read the section and tell me what you are doing and thinking about as you try to see where this section fits in the entire story. I will just listen and not nod or say anything at all: in fact, this is more like talking to yourself—"thinking aloud." I am interested in what you say to yourself as you read, what you are thinking about as you go along.

After you have read the first color-coded section and told everything you are thinking, go on to the next section mentioning its color. In a way, you are then telling what you are thinking about two sections of the story (or text), and then three, and so on—kind of news bulletins or play-by-play descriptions of where you are in your thoughts as you try to figure out how to put the story together so that it makes sense.

If you get stuck or have trouble understanding, I would like to hear about that also and try to figure out a solution to what's puzzling you.

After you have read and talked about each section, and put the story together the way you as an author think it should go, I'd like to have you reflect for awhile and then tell me your own sense of what the story was about. You can look back at the story if you like, but try to recall the basic ideas in your own words.

While you are doing this, I will say nothing. I will have a small notebook open because I may want to write a few notes to myself—things that occur to me as you talk about the story. I know I will have the tape to listen to but I have found that I sometimes can't remember ideas unless I write them down.[22]

REPRODUCIBLE EXAMPLE OF A STORY THAT CAN BE USED FOR A "THINK-ALOUD"

The following is a reproducible story at approximately the fifth-grade reading level that you can use for a "think-aloud." You should first reproduce it, cut it apart at the dotted lines, color code it, and then laminate it for durability. Then have the child follow the procedure for reading it and "thinking-aloud" which was described earlier. You can then tape record it and also take notes on the commentaries if you wish. The same procedure can be followed for any reading material you want to reproduce and cut apart.

---

[22]S. L. Lytle, "Exploring Comprehension Style: A Study of Twelfth Grade Readers' Transactions with Text," Unpublished doctoral dissertation, University of Pennsylvania, 1982. *Dissertation Abstract International,* 43, 2205-A.

KANGAROOS

Kangaroos are truly fascinating animals. These interesting animals live in the countries of Australia, New Zealand, Tasmania, and New Guinea. All kangaroos belong to the family of <u>marsupials,</u> or animals with pouches.

A baby kangaroo is born after only about thirty days. It is called a <u>joey</u> and is so small that it is only the size of a quarter and weighs much less than an ounce. In fact, six newborn baby kangaroos could fit into only one teaspoon!

The joey lives all of the time in its mother's pouch where it gets its food, warmth, and protection for about six months. Then it leaves for the first time but returns to her pouch at the first sign of danger.

When a kangaroo is fully grown, it moves by hopping on its powerful hind legs. Most kangaroos do not eat meat, but are vegetarians. Kangaroos usually live about four to six years in the wild, and their main enemy are packs of wild dogs called <u>dingoes</u>. However, kangaroos can protect themselves by kicking with their strong hind legs and also by biting.

In summary, kangaroos fascinate most people whether they live in zoos, an animal preserve, or the wild. They are just so unique that most people find learning about them very interesting.

Brief Description of Creative Book Sharing

Children should be given many opportunities to share the books they have read independently to acknowledge their efforts and accomplishments in reading. They also can learn much from hearing about what their classmates have read. Traditional book reports have mainly been replaced by many different kinds of creative, naturalistic responses to literature. Indeed, many adults have told me that traditional book reports more than any single other factor have turned them off reading for pleasure.

Responses to children's literature can be evaluated in the following ways:

- Did the response show that the student knew the story line (narrative material) or main idea (expository material)?
- Did the student simply retell the text or relate it to his or her own experiences?
- Did the response show that the child is thinking clearly and logically?
- Did the response show that the child is making connections between this book and other pieces of literature?

Students can react thoughtfully to what they have read by writing in *reading (literature) logs* or critically reviewing books on note cards that are filed for other students to read. Children should keep *reading logs (records)* of books they have read. The following is a good way for a *primary-grade child* to keep records of his or her reading:

Books I've Read
Title **Author**

Here is a good way for an *intermediate-grade child* to keep records of his or her reading:

Recreational Reading Record			
Title	**Author/Illustrator**	**Publisher**	**Comments**

There are numerous creative ways for a child to share his or her reading that can take the place of the traditional book report. Here are some of the more useful ways:

- Let children make original book jackets for favorite books by illustrating the cover, writing a brief biographical sketch of the author on one flap, and writing a "blurb" on the other flap to make the book sound appealing.
- Ask each child to prepare an annotated list of his or her favorite books and then get together with other students to alphabetize the combined lists and compile a class bibliography for other students to use. A computer would be helpful for this activity since it would make changes very easy.

- Have the child write a letter to the author or a character in the book.
- Have the child create an advertisement or poster to sell the book to other children.
- Have the child write a poem about one of the characters in the book.
- Have the child design a travel brochure for one of the locations mentioned in the book.
- Have the child write a cinquain about his or her book. Here is an example of a cinquain from the book *Charlotte's Web* by E. B. White.

> Charlotte (*one noun*)
> Unselfish, kind (*two adjectives*)
> Killing, weaving, dying (*three verbs*)
> She was very caring. (*four-word sentence*)
> Spider (*one noun*)

- Have the child write captions for the illustrations in the book.
- Have one child pantomime a character as another child reads a portion of the book aloud. For example, a child can pantomime the peddler Solomon Joseph Azar as he searches for the American dream after leaving his homeland of Lebanon, while another student reads a portion of the book *A Peddler's Dream* by Tom Schefelman (Houghton Mifflin, 1992).
- Have a child read a biography of a famous person from history and write a story about what might happen if that person lived today.
- Have a group of students present a Reader's Theater production of a book they have read. They should write a script by removing extraneous parts of the material, shortening long speeches, and eliminating unnecessary descriptions or transitional material. They can gather minimal props if they will enhance the production, practice their parts, and present the Reader's Theater to other class members and other audiences. *The Bracelet* by Yoshiko Uchida (Philomel, 1993) is a good book for intermediate-grade children to present in this format.
- Have the child develop alternate endings to books.
- Have the child add or take out characters and rewrite books.
- Have the child make a diorama from the book. This requires the child to study the descriptive passages of the book and do additional research if necessary.
- Puppetry is very helpful in dramatizing a book. The following are various kinds of puppets:

    hand puppets (the head is moved by the index finger and the arms by the third finger and thumb)

    rod puppets (controlled by one or more rigid rods to which the puppet is attached)

    paper bag puppets

    Styrofoam puppets

papier-mâché puppets

sock puppets

A Puppet Theater may be a sturdy wooden theater mounted on wheels that can be moved from room to room or a cardboard carton that is kept in the classroom.

- Have several children create a mural about one book or several books.

- Have the child design cartoon representations of a book that he or she has read.

- Have the child design a mobile beginning with a theme and a plan for developing that theme. Tiny objects or two-dimensional cutouts of characters are attached to nylon thread, fishing line, or fine wire and are suspended from rods or some sort of frame. The balancing rods may be cut from metal coat hangers, or children can use a tree branch or umbrella frame for support. The mobile must be carefully balanced so that objects can move freely.

- Have the children place mini-reviews of favorite books they want to recommend to classmates on a bulletin board.

- There are many creative artistic ways for a child to respond to a book, which can vary depending upon the content of the book. For example, in the book *Switching Stars,* Mary Lyons writes about the life of Harriet Powers, who created her stories through quilts. Harriet took quilting to new levels with her creative story quilts. Have the child(ren) make a quilt out of pieces of cloth or construction paper. This book is part of a series about African-American artists and artisans (Scribner, 1993).

There are countless other ways in which a child can share his or her reactions and feelings about a book. If you want additional creative ways for children to share their reading, here are some useful resources:

Bernice E. Cullinan, ed., *Children's Literature in the Reading Program.* Newark, DE: International Reading Association, 1987.

Patricia Tyler Muncy, *Hooked on Books! Activities and Projects That Make Kids Love to Read.* West Nyack, NY: The Center for Applied Research in Education, 1995.

Mary Lou Olsen, *Creative Connections: Literature and the Reading Program, Grades 1–3.* Littleton, CO: Libraries Unlimited, 1987.

Shirley C. Raines and Robert J. Canady, *Story Stretchers: Activities to Expand Children's Favorite Books.* Mt. Rainier, MD: Gryphon House, 1989.

REPRODUCIBLE EXAMPLES OF CREATIVE BOOK SHARING

Here are several reproducible examples of creative book sharing. You can duplicate and use them in their present form if you wish or modify them in any way you want. Remember, they are just examples of what can be done.

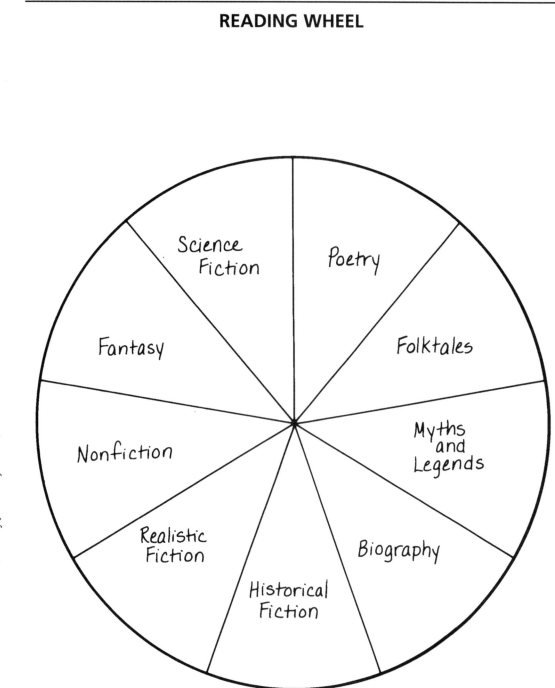

BOOKWORM

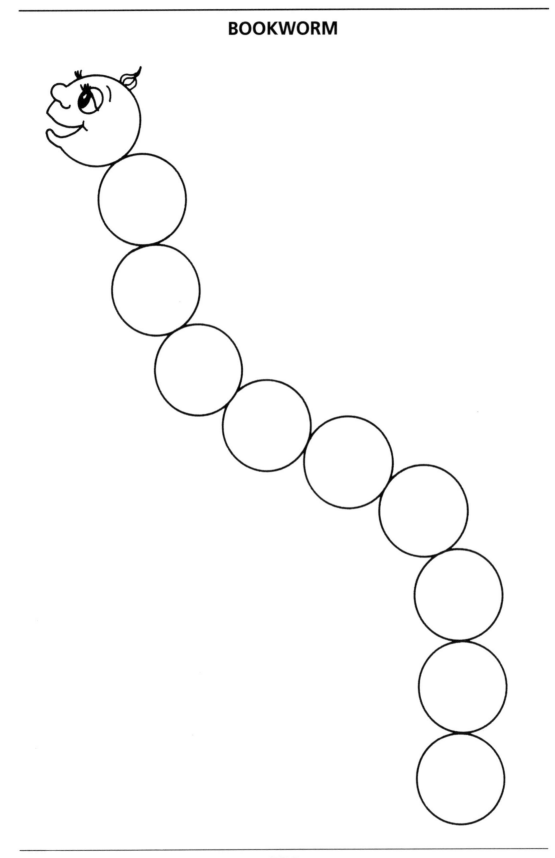

ROCKET SHIP

Read eight books to make your rocket ship blast off!

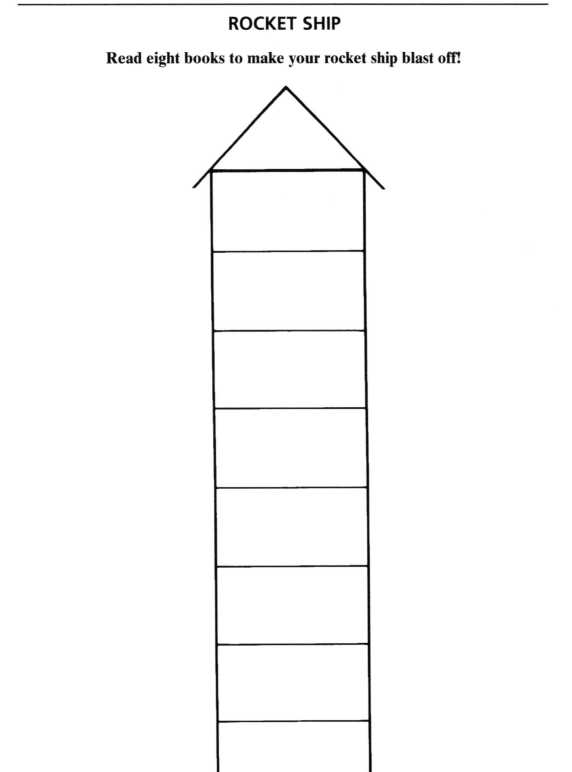

Brief Description of Story Frames

Gerald W. Fowler wrote a valuable article in which he showed how *story frames* can be used to assess both story grammar skills and comprehension skills. A story frame consists of a series of incomplete sentences that deal with the elements of a story. After a child has read a story, he or she can fill in the blank spaces in the frame. Oral discussion can either precede or follow the story frame activity. Evaluation of a child's responses on the story frame should include an examination of his or her knowledge of story structure and comprehension of the story.

Fowler illustrated several types of story frames, several of which are reproduced next in this section. He suggested using only one story frame at the beginning. Probably the first story could be placed on an overhead projector following the reading of a story so that a group of children can complete it with teacher direction. There often is no exact response for a blank in a story frame. After a child has had some experience with this technique, he or she often can complete the story frame independently after reading a story. After a child has had some practice with story frames, he or she can work on more than one story frame simultaneously. However, not all story frames are equally appropriate for all stories.[23]

REPRODUCIBLE STORY FRAMES

Here are a number of reproducible story frames. You can duplicate any of them in their present form or modify them in any way you wish.

---

[23]Adapted from story frames from "Developing comprehension skills in primary students through the use of story frames," Gerald W. Fowler, *The Reading Teacher*, November 1982. Copyright by the International Reading Association.

STORY FRAMES[24]
(Intermediate-Grade Reading Level)

Story Summary with One Character Included

The story is about _____. _____ is an important character in the story. _____ tried to _____. The story ends when _____.

Important Idea or Plot

In this story the problem starts when _____. Next, _____. Then, _____. The problem is finally solved when _____. The story ends _____.

Setting

This story takes place _____. I know this because the author uses the words "_____." Other clues that show when the story takes place are _____ _____.

Character Analysis

_____ is an important character in the story. _____ is important because _____. Once, he/she _____ _____Another time, he/she _____ _____. I think that _____ (character's name) is _____ because _____ (character trait) _____.

Character Comparison

_____ and _____ are two characters in the story. _____ (another character's name) is _____ (character trait) while _____ (another character's name) is _____ (character trait). For example, _____ tries to _____ and _____ tries to _____. _____ learns a lesson when _____.

© 1995 by John Wiley & Sons, Inc.

---

[24]Adapted from the article by Gerald W. Fowler which was cited in footnote 23.

Name _____ Grade _____ Teacher _____ Date _____

BASIC STORY FRAME

(Intermediate-Grade Reading Level)

The most important character in this story is _____.

The supporting characters are _____

_____.

The story takes place _____

_____.

The major problem in the story is _____

_____

_____.

Some of the most important events in the story are _____

_____

_____

_____

_____

_____.

The problem is solved when _____

_____

_____

_____.

The author wanted me to believe that _____

_____

_____.

I liked (didn't like) this story because _____

_____

_____.

Brief Description of a QAD Chart

Question-answer-detail (QAD) charts require children to provide details that support their answers to specific questions. Although a QAD chart can be used with either narrative or expository (content) material, it may be more useful with expository material. In constructing a QAD, the teacher or the child formulate questions to important points in the reading material. After reading the material, the child with a partner(s) or independently writes the answers to the questions with the supporting details without referring to the material.

The inability to answer questions on a QAD chart may indicate inadequate retention of the reading material. For example, a child's responses may be logical but derived from experiences other than from the material. Some children will answer the questions quickly and accurately but have difficulty in supplying the details. They are not able to justify the responses they have made. Since the purpose of a QAD chart is to elicit responses that are accurate, children may need to refer to the reading material to complete the chart. However, the main reason for using the QAD technique is to help children organize information and develop retention. Therefore, they should gradually refer less and less to the reading material as they complete QAD charts.

QAD charts can provide diagnostic information about a child's *comprehension, retention, and understanding of relationships among the details* in the material. The charts provide an organizational structure that facilitates *remembering*. According to schema theory, this type of structure is necessary for the remembering and retrieval of information. In addition, QAD charts may improve metacognitive thinking strategies because readers must justify answers when they supply supporting details.

REPRODUCIBLE EXAMPLE OF A QAD CHART

The chapter now contains a reproducible model of a QAD chart at about the sixth-grade level. Have the child read the material about the Panama Canal first and then attempt to complete the QAD chart. It will probably be helpful to have several children read the material and then try to complete the QAD chart together, although it also is possible for a child to complete it independently.

You can use this material in its present form or modify it in any way you wish. More important, you can use it as a model for constructing your own QAD charts based on the narrative or expository (content) reading material you are using in your own classroom.

The answers are:

Answer	Detail
1. the Panama Canal	a way for ships to travel between the Atlantic and Pacific Oceans
2. George Washington Goethels	he was in charge of the construction of the Panama Canal; a great engineer

3. the workers getting ill

malaria; yellow fever; both diseases could have killed many of the workers building the Panama Canal

4. make a cut through them

landslides; lots of dirt fell on the machinery and filled the cut again; took a lot of time and work

5. the big locks

they fill and empty with water; raise and lower the ships 85 feet

6. 1914

took two years to build

7. "mules"

electric locomotives; 4 to 10 are needed to pull each ship

8. seven to eight hours

must go through a series of locks; must be pulled by "mules"; ships cannot travel through the canal without help

9. cruise ships

cruise ships and freighters still travel through the canal regularly

QAD CHART

(Sixth-Grade Reading Level)

Read the following passage about the Panama Canal to yourself. Then complete the **QAD Chart** on the next page. You will need to answer each question and then write the details that helped you to answer that question. <u>Do not look back at the passage unless your teacher tells you that you can. You should be able to complete the chart without referring back to the material. You can work with one or several partners if you want to.</u>

THE PANAMA CANAL

For many years the United States had wanted a short, quick way for ships to travel between the Atlantic and Pacific Oceans instead of having to sail all the way around South America. In 1904 the construction of the Panama Canal was begun under the direction of John F. Wallace, an American engineer with an international reputation. However, after awhile George Washington Goethals became the chief engineer, and it was he who really was in charge of the construction of the canal.

One of the greatest difficulties in building the canal was trying to eliminate malaria and yellow fever from the Canal Zone that otherwise would have killed many construction workers. This chiefly was accomplished by Dr. William Gorgas who literally made the construction of the Panama Canal possible.

There were three major challenges to be overcome in building the canal. They were constructing an enormous dam to control the dangerous Chagres River and create a lake, making a deep cut through the mountains whose top was the Continental Divide, and building giant locks at each end of the canal to move ships up and down 85 feet.

The actual construction of the canal presented many difficult problems. For example, making the cut through the mountains caused many landslides that made many thousands of tons of earth to plunge into the cut, making much extra work and destroying machinery.

The Panama Canal was finished in 1914 at a cost of $366,650,000. The canal is just over forty miles long from shore to shore with ten miles more of deepened channel entrances at the two ends. Ships are towed through the locks by electric locomotives called "mules." About four to ten "mules" are required to tow each ship, and the entire trip through the canal takes about seven to eight hours, with the ship being raised and lowered by a series of locks that are filled and emptied of water.

Even today people are very interested in traveling through the Panama Canal. For example, a number of cruise ships make ten-day cruises that feature traveling through the canal, and these cruises are very popular.

QAD CHART

Question	Answer	Detail
1. What was this passage about?		
2. Who was the chief engineer of the Panama Canal?		
3. What was the greatest difficulty in building the Panama Canal?		
4. What did the workers have to do to the top of the mountains?		
5. What helps a ship go up and down as it travels between the Atlantic and Pacific Oceans?		
6. In what year was the Panama Canal finished?		
7. What pulls a ship through the locks of the Panama Canal?		
8. How long does it usually take a ship to travel through the Panama Canal?		
9. How do you know that after more than 80 years the Panama Canal is still being used?		

Brief Description of the Reading Autobiography

The *reading autobiography* can be used to determine information about how a student learned to read. This type of information may be useful in understanding the types of reading difficulties a student has at the present time. If you understand the types of reading problems a student has and their causes, you may be better able to help the child correct them.

There are two types of reading autobiographies—the *structured reading autobiography* and the *open-ended reading autobiography.* Although either of them is most useful with students in the intermediate grades, children in the primary grades may be able to respond to the structured reading autobiography, especially if the questions are read aloud to him or her.

In administering a structured reading autobiography, you simply ask the student to read each question silently and then check *yes* or *no.* If you wish to give this type of device to a younger child, as stated earlier, or to a severely disabled reader, you may have to read each question aloud to the student. In evaluating this device, you can determine when a student began to have difficulty with reading instruction. You also may be able to determine which reading skills, such as graphophonic analysis or comprehension, cause a student the greatest amount of difficulty. You also can ascertain his or her present attitudes toward reading.

The open-ended reading autobiography is very easy to administer since the student reads the directions silently. In evaluating this device, you can notice the student's sentence structure and spelling to ascertain his or her achievement in these language arts. You also can notice the grade level at which he or she began having difficulty with reading. You may also be able to determine the student's present attitudes toward reading.

REPRODUCIBLE EXAMPLES OF READING AUTOBIOGRAPHIES

Here are reproducible examples of both the structured and open-ended reading autobiographies. You can use them in their present form or modify them in any way you wish. You also may be able to adapt them for use at the primary-grade reading level.

STRUCTURED READING AUTOBIOGRAPHY

(Intermediate-Grade Level)

	Yes	No
1. When you were small, did anyone in your family read to you quite often?	❏	❏
2. When you were small, were there books in your home for you to look at and read?	❏	❏
3. When you were in first grade, did you like learning to read?	❏	❏
4. When you were in the primary grades, was it hard for you to remember words you saw in books?	❏	❏
5. When you were in the primary grades, did you have trouble sounding out words?	❏	❏
6. When you were in the primary grades, did you have trouble understanding what you read?	❏	❏
7. Do you think you are a good reader now?	❏	❏
8. Do you have any difficulty with reading now? If you do, what about reading is hard for you?	❏	❏
9. Do you now enjoy reading for pleasure?	❏	❏
10. Do you have a library card now?	❏	❏
11. Have you been to the public library within the last month?	❏	❏
12. Would you rather watch television than read?	❏	❏
13. Do you enjoy reading in bed?	❏	❏
14. Do you read as fast as you would like to?	❏	❏
15. Do you ever read aloud to younger children?	❏	❏
16. Are there books and magazines in your home for you to read?	❏	❏
17. Do you enjoy reading paperback books?	❏	❏
18. Do you read the newspaper regularly?	❏	❏
19. Do you like to read assignments in social studies textbooks?	❏	❏
20. Do you like to read assignments in science textbooks?	❏	❏

OPEN-ENDED READING AUTOBIOGRAPHY

(Intermediate-Grade Level)

You can write at this time about how you learned to read and how you feel about reading now. Do you remember how you were taught to read in first grade? How did you do in reading in first grade? At that time, do you remember what part of reading was the hardest for you? Did you have trouble remembering the words you saw in your books? How did you do in reading in second and third grades? Did you ever have trouble sounding out words? Have you ever had trouble understanding what you read? Today, what do you enjoy most about reading? What kind of books do you enjoy reading? Today, what is the hardest part about reading for you? Why do you think you have trouble with this part of reading, if you do?

_____

_____

_____

_____

_____

_____

_____

_____

_____

_____

_____

_____

_____

_____

_____

_____

_____

Continue on another sheet of paper if necessary.

Brief Description of a Self-Appraisal of Reading Ability

Assessment should help students develop the ability to evaluate their own accomplishments—to formulate their own goals, decide on how to achieve those goals, and assess their progress toward attaining those goals—in order to experience a sense of ownership in the assessment process. In many ways a student's own assessment of his or her work is the most important aspect of evaluation because when a student knows what he or she does well and is able to determine what he or she still needs to learn, the student can be a truly independent learner.

Students who display this kind of self-appraisal are aware of how they learn and of their own strengths and weaknesses in relation to specific learning tasks. They ask themselves questions about what they need to accomplish while completing an assignment, what strategies they might use to reach their goals, any potential problems that might arise, and their likelihood of success. Students who learn to monitor their reading and studying through generating their own questions are usually more successful in all reading tasks than are other students.

REPRODUCIBLE SELF-APPRAISAL DEVICES

On pages 369 and 370 are reproducible self-appraisal devices for use at both the primary- and intermediate-grade reading levels. You can duplicate and use them in their present form if they seem applicable or modify them in any way you want.

Reproducible Book-Selection Device

The chapter closes with a reproducible *book-selection device* on page 371. It is a simple way for a reading teacher to evaluate the criteria an intermediate-grade student uses in choosing a book to read for either pleasure or information. It should help you to evaluate a student's ability in book-selection behaviors.

You can duplicate this device in its present form or modify it in any way you want.

Name _____ Grade _____ Teacher _____ Date _____

SELF-APPRAISAL OF READING ABILITY
(Upper Primary-Grade Reading Level)

Answer each of these questions by placing a ✓ in the box under the word **Yes** or **No**.

	Yes	No
1. I know most of the words in the books I read when I see them.	❏	❏
2. I can sound out the words in the books I read when I need to.	❏	❏
3. I can use the rest of the sentence to figure out a word I don't know.	❏	❏
4. I can understand what I read.	❏	❏
5. I use what I already know to help me understand what I'm reading.	❏	❏
6. When I'm reading, I know when a word I've read doesn't make sense.	❏	❏
7. I know what to do when I don't understand what I'm reading.	❏	❏
8. I can read aloud well.	❏	❏
9. I can find books that I like to read in my room and in the school library.	❏	❏
10. I like to read for fun.	❏	❏

Name _____ Grade _____ Teacher _____ Date _____

SELF-APPRAISAL OF READING ABILITY
(Intermediate-Grade Reading Level)

Answer each of these questions by placing a ✓ in the box under the word **Yes** or **No**.

	Yes	**No**
1. I know most of the words in the books I read when I meet them.	❑	❑
2. I can sound out the words in the books that I read when I need to.	❑	❑
3. I can use the rest of the sentence to figure out a word I don't recognize or understand.	❑	❑
4. I can understand what I read.	❑	❑
5. I use what I already know to help me understand what I'm reading.	❑	❑
6. I can "read between the lines" and understand what the author is trying to say.	❑	❑
7. I think about what I read and what it really means to me.	❑	❑
8. I can find the main idea of a paragraph.	❑	❑
9. I can find the important details in a paragraph.	❑	❑
10. I ask myself questions as I read to make sure that I understand.	❑	❑
11. I know what is important to remember from reading my textbooks.	❑	❑
12. I know how to use the table of contents, indexes, and glossary of my textbooks.	❑	❑
13. I know how to study for a test.	❑	❑
14. I can use a dictionary to learn how to pronounce new words.	❑	❑
15. I can use a dictionary to find word meanings.	❑	❑
16. I can read aloud well and with good expression.	❑	❑
17. I can change my reading speed depending upon my purpose for reading and how hard it is.	❑	❑
18. I can find books I like to read in my classroom, the school library, and the public library.	❑	❑
19. I know how to locate information in a library.	❑	❑
20. I know how to read social studies textbooks, science textbooks, and math verbal problems.	❑	❑

Name _____ Grade _____ Teacher _____ Date _____

BOOK-SELECTION DEVICE
Intermediate-Grade Level

Location of Book Selection:

Looks At	**Asks for Advice**	**Time Spent**
Cover of book	Classmates	0-5 minutes
Information of the book jacket	Teacher	5-10 minutes
Chapter title	Librarian	10-15 minutes
First few pages	Students from other classes	15-20 minutes
Middle of the book		Over 20 minutes
Ending of the book		

Books Considered

1

2

3

4

5 or more

Title of Book Selected

_____

_____

Teacher Comments_____

_____

_____

_____

_____

_____

PART TWO

Assessing Competencies and Weaknesses in Writing and Spelling

CHAPTER EIGHT

Using Checklists to Assess Competencies and Weaknesses in Drawing, Writing, and Spelling

One of the most critical and useful emphases of the 1980s and 1990s has been the attempt to integrate the teaching of all the elements of literacy—**listening, speaking, reading,** and **writing.** For far too long, for example, reading and writing have been taught in most elementary schools as separate entities with by far the most emphasis being placed on reading instruction. It is interesting to note that "for every $3000 spent on children's ability to receive information, $1.00 was spent on their power to send it in writing."[25] Even today after the recent renewed emphasis on the integration of the teaching of literacy and the increased time and effort being spent in the teaching of writing, reading instruction receives much more stress with both competent and disabled readers.

This chapter provides numerous reproducible checklists the literacy teacher can use in assessing competencies and weaknesses in **drawing** (a beginning stage of writing), all of the elements of writing and spelling including **scribbling, letter strings, invented spelling,** and **traditional spelling,** and all of the elements of creative and content writing at the primary, intermediate, and middle–upper levels.

The literacy teacher should find this chapter extremely useful in assessing the various aspects of a student's drawing, writing, and spelling behaviors. This assessment should, of course, point the way toward correct prescriptive instruction in any of the areas in which a student lacks competence.

---

[25]Donald H. Graves, "A New Look at Writing Research," *Language Arts,* 57 (November/December 1980), p. 914.

Brief Description of Emergent Writing Behaviors

For many years it was believed that the acquisition of early reading skills occurred earlier than that of early writing skills. Now it is known that the development of writing skills may even predate those of reading skills or they may be acquired at about the same time. The development of early writing skills is one aspect of what is now called *emergent literacy development.*

In any case, most children acquire *emergent writing behaviors* in a number of stages, some of which may overlap. Here is a very brief description of the **emergent writing stages:**

- *Writing via drawing*—The child uses drawing to stand for writing. Actually the child is working out the relationship between writing and drawing and not truly confusing the two of them. The child believes that drawing/writing is a communication of a specific and purposeful message. Children who participate in writing via drawing read their drawings as if there is writing on them. Here is an illustration of this stage:

- *Writing via scribbling*—The child scribbles but intends it as writing. The child may appear to be writing as he or she scribbles from left to right. The child moves the pencil just like an adult does, and the pencil makes sounds that sound like those of writing. The scribbling resembles writing in some ways. Here is an illustration of this stage:

- *Writing via making letter-like forms*—At this stage, the shapes in the child's writing actually resemble letters. Careful observation, however, reveals that they only look like letters; they are not actually letters. In addition, they are not just poorly formed letters, but are actually unique creations. Here is an illustration of this stage:

- *Writing via making random letters or letter strings*—At this stage, the child uses letter sequences learned from such sources as his or her own first name. The child sometimes changes the order of the letters, writing the same letters in a number of different ways, or reproduces letters in long strings or in random order. Here is an illustration of this stage:

- *Writing via invented spelling*—Children demonstrate many different varieties and levels of invented spelling. Usually a child creates his or her own spelling for words when he or she does not know the conventional spelling. In invented spelling, one letter may represent an entire syllable, and words may overlap and not be properly spaced. As the child's writing matures, the words look more like conventional spelling with perhaps only one or two letters invented or omitted. Here is an illustration of this stage:

- *Writing via conventional (traditional) spelling*—At this stage, the child's writing resembles adult writing, in most instances. Here is an example of this stage:

Although there obviously are great differences among children, usually children at the ages **three to five** scribble, string letters together, and make letter-like forms. At the ages of **five and six** they begin to demonstrate a rudimentary understanding of the alphabet principle that links letters and sounds. At about the age of **six** children use phonetic spelling, while children **seven and eight** typically stop relying only on grapho-phonic information and also use visual and structural clues. Normally most children will use mainly conventional spelling by the age of about **eight or (at the latest) nine.** It is very important to encourage children to write on a regular basis no matter what their stage of writing. They should never be discouraged from exploring writing by the means they are able to do, whether it be scribbling, letter strings, invented spelling, or conventional spelling.

REPRODUCIBLE CHECKLIST OF EMERGENT WRITING BEHAVIORS

Here is a reproducible checklist of emergent writing behaviors. It usually is the most applicable at the kindergarten or first-grade level; however, it may still be applicable with some children in second grade. You can duplicate and use this checklist in its present form if it seems applicable or modify it in any way you wish.

Name _____ Grade _____ Teacher _____ Date _____

CHECKLIST OF EMERGENT WRITING BEHAVIORS

(Emergent Literacy Level)

PART I: Level of Writing

Check the level or levels at which the child is currently writing:

1. _____ Uses drawing both for writing and drawing
2. _____ Is able to differentiate between writing and drawing
3. _____ Uses scribble writing for writing
4. _____ Uses letter-like forms for writing
5. _____ Uses learned letters in a random way (letter strings) for writing
6. _____ Uses invented spelling while writing
7. _____ Uses conventional (traditional) spelling while writing

	Always	Sometimes	Never
PART II: COMPETENCY IN WRITING			
8. Demonstrates an interest in writing for real purposes such as writing notes, cards, letters, lists, etc.	❑	❑	❑
9. Explores with writing materials such as unlined and lined paper, pencils, markers, and crayons	❑	❑	❑
10. Dictates words, sentences, or stories that he/she wants to have written down	❑	❑	❑
11. Attempts to copy letters, numbers, words, and sentences	❑	❑	❑
12. Attempts to write independently whether using drawing, scribbling, random letters (letter strings), invented spelling, or conventional (traditional) spelling	❑	❑	❑
13. Is able to print his/her own first name legibly	❑	❑	❑
14. Sometimes works with other children while writing	❑	❑	❑
PART III: WRITING MECHANICS			
15. Is able to form all or most of the capital letters correctly	❑	❑	❑
16. Is able to form all or most of the lower-case letters correctly	❑	❑	❑
17. Writes from left to right	❑	❑	❑
18. Leaves spaces between word boundaries	❑	❑	❑
19. Uses capital letters when appropriate	❑	❑	❑
20. Uses periods when appropriate	❑	❑	❑
21. Uses commas when appropriate	❑	❑	❑

Brief Description of Creative and Content Writing at the Primary, Intermediate, and Middle–Upper Levels

Writing instruction today is considered a *process* rather than a *product*. Although the product of the writing process obviously has importance, in contemporary literacy instruction the writing process is considered to be more important.

There are several different types of writing in which students in elementary and middle schools may engage. Here is one way of classifying them:

- *Creative expression*—This is the personal product of the student's experience or imagination. Creative writing may be in the form of original poetry or prose of a realistic, fanciful, fictional, or factual nature.

- *Narration*—In narrative writing, the students tell a story or recount personal experiences or report on observed events. Usually narrative writing is a chronological account of events, although students may use other organizing strategies.

- *Exposition*—In expository writing, the aim is to inform or explain. A student must select the best method to present factual information.

- *Persuasion*—A persuasive composition is written to influence, motivate, or convince an individual or a group to act in a certain manner.

- *Description*—In descriptive writing, the aim is to help the reader visualize what is being described. A student may describe a person, place, or object by using details that appeal to the senses to support and elaborate.

At the primary-grade level, most of children's writing is some variation of creative expression, while at the intermediate and middle–upper levels both creative and informative writing of the types described earlier are done. In either case, motivation for many types of writing can be found in literature-rich classrooms that contain numerous narrative and expository (content) reading materials.

All writing can be evaluated in terms of the following criteria:

- *Clarity*—Does the writing seem clear, well-organized, and easy to understand?

- *Interest Appeal*—Is the writing interesting to the readers who ultimately are to read it?

- *Correctness*—Is the writing mechanically correct (spelling, sentence structure, and grammar)?

Of course, at the primary-grade level *correctness* is not of as much concern as is the *content of the writing*. At the emergent literacy level and into the upper primary grades, *invented spelling* and *incorrect mechanics* should be de-emphasized in relation to the content of the writing. If too much emphasis is placed on correct mechanics too early, children will be turned off writing and usually will not want to write anything. In many cases, invented spelling can be called a *good way to spell a word,* while correct spelling can be called the *grown-up way to spell a word.* In the upper primary grades, however, children can be helped to rewrite and publish some, but certainly not all, of their writing.

Here are the steps children should use to write a finished product. They should not be followed while doing all writing. Sometimes a first draft is sufficient.

- *Prewriting (brainstorming)*—The child attempts to come up with the topic to write about. In many cases, a number of ideas will be discarded before the final topic is selected.
- *Rough draft (sloppy copy)*—The child writes a rough draft without paying attention to correct spelling, sentence structure, or grammar.
- *Conferencing*—During a conference either with the teacher or his or her peers, the child attempts to determine how to improve his or her written product. The goal in the conference is to locate all of the mechanical errors and to organize the product into a polished final form.
- *Final draft*—The child writes a final draft of the writing, trying to use correct mechanics and to organize it in the best possible manner.
- *Editing the final draft*—After the final draft is completed, the child either alone or with a peer(s) goes over the writing very carefully to be sure that it is written in the best possible manner and that there are no mechanical errors.
- *Publishing and sharing the final draft*—Since writing is usually, but not always, written to be shared with others, the final polished draft should be published in some type of book form and shared by reading it aloud to other students or by placing it in the classroom library or literacy center.

The writing workshop is used in many contemporary elementary and middle-school classrooms to foster an interest in all types of writing. The term "workshop" calls to mind an image of cooperation among members of a group of people who are striving to master a craft—*the craft of writing.* Community implies cooperation or working toward the central goal of *creating and improving writers.* In this atmosphere students discuss each other's writing in a spirit of mutual growth rather than criticism. Teachers work with students as fellow writers and as members of the literate community that has been established in the classroom. The context that supports a writing workshop includes:

- a supportive environment in which students and teachers work together to become better writers
- constant and self-directed practice in the craft of writing
- regular blocks of time devoted to the craft of writing
- regular blocks of time devoted to literature and reading

An effective writing workshop also must have space for writing and all types of writing materials such as unlined and lined papers; pencils; markers; crayons; paints and other art supplies; staplers and staples; tape; correction fluid; scissors; cardboard and other thick paper for binding books; hole punches; heavy yarns, thread, or dental floss for binding books; large embroidery needles for binding books; dictionaries; thesauruses; and writing folders.

Contests such as the "Young Author's Contest" can be extremely effective in motivating students to write. Each year my teacher-trainees judge all of the entries in the "Young Author's Contest" at Sugar Creek Elementary School in Normal, Illinois, and are amazed by the quality of the children's creative and informative writing. It seems to be one of the best ways to motivate children to work hard toward producing a polished published product.

There are several other techniques that are effective in motivating all kinds of writing. *Response journals* in which a child writes his or her individual response to some of the reading that he or she does are very useful. A notebook is a convenient form for the response journal to take. We have found *journal writing* in which the teacher and/or peers may or may not read a student's writing to be very effective. A *dialogue journal* in which a teacher writes regular responses to the child is often useful. *Story starters* and *unfinished stories* may also motivate creative writing. *Semantic webs or maps* may be very helpful in motivating a student to do summary or report writing. They are often much more motivating for this purpose than is the traditional outline. A student also may want to keep *daily logs of his or her content writing* in which each day he or she summarizes the important points about what was read from the content textbook that day. The child may also keep his or her own *notebook* in which he or she jots down important ideas and concepts that may be written about later in various ways.

Finally, the *computer* may be an extremely valuable tool to use in motivating students to do all kinds of writing. Children as young as the kindergarten level can easily learn keyboarding skills. Obviously, the computer is very motivational and makes editing much simpler—as well as provide a spelling and grammar check. Here is a list of several computer programs that can be used in the elementary school as an aid to writing:

* *Clifford's Big Book Publisher* (Scholastics, 730 Broadway, New York, NY 10003)—Create Big Books with Clifford, the big red dog, and other characters. (Apple, MS-DOS)

* *The Children's Writing and Publishing Center* (The Learning Company, P.O. Box 6187, Santa Barbara, CA 93160)—Create stories, reports, and newsletters with a variety of headings, clip art, and fonts available. (Apple, MS-DOS)

* *The New Print Shop* (The Brøderbund Company, 17 Paul Drive, San Rafael, CA 94904)—Create signs, posters, banners, cards, and calendars. Variety of graphics and graphic layouts available. (Apple, MS-DOS)

* *POW! ZAP! Ker Plunk! The Comic Book Maker* (Pelican/Queue, P.O. Box 3110, Gretna, LA 70054)—Create comic books with classic comic-book components: speech bubbles, sound and special effects, props, heroes, and heroines. (Apple, MS-DOS)

REPRODUCIBLE CHECKLISTS OF WRITING BEHAVIORS

The chapter now contains reproducible checklists of writing behaviors at the primary-grade, intermediate-grade, and middle–upper levels. You can duplicate and use any of these checklists in their present form if they are applicable for your use or you can modify them in any way you wish.

Name _____ Grade _____ Teacher _____ Date _____

CHECKLIST OF PRIMARY-GRADE WRITING BEHAVIORS

	Always	**Sometimes**	**Never**
1. Holds the writing implement correctly	❑	❑	❑
2. Is able to print his/her own first and last names correctly	❑	❑	❑
3. Dictates words, phrases, sentences, and stories that he/she wants to be recorded	❑	❑	❑
4. Enjoys exploring with writing materials such as unlined and lined paper, a variety of pencils, markers, and materials for binding books	❑	❑	❑
5. Uses invented spelling when necessary instead of asking for teacher or peer assistance	❑	❑	❑
6. Uses conventional spelling when writing most familiar words	❑	❑	❑
7. Is able to use correct segmentation between words, sentences, lines, and the end of the page while writing	❑	❑	❑
8. Displays a willing attitude toward writing activities	❑	❑	❑
9. Is able to write attentively for about 15–20 minutes	❑	❑	❑
10. Writes in varied genres such as creative expression, narration, exposition, persuasion, and description	❑	❑	❑
11. Is willing to receive and give advice to his/her classmates about writing in writing conferences	❑	❑	❑
12. Is able to brainstorm to select a topic for writing	❑	❑	❑
13. Is able to write an acceptable rough (first) draft	❑	❑	❑
14. Is able to effectively edit his/her rough (first) draft, making additions, deletions, and reorganizations	❑	❑	❑
15. Understands and effectively uses correct mechanics such as complete sentences, capital letters, periods, commas, question marks, and exclamation points	❑	❑	❑
16. Demonstrates a growing vocabulary commensurate with his/her level of maturity	❑	❑	❑
17. Demonstrates some organization in story form (beginning, middle, and ending)	❑	❑	❑
18. Is able to publish his/her writing in acceptable form when it is appropriate	❑	❑	❑
19. Writes to arouse the interest of his/her classmates	❑	❑	❑
20. Is able to reread his/her own writing effectively	❑	❑	❑
21. Is able to share his/her writing with classmates	❑	❑	❑
22. Listens attentively to the writing of his/her peers	❑	❑	❑
23. Responds appropriately to the writing of his/her peers	❑	❑	❑
24. Is able to use a computer for writing when appropriate	❑	❑	❑
25. Is willing to enter his/her writing in some type of informal competition such as the "Young Author's Contest" if he/she has the opportunity to do so	❑	❑	❑

Name _____ Grade _____ Teacher _____ Date _____

CHECKLIST OF INTERMEDIATE-GRADE WRITING BEHAVIORS

	Always	Sometimes	Never
1. Displays a willing attitude toward writing activities	❏	❏	❏
2. Is able to write attentively for about thirty minutes	❏	❏	❏
3. Writes competently in the varied genres of creative expression, narration, exposition, persuasion, and description	❏	❏	❏
4. Uses semantic webs (maps) as a technique for motivating writing	❏	❏	❏
5. Is able to brainstorm to select an appropriate topic for the type of writing to be done	❏	❏	❏
6. Is able to write an acceptable rough (first) draft	❏	❏	❏
7. Is able to effectively edit his/her rough (first) draft by making additions, deletions, and reorganization	❏	❏	❏
8. Is willing to receive and give advice to his/her peers about writing during writing conferences	❏	❏	❏
9. Uses conventional spelling while writing	❏	❏	❏
10. Understands and uses correct mechanics such as grammar, complex sentence structure, and punctuation marks	❏	❏	❏
11. Demonstrates a growing vocabulary in his/her writing commensurate with his/her level of maturity	❏	❏	❏
12. Structures a paragraph using a topic sentence	❏	❏	❏
13. Demonstrates the proper organization for the type of writing he/she is attempting to do	❏	❏	❏
14. Consults a variety of sources in search of information for his/her writing	❏	❏	❏
15. Sequences ideas logically while writing	❏	❏	❏
16. Writes satisfactory endings or conclusions	❏	❏	❏
17. Is able to publish his/her writing in an acceptable form when it is appropriate	❏	❏	❏
18. Writes to arouse the interest of his/her classmates	❏	❏	❏
19. Is able to reread his/her own writing effectively	❏	❏	❏
20. Is able to effectively share his/her writing with classmates	❏	❏	❏
21. Listens attentively to the writing of his/her classmates	❏	❏	❏
22. Responds appropriately to the writing of his/her classmates	❏	❏	❏
23. Keeps a writing folder that demonstrates writing improvement over time	❏	❏	❏
24. Is able to use a computer for writing	❏	❏	❏
25. Is willing to enter his/her writing in some type of informal competition such as the "Young Author's Contest" if he/she has the opportunity to do so	❏	❏	❏

Name _____ Grade _____ Teacher _____ Date _____

CHECKLIST OF MIDDLE–UPPER LEVEL WRITING BEHAVIORS

	Always	Sometimes	Never
1. Displays a willing attitude toward all writing activities	❑	❑	❑
2. Is able to write effectively for more than thirty minutes if the level of writing requires it	❑	❑	❑
3. Writes at an advanced level of competency in the varied genres of creative expression, narration, exposition, persuasion, and description	❑	❑	❑
4. Uses semantic webs (maps) or outlines as a motivation and/or aid in various genres of writing	❑	❑	❑
5. Is able to brainstorm at an advanced level to select an appropriate topic for the genre of writing to be done	❑	❑	❑
6. Is able to write a good rough (first) draft	❑	❑	❑
7. Is able to edit his/her writing at an advanced level by making appropriate additions, deletions, and reorganizations	❑	❑	❑
8. Demonstrates complex, precise general and specialized vocabulary while writing commensurate with his/her level of maturity and the genre in which he/she is writing	❑	❑	❑
9. Is willing to receive and give advice to his/her peers about writing during writing conferences	❑	❑	❑
10. Understands and can use correct mechanics such as spelling of general and specialized vocabulary terms, complex sentence structure, and punctuation marks at an advanced level	❑	❑	❑
11. Sequences ideas logically while writing	❑	❑	❑
12. Demonstrates the proper organization for the type of writing to be done, whether it is creative expression of prose or poetry, narration, exposition, persuasion, or description	❑	❑	❑
13. If appropriate, consults a variety of sources such as the library card catalog, encyclopedia, or computer software for information while writing	❑	❑	❑
14. If appropriate to the genre of writing being done, sequences ideas logically while writing	❑	❑	❑
15. Writes good endings or conclusions depending upon what is required in a specific genre	❑	❑	❑
16. Is able to publish his/her writing in a polished format when appropriate	❑	❑	❑
17. Writes to inform, motivate, persuade, or interest his/her classmates	❑	❑	❑
18. Is able to reread his/her writing effectively	❑	❑	❑
19. Is able to effectively share his/her writing with classmates in either an oral or published form	❑	❑	❑
20. Listens attentively to the writing of his/her classmates	❑	❑	❑
21. Structures paragraphs with directly stated or implied main ideas and satisfactory supporting details	❑	❑	❑
22. Uses writing as an aid to retaining information gained from reading social studies and science textbooks	❑	❑	❑
23. Keeps a sophisticated writing folder that shows improvement in writing over time	❑	❑	❑
24. Is able to use a computer for writing	❑	❑	❑
25. Is willing to attempt to have his/her writing published in publications of various sorts such as newspapers, newsletters, or magazines or to enter his/her writing in some type of formal or informal competition if he/she has the opportunity to do so	❑	❑	❑

Reproducible Checklist for Computer Word Processing

Page 387 is a reproducible checklist for computer word processing that would be most applicable with students at the intermediate-grade level and above. You may duplicate and use this checklist in its present form if it seems applicable or modify it in any way you wish.

Reproducible Checklist of Editing Behaviors

Page 388 is a reproducible checklist of a student's editing behaviors while writing. It is probably most applicable for the intermediate-grade level and above. You can duplicate and use this checklist in its present form if it seems applicable or change it in any way you wish.

Name _____ Grade _____ Teacher _____ Date _____

CHECKLIST FOR COMPUTER WORD PROCESSING
(Intermediate and Middle–Upper Grade Levels)

	Yes	No
1. Willingly chooses to write using the computer	☐	☐
2. Takes pride in his/her completed writing product	☐	☐
3. Organizes his/her thoughts before using the computer to write	☐	☐
4. Writes from notes or an outline	☐	☐
5. Writes creatively in the form of prose or poetry	☐	☐
6. Can do informative writing in the form of narration, exposition, persuasion, and description	☐	☐
7. Writing reflects his/her own language patterns	☐	☐
8. Effectively uses word-processing editing techniques	☐	☐
9. Effectively uses word-processing revision techniques	☐	☐
10. Uses varied sentence length and sentence structure in his/her writing	☐	☐

Name _____ Grade _____ Teacher _____ Date _____

CHECKLIST OF EDITING BEHAVIORS
(Intermediate and Middle–Upper Grade Levels)

		Yes	No
1.	Locates his/her own spelling errors while writing	☐	☐
2.	Corrects his/her own spelling errors while writing	☐	☐
3.	Approximate percentage of spelling errors corrected	_____ %	
4.	Locates his/her own grammar errors while writing	☐	☐
5.	Corrects his/her own grammar errors while writing	☐	☐
6.	Approximate percentage of grammar errors corrected	_____ %	
7.	Locates his/her own punctuation errors while writing	☐	☐
8.	Corrects his/her own punctuation errors while writing	☐	☐
9.	Approximate percentage of punctuation errors corrected	_____ %	
10.	Locates his/her own organization errors while writing	☐	☐
11.	Corrects his/her own organization errors while writing	☐	☐
12.	Approximate percentage of organization errors corrected	_____ %	

CHAPTER NINE

Using Holistic Scoring and the Informal Writing Inventory to Assess Writing

When one of your students has written a composition, how are you to know if it is very good, average, or perhaps even slightly below average for his or her grade level? Of course, if you have taught at that grade level for a number of years, you may have a good idea. However, you may want a more precise way of determining a student's writing performance. Unfortunately at the present time, there is no exact way to assess writing skills with precision. However, undoubtedly *the holistic scoring of writing* is one of the most promising and effective ways of doing this despite the great amount of subjectivity teachers must use in making the assessment. At this time even the state of Illinois uses holistic scoring with trained evaluators of writing in the evaluation of the Illinois Goal Assessment Program—Writing (IGAP—Writing) which is given to all students in the state. Therefore, in spite of its limitations, holistic scoring remains one of the best ways to evaluate composition writing competency at this time.

This chapter is devoted to using holistic scoring in the assessment of writing. After reading and studying it carefully, you should be much better able to use this assessment system in evaluating the writing of your students in the primary, intermediate, and middle–upper grades.

Description of Holistic Scoring Used in This Handbook

The holistic scoring used in this handbook has five main elements: **clarity, support, organization, mechanics,** and **overall rating.** Here is a comprehensive description of each of these elements so that you can use them in the assessment of your students' writing.

Clarity

A well-executed composition has a clear and well-defined topic. The composition has a unified opening and summary. The rating scale for evaluating the **clarity** of a piece of writing ranges from **5** as the highest to **1** as the lowest.

- **5** The topic is very clear. The main idea and the major points to be developed are correctly stated in the opening. The opening and concluding statements are related to the content of the composition and to each other.

- **4** The topic is fairly clear. The main idea is stated satisfactorily; however, the major points developed are not all included in the beginning. Although the concluding statement does support the main idea to a degree, the relationship between them may not be completely clear.

- **3** The topic is fairly clear; however, the main idea may have to be inferred to some extent. The main points that are developed are not all included in the opening. Irrelevant details may well be included. The conclusion may not be included or be irrelevant.

- **2** The topic is fairly clear; however, the main idea must be completely inferred. There are no main points and no conclusion to the composition.

- **1** The topic is unclear and there is no main idea at all.

Support

A good composition contains details that support the main idea and subpoints. Additional information can be provided through the use of *explanations, examples, reasons, and descriptions*. The rating scale for evaluating the support of a composition ranges from **5** as the highest to **1** as the lowest.

- **5** There are explanations, examples, reasons, details, and descriptions that directly support the main idea. Main points are elaborated upon and explained in detail. All of the explanations, examples, reasons, and descriptions are accurate and appropriate.

- **4** There are many explanations, examples, reasons, details, and descriptions that support the main idea. Although some of the support is not entirely complete, it is usually accurate.

- **3** Some explanations, examples, reasons, details, and descriptions are provided for the main idea. However, some of the support may be incomplete or inaccurate.

- **2** Support has been attempted but only a few of the main points have been expanded upon. Some of the supporting points may be inaccurate or inappropriate.

- **1** There is little or no support for the main idea, and much of the support may be questionable or inaccurate.

Organization

A well-organized composition exhibits a well-thought-out plan of development. The ideas are logically sequenced and related and have correctly constructed paragraphs. The length of the composition should be appropriate for the grade level and the type of writing that is required. The rating scale for organization ranges from **5** as the highest to **1** as the lowest.

- **5** The organization of the composition is very clear. The main points are developed by the correct use of paragraphs. Transitional words and phrases also are used. All of the points are developed logically.

- **4** The organization of the composition is fairly clear. Many of the main points are developed in accurate paragraphs, and there may be some transitional words and phrases. Although most of the points are developed logically, there may be a few omissions or irrelevancies.

- **3** Although the composition may have some organization, it is not really evident. There may be some incorrect paragraphing, and a limited use of transitional words and phrases. Many of the points may not be developed logically.

- **2** Although some organization may have been attempted, it is not clear. There are very few transitional words and phrases and inaccurate paragraphing.

- **1** There is no evidence of organization and no logical sequence in the composition.

Mechanics

A good composition has correct spelling, sentence structure, paragraphing, grammatical usage, punctuation, and capitalization. Mechanics develop through the grade levels and must be evaluated on a cumulative basis considering the grade level of the child who wrote the composition. *Major errors* are those that interfere with communication and include those mechanics a student should have mastered by a specific grade level. *Minor errors* do not interfere with communication. They include errors in which a child is not supposed to have mastered at a specific age. The rating scores in mechanics range from **5** as the highest to **1** as the lowest.

- **5** There are no major or important errors and very few minor or unimportant errors.

- **4** There are a few major or important errors and some minor or unimportant errors.

- **3** There are some major or important errors and a number of minor or unimportant errors.

- **2** There are many major or important errors that may cause considerable confusion in attempting to understand the composition.

- **1** There are numerous serious errors that interfere significantly with communication.

Errors in Mechanics

- **Spelling**—Misspelling of words common for that specific grade level
- **Punctuation and Capitalization**—Incorrect or totally lacking in the various marks of capitalization and in using capitalization when appropriate
- **Grammatical Usage**—Incorrect tense usage, incorrect verb usage indicating singular or plural, incorrect pronoun referents, and incorrect usage of common words
- **Sentence Structure**—Lack of agreement with a subject and verb, run-on sentences, and sentence fragments

The Overall Rating

The purpose of the **holistic rating** is to form an overall assessment of how adequately the student performed the specific writing task. The teacher should read the paper from beginning to end to make an assessment of how well the student met the requirements of the four previously mentioned features. The rating for the holistic component are **5** for the highest to **1** as the lowest.

Overall Rating	Clarity, Support, Organization	Mechanics
5	Two features must be a 5; one may be a 4	Must be 4 or 5
4	Two features must be a 4; one may be a 3	Must be 3, 4, or 5
3	Two features must be a 3; one may be a 2	Must be 3, 4, or 5
2	Two features must be a 2; one may be a 1	Must be 2, 3, 4 or 5
1	Two features must be a 1; one may be a 2	Usually will be no higher than a 2

There are other **holistic classification schemes** in addition to the one just described and will be illustrated later in this chapter. Some of them use a **1–4, 1–6,** or **1–8** rating scale. If you would like more information about two such schemes we have found useful, you can consult the following resources:

Robert L. Hillerich, *Teaching Children to Write, K–8.* Englewood Cliffs, NJ: Prentice Hall, 1985, pp. 234–241.

Michael Sampson, Roach Van Allen, and Mary Beth Sampson, *Pathways to Literacy.* Fort Worth, TX: Holt, Rinehart and Winston, 1991, pp. 264–270.

ACTUAL CHILDREN'S WRITING SAMPLES THAT HAVE BEEN SCORED HOLISTICALLY

NOTE: All of the *holistic scores* from first-grade children must be considered *very tentative.* Indeed, I do not recommend using holistic scoring until near the end of the second semester of first grade. It is not possible to obtain even a fairly accurate holistic score earlier than that.

"Mother"

A first-grade-child wrote the narrative composition entitled "Mother" without teacher assistance near the end of April 1994.

Holistic Analysis of the First-Grade Narrative "Mother"

- **Clarity 5**   The topic is clear, and all of the main points seem to be developed satisfactorily.
- **Support 3**   Although there is some support in this composition, more elaboration could have been included.
- **Organization 4**   The organization is fairly clear for the first-grade level.
- **Mechanics 5**   There are no major mechanical errors and only two minor errors that do not interfere with comprehension.
- **Overall Rating 4**   This is a good narrative composition for the first-grade level. It could have had better support and somewhat better organization.

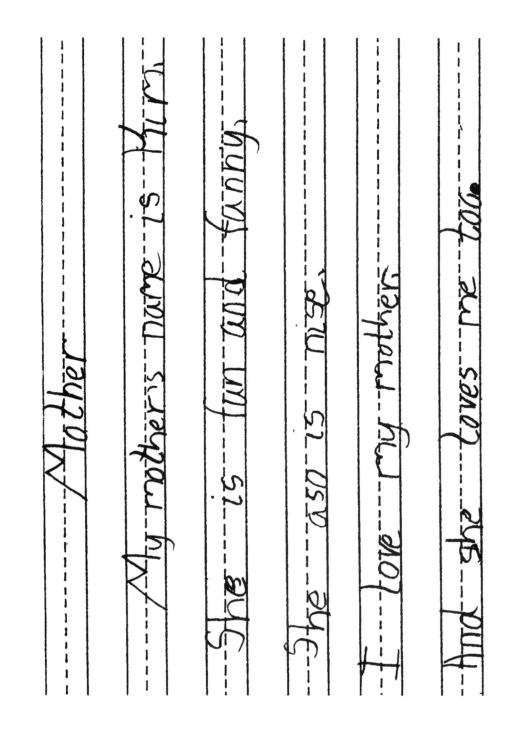

Mother

My mother's name is Kim.

She is fun and funny.

She also is nice.

I love my mother

And she loves me too.

"The Candy Monster"

A second-grade child wrote the creative expression composition entitled "The Candy Monster" without teacher assistance near the end of April 1994.

Holistic Analysis of the Creative Expression Composition "The Candy Monster"

- **Clarity 3**   The topic is clear to an extent. However, its development is not always logical or understandable.

- **Support 2**   The support is not entirely logical or understandable. There is much repetition in the support.

- **Organization 2**   The organization is very difficult to follow. It does not really seem to have a logical organization.

- **Mechanics 3**   There are some major and numerous minor mechanical errors. The major errors cause considerable confusion in understanding this composition. None of the evaluators were able to decipher the word "aloins," although it may be the word "allowance."

- **Overall Rating 2**   This composition is not very well organized and fairly difficult to understand.

The Candy Monster

One day there was a monster who ate and ate candy. He ate so much candy his parents told him not to eat so much candy. Some time went much candy to much candy. He ate his parents rech him no good at all. He freed they to tak his candy away but he cept criyying it awy but he aboind so that took away his aboind so he cant buy it.

"Soccer"

A third-grade child wrote the persuasive composition "Soccer" without teacher assistance near the end of April 1994.

Holistic Analysis of the Persuasive Composition "Soccer"

- **Clarity 5**   The topic is very clear, and the major ideas and points are well developed and relate to the content of the composition and each other well.
- **Support 5**   The main idea is very well supported with explanations, details, examples, and reasons.
- **Organization 5**   This composition is very well organized in a logical and clear manner. The main points are well developed by paragraphs and transitional words are included.
- **Mechanics 5**   Although there are several omitted words and a few minor spelling errors, this composition is easy to understand. These errors in mechanics do not significantly interfere with comprehension.
- **Overall Rating 5**

Soccer

Soccer is a very fun sport. The best things to do in soccer are to kick, pass, and score. If you do all those things you'll score. That is the object of the game.

First you have to kick the ball. To kick it, you usually do it with the toe of your foot. When you kick it you usually try to score. I'll tell you about scoring in a minute, though.

Next you have to pass the ball. It is what gets you down the feild so you can score. You have to pass with the inside of your foot to really pass good. Passing helps when you have the ball and there people around you.

Then you have to score. To score you have to kick hard with your toe down. That way you'll the ball high into the goal. Then you'll score. To win you have to get the most points.

Finally you have to kick,

pass, and score. See how fun soccer really is? So far this season my team has been undefeatable. It's fun when you win.

The
End

A fourth-grade child wrote this expository compostion "Illinois" without teacher assistance near the end of April 1994.

Holistic Analysis of the Expository Composition "Illinois"

- **Clarity 3**   Although the topic is fairly clear, the opening does not express it well. Most of the main points in the composition must be inferred.

- **Support 2**   Support has been attempted for this competition, but very few of the main points have been expanded upon to any degree, and there is repetition in the support.

- **Organization 1**   This composition is very poorly organized. It contains no logical sequence, making it very difficult to understand.

- **Mechanics 1**   There are numerous major mechanical errors in this composition, causing great difficulty in understanding it. It has many spelling, punctuation, grammatical usage, and sentence structure errors and no paragraphing which make it hard to understand.

- **Overall Rating 1**   This is a poorly organized expository for the fourth-grade level with numerous mechanical errors, and it is difficult to understand.

Illinois

by Tim Salomone

Illinois is such a betiful state. Like Chicagos tall building and skyscapers and also the tallest building in the united states. then then is the Aple. Most of Illinois is caverd by flat land which is were farmers here grow corn and soybeans. Illinois capital is Springfeild Home of are sixenth President Abrham Lincoln. You can see his home their and are capital building. Illinois city Chicago has the shedd Aqurim. and the Mueson of science and industy. The Sears Tower the tallest building in the united states. The climate in Illinois is just right cold winters hot summers I Love Illinois

"An Imaginery [sic] Trip"

A fifth-grade child wrote the creative expression composition "An Imaginery [sic] Trip" without teacher assistance near the end of April 1994.

Holistic Analysis of the Creative Expression Composition "An Imaginery [sic] Trip"

- **Clarity 4**   The topic is fairly clear, but the main idea is found in the title rather than in the opening. Although the ending does not really relate to the opening, it is satisfactory.

- **Support 5**   There are sufficient details and descriptions to support the main idea of this composition.

- **Organization 5**   This composition is well organized and understandable. Although the first long paragraph probably should have been subdivided, this organization is still easy to understand.

- **Mechanics 5**   The spelling, grammatical usage, and sentence structure in this composition are very good for the fifth-grade level. There are no major mechanical errors and only a few minor ones, none of which interfere with understanding.

- **Overall Rating 5**   Although the long paragraph could have been divided, this is a good creative expression composition for the fifth-grade level. It is well organized and supported, easy to understand, and creative.

An Imaginary Trip

One day I was walking through the forest and I saw a bright, shiny light. I followed it until I was half way in the forest. I stopped. It was getting duller and duller every step I took. I wondered what it could be. I finally was there, as close as I could be. If I went any closer, would it be dangerous, or maybe even surprizing. I thought and I thought wondering if I should go any closer or run back and tell my parents. I decided to go on and see what was behind the light. I asked myself many questions like "What if I am stuck there forever" or "What will happen to me when I go in." It was hard to decide, but I wanted to go on and see what was there behind the bright, shiny light.

As soon as I started to walk on I slipped and fell. I opened my eyes and there I was in the middle of the street. I was rollar blading with a friend and I fell right there in the street. I wasn't in a forset and there was no bright, shiny light. Just then I figured it out, it was a dream, an imaginery trip. I felt really dumb sitting in the middle of the street. I got up and went back rollar blading with my friend. I never thought about it again

The End

"Earth"

A sixth-grade student wrote the expository composition about the "Earth" without teacher assistance near the end of April 1994.

Holistic Analysis of the Expository Composition "Earth"

- **Clarity 5** This composition has a very clearly stated main idea, with the main idea and major details stated in the opening, and a very well-related concluding statement.

- **Support 5** This composition contains many examples, reasons, and details that support the main idea very well.

- **Organization 5** This composition is very well organized with correct paragraphing and transitional phrases. All of the major points are developed logically.

- **Mechanics 5** This composition has no major mechanical errors and only a few minor errors that do not interfere with understanding. It has generally correct sentence structure, paragraphing, grammatical usage, punctuation, and capitalization.

- **Overall Rating 5** This is a very good expository composition for the sixth-grade level. It is very well constructed, supported, and thought provoking. It demonstrates the maturity of the student who wrote it.

What can you do to help keep the Earth clean and beautiful? Everyone can do many things to help the Earth. I could pick-up any garbage I see, and throw it in the nearest trash can, walk more instead of taking a car, and also plant flowers and trees, helping keep our planet pretty, everyone should do their part.

The first thing I should do when I see trash is throw it away or take it to a recycling bin. If you're just walking along and see an empty pop can pick it up and save it to recycle. Just picking up trash can prevent our Earth from getting worse, it keeps the streets and sidewalks clean, so we can have a more beautiful planet.

Car pollution is a very bad problem in this world today. Just taking a walk or bike ride instead of driving a car can cut down on pollution. Walking more can also help you get more exercise to keep you in shape. Just think about the next time you could ride your bike instead of taking a car.

Another project I could do to help the Earth is planting more flowers or trees. Trees give us oxygen, and we need oxygen to live. Also, planting flowers and trees might make your yard look nicer. Our Earth needs all the help it can get and by planting more trees and things you can do that.

The Earth is ours and we want to show it off. But how can we do that if it isn't very nice to look at. Everyone should pitch in and do some work to keep the Earth clean. Like, picking up trash, walking even when you don't have to, and planting more trees. Let's do these things to keep our Earth looking beautiful.

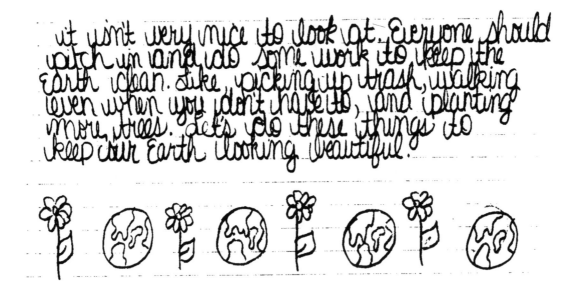

EXAMPLES OF COMPOSITIONS THAT GIVE YOU PRACTICE IN USING HOLISTIC SCORING

The chapter now includes compositions at the first-grade, second-grade, third-grade, fourth-grade, fifth-grade, and sixth-grade levels you can score holistically using the criteria described and illustrated in this chapter. For your information, the holistic scores assigned to each of these compositions by trained evaluators and their comments are found at the end of this section.

"My Mother"

A first-grade child wrote the narrative composition "My Mother" without teacher assistance near the end of April 1994.

"The Mystery of the Green Gass" [sic]

A second-grade child wrote the creative expression composition "The Mystery of the Green Gass" [sic] without teacher assistance near the end of April 1994.

"Motorcycles"

A third-grade child wrote the persuasive composition "Motorcycles" without teacher assistance near the end of April 1994.

"Save Our Earth"

A fourth-grade child wrote the expository composition "Save Our Earth" without teacher assistance near the end of April 1994.

"Social Studies"

A fifth-grade student wrote the expository composition "Social Studies" without teacher assistance near the end of April 1994.

"Friendship"

A sixth-grade student wrote the persuasive composition "Friendship" without teacher assistance near the end of April 1994.

My Mother is paretty and nice.

I love her and she lues me.

Her name is Lorrane lee Henricks.

She snoggles me evry night.

She has one brother but no sisters.

Her rell last name is Studer.

She is the best mom in the world.

The Mystery of the ___

Once there was a man that put poison...

...grass in all of the toilets so when our...

...flush green gas would scream over...

house. The only way to get rid of it...

...spray bug spray...

...I have never about it anyway...

...got him. Everybody lived in pieces...

...was a ___ now they have to...

...people because when they were trying...

...get him they didn't want any trouble they...

...haven't made enough money to rate them because...

...they hid some of the ___ the ___ thing he...

...stayed in jail for the rest of his life and every...

...one lived in peace.

The End

Motocycles

I like motocycles a lot. One day I was in a motocycle race. Later I will tell you three things I like about them. There are many thing I like about them but I can only tell you three. I'll tell ya later. I have only raced in one race befor. The three thing I like about motocycles are how fast they go, the jumps, and the colors of it.

First motorcycles go fast. They go 30-35 miles per hour. They go so fast that the first time I rode one I fell off because at the start it went so fast. It took me a wile to get use to the speed. Next I like the jumps, I awarys go high when I go off a jump. one time I double jumped. that means to jump from one jump to athor jump. but then I fell it hurt. I only fell a cuple times.

Then I like the colors of motorcycles. The colors of my motorcycle is red, white and blue. You can coose what color you want it to be. my uncle coose the color of my motorcyde. I like the colors of my motorcycle.

Finally I like
the speed, the jump
and colors!
If you want
to watch me my
number is 752.

The

End

Save Our Earth

There are many ways to save the earth. For one thing we can stop using styrofoam trays for lunch at school, We can stop buying six packs for coke & pop, & we can recycle a whole lot more.

Instead of using styrofoam trays we could just bring cold lunches every day to school like my moms school does, Then in the cafeteria there can be trash cans for certain things we can recycle.

Next, we can stop buying six packs because the plastic thing around the cans can get caught on a duck. But if we buy 2 litter bottles, they last longer and then we can recycle them. And it doesn't hurt the enviorment if we recycle it. But if we leave it in the middle of nowhere that would be polluting & it will hurt the earth.

Last, of all we can recycle more because pretty soon we won't have any land to build a house on. Because if nobody recycles the trash will take up more room. And nobody will want to live on trash!

In conclusion, if schools stop using styrofoam trays, people stop buying six packs, and recycle a whole lot more we can save the earth!

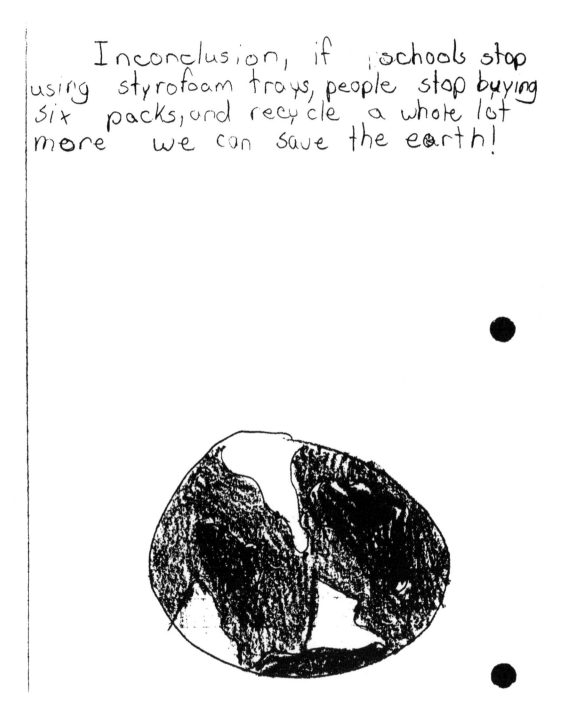

SOCIAL STUDIES

Hi! I will be writing about social studies. We are learning about the war of 1812. In the battle we were nutral.

Now the british were stealing ships. So the united states are going to war with the British soldiers.

We decided to meet the British and fight them in New orleans.

First we marched down the mississipi river to fight them. When we found them we were fighting our best fight we could ever fight.

We had a verry few men died and a amount of them were wounded. But we won the war of 1812 at new oliars, and now the british should now were are the best fight ever

417

Do you have an idea of some qualities you want your friendship to have? A lot of people don't think about it, some people just take these qualities for granted. I think about them every once in a while. Some of the things I think friendships should have are honesty, belief, and commitment.

All friendships should have honesty. Friends should always tell the truth, even if it might hurt them. The longer you tell a lie, the more you would hurt your friend. If you lie you might talk about your friend behind their back or tell people you don't like your friend when you really do. That's why friendships should have honesty.

Belief is another quality friendships should have. You and your friend have to believe in each other so your friendship will be a good one. If people didn't have belief in each other everybody would feel bad and fight. So belief is a major qualities in every friendship.

Then, the last quality is commitment. Commitment is something you definitely need to have in a friendship because it's what keeps friends together. Friendships have to have commitment or else there would only be "two-week-friendships" for everybody. Then that would make commitment a necessary quality in friendships.

So you now know that I think friendships should have honesty, belief, and commitment. Do you have a good relationship with your friend? I sure do because of the qualities I think are good. If you take your friendships for granted, don't because it might not be there someday.

Scores for the Holistic Writing Samples

FIRST-GRADE NARRATIVE COMPOSITION "MY MOTHER"

- **Clarity 5**   The topic is clear, and all of the points are well developed.
- **Support 5**   There is sufficient support in this composition for the first-grade level.
- **Organization 5**   This is a well-organized composition.
- **Mechanics 5**   There are no major mechanical errors and four minor errors that do not interfere with communication (pretty, loves, snuggles, real). However, these all could not reasonably be expected to be in a first-grade child's spelling vocabulary.
- **Overall Rating 5**   This is a very well-constructed composition for the first-grade level.

SECOND-GRADE CREATIVE EXPRESSION COMPOSITION "THE MYSTERY OF THE GREEN GASS" [SIC]

- **Clarity 4**   The topic is fairly clear and fairly easy to understand.
- **Support 3**   Although there is some support in this composition, it is not completely logical or understandable.
- **Organization 2**   The organization in this composition is very difficult to follow. It does not really seem to have a logical organization.
- **Mechanics 4**   Although there are a few major and minor errors in this composition, it is generally understandable and is fairly good for the second-grade level.
- **Overall Rating 3**   This composition is fairly good for the second-grade level. Although its topic is creative, it could be better organized and supported. It is, however, fairly easy to understand.

THIRD-GRADE PERSUASIVE COMPOSITION "MOTORCYCLES"

- **Clarity 4**   Although the topic is fairly clear, it is not entirely clear whether the child is writing about all motorcycles or only his own.
- **Support 4**   This composition is well supported. It includes a number of supporting examples and details.
- **Organization 4**   This composition is fairly well organized. However, the first paragraph is somewhat disorganized in comparison to the rest of the composition.
- **Mechanics 4**   Although this composition has a few major mechanical errors and a number of minor errors, it is still easy to understand.
- **Overall Rating 4**   This is a good persuasive composition for the third-grade level. It is fairly clear and well organized and is very interesting to read.

FOURTH-GRADE EXPOSITORY COMPOSITION "SAVE OUR EARTH"

- **Clarity 5**   This composition has a clear topic, and the opening and concluding statements are both logical and related.

- **Support 5**   There are sufficient well-explained support examples and details to make this composition very clear and effective.

- **Organization 5**   This composition is very well organized. It has logically sequenced ideas with correct paragraphing. It also uses transitional words and phrases effectively.

- **Mechanics 5**   This composition has no major mechanical errors and very few minor ones. The mechanics demonstrated by the child are very good for the fourth-grade level.

- **Overall Rating 5**   This is a very well-done expository composition for the fourth-grade level. It is clear, well organized, timely, and very informative.

FIFTH-GRADE EXPOSITORY COMPOSITION "SOCIAL STUDIES"

- **Clarity 2**   Although the topic of this composition ("The War of 1812") is clear enough, it is not expressed in either the title or the opening. The ending does not really relate to the opening either.

- **Support 1**   The support in this composition is very limited and, in one case, inaccurate. The support does not demonstrate a complete picture of the topic.

- **Organization 1**   This is a poorly organized expository composition that is very difficult to follow and understand.

- **Mechanics 1**   There are numerous major and minor mechanical errors in capitalization, sentence structure, and paragraphing that make this composition very difficult to understand.

- **Overall Rating 1**   It is very difficult to understand this disorganized, unsupported expository composition.

SIXTH-GRADE PERSUASIVE COMPOSITION "FRIENDSHIP"

- **Clarity 5**   The topic is very clear, and the opening and concluding statements relate well to each other.

- **Support 5**   There is sufficient support for the main idea in this composition in the form of examples and explanations. All of the examples and explanations are accurate and insightful.

- **Organization 5**   This composition is very well organized. Correct paragraphing and appropriate transitional words are used. All of the major points are developed logically.

- **Mechanics 5**   There are no major mechanical errors and only a few minor ones that do not interfere with understanding this composition. It contains generally correct spelling, punctuation, capitalization, grammatical usage, and sentence structure.

- **Overall Rating 5**   This is a very good persuasive composition for the sixth-grade level. It demonstrates good organization, support, and mechanics, and a true emotional maturity on the part of the student who wrote it.

Brief Description of an Individual Writing Inventory

In their book, Manzo and Manzo describe a version of an *Individual Writing Inventory.*[26] Their inventory consists of two levels: *Primer through the Fourth Grade* and *Fifth Grade through High School.* This inventory is a very simple way to make an assessment of some of the aspects of a student's writing skills and may be of some use in making such an assessment.

As with all such reading and writing inventories, it is an *informal assessment device* and, therefore, must be thought of as such. It is neither statistically valid or reliable. However, that does not mean it is of no use for making an informal assessment of writing skills. This inventory merely contains all of the limitations characteristic of an informal assessment device. If you want to examine Manzo and Manzo's *Individual Writing Inventory,* consult their book.

REPRODUCIBLE INDIVIDUAL WRITING INVENTORY DEVELOPED FOR THIS HANDBOOK

This handbook now includes a reproducible example of my own Individual Writing Inventory that is only minimally based on the model contained in the Manzo and Manzo book. You can duplicate and use this informal writing assessment device in it present form if it seems applicable or modify it in any way you wish.

---

[26]Anthony V. Manzo and Ula C. Manzo, *Literacy Disorders: Holistic Diagnosis and Remediation.* Fort Worth, TX: Harcourt Brace Jovanovich College Publishers, 1993, pp. 107–112.

Name _____ Grade _____ Teacher _____ Date _____

INDIVIDUAL WRITING INVENTORY
Part I: Second- and Third-Grade Levels

I. Have the child write out his/her own first and last names and addresses (if able).

	below average	average	above average
1. accuracy	❑	❑	❑
2. legibility	❑	❑	❑
3. spelling	❑	❑	❑
4. Teacher comments_____			

II. Have the child write a description of something pictured.

	below average	average	above average
1. accuracy of the details	❑	❑	❑
2. mechanics*	❑	❑	❑
3. correct sequence	❑	❑	❑
4. lack of irrelevant details	❑	❑	❑
5. Teacher comments			

III. Have the child complete the following two sentences.
An automobile _____
Television is _____

	below average	average	above average
1. mechanics	❑	❑	❑
2. appropriateness	❑	❑	❑

IV. Have the child fill in an omitted word from each of three sentences and then rate:
It is a beautiful, clear, _____ day today.
It is often _____ and snowy in the winter.
My _____ had five cute puppies last week.

	below average	average	above average
1. accuracy	❑	❑	❑
2. semantic acceptability	❑	❑	❑
3. syntactic acceptability	❑	❑	❑
4. prior knowledge	❑	❑	❑
5. Teacher comments _____			

V. Dictate three sentences, repeating each sentence three times. Rate the child's transcription for:

	below average	average	above average
1. accuracy	❑	❑	❑
2. mechanics	❑	❑	❑
3. penmanship	❑	❑	❑
4. Teacher comments_____			

*Mechanics in this Individual Writing Inventory means spelling, capitalization, grammatical usage, and punctuation.

Name _____ Grade _____ Teacher _____ Date _____

INDIVIDUAL WRITING INVENTORY
Part II: Fourth- Through Sixth-Grade Levels

I.   Have the student write a description of a picture.

	below average	average	above average
1. accuracy of details	❑	❑	❑
2. organization	❑	❑	❑
3. mechanics*	❑	❑	❑
4. overall evaluation	❑	❑	❑

   5. Teacher comments_____

II. Have the student write a summary of a passage (250–500 words) on the student's independent or low instructional reading level.

	below average	average	above average
1. accuracy	❑	❑	❑
2. correct sequence	❑	❑	❑
3. lack of irrelevant statements	❑	❑	❑
4. mechanics	❑	❑	❑
5. overall evaluation	❑	❑	❑

   6. Teacher comments _____

III. Have the student write a brief reaction composition to the statement: "Every student in the United States should learn at least one foreign language, such as Spanish or French, in elementary school."

	below average	average	above average
1. persuasiveness	❑	❑	❑
2. maturity of judgment	❑	❑	❑
3. mechanics	❑	❑	❑
4. overall reaction	❑	❑	❑

   5. Teacher comments _____

IV. Have the student offer a resolution to the problem: "In what ways can our society encourage people to recycle in order to preserve the environment?"

	below average	average	above average
1. maturity of judgment	❑	❑	❑
2. thoughtfulness	❑	❑	❑
3. inventiveness	❑	❑	❑
4. relevance of facts	❑	❑	❑
5. mechanics	❑	❑	❑
6. overall reaction	❑	❑	❑

   7. Teacher comments _____

V.   Have the student write a description of his/her favorite person.

	below average	average	above average
1. imagination	❑	❑	❑
2. maturity of judgment	❑	❑	❑
3. mechanics	❑	❑	❑
4. overall reaction	❑	❑	❑

   5. Teacher comments _____

*Mechanics in this Individual Writing Inventory means spelling, capitalization, grammatical usage, and punctuation.

CHAPTER TEN

Other Alternative Means
of Assessing Writing and Spelling Ability

In addition to using checklists and holistic scoring there are other informal ways of assessing competency in writing and spelling. This chapter is designed to acquaint you with these useful alternative informal ways so that you can use them effectively in your elementary or middle school literacy program. After reading this chapter and the previous two chapters carefully, you should have a very good understanding of how to effectively evaluate the writing and spelling skills of your students.

Have the Child at the Emergent Literacy Level
Write All the Words He/She Can

As part of the assessment program for entrance into the contemporary Reading Recovery Program™, each child is given a sheet of paper and asked to write all the words he or she is able to write on the paper. The Reading Recovery™ assessment program also includes the knowledge of capital and lower-case letter names and sight-word identification among other emergent literacy skills.

Normally when you ask a child at the emergent literacy level to write all of the words he or she can, invented spelling should be considered correct if it is decipherable. The following book will give you precise instructions about how to evaluate this part of the assessment:

Marie M. Clay, *An Observation Survey of Early Literacy Achievements*. Portsmouth, NH: Heinemann, 1993.

However, for the purposes of the typical literacy teacher, an informal assessment with simple examination and ranking of the children's responses in your classroom should be sufficient. An emergent literacy teacher can learn a great deal about a child's sight word identification ability, phonic analysis ability, and spelling ability by this very simple, quick assessment technique.

Words Per T-Unit

One of the best measures of sophistication competency either in oral or written language is the number of *words used per T-unit.* A *T-unit* is defined as any independent clause with all of its subordinate clauses and modifiers. Not only is this technique for determining sophistication of language supported by research, it also is logical as can be seen from the following two eleven-word sentences, containing about the same basic idea.

It is hot today, and I went swimming in the lake.
Since it is hot today, I went swimming in the lake.

The first sentence is a compound sentence and consists of two T-units: *"It is hot today"* and *"and I went swimming in the lake."* Thus, this writer used an average of *5.5 words* per T-unit. However, in the second sentence which is a complex sentence containing a subordinate clause, there is only one *independent clause* which contains a T-unit of eleven words. It is more sophisticated to subordinate ideas within the same sentence, and more sophisticated thinking tends to be expressed in more complex sentences.

Of course, evaluation by the use of T-units is not appropriate to atypical pieces of writing such as poetry or some types of prose. However, the T-unit measure is objective and reliable for individuals or for groups of students if the goal is to determine relative status of writing ability or writing growth over a period of time. Thus, T-units can be a useful and inexpensive assessment device for randomly assessing the effectiveness of the writing program in terms of improvement from year to year in a classroom or school district as long as the same type of writing is used in the evaluation.

However, the research of Crowhurst and Piche found that some students used more words per T-unit when writing persuasive compositions than when writing narrative or descriptive ones. The table shown on the next page, although not intended as a statistical table of norms, may give the literacy teacher some indication of the number of words per T-unit that might be expected at various grade levels.

As indicated in this table, there is no precise agreement as to the number of words per T-unit that students at any given grade level will use. Although all of these figures can be used as a basis of comparison, any school district planning to use this assessment technique to evaluate the success of its writing program should develop its own criteria in order to determine how students in that district are progressing from year to year and how the program is improving writing skills at each grade level from year to year.

Words Per T-unit Written at Various Grade Levels

	Crowhurst and Piche[27]	Hillerich[28]	Hunt[29]	Loban[30]
Grade				
3				7.60
4		10.08	8.6	8.02
5		10.44		8.76
6	10.13–11.75	10.98		9.04
7		11.48		8.94
8		11.65	11.5	10.37
9				10.05
10	11.15–14.26			11.79

Brief Description of Writing Coaching/Conferencing

The *writing conference* is the time when the teacher and the student(s) can discuss some aspect of the student's writing and the teacher can ask guiding questions that will help the student to formulate his or her thoughts. *Teacher-student and peer conferences are the cornerstone of the writing process.* The following suggestions may be helpful in planning your writing conferences:

1. Before beginning to use writing conferences, explain their purposes to the students and role play a number of different types of writing conferences.

2. Keep the writing conferences brief and on task. In most instances a writing conference should not last more than about 5 minutes.

3. Keep the writing conferences positive and interactive. Use thought-provoking questions that encourage students to think about and talk about their writing.

4. Have a definite plan in mind for each of the writing conferences. Most writing conferences can follow this approximate plan:

   a. *opening*—Have the student read his or her composition. Listen or read along with the student.

---

[27]Marion Crowhurst and Gene L. Piche, "Audience and Mode of Discourse Effects on Syntactic Complexity in Writing at Two Grade Levels," *Research in the Writing of English,* 13 (May 1979), pp. 101–109.

[28]Robert L. Hillerich, "Evaluation of Written Language," *Elementary English,* 48 (November 1971), pp. 839–842.

[29]Kellogg W. Hunt, *Grammatical Structures Written at Three Grade Levels.* Urbana, IL: National Council of Teachers of English, 1965.

[30]Walter D. Loban, *Language Development: Kindergarten Through Twelfth Grade.* Urbana, IL: National Council of Teachers of English, 1976.

b. *discussion*—Talk with the student about the purpose, content, and sequence of his or her composition. You can ask such questions as these during a writing conference:

—What part of the composition do you think is the most important?
—What part of the composition do you think is the most interesting?
—What ideas do you want your readers to get from this composition?
—How might you put these different parts of the composition together?
—Can you open your composition in a more interesting way?
—Did you end your composition with the most important idea you wanted the reader to get from your writing?
—How many of your sentences begin in the same way?
—How could you begin some of these sentences in a different way?
—How could you break this long sentence into shorter ones?
—How could you combine two or three short sentences into a more complex, interesting sentence?

c. *closing*—Help the student to focus attention on one or two items that he or she can easily do to improve the quality of the composition.

5. Keep a simple record sheet for each student's writing. (This chapter contains a reproducible sample record sheet for writing.)

6. On occasion have group conferences during which you talk to several students about their writing. This may be especially helpful if several students are doing the same type of writing such as creative expression, persuasive, expository, narrative, or descriptive writing.

7. Have two or three peers conduct writing conferences without teacher input. The following brief guidelines may be of help in this regard:

a. Don't try to rewrite your friend's work. It is his or her work, not yours.
b. Allow the writer to read his or her composition aloud if he or she wants to do so.
c. Tactfully tell the writer what you do and do not like about his or her writing.
d. If you feel the composition can be improved, make only *one or two* really useful suggestions. Don't criticize a composition just to be negative.
e. If you are supposed to proofread the composition for errors, do it silently.
f. If you don't understand some part of the composition, be sure to ask questions.
g. Always make a peer conference a positive experience for the writer and yourself.

REPRODUCIBLE SHEET FOR RECORDING INFORMATION ABOUT A STUDENT'S WRITING

The chapter now contains a reproducible sheet for recording important information about a student's writing. You can duplicate and use this record sheet in its present form if it seems applicable or modify it in any way you wish.

Name _____ Grade _____ Teacher _____ Date _____

STUDENT WRITING RECORD SHEET
(Upper Primary-Grade and Intermediate-Grade Levels)

Date	Name of Composition	Suggestions and Needs	Comments

Brief Description of a Writing Survey

If you want to learn about a student's attitudes toward all types of writing activities, you can have any student at the intermediate-grade or middle-school level complete a simple "Writing Survey." This type of survey can be very helpful in learning in what elements of writing a student feels competent and in what elements of writing he or she believes help is needed. Most students at this level are easily able to answer a few open-ended questions about their feelings and attitudes toward writing activities.

REPRODUCIBLE EXAMPLE OF A WRITING SURVEY

Here is a reproducible example of a writing survey that can be used with students at the intermediate-grade or middle-school level. You can duplicate and use this survey in its present form if it seems applicable or modify it in any way you wish.

WRITING SURVEY
(Intermediate-Grade or Middle-School Levels)

1. How do you think a person learns to write?

2. What kind of a writer do you think you are?

3. What do you think a good writer needs to do in order to write well?

4. What kind of compositions do you like to write the best—creative expression, persuasive, narrative, descriptive, or expository (content)? Why do you feel as you do?

5. What kind of compositions do you like to write the least—creative expression, persuasive, narrative, descriptive, or expository (content)? Why do you feel as you do?

6. What is the most difficult part of writing for you?

7. What is the easiest part of writing for you?

8. Do you enjoy reading your writing to other people? Why? Why not?

9. What do you like and dislike about participating in a peer writing conference?

10. What is your main goal in writing for the next two months?

Brief Description and Model of a Dialogue Journal

A *dialogue journal* is a type of writing activity designed to give a student the opportunity to share privately in writing his or her reactions, questions, and concerns about school experiences and sometimes personal matters without any threat of formal teacher evaluation. A dialogue journal, however, can be used as an *informal assessment measure* of a student's competency in writing **if the student allows the teacher to read his or her writing.** It also can give the teacher the opportunity to learn what each student is thinking and doing and then to offer help if this is possible.

Although the term *dialogue journal* has been coined fairly recently, journals have been kept for time immemorial, ever since individuals began to use writing as a way of keeping a record of their lives. The main difference between *traditional journals* and *dialogue journals* is the importance given to **providing communication between teacher and student.** Dialogue journals are like a daily letter or memo between teacher and student. In a dialogue journal a student writes to his or her teacher, and the teacher tries to write a timely, sincere response to the student.

To illustrate the possible use of a dialogue journal, examples from dialogue journals used in a typical fifth-grade classroom are shown below and on the next page.

It is important to allow some uninterrupted time each day or at least several times a week for the dialogue journal writing. In most classes, each student has a special folder in which the material is placed. As much as possible, the journals should focus on *writing about reading, books, authors, and writing.*

January 23, 1995

Last week I wrote a story trying to persuade my parents to send me to summer camp in the mountains next year. I hope that they will since it would be a lot of fun I think.

Casey,

I read your story on Friday, and I thought that it was very, very good.

I hope that your parents will send you to summer camp since you want to go so very much.

I think that your persuasive composition may help some to persuade them.

C. Harrington

> January 25, 1995
> Matt and I worked together on our writing yesterday. I think he helped me improve my descriptive story a lot. I'm pretty sure that it's good now. I liked working with Matt.

> Ben,
> I'm really looking forward to reading your descriptive composition. I bet that it is very good now. I'm also glad that you and Matt can work together so very well.
> C. Harrington

Here are several cautions you may want to consider in using dialogue journals in your classroom:

- *Always protect the privacy of the journal.* Never read aloud any part of a student's journal without first obtaining his or her permission.

- *Be an active reader and a prompt, sincere responder to the journal.* Write general comments rather than correct or criticize.

- *Always be honest with students.* Do not encourage a student to tell you more than you want to know and do not allow him or her to use offensive language.

- *Accentuate the positive in a student's journal.* Always try to encourage rather than discourage a student.

- *Try to make journal writing interesting and unique.* Be careful not to allow this activity to become tedious and boring by being sure to respond to the student's writing with interest and sincerity.

- *Do not promise to respond to students more often than is truly possible.*[31]

Brief Description and Sample of a Developmental Spelling Test

The "Developmental Spelling Test" is a very useful informal assessment device at the beginning stages of literacy. By studying the relation between the letters written and

---

[31]J. Joan Staton, "Writing and Counseling: Using a Dialogue Journal," *Language Arts,* 57 (April 1980), pp. 514–518.

the letters that are expected, you can make some tentative inferences about what a child understands about letter-sound relationships. You also can infer the developmental stage that they have achieved in understanding conventional English spelling. While this procedure may be especially useful near the beginning of a school year, it also can be used during the school year to assess the development of a child's knowledge of spelling.

The "Developmental Spelling Test" may be especially useful because it includes words that differ in complexity and because it is sensitive to changes that occur in the beginning stages of spelling. This spelling test has been used successfully with both kindergartners and first-graders. In a research study Morris and Perney found it to be a good predictor of later first-grade reading achievements.[32]

This spelling test is composed of 12 words. Before giving it, prepare children through a simple demonstration of spelling. First ask them to list the letter names they hear in a few sample words not found on the list, such as *sat* and *bet*. Then write these letters on the chalkboard, supplying any unknown letters if necessary. As an example, if the children hear only the /s/ and /t/ in *sat*, you might say "Fine," write *s_t* on the chalkboard, and say, "There also is an *a* in the middle of the word *sat*." After such a demonstration, the child should be asked to write each word "the best he or she can" by writing all the letter names that they are able to hear as you pronounce the twelve words on the list. Pronounce each word several times and allow the children enough time to think and to write what they hear. The early spelling responses of children can be classified developmentally according to several different stages. In the first stage, words are represented by letters and numbers, and the spellings do not resemble correct spellings. Such answers indicate that children understand that words are represented by a series of characters, but they have not yet learned that the elements within spoken words are represented by *letters*.

The second stage is alphabetic writing in which children represent some sounds of words in a systematic way, mainly those at the beginnings of words. The second stage can be divided into the following two substages: the stage in which only the initial consonants are represented and the stage in which both the initial and final consonants are represented, which is sometimes called a *consonant frame*.

In the third stage, children represent within-word patterns· more completely. At this stage letters representing *vowels* are included. Next in the transitional stage, the correct vowels and letters marking the pronunciation of words are represented; however, the spellings still differ in systematic ways from standard spelling for some words. Finally, children learn to spell words in the *conventional way*.

Therefore, from a child's responses to the "Developmental Spelling Test," you can ascertain whether most of a child's responses are *preliterate, initial consonant, consonant frame, phonetic, transitional,* or *standard*. After making this assessment, you then can direct the child's instruction in letter-sound relationships to his or her stage of development. As an example, in the preliterate stage, you can determine which, if any,

---

[32]Darrell Morris and Jan Perney, "Developmental Spelling as a Predictor of First-Grade Reading Achievement," *Elementary School Journal,* 84 (March 1984), pp. 441–457. Copyright © 1984 by The University of Chicago Press.

of the letter names the child still needs to learn, while in the phonetic stage you can determine which short and long vowel sounds the child still needs to learn.

The following table will provide you with some guidelines for evaluating the results of the "Developmental Spelling Test."

**DEVELOPMENTAL SPELLING TEST ITEMS
AND ILLUSTRATIVE SPELLINGS AT EACH STAGE**

Correct	Preliterate	Initial Consonant	Consonant Frame	Phonetic	Transitional
BACK	RE	BET	BC	BAK	*
SINK	E	C	SE	SEK	SINCK
MAIL	A	MM	MOL	MAL	MAEL
DRESS	S	DN	JS	GAS	DRES
LAKE	AH	L	LAE	LAK	LACE
PEEKED	TTT	PF	PT	PECT	PEKED
LIGHT	IEIX	LSIE	LAT	LIT	LIET
DRAGON	ATJA	JK	GAN	DAGN	DRAGIN
STICK	F	S	STC	SED	STIK
SIDE	TC	ST	CI	SID	CIDE
FEET	V	F	FT	FET	*
TEST	ABT	TS	TST	TAST	TEEST

*No transitional spellings were produced by the subjects for these words.

Source: Lou Ferroli and Timothy Shanahan, 1987. "Kindergarten Spelling: Explaining its Relation to First-Grade Reading" in J. E. Readence and R. S. Baldwin, Editors, *Research in Literacy: Merging Perspectives.* Thirty-Sixth Yearbook of the National Reading Conference. Rochester, NY: National Reading Conference, pp. 93–99. Based on Darrell Morris and Jan Perney, 1984, "Developmental Spelling as a Predictor of First-Grade Reading Achievement," *Elementary School Journal,* 84 (March 1984) pp. 441–457. Copyright © 1984 by The University of Chicago Press.

DEVELOPMENTAL SPELLING TEST

Teacher Directions

Pronounce each of these words slowly and carefully, allowing the child(ren) enough time to write it the best they can.

1. BACK
2. SINK
3. MAIL
4. DRESS
5. LAKE
6. PEEKED
7. LIGHT
8. DRAGON
9. STICK
10. SIDE
11. FEET
12. TEST

Answer Key

Children's responses at the various spelling stages are found in the table entitled: "Developmental Spelling Test Items and Illustrative Spellings at Each Stage."

DEVELOPMENTAL SPELLING TEST
(Beginning Literacy Level)

As your teacher says each word, write it the best you can on the line beside the number.

1. _____

2. _____

3. _____

4. _____

5. _____

6. _____

7. _____

8. _____

9. _____

10. _____

11. _____

12. _____

Brief Description of Sentence-Combining as a Writing Assessment Strategy

Sentence-combining is one strategy that can be used to informally assess a student's writing ability and also improve his or her reading comprehension ability. It also very effectively stresses the relationships between reading and writing. Sentence-combining instruction encourages students to read two or more short sentences and combine them into one longer, more complex sentence. Sentence-combining is based on the assumption that sensitizing students to the methods by which ideas are expressed and related in reading material will develop their ability to compose and comprehend.

Students should be introduced to the concept of sentence-combining through examples given by the literacy teacher that demonstrate the use of a connective or some other method of combining sentences, such as the use of subordinate clauses. Students should learn to notice how sentences are combined based upon the meaning they imply and "how they sound" rather than on any set rule. To help students determine the usefulness of certain combinations, they can share their combinations and judge as a group which combinations of the same sentence are the most preferable. Sentence-combining can be taught by units dealing with separate and somewhat distinct skills. As an example, one unit might concern the use of a connective such as *and, but,* or *or,* while another might deal with the use of subordinate clauses beginning with such words as *because, since, although, even though,* and *as soon as.* The sentence always should be emphasized as the meaning-bearing unit instead of the word when teaching sentence-combining.

REPRODUCIBLE ACTIVITY SHEET EMPHASIZING SENTENCE-COMBINING

The following is an activity sheet at about the fifth-grade level that emphasizes sentence-combining as an assessment and teaching technique. You can use this activity sheet in its present form if it seems applicable or modify it in any way you wish.

> **NOTE:** The following answers are only for illustrative purposes. There are other possible correct answers.

2. Since Mahalia's mother died when she was only five, she had a very difficult life as a child.

3. Since even as a child Mahalia had a very good singing voice, she began singing in a church choir at the age of five.

4. As a young girl Mahalia worked very hard cleaning houses and caring for children.

5. At the age of sixteen Mahalia left New Orleans so that she could study nursing in Chicago.

6. Since Mahalia needed money to live, she did laundry for white families using an old-fashioned washboard.

7. Since Mahalia always loved music very much, she became a soloist in the Greater Salem Baptist Church choir.

8. Mahalia earned money by singing in black churches and at funerals and by making religious records that were sold to black people.

9. Since Mahalia vowed that she would only sing religious music, she only sang religious music for the rest of her life.

10. Near the end of her life Mahalia became deeply involved with the Civil Rights Movement headed by Dr. Martin Luther King, and she donated a good portion of her money to that movement.

ACTIVITY SHEET FOR SENTENCE-COMBINING
(Approximately Fifth-Grade Level)

Read each of the following sets of sentences to yourself. Then <u>combine each set of sentences into one longer, more interesting sentence and write it on the lines below.</u> The first one is done for you as an example.

1. Mahalia Jackson was a famous African-American gospel singer.

   Mahalia Jackson's life provides a model of faith, determination, and courage.

   Mahalia Jackson was a famous African-American gospel singer, and her life provides a model of faith, determination, and courage.

2. Mahalia had a very difficult life as a child.

   Mahalia's mother died when she was only five years old.

   _____

   _____

   _____

3. Even as a child, Mahalia had a very good singing voice.

   Mahalia began singing in a church choir at the age of five.

   _____

   _____

   _____

4. As a young girl Mahalia worked very hard.

   As a young girl Mahalia cleaned houses and cared for children.

   _____

   _____

   _____

5. At the age of sixteen Mahalia left New Orleans for Chicago.

   Mahalia wanted to study nursing in Chicago.

   _____

   _____

   _____

ACTIVITY SHEET FOR SENTENCE-COMBINING
(Approximately Fifth-Grade Level) (Cont.)

6. In Chicago Mahalia needed money to live.

   In Chicago Mahalia did laundry for white families using an old-fashioned washboard.

   _____

   _____

   _____

7. Mahalia always loved music very much.

   Mahalia became a soloist in the Greater Salem Baptist Church choir.

   _____

   _____

   _____

8. Mahalia later earned some money singing in black churches and at funerals.

   Mahalia also earned money by making religious records that were sold to black people.

   _____

   _____

   _____

9. Mahalia vowed that she would only sing religious music.

   Mahalia only sang religious music for the rest of her life.

   _____

   _____

   _____

10. Near the end of her life Mahalia became deeply involved in the Civil Rights Movement headed by Dr. Martin Luther King.

    She donated a good portion of her money to the Civil Rights Movement.

    _____

    _____

    _____

    _____

PART THREE

Portfolio Assessment

CHAPTER ELEVEN

Using Portfolio Assessment in Any Literacy Program

"Since I'm using a whole language program now, the standardized tests my students have to take just do not really reflect their literacy accomplishments! I just don't know what to do about this." If you are a contemporary literacy teacher, you may very well have made a statement similar to this in the recent past. Many literacy teachers who are using variations of whole language have found the standardized tests they are required to give not to be compatible with this type of literacy program. However, the use of portfolio assessment in combination with various required standardized tests may help you and your students to assess their literacy accomplishments much more effectively and accurately.

After reading this chapter carefully, any literacy teacher should feel competent to implement portfolio assessment in his or her literacy program. This added dimension of assessment should greatly benefit students, teachers, and parents in understanding a student's accomplishments and self-evaluation skills. Portfolio assessment is a very important addition to traditional assessment programs, which often place far too much emphasis on standardized tests of various kinds.

Brief Description of Some of the Basic Characteristics of a Literacy Portfolio

A *literacy portfolio* can be defined as a collection of a student's work such as reading, writing, and thinking. The use of a literacy portfolio is part of what can be called *authentic assessment of literacy*. The use of portfolios should not entirely replace traditional assessment such as the use of standardized and informal tests of various types. Instead, portfolios should be an important part of a *comprehensive assessment program.*

A literacy portfolio, which is a record of a student's progress and self-assessment over time, is usually kept in some type of holder. Perhaps the most common type of holder for a portfolio is an accordion-type with compartments or sections. However, the holder also can be a folder, a box, or even a paper bag. The holder should be large enough to keep numerous papers, tapes, and drawings, and the student also can design and illustrate its cover. In any case, the folders, boxes, or containers should be easily accessible to the students in any classroom in which portfolios play a major role. It is essential that students be able to take them out, look through them, organize them, and add or delete material when they need or want to do so.

Although the use of portfolios in instruction and assessment is not entirely new, portfolios are now being used much more often because they are very compatible with the increased understanding of how language develops and the more widespread use of the whole language philosophy in both elementary and special literacy classes. As you undoubtedly know, whole language emphasizes instruction that stresses the use of "real" reading materials, the integration of the literacy skills, and constructing and reconstructing of meaning.

The idea of using portfolios in instruction and assessment in education undoubtedly stems from their use by other professionals such as artists, photographers, architects, and models. However, when portfolios are used in such professions as these, they normally are *show portfolios*, which display a range of the very best work done by that professional. However, most of these professionals also have a *working portfolio* somewhere from which the material for the show portfolio is derived.

Both *working portfolios* and *show portfolios* can be used in literacy instruction and assessment. However, *working portfolios* are much more relevant for students in the elementary and middle school. A working portfolio contains all of the materials with which the student is currently engaged. On the other hand, a show portfolio can be derived by selecting certain materials from the working portfolio preferably by the student him- or herself and occasionally by the teacher to be shown at parent-teacher conferences, to administrators, to school board members, or to various parent groups. A teacher can learn a great deal about a student's abilities and interests by carefully examining his or her portfolio on a regular basis and by having regularly scheduled conferences of about ten to fifteen minutes with the student about the portfolio at least four times a year.

Certainly, however, *working portfolios* are much more relevant and useful for students in the elementary and middle school. Although the possible content of a working portfolio is explained in some detail in the next section, very briefly here are some of the elements that can comprise a working portfolio:

- a table of contents to show the organization of the portfolio
- a reading/writing log
- various drafts of all types of writing that a student might do
- reading response journals
- dialogue journals

- writing done outside of class
- checklists and surveys of various types
- tape-recorded oral-reading protocols
- audiotapes
- videotapes
- student-teacher conference notes
- various types of self-assessment devices
- teacher anecdotes and observations
- graphs of progress

It should always be remembered that the **major purpose of using a portfolio is the opportunity for a student to self-assess his or her work**. Without allowing the student the opportunity and time to make such self-assessments, portfolios have very little meaning, making them merely a collection of a student's work. It also is essential for both the student and teacher to have input into selecting what is going to be placed in the student's working portfolio; however, **the student always should have the major input in the selection process**. Each student also should thoroughly understand that his or her portfolio is going to be readily available for inspection by his or her teacher, classmates, and parents, among others. Sometimes material from a student's working portfolio can be gathered and sent home after the student has decided—with or without teacher input—that it is no longer relevant for inclusion in his or her portfolio.

Parents must be thoroughly informed before implementing portfolio assessment in a classroom. Such information can be given to them by using a letter to parents, newsletters, a back-to-school meeting at the beginning of the school year, or some other means. It is crucial that parents understand the purpose and content of portfolios before a literacy teacher attempts to implement their use in either a regular or special literacy classroom.

In summary, *portfolios can be an integral part of a total assessment program*. Their use has unique advantages that are summarized later in this chapter. I urge you to consider implementing portfolios as one important part of your assessment of literacy skills.

Description of Some of the Elements That Can Comprise a Useful Working Portfolio

The chapter now contains a fairly comprehensive discussion of some of the elements that can comprise a useful working portfolio at either the elementary- or middle-school level.

PORTFOLIO HOLDER

The student always should have as much input as possible in selecting his or her *portfolio holder*. It is important for the student to have a container of some type because it keeps together what will become an assortment of different-sized materials, provides some privacy for him or her, and establishes some sense of ownership.

Although paper briefcases or file holders with flaps and attached bands or strings for holding them may be useful, they also may be fairly expensive. Some teachers provide each student with a half-open cardboard file box, but they may be fairly expensive too. One teacher obtained the corrugated boxes that contained fanned computer-printer paper and cut the flaps off the top. A first-grade teacher gave each child two paper grocery bags—one placed inside of the other to make it stronger. The upper edges were folded down to give more structure, and each child decorated his or her bag, which was then placed on the floor of the classroom. Self-stick vinyl can be applied to the bag if the child wishes to make it prettier. Flat-bottomed shopping bags from a department store also can be used. The upper edges can be fringed and colored construction paper can be placed over the handles. If the child wants, he or she can write his or her name over the store's logo. Many different types of boxes can be decorated with construction paper cut-outs, crayons, or paints, and many of these boxes contain lids that are attached at one side. You can see that the possibilities for portfolio holders are indeed limitless and should reflect the ingenuity and creativity of each student.

In summary, here are some considerations about portfolio holders:

- The portfolio should be large enough to hold a wide variety of different-sized papers without folding them and also large enough to accommodate other materials, such as audiotapes and videotapes.

- Each student should be encouraged to decorate his or her portfolio in some way to make it individualized and to give the student a sense of ownership.

- The portfolio should be strong enough to withstand frequent handling by the student, teacher, and other students.

- If possible, each student should be allowed to select the type of holder for his or her portfolio that he or she wants within the capability of the teacher to easily store them in the classroom and still make them accessible to the students.

TABLE OF CONTENTS

The teacher can introduce the concept of a table of contents to students after most of them have collected enough material for their portfolios so that they can organize it. One of the major purposes of having a table of contents for a portfolio is to encourage students to do *self-evaluation* of the items it contains. Obviously, students must have considerable direction when they first begin trying to develop a table of contents, and the teacher must be very patient and understanding.

A student can begin to develop his or her table of contents for the portfolio after he or she has accumulated enough material to sort and organize or categorize. The student also can create a written explanation to accompany a table of contents if he or she wants to do so and thinks it appropriate. Since the table of contents mainly should encourage *self-assessment*, there can be room on the table of contents for an explanation if the student desires it. Obviously, the table of contents should list the items actually contained in the portfolio, and all of the pages in the portfolio can be numbered, although this may create some difficulty as the student adds or deletes material. If possible, the classification scheme for the table of contents should be flexible enough to allow for additional material to be easily added or deleted.

The student can create his or her own categories for a table of contents. However, you also can help the student if he or she seems to have a great deal of difficulty with it. If a student has great difficulty creating a table of contents, it may indicate that he or she does not think much about his or her reading and writing. However, when you allow a student to create his or her own table of contents, it indicates that you trust the student's judgment.

Here are some of the ways in which a student can develop a table of contents:

- **sequential/chronological**—This is a time sequence in which the material in the portfolio was created. This may indicate how a student's writing has progressed over a semester or a school year. It also is useful in helping the student keep drafts of writing in the order in which they were written.

- **preferences (likes/dislikes)**—Two categories in this type of table of contents may be "Here Is My Best Work" and "Here Is My Worst Work."

- **topical**—The student's favorite subject matter or type of material.

- **genres**—An organization in terms of different types of writing such as fiction and nonfiction.

- **difficulty**—In this organization the student can place all of the difficult work in one section and the easy work in another section.

- **uses**—This organization indicates how different materials have different uses. For example, it can be organized with pictures and clippings used for writing and writing that is unfinished or finished.

- **other**—Any organization that is meaningful or useful to the student. The teacher can give guidance on the organization during the student-teacher conference, if necessary.

If you like, several students can work together in trying to develop a table of contents for their portfolios. Each student should be given the time and opportunity for thoughtful review of the table of contents and the content of his or her portfolio *before* the regularly scheduled student-teacher conference for the portfolio, which should occur at least four times during a school year. The table of contents can serve as a focus for discussion and can set a direction for the conference as well as indicate to the teacher some of the student's interests. It is very important that the student has given much thought to formulating the table of contents and can discuss his or her reasons for it.

You will find a reproducible table of contents sheet later in this chapter. This sample table of contents should help you determine what can be included in such a sheet and can be duplicated in its present form or modified in any way you wish.

READING/WRITING LOG

Each student should regularly keep a reading/writing log in which he or she briefly summaries all of the *reading and writing* that he or she does. A reading/writing log is simply a very brief account of everything that the student reads and writes with room for notes, comments, and reactions. A number of literacy specialists recommend that students keep separate logs for reading and writing. You certainly can have your students do this, but the reading/writing log has the advantage of showing the relationships between reading and writing and then becomes a true *literacy log*. The reading/writing log may lead to more integration between reading and writing.

In any case, any type of log to be included in a portfolio should be very simple for students to keep. A very detailed log almost certainly will discourage students from keeping any type of log because of the time involved in keeping it up to date. In addition, you should give students considerable help while they are making the first few entries in a log. You also must allow plenty of class time every few days for students to update their logs. You can have them make up tag names for writing that does not have a title.

The student can list the material he or she has read on lines that are interspersed with entries for pieces of writing that they have done. Most reading/writing logs have a column for indicating *reading* or *writing* so that the child can either print an **R** or **W** in that column. The student can write his or her name on top of each page he or she uses and then number the page. The student then enters the title in the left-hand column and the author's name in the column to the right. The student also can write reactions or annotations about the reading material to the right of the sheet. A reading/writing log can be simplified for first-grade children by using faces that indicate different emotions, such as happy and unhappy faces.

Obviously, there are countless different types of reading/writing logs or separate reading and writing logs that you can construct either alone or with the help of your students. **However, a useful reading/writing log that you can duplicate and use in its present form or modify in any way you wish is found later in this chapter**. If you do not choose to use this particular reading/writing log, it probably will provide you with an idea about how to construct your own version of a log.

DRAFTS OF ALL TYPES OF WRITING

A portfolio also can contain drafts of all types of writing a student does. Certainly, all of the drafts in process writing—including the rough draft, a revised draft, an edited draft, and the final product—should be included in a *working portfolio* to indicate a student's progress in writing. However, perhaps the student may want to include only the final, polished product in his or her *show portfolio*.

As much as possible, the writing included in a portfolio should relate to the reading the student does. In this way, the **assessment** of the student's writing becomes truly **authentic**. The writing contained in a student's portfolio also will indicate to you whether or not the student is doing all of the different types of writing and not just one type, such as narration. Occasionally, it also is important for a single piece of writing to respond to more than one type of reading on occasion.

Many different types of writing can be included in a portfolio. All of the various types of compositions that were explained and scored holistically in Chapter 9, including creative expression of prose and poetry, narration, exposition, persuasion, and description, can be included. Additional types of writing that can be placed in a student's portfolio are parodies of favorite poems or stories, thought-for-the-day journals, new lyrics for songs, new rap copy, or scripts for scenes in a play.

READING RESPONSE JOURNALS

A reading response journal also can be included in a portfolio. Such a journal contains writing that is *in response* to some type of reading. As an example, the student reads a book or selection and then writes some type of personal response to it.

Here are several suggestions of inclusions for a reading response journal:

- a summary of the reading
- a new beginning for the reading
- a new ending for the reading
- including him- or herself as a character in the reading
- a summary of his or her favorite part of the reading
- a summary of his or her least favorite part of the reading
- changing the time or place setting of the reading
- writing a Reader's Theater script or a play that was based on the reading

DIALOGUE JOURNAL

A student's portfolio can contain dialogue journals. As you may remember, dialogue journals were explained and illustrated in some detail in Chapter 10. However, very briefly a dialogue journal is a written interaction between a student and teacher in which each person writes or responds to the other person in a truthful, timely manner. The teacher can ask questions in a dialogue journal that the student is then motivated to answer, giving him or her a topic to write about. A dialogue journal is a technique that *may* eliminate the threat of exposing personal feelings and thoughts.

A dialogue journal that is contained in a portfolio also conceivably may be between two classmates instead of between student and teacher. Two students who have worked together on constructing certain materials for their portfolios, such as the table of contents, could also easily be two students who would benefit from working on a dialogue journal together.

WRITING DONE OUTSIDE OF CLASS

A student should include in his or her portfolio all types of writing done outside of class. If a student does not include writing done outside of class time, such as writing about family experiences or unassigned stories done at home, he or she probably is not very involved in his or her portfolio and does not feel any great sense of ownership in it.

If a student does not include writing done outside of class in the portfolio, he or she certainly should be encouraged to do so. A student also should be encouraged to compare writing done at school and at home. One way of motivating writing at home is by giving the student time at school to begin some type of writing that will be completed at home. Some students may work on types of writing at home that were introduced in school, such as journals, various kinds of compositions, and letters. The student should be encouraged to tag work done at home so that it can be properly included in his or her portfolio.

CHECKLISTS AND SURVEYS OF VARIOUS TYPES

A student's portfolio can include checklists and surveys of various types. Some of them can be completed by the student him- or herself, while others can be completed by the teacher. The teacher can construct an almost limitless variety of checklists and surveys related to a student's achievement in and attitudes toward both reading and writing.

This handbook also contains a number of different checklists and surveys that can be completed either by the student or teacher and placed in his or her portfolio. For example, the checklists at various levels in letter identification and word identification found in Chapter 2 can be completed by the teacher and included in a student's portfolio. Chapter 3 contains checklists at the various reading levels for informally assessing a student's competencies and weaknesses in vocabulary, the various elements of comprehension, and the basic study skills. The student usually can independently complete the interest inventory found in Chapter 5. Chapter 7 contains reading attitude surveys and the reading autobiography. That chapter also includes a self-monitoring checklist a student can complete and then place in his or her portfolio.

In summary, any commercial or teacher-constructed checklist or survey that either the student or teacher fills in has an appropriate place in a working portfolio or perhaps a show portfolio.

TAPE-RECORDED ORAL READING PROTOCOLS

Either a working or show portfolio can include tape-recorded oral-reading protocols. These are audiotapes of a student's unrehearsed or rehearsed reading. They are extremely useful in showing the student and his or her parents the student's reading progress over time. Usually the student makes taped oral reading samples starting near the beginning of the school year, and at periodic intervals after that, such as once a month. Unrehearsed protocols should be compared only with unrehearsed protocols, while rehearsed protocols should be compared only with rehearsed protocols to obtain a more accurate assessment of the student's actual oral-reading progress.

When a student or parents replay earlier tape-recorded oral reading protocols and compare them to one done at the present time, the student or parents often are pleasantly surprised at the amount of improvement the student has made. The student and/or parent can observe such characteristics of oral reading as these:

- increased oral reading fluency
- better expression and phrasing while reading orally
- lack of word-by-word reading while reading orally
- fewer hesitations, substitutions, mispronunciations, repetitions, and reversals while reading orally

AUDIOTAPES

A student can include several different types of audiotapes in his or her portfolio. For example, if the teacher wishes, he or she can include an audiotape of an Individual

Reading Inventory such as that contained in Forms L and M in Chapter 5 of this handbook. Perhaps the student or parent then can concretely see the improvement over time that the student has made while taking such an informal assessment device.

A taped copy of a student's running record as was described and illustrated in Chapter 4 also can be included in a student's portfolio as well as tapes of other types of miscue analysis, such as were also described and illustrated in Chapter 4 of this handbook. In addition, the student can include an audiotape of him- or herself and several other students orally reading material in parts or a tape of him or her orally reading along with a commercial or teacher-prepared read-along tape.

STUDENT-TEACHER CONFERENCE NOTES

As has been stated earlier, the student and teacher should conference about the student's portfolio on a regular basis for about ten to fifteen minutes at least four times a year. The student should always carefully prepare for this conference by being sure that his or her portfolio has a current table of contents and that he or she is very familiar and comfortable with its contents.

During a student-teacher conference about a portfolio, the student and teacher both write notes on a sheet that has been especially constructed for this purpose. **Later in this chapter you will find a student-teacher conference notes sheet that you can duplicate and use in its present form or modify it in any way you wish.** If you do not want to use it, at least it should serve as a useful model of this type of form.

When using such a sheet, the student and teacher pass it back and forth to *record observations and decisions about the portfolio that were made during the conference.* Although it may seem cumbersome to pass the sheet back and forth, it is important to assure that both student and teacher are able to see what the other has written.

The conference notes should cite improvements and other areas that either student or teacher discuss and agree upon. Try to help the student set several literacy goals for the near future and write them on the sheet. By the end of the school year each student's portfolio should contain at least four completed student-teacher conference note sheets to indicate four successfully completed student-teacher conferences about the portfolio.

SELF-ASSESSMENT DEVICES

A student's portfolio also can include a variety of self-assessment devices in both reading and writing. Since it was stated earlier that one of the main purposes of using portfolios is to help students learn to assess their progress in reading and writing skills effectively, it is obvious that self-assessment devices have a very important part in a student's portfolio. Any type of device that the student can use to assess his or her progress in literacy can be placed in a portfolio.

Several such self-assessment devices have been included in this handbook. For example, Chapter 7 contains a reading attitude survey, a reading autobiography, and a self-monitoring checklist, any of which a student can complete and place in his or her portfolio. As you know, each of these informal devices can be used to assess different elements of literacy. You also can construct many other types of informal self-assessment devices a student can complete and place in the portfolio.

Any way in which a student evaluates his or her literacy product can promote self-assessment. For example, responding to reading, reacting to reading, expressing opinions for classroom publications, and writing and editing class publications all promote self-assessment of literacy.

Various Types of Notes and Memos

Several different types of notes and memos may have an important place in a student's portfolio. For example, notes in which a student writes a summary of what he or she has learned recently in literacy can be evidence of self-assessment and can be placed in the portfolio. Some teachers require notes such as these to be placed in the portfolio before a regularly scheduled student-teacher portfolio conference or any time in which the portfolio is to be examined by someone, such as by parents or administrators.

Teachers, parents, and administrators also can write brief notes, giving their reactions to the portfolio as a whole or any specific item contained in it, which then can be included in a student's portfolio. The student also can include notes in his or her portfolio explaining why he or she included certain items in it. These notes may be stapled to the entries in the portfolio.

> **CAUTION**: Be sure not to require the student to do an excessive amount of writing for his or her portfolio or you may discourage him or her from keeping a good one.

Teacher Anecdotes and Observations

A student's portfolio can include any teacher anecdotes and observations you consider to be relevant in evaluating the student's competency or growth in either reading or writing, or his or her ability or improvement in self-assessment.

However, you must be certain not to include any statements that may be potentially damaging to the student, as he or she will certainly read them. As much as possible, these anecdotes and observations should be complimentary although as objective as possible. Certainly the student's own portfolio is *not* the place to include material that will be potentially damaging to him or her.

Graphs (Records) of Progress

Finally, the student either independently or with peers should be encouraged to show his or her progress in both reading and writing in a concrete, creative way. For example, these records can demonstrate the number of books read or the number of compositions written. Although this is not entirely compatible with the *whole language* approach, the student also can record the number of sight words identified or phonic rules learned.

There are countless creative ways for a student to record the books he or she has read. Chapter 7 of this handbook contains many several creative ways to do this. However, a few of them are as follows:

- traditional graphs of progress
- reading wheel (illustrated in Chapter 7)
- bookworm (illustrated in Chapter 7)
- rocket ship (illustrated in Chapter 7)
- a hot air balloon

The following resource, also cited in Chapter 7, contains numerous creative ways of recording books read and reported on:

Patricia Tyler Muncy, *Hooked on Books! Activities and Projects That Make Kids Love to Read.* West Nyack, NY: The Center for Applied Research in Education, 1995.

NOTE: It is especially motivating for a disabled reader, a reluctant reader, or a learning-handicapped student to record his or her reading and writing progress in a concrete, tangible way.

Should Standardized and Informal Test Scores Be Included in a Student's Portfolio?

Both literacy specialists and literacy teachers differ on whether or not standardized and informal test scores of various types should be included either in a student's *working portfolio or show portfolio.* Some of them recommend including all of a student's test scores, including achievement test scores, criterion-referenced test scores, and basal reader test scores, in portfolios. In addition, they recommend that all informal test scores such as running records, the results of miscue analysis, Individual Reading Inventory scores, and results from all other informal assessment devices should be included. They may recommend that any of these results be included in either a student's working portfolio or show portfolio.

There are several valid reasons that may support this point of view. For example, it can be argued that a student has a right to know how well or poorly he or she performed on any type of assessment device he or she is required to take. Then, too, all of these scores are then readily available in the student's portfolio to be shown to parents during parent-teacher conferences. It can also be stated that all such test results are part of an entire assessment program and should be included in a portfolio since it also is devoted to being a record of the student's performance.

However, there are equally compelling reasons why test scores should *not* be included in a student's portfolio. For example, test scores may detract from a student's analysis of his or her own reactions to his or her reading, writing, and thinking. The inclusion of test scores, perhaps especially standardized test scores, in a portfolio really is a contradiction of the major purpose of using portfolios—that of the student as a *self-assessor.*

In any case, the portfolio may qualify and enlighten test scores, but test scores really add little to the meaning and value of any portfolio collection. However, the portfolio has great value as a back-up when a student's test scores seem inaccurate in light of a teacher's observations about him or her. Certainly all types of *performance assessments*, which sometimes can be in the form of teacher-prepared paper-and-pencil tests, are relevant for inclusion in a student's portfolio.

In summary, each literacy teacher should him- or herself make the decision about whether or not to include standardized and informal test scores in the portfolios of his or her students. This decision should be made in terms of a teacher's beliefs and the possible requirements of his or her school system.

The Advantages and Limitations of Using Literacy Portfolios

A literacy portfolio has many unique *advantages*. Very briefly, here are some of them:

- It aids a student in self-assessment, a crucial life skill.
- It is a highly effective instructional tool as well as an assessment tool.
- It exemplifies language use as meaning-constructed behavior.
- It supports student ownership for his or her reading or writing improvement.
- It is an example of authentic assessment since it keeps the focus on genuine, student-oriented purposes for reading and writing.
- It promotes writing with an audience awareness.
- It emphasizes reading and writing activities that reflect each student's unique background and interests.
- It helps a student develop a very positive attitude toward reading and writing activities.
- It promotes student-teacher interaction and collaboration among students.
- It shows a student his or her reading and writing progress in a concrete way.
- It is useful in parent-teacher conferences and in enlisting parent support for the student's instruction and evaluation processes.
- It can be useful in conferences about students with principals, supervisors, and consultants.
- It can provide much useful information about a student to his or her teacher.

However, literacy portfolios have several *limitations* you should consider before implementing them in a regular classroom literacy program, special literacy program, or learning disability classroom:

- It takes a great deal of time and effort to implement portfolio assessment in any type of literacy program. Therefore, it is best to start portfolio assessment gradually, as is explained later in this chapter.
- It takes time for a student to compile, self-assess, and prepare his or her portfolio for student-teacher portfolio conferences.

- It is very time-consuming for the teacher to conduct twenty to thirty 10- to 15-minute student-teacher portfolio conferences at least four times a year.

- It must be thoroughly explained both to parents and school administrators before it is selected for use in any type of literacy program.

- It is fairly difficult to accurately grade a literacy portfolio if this is required by a teacher's school system for some reason.

In summary, I believe the many advantages of portfolio assessment greatly outweigh its limitations. Therefore, I recommend you use it as *one means of assessment in any kind of literacy program.* However, standardized tests and informal tests of various types should also be used in any literacy assessment program. Each has unique advantages and limitations and may meet the requirements of different constituencies such as students, teachers, parents, school administrators, school boards, or state boards of education.

The Importance of Using Portfolio Assessment in a Whole Language Program

Portfolio assessment has a number of unique advantages that make it especially useful in a whole language (literature-based) program. Traditional assessment often does not reflect the whole language philosophy well for a number of reasons. That is why many teachers have found it difficult to use only traditional assessment devices while using a whole language program.

Here are some of the main reasons why standardized tests of various types are *not* reflective of a whole language program:

- Tests usually employ short passages while a whole language program uses entire passages of different genres of children's literature.

- Tests normally evaluate isolated reading skills such as sight-word recognition, phonic analysis, word structure, and discrete elements of comprehension and the study skills. A whole language program does not teach to reinforce literacy skills in isolation but rather in the context of whole language, such as sentences or passages.

- Tests usually separate reading and writing skills while a whole language program stresses all literacy skills such as listening, speaking, reading, and writing equally.

- Tests usually do not stress a student's decision-making ability, while a whole language program emphasizes each student's decision-making skills to a great degree.

- Tests often do not evaluate a student's ability to apply knowledge, but rather just to recall it, while a whole language program stresses the application of knowledge often using thematic units in social studies and science.

- Many tests do not allow students to use background knowledge or construct meaning. A whole language program usually stresses both prior knowledge and the construction of meaning.

- Some tests may use "artificial language" while a whole language program uses the language found in quality children's literature of various narrative and expository (content) genres.

- Many tests stress explicit (literal or lower-level) thinking since an explicit question usually has only one correct answer. However, a whole language program requires that a student do much interpretive (higher-level) thinking in planning and executing the thematic units that comprise a large portion of the program.

- Any test may not be normed using students that represent the particular balance of students in many schools and districts that will nonetheless be comparing their students' scores to those of the norming sample.

In summary: Most standardized tests do not emphasize the *authentic assessment* that is necessitated by the content of a whole language program.

However, portfolio assessment *is* very well suited for assessment in a whole language program for the following main reasons:

- It emphasizes *authentic assessment*.
- It stresses a student's self-assessment and decision-making abilities.
- It encourages the reading of actual children's literature of various genres.
- It stresses the integration of reading and writing skills.
- It stresses the use of the student's own prior knowledge.
- It stresses the application of a student's learning.
- It encourages various higher-level thought processes.
- It compares the student's performance only with him- or herself instead of with a norm group that may not be comparable to the student.

In summary: Portfolio assessment is extremely well suited for use in any contemporary whole language (literature-based) program. It seems to meet the special requirements of such a program.

However, it is obvious that such programs also must give standardized tests of various types to meet the needs of other various constituencies as was discussed earlier.

Some Guidelines for Starting Portfolio Assessment in Any Literacy Program

A number of teachers are hesitant about implementing literacy portfolios in their classrooms if they have not had any previous experience with them. However, remember that since portfolios bring *literacy instruction and assessment together*, as students become familiarized with them and with self-assessment, much of the management in a portfolio assessment program can be done by the students themselves. Of course, you always will need to provide students with guidance and feedback during the process by using brief, informal conferences and the regularly scheduled student-teacher portfolio conferences.

In any case, here are the main steps any literacy teacher can take in beginning to use portfolios with his or her students:

1. **Introduce the literacy portfolio concept to your students.** Before beginning to use portfolios with your students, introduce them by explaining that the use of portfolios can help them and their teacher to improve the teaching and learning of reading and writing skills. Tell students why portfolios are very effective and how they promote a student's *self-assessment* of his or her reading and writing skills. Tell them that the portfolios will be used to show their teacher, classmates, and parents the type of literacy activities in which they are engaging. Also tell them that you will be working closely with them, helping them learn to select and assess materials for the portfolio regularly and by using ten- to fifteen-minute student-teacher portfolio conferences. You also may want to show several different types of portfolio holders and several model portfolios that have been kept by students at about the same grade level. This introduction should reassure students about the entire portfolio assessment system.

2. **Identify the categories of information to be included in the portfolio.** Next, explain and demonstrate models of the various types of materials that can be included in a portfolio. Discuss and perhaps demonstrate for your students the following categories, which have been explained earlier in this chapter.

   a. the portfolio holder
   b. formulating a table of contents after some materials have been collected
   c. a reading/writing log
   d. drafts of writing
   e. a reading response journal
   f. a dialogue journal
   g. writing done outside of class
   h. checklists and surveys
   i. tape-recorded oral reading protocols
   j. audiotapes
   k. videotapes
   l. student-teacher conference notes (explain that you will be holding at least four ten- to fifteen-minute student-teacher literacy portfolio conferences during the school year)
   m. self-assessment devices the student can complete
   n. notes and memos of various types, some of which can be used to tag and briefly explain why the student selected certain items for his or her portfolio
   o. kinds of records of the student's reading and writing process

NOTE: You may want to begin with having the student only select appropriate materials relating to a few categories and gradually expand on these categories as he or she becomes more familiar with portfolios. I recommend starting with these categories: a reading/writing log; drafts of writing; a reading response journal; and tape-recorded oral reading protocols.

3. **Plan the procedure for using portfolio assessment with your students**. Next, plan *with your students* just how to implement portfolio assessment in your classroom. It is very important that this procedure be *student controlled* as much as possible. Then discuss with your students how to obtain a *holder for the portfolio*. Also discuss a location in the classroom for housing all of the portfolios. Next, discuss how each student will select the materials for his or her portfolio. Although there are some materials you must require to be included in the portfolios, the decision about what to include should be left to the students as much as possible. You also need to discuss the placing of materials in the portfolio and the use of entry slips or tag names to explain the inclusion of certain materials. The students need directions as to how and when they will work with their portfolios and when you will allot time especially for this purpose. You should also briefly explain the concept and procedures for the student-teacher literacy portfolio conferences and how the entire portfolio experience will be periodically evaluated.

4. **Holding the student-teacher literacy portfolio conferences**. When the portfolios have been started and the basic routines have been established, you can begin to plan these conferences. If possible, begin the portfolio conferences several weeks after implementing portfolios in your classroom. At the beginning try to have fairly frequent, brief conferences, giving each student guidance, then moving later to the regularly scheduled longer conferences. One common problem at the beginning of using portfolios is a student's tendency to *include too much material in the portfolio* and perhaps to *miss some important material*. However, the conferences should fairly easily eliminate these problems. The portfolio conferences should be both *reflective and collaborative*. You can try to ascertain such information as the following from these conferences:

—How does the student feel about what he or she is doing?
—What student strengths can you and the student locate?
—What does the *student* think he or she needs to do to improve?
—What future goals for the portfolio would you and the student like to establish?

5. **Review, evaluate, and revise the portfolio process**. Since portfolio assessment is a continuous, ongoing process, it is important to talk to the entire class about how they believe it is working and how they believe it could best be improved. You can also discuss your program of portfolio assessment with other teachers who are also using it to hear their thoughts and suggestions.

The Importance of Student Self-Selection and Self-Assessment of Materials in His or Her Literacy Portfolio

As has been emphasized throughout this chapter, a student's literacy portfolio should be his or her own. Therefore, a student should be able to choose almost any type of material for inclusion in his or her *working portfolio* and perhaps also for his or her *show portfolio*. Of course, the teacher will have to establish a minimum of materials that also must be included in a literacy portfolio, such as a table of contents, reading/writing log, drafts of writing, a reading response journal, tape-recorded oral reading protocols, and notes and entry slips justifying including material selected for the portfolio.

Self-selection of material for a literacy portfolio helps student's decision-making ability, which is a major purpose of using portfolio assessment. As stated earlier, although a student sometimes may place too much material in the portfolio, with informal teacher guidance and the regularly scheduled student-teacher conferences, this problem should easily be eliminated. When the teacher believes that a student is "stuffing" his or her portfolio with material that is unrelated to his or her reading or writing or overlooking good material, you can have him or her write notes or entry slips rationalizing the selections. These notes or entry slips may help the student become more selective about what he or she includes in the portfolio.

In summary, since the portfolio truly belongs to the student who created it, he or she should be allowed to control its contents as much as possible with some teacher guidance and requirements.

Self-assessment of the material included in a literacy portfolio is probably the major goal of portfolio assessment. This is extremely important because the major goal of education is to develop students who will continue to learn throughout their lives. If a student is to improve in any literacy skill, he or she must consider how to make the required improvement. Allowing a student to self-assess the materials in the literacy portfolio can enhance his or her self-esteem as a reader and writer. *Self-assessment begins* when the student starts to select the work to be contained in the portfolio and *continues* when a student:

- organizes his or her portfolio
- formulates the table of contents for the portfolio
- completes self-assessment devices that will be included in the portfolio (several reproducible self-assessment devices are included later in this chapter)
- thinks about his or her reading and writing goals and reviews his or her work

In summary, the self-assessment that is an integral part of portfolio assessment *promotes ongoing analysis of the materials to be placed in the portfolio* and *encourages critical thinking about why the student selected certain materials.*

Various Types of Reproducible Devices That Can Be Included in a Portfolio Assessment Program

The chapter now includes a number of reproducible forms that may be useful in any portfolio assessment program. It includes reproducible examples of a sample letter to be sent to parents before using portfolio assessment, a table of contents sheet for a portfolio, a sheet for organizing a portfolio, a student welcome sheet to the portfolio, a reading/writing log, a student-teacher conference form, several self-evaluation devices for a portfolio, a portfolio peer review sheet, a parent review form for a portfolio, and a form for evaluating a portfolio.

You can duplicate and use any of these examples in their present form or modify them in any way you wish in light of the interests and needs of your students.

Date _____

Dear Parent,

In your child's class this year each student will collect pieces of writing and other materials in a portfolio. Some of the papers may be drawings or writing that was done after the student read something that was very interesting to him or her. As an example, your child may write a different ending to a book or story or write why he or she particularly liked a book or story. In some cases, the child may write about nonfiction that especially interests him or her.

The students will be collecting many other things in their portfolios such as clippings from old magazines and other sources as ideas for stories to write. *I hope that some of the pieces of writing and other materials will be done or found at home. However, these activities should <u>not</u> be thought of as <u>homework</u> because all reading, writing, and thinking about things should be fun and interesting.*

Another important part of the student portfolios will be some simple records. As an example, your child will keep a log of all things he or she reads and writes both at school and at home. It also will include comments by your child about the books, stories, and other materials read and about the papers he or she wrote. There also may be longer notes in the portfolio that tell about writing particular pieces of work contained in it and that analyze his or her progress as a reader and writer. There also will be notes from some other people who look at the portfolio. I will write some notes, and your child's classmates also may write some. Your child and I also will make notes at the conferences we will be having about the portfolio. Although we will probably be talking about the portfolio nearly every day, we also will have regular conferences in which your child and I together evaluate his or her reading and writing progress and set some goals for the future.

You will also have opportunities to write comments that can be included in the portfolio. It will be a <u>working portfolio</u> which means that it is a full collection that encourages self-assessment by your child. It is not a <u>show portfolio</u> to be evaluated by either of us. The *major purpose of portfolios is to help a student <u>assess or evaluate</u> his or her work better so that he or she will become a better reader and writer.*

During this year there will be several opportunities for you to look at the portfolios and ask questions about what they contain. You can then also talk with me about your child's performance as a reader and writer. However, if you have any questions now, please feel free to let me know.

There are many ways in which you can become involved in your child's portfolio. You should always encourage your child to read and write at home as often as possible. It also is very important for your child to include things read and written at home in his or her portfolio. Things that are read at home can be added to the reading/writing log, and things written at home can be brought to school to be added to the portfolio if your child wants. *In any case, always continue to praise the strengths and improvements you notice in your child's reading and writing.*

Sincerely,

© 1995 by John Wiley & Sons, Inc.

Name _____ Grade _____ Teacher _____ Date _____

MY PORTFOLIO
Table of Contents

Decide how you want to organize your portfolio. Sort everything in your portfolio and put them in piles that seem to go together in some way. Then try to think of a good title for each chapter. Include the books and stories you have read and all the different kinds of writing you have done.

Title for Chapter 1: _____

What I included in this chapter: _____

_____

_____

_____

_____

The reasons I included these things in this

chapter: _____

_____

_____

_____

Title for Chapter 2: _____

What I included in this chapter: _____

_____

_____

_____

_____

The reasons I included these things in this

chapter: _____

_____

_____

_____

Title for Chapter 3: _____

What I included in this chapter: _____

_____

_____

_____

_____

The reasons I included these things in this

chapter: _____

_____

_____

_____

Title for Chapter 4: _____

What I included in this chapter: _____

_____

_____

_____

_____

The reasons I included these things in this

chapter: _____

_____

_____

_____

Name _____ Grade _____ Teacher _____ Date _____

HOW I AM ORGANIZING MY PORTFOLIO

These are some of the things in my portfolio

Here Is What I Like to Read About:

1. _____

2. _____

3. _____

4. _____

5. _____

Here Is What I Like to Write About:

1. _____

2. _____

3. _____

4. _____

5. _____

These Are the Names of the Favorite Books and Stories I Read:

1. _____

2. _____

3. _____

4. _____

5. _____

These Are the Titles of the Favorite Things I Wrote:

1. _____

2. _____

3. _____

4. _____

5. _____

Here Are the Kinds of Books and Stories I Hope I Can Read Soon:

1. _____

2. _____

3. _____

4. _____

5. _____

Here Is What I Want to Write About Soon:

1. _____

2. _____

3. _____

4. _____

5. _____

THIS IS MY PORTFOLIO

My name is _____

I am in grade_____at _____ School.

My teacher's name is _____

I filled in this sheet on _____

I started my portfolio on _____

This is how I organized my portfolio: _____

_____

_____

_____

This is what my portfolio shows about my reading: _____

_____

_____

_____

This is what my portfolio shows about my writing:

_____

_____

_____

_____

This is what I think are the best things in my portfolio:

_____

_____

_____

_____

Name _____ Grade _____ Teacher _____

MY READING/WRITING LOG

RATINGS:

Great	☆ ☆ ☆ ☆
Good	☆ ☆ ☆
All Right	☆ ☆
Poor	☆

Date	Title and Author	R or W	My Comments: Why I Read or Wrote It; Why I Like or Didn't Like It; My Other Comments	My Overall Rating

Name _____ Grade _____ Teacher _____ Date _____

STUDENT-TEACHER LITERACY PORTFOLIO
Conference Notes

Student's Conference Notes	Teacher's Conference Notes

SELF-ASSESSMENT DEVICE
(Intermediate-Grade Level)

1. What does a person have to do to be a good reader?

2. Who is my favorite author? Why do I like to read books or stories written by him or her?

3. What are the three best things I have read this semester? Why did I like them?

4. What are the easiest and hardest things about reading for me?

5. What kinds of books and stories would I like to read in the future?

6. What does a person have to do to be a good writer?

7. What kinds of writing have I done this year?

8. What kinds of writing do I like to do the most?

9. What piece of writing would I like most to do over to make it better?

10. What kinds of writing would I like to do in the future?

11. What are the easiest and hardest things for me about writing?

12. What do I need to work on the hardest to improve my writing?

Name _____ Grade _____ Teacher _____ Date _____

WHAT I THINK ABOUT MY READING AND WRITING
(Intermediate-Grade Level)

Write how you think you have become a better reader and writer this year. In what ways do you think you have improved the most this year as a reader and writer? What new goals do you still have for yourself as a reader and writer?

_____

_____

_____

_____

_____

_____

_____

_____

_____

_____

_____

_____

_____

_____

_____

_____

_____

Continue on the back of this sheet if necessary.

CLASSMATE REVIEW SHEET
(Intermediate-Grade Level)

Name of Portfolio Owner _____ Grade _____ Teacher _____

Name of Student Who Reviewed This Piece of Writing _____

Title of Paper _____

Date Written _____

Date Evaluated _____

1. What do you think was especially good about this piece of writing?

2. Why do you think the writer chose to do this piece of writing?

3. Suggest **one** thing for the writer to work on next in his or her writing.

PARENT PORTFOLIO REVIEW FORM

Name of Student _____

Name of Reader _____

Grade _____ Teacher _____ Date _____

Please read everything in your child's portfolio. A number of the materials are accompanied either by student or teacher comments. The portfolio includes many materials related to the reading and writing that he or she has done this year. It also includes self-assessment devices that help a student analyze his or her strengths and weaknesses as a reader and writer.

The best assessment of a student's reading and writing begins with him- or herself but also should be broadened to include the widest possible audience. I encourage you to become part of that audience.

When you have read your child's portfolio, please talk with him or her about it. In addition, please take a few minutes to respond to these questions:

- **What do you think are your child's strengths in reading?**
- **How do you think your child could best improve his or her reading?**
- **In what ways do you think you could help your child improve his or her reading?**
- **What do you think are your child's strengths in writing?**
- **How do you think your child could best improve his or her writing?**
- **In what ways do you think you could help your child improve his or her writing?**

Thank you so much for taking the time to look at your child's portfolio.

Sincerely yours,

Name _____ Grade _____ Teacher _____ Date _____

EVALUATION OF A PORTFOLIO

Evaluation of the portfolio compiled between _____ and _____

	READING			WRITING		
Quantity of Reading and Writing	Excellent	Good	Fair	Excellent	Good	Fair
	___	___	___	___	___	___

Teacher Comments: _____

_____

_____

_____

	READING			WRITING		
Progress as a Reader and Writer	Excellent	Good	Fair	Excellent	Good	Fair
	___	___	___	___	___	___

Teacher Comments: _____

_____

_____

_____

	READING			WRITING		
Overall Evaluation of the Portfolio	Excellent	Good	Fair	Excellent	Good	Fair
	___	___	___	___	___	___

Teacher Comments: _____

_____

_____

_____

PART FOUR

Closing

Thoughts

CHAPTER TWELVE

Closing Thoughts

It should be reiterated that the sole use of various types of standardized tests simply does not accurately and completely evaluate a student's accomplishments and weaknesses in the literacy skills of reading, writing, and spelling. As stated clearly in the introduction to this handbook, many, many students have been judged very unfairly by the arbitrary standards imposed by the use of standardized tests. Such students have been wrongly labeled or assigned because of the tendency of many educators to place far too much emphasis on the supposed accuracy of all types of standardized tests. *This has been one very important message of this literacy teacher's resource.*

Instead, this book has provided you with a wealth of classroom-tested strategies and reproducible materials for *informally assessing* each student's competencies and weaknesses in all of the literacy skills that are crucial to a student's later becoming a truly literate adult. Using the appropriate strategies and materials with your students in any elementary classroom, special literacy program, or learning disabilities classroom should help you easily and accurately determine the literacy skills in which a student is competent and those in which he or she is weak.

There is little value to using any or all of the assessment devices included in this handbook if the informal assessment is not followed up by appropriate instruction and/or reinforcement in reading, writing, or spelling.

Far too many standardized test scores are simply in a student's cumulative folder or sent to the appropriate school district offices or state boards of education with no changes ever being made in a student's literacy program. When the results of tests are used in this way, there can be **no** justification for the teacher time, student time and effort, and expense that their use requires. Only when a student's instruction is *significantly altered for the better* can either standardized testing or informal assessment ever be justified.

Grading in a Whole Language Program That Mainly Uses Informal Assessment

Even with new informal techniques and materials, the issue of **grading** continues to frustrate many literacy teachers. Almost all schools continue to give grades even after they have adopted widespread use of portfolios in their assessment program. In many cases the report cards do *not* match the informal assessment program they have begun. However, grading always has been a very difficult issue to teachers to deal with whether they teach in the primary grades or at the university level.

Under the old method of evaluation, teachers easily could take numerical scores from activity sheets, workbooks, and tests, record them in a grade book, total them, and average them for a percentage that could then correspond to a letter grade. Thus, they could show something concrete to students, parents, and administrators without having to worry whether or not they could justify these grades. However, although this may have been fairly simple, it did not actually reflect the true achievement of students.

The report card system (A-B-C-D-F letter grades) used by many schools does not fit in with whole language instruction or a number of the informal assessment devices described and illustrated in this handbook. Therefore, many schools should rethink their report card system. Although letter grades really do not reflect either whole language or informal assessment techniques well, if letter grades must be given in a whole language program, evaluation should be viewed as being more subjective. Therefore, you could consider these factors:

- Written descriptions for each letter grade should be developed that vary depending upon grade level and that are based on the objectives of the school. The descriptions can use some of the characteristics included in various checklists found in this handbook. For example, an **A** at Grade 5 might be as follows: **A** = Reads many self-selected narrative and content books with higher-level understandings including predicting outcomes, interpreting, and conclusions and generalizations; is able to critically analyze what was read and to compare material from several different sources; is able to apply what has been read to his or her own life.

- If you must use letter grades, use a rating scale to evaluate written and oral responses to narrative and content material. For example: **A** = Shows a complete understanding of what was read; **B** = Shows a good understanding of what was read; **C** = Shows a fair understanding of what was read; **D** = Shows a below-average understanding of what was read; and **F** = Shows a poor understanding of what was read.

- Involve students in their own grading. After discussing your grading criteria with your students, ask each student to determine his or her own literacy grade and write it in his or her portfolio with the reasons for it.

Sample Report Card Showing Some Literacy Behaviors

Here is a portion of a contemporary report card that stresses some aspects of reading, writing, spelling, speaking, and listening. Although you certainly are welcome to duplicate and use it, it is provided only as a model of some of the elements that can be included in a contemporary report card at about the intermediate-grade level.

CONTEMPORARY REPORT CARD STRESSING
THE LITERACY SKILLS

THE LITERACY SKILLS	Semesters				
	1	2	3	4	Avg.
Reading					
Is able to read about on grade level					
Shows an understanding of what is read					
Can read silently for a sustained period of time					
Chooses to read a variety of narrative and content materials					
Is willing to read independently					
Has sufficient vocabulary skills to comprehend what is read					
Writing					
Will write regularly					
Writes varied types of compositions such as creative expression, narration, exposition, persuasion, and description					
Uses correct mechanics					
Spelling					
Uses appropriate invented spelling for unfamiliar words					
Uses learned spelling words correctly while writing					
Spells words correctly that are typical for his or her grade level					
Applies spelling strategies correctly					
Speaking					
Stays on the topic during conversations					
Expresses his or her ideas appropriately					
Asks appropriate questions					
Listening					
Listens attentively to classmates and adults					
Responds appropriately while listening to others					